Mastery, Tyranny, and Desire

A little before last Christmas a doctor Richard Renton, who settled at Savanna-la-Mar about half a dozen years ago, and had a considerable share of the practice in the Neighbourhood, being engaged in a work on the diseases of this country, and knowing I had kept a journal of the weather for many years past, made application to me for a copy from the beginning of 1770, which I readily granted, and lent him for his — to copy; & myself wrote out the height of the thermometer &c for him. But about a month ago, when he expected to sail for England in a few days, he unfortunately died (having been long in a very poor state of health) which probably has deprived the world of a valuable performance, as he was a sensible man and very capable of such an undertaking. After his decease these copys became useless, when seeing inserted in the history of Jamaica the quantity of rain, that I had observed fell in 1761 at Egypt, which imagine was communicated by my worthy friend Dr. Anthony Robinson, determined to send them to you, thinking they might not be altogether unacceptable, and hope you will pardon this boldness in an entire stranger. Have since added the general account of rain fallen since the beginning 1761, and some other small matters; also beg leave to assure you the observations were made with all the care and exactness I was able, and should they afford you the least entertainment or satisfaction, will be a pleasure, to

Sir,

your most humble servant,

Thos. Thistlewood

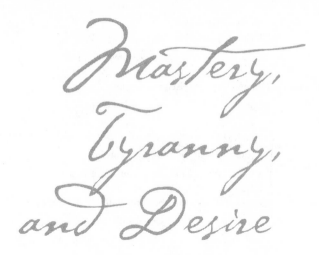

Mastery, Tyranny, and Desire

Thomas Thistlewood
and His Slaves in the
Anglo-Jamaican World

Trevor Burnard

The University of North Carolina Press
Chapel Hill and London

Designed by April Leidig-Higgins

Set in Ehrhardt by Copperline Book Services, Inc.

The paper in this book meets the guidelines for permanence
and durability of the Committee on Production Guidelines
for Book Longevity of the Council on Library Resources.

Parts of this book have been reprinted with permission in re-
vised form from "The Sexual Life of an Eighteenth-Century
Jamaican Overseer," in Merril D. Smith, ed., *Sex and Sexuality in Early America* (New York: New York University
Press, 1999), 163–89.

Frontispiece: Thomas Thistlewood to Edward Long, 17 June
1777, Long Papers, Add. MSS 18275A, f. 126, British Library.

Library of Congress Cataloging-in-Publication Data
Burnard, Trevor.
Mastery, tyranny, and desire: Thomas Thistlewood and his
slaves in the Anglo-Jamaican world / Trevor Burnard.
    p. cm.   Includes bibliographical references and index.
ISBN 0-8078-2856-4 (cloth: alk. paper)
ISBN 0-8078-5525-1 (pbk.: alk. paper)
1. Thistlewood, Thomas, 1721–1786.   2. Slaveholders—
Jamaica—Biography.   3. Plantation owners—Jamaica—
Biography.   4. Plantation life—Jamaica—History—18th
century.   5. Slaves—Jamaica—Social conditions—19th
century.   6. Jamaica—Race relations.   I. Title.
HT1096.B86   2004
306.3'62'097292—dc22   2003022319

cloth   08 07 06 05 04   5 4 3 2 1
paper   08 07 06 05 04   5 4 3 2 1

Contents

Illustrations and Tables

Acknowledgments

I never intended to write a book on the life and diaries of Thomas Thistlewood. As an early Americanist with an interest in the history of the West Indies in the seventeenth and eighteenth centuries, I had been aware of the importance of Thomas Thistlewood's diaries as a source for Jamaican history and the history of slavery in the Americas since reading Douglas Hall's pathbreaking compendium of the diaries, published in 1988. My first thought was that these diaries would be a marvelous resource for teaching, and I applied to my department at the University of Canterbury in New Zealand for funds to purchase microfilm copies of the diaries for use in my honors course on slavery in British America and the United States. In their essays written over several years in the early 1990s, my students proved that the diaries were a treasure trove of information not only about slavery but also about white society in mid-eighteenth-century Jamaica, a special research interest of mine. Their essays convinced me to have the diaries transcribed, with the crucial assistance of two masters' students, Michael Peck and Karen Rule, to whom I owe a big vote of thanks. They also convinced me that a book was waiting to be written about the fascinating life and times of Mr. Thistlewood. We academics often claim that we need funding to do research so we can use the fruits of our research in our teaching; here is an example of how investment in teaching led to the development of research that otherwise might not have been contemplated. The two activities—research and teaching—are symbiotically linked, as everyone save government representatives seems to realize.

I would not have been able to develop this research into a book without obtaining permission to use the diaries for these purposes. I am extremely grateful to Lord and Lady Monson for granting me permission to purchase microfilm copies of the diaries and to use them as a basis for this book. The diaries are held at Lincolnshire County Archives, and I am grateful to the Lincolnshire

County archivist for securing Lord Monson's assent to my access to the diaries. Other materials necessary for the preparation of this book are held at the Jamaica Archives and the Island Record Office in Jamaica, the British Library and Public Record Office in Britain, and the John Carter Brown Library in the United States. I am grateful to the archivists at these institutions for allowing me to use material from their collections. I am also grateful to Valerie Facey of Mill Hill Press in Jamaica for her help in getting copies of the prints by Thomas Vivares of 1778 paintings by William Robertson that adorn this book.

The completion of any project such as this requires both time and money. My employers during the course of this project, the University of Canterbury and Brunel University, have generously provided the assistance I needed to get the book done. It would not have been completed without the fellowship I was awarded to visit the Australian National University in the northern summer and southern winter of 2002. It was in the peaceful surroundings of the Research School of Social Sciences in Canberra that the first draft was completed. I am indebted to Barry Higman for securing this fellowship (and for much else besides, not least hiring me in my first position, at the University of the West Indies at Mona) and to my dean at Brunel, Alan Irwin, for allowing me to abscond so shamefully from important head-of-department duties for such a long period. I was also galvanized into finishing the book by being asked to do a television program on Thistlewood for Channel 4 in Britain. This invitation allowed me to see for the first time, despite many trips to Jamaica, where Thistlewood had lived. It put many things that I had been studying into context. I am grateful to Neil Crombie of Diverse Productions for his encouragement and interest in the project and to Sarah Manley for her assistance in Jamaica. I also thank Jonathan Dalby and Juliet Williams for generously hosting me on my trips to Kingston and providing transportation to the Jamaica Archives. I owe them a very large debt.

Many friends and colleagues have listened to me talk about Thomas Thistlewood and his world at lectures in Britain, New Zealand, Australia, and the United States. It is invidious to single out the few from the many in this list, but some people deserve special mention. In Jamaica, my former colleagues at the University of the West Indies have been uniformly helpful. In New Zealand and Australia, my colleagues in the Department of History at the University of Canterbury and in the Australian and New Zealand American Studies Association have listened without complaint to a great deal about Thistlewood. Shane White has been especially solicitous of my interests. John Salmond encouraged me in my first work on Thistlewood and has been interested in him ever since. John Lean at Canterbury has been an inspiring student who not only helped me with this project but also through his own work on British Guiana forced me to reconsider much of what I thought I knew about slavery and the West Indies. In Britain, I have learned much from fellow early Americanists, especially Betty Wood, Chris Clark, Mary Turner, Gad Heuman, Michael McDonnell, Steve Sarson, Julie Flavell, and Sarah Pearsall. My colleague at Brunel University, Kenneth Morgan, has been a tower of support in this and many other endeavors. In America, Merril Smith, Christine Daniels, and Barry Gaspar have been of assistance as editors of volumes in which I published essays on Thistlewood. Peter Mancall, Tommaso Astarita, Alison Games, Ann Plane, and Anne Lombard have helped me in numerous ways on trips to the United States. I have also had several interesting and insightful discussions with Philip Morgan, a fellow devotee of Thistlewood, on whites in Jamaica and the slaves they controlled, especially at a conference I organized at Christchurch in 1999 where he was a keynote speaker.

I am grateful to several people who commented on various drafts of this book. Barry Higman, Sheryllynne Haggerty, Stanley Engerman, and Jay Kleinberg have all given me very useful advice. Some of it I have taken, some I have not, possibly to the detriment of my writing and my argument. Andrew O'Shaughnessy has read the entire manuscript with his usual care and precision and has given me both encouragement and valuable advice. Betty Wood and Ron Hoffman were especially acute readers of the manuscript at its final stages of revision. Jerry Handler allowed me to draw on his vast knowledge of the Caribbean in his critiques of the manuscript and introduced me to Elaine Maisner of the University of North Carolina Press. Elaine has been an exemplary editor. I owe a lot more to Jerry than the occasional lunches he demands from me and hope that this work approaches his high standards.

One is always aware in any form of scholarship that one stands on the shoulders of giants who went before. It would have been difficult to undertake this task without the pioneering efforts of the late Douglas Hall, whose book on Thistlewood this work does not so much supersede as supplement. It would have been impossible to contemplate doing this book without the lifetime of work on the Caribbean of the late Richard Sheridan, whose friendship and support in the last years of his life I greatly value.

Finally, I dedicate this book to my dear wife, Deborah. It feels strange dedicating a book on Thistlewood to her, knowing that the hero could be a brutal sadist and occasional rapist and that the world that he and his slaves lived in was characterized by the full range of man's inhumanity to man. I don't imagine that she would have liked Thistlewood one bit. But I hope she appreciates that this dedication has nothing to do with the subject matter that will dominate the following pages and everything to do with my thanks for her continuing support for my strange fixations over many years.

Mastery, Tyranny, and Desire

chapter one

The Gray Zone

An Introduction to Thomas Thistlewood and His Diaries

[A] Good Ship and easy gales have at last brought me to this part of the New
World. New indeed in regard of ours, for here I find everything alter'd. . . .
Britannia rose to my View all gay, with native Freedom blest, the seat of Arts,
The Nurse of Learning, the Seat of Liberty, and Friend of every Virtue,
where the meanest swain, with quiet Ease, possesses the Fruits of his hard
Toil, contented with his Lot; while I was now to settle in a Place not half in-
habited, cursed with intestine Broils, where slavery was establish'd, and the
poor toiling Wretches work'd in the sultry Heat, and never knew the Sweets
of Life or the advantage of their Painful Industry in a Place which, except the
Verdure of its Fields, had nothing to recommend it.—Charles Leslie, *A new
and exact account of Jamaica*

A Year in the Tropics

On 24 April 1750 at about noon, the *Flying Flamborough* docked at Kingston, Jamaica, after a long and troublesome voyage from London. Aboard was Thomas Thistlewood, age twenty-nine, the second son of a tenant farmer from Tupholme, Lincolnshire. Having failed to establish himself as a farmer in his home district, he had resolved to seek his fortune in the wider world. A trip to India as a supercargo on an East India ship had come to nothing. By late 1749, he had decided to set off for Jamaica.[1] His baggage was not impressive. After paying for his passage, he had £14 18s. 5d. He hoped to supplement this small sum by selling "36 cases of razors" he had bought from a merchant in Ghent, which were worth £28 16s. and had been "made over to Mr. henry Hewitt of Brompton in lieu of £25 and its interest at 5% till paid." He also had a promissory note of £60 from his older brother, William, which was all that remained of his inheritance from his deceased parents. In addition, he brought a bed; a liquor case with arrack, Brazilian rum, and Lisbon wine; two large sea chests crammed with books and four pictures, including "a very fine print of ye pretender, bought at Ghent"; surveying instruments; kitchen gear; mementos from his trip to the Orient; and an impressive collection of clothes that included nine waistcoats in various fabrics and colors. Most important for our purposes, he took with him a "Marble cover'd book for a journal." Through this "Marble cover'd book" and thirty-six others just like it, we are afforded a rare entrée into the life and times of an ordinary man in an extraordinary society.

Thistlewood was no stranger to exotic locales. Nevertheless, the Caribbean presented him with novel sights and sounds. On a brief stopover in St. John's, Antigua, he ventured into town with a fellow passenger to see "a pretty piece of modern architecture" that was to be the state house and spent "6d. which here is 9d." at a rum house. He was not impressed. St. John's was "an indifferent sort of place; streets rugged and stony and everything dear." He visited a slave market, where he saw "yams, cashoo apples, guinea corn, plantains &c." and first encountered West Indian slaves—"black girls" who "laid hold of us and would gladly have had us gone in with them." Kingston was more agreeable. It was larger, with "24 ships . . . and other craft in abundance" in the harbor.[2] He visited two of the oldest residents of Kingston—the eighty-one-year-old William Cornish, who had been in Kingston since at least 1700, and the Reverend William May, rector of Kingston Parish since 1722, who gave him advice about how to survive—drink only water and eat lots of chocolate. He also started to learn about the culture of the majority of the inhabitants of his new land. He went "to the westward of the Town, to see Negro Diversions—odd Music, Motions &c. The Negroes of each Nation by themselves."[3]

He learned even more when he traveled to Savanna-la-Mar in Westmoreland Parish in the southwest corner of the island. Within hours of arriving at noon on Friday, 4 May 1750, he was offered a job as an overseer on one of the properties of wealthy sugar planter William Dorrill. Dorrill lent him a horse, gave him a meal, and let him stay at his plantation, "ready to succeed his overseer who leaves him in about two months." As it turned out, Dorrill's position did not become vacant until September 1751. In the meantime, Thistlewood accepted a position from another wealthy planter, Florentius Vassall, as pen keeper at Vineyard Pen ("pen" is a Jamaican term for a property producing livestock or garden produce) in neighboring St. Elizabeth Parish on 2 July 1750. In the two months he lived at Dorrill's, however, he began to understand the extent to which white dominance rested on naked force. Twelve days after Thistlewood's arrival in Westmoreland Parish, Dorrill meted out "justice" to "runaway Negroes." He whipped them severely and then rubbed pepper, salt, and lime juice into their wounds. Three days later, the body of a dead runaway slave was brought to Dorrill. He cut off the slave's head and stuck it on a pole and then burned the body. These lessons on the necessity of controlling slaves through fear and violence were reinforced at Vineyard Pen. In mid-July 1750, less than two weeks after becoming pen keeper at Vineyard, he watched his first employer, the scion of one of the richest and most distinguished families on the island, give the leading slave on the pen, Dick, a mulatto driver, "300 lashes for his many crimes and negligences." In the nearby town of Lacovia on 1 October, he "Saw a Negroe fellow named English . . . Tried [in] Court and hang'd upon ye 1st tree immediately (drawing his knife upon a White Man) his hand cutt off, Body left unbury'd." Given these examples, it is not surprising that Thistlewood also maintained his authority with a heavy hand. On 20 July, already convinced that his slaves were "a Nest of Thieves and Villains," he whipped his first slave. He gave Titus, a slave who harbored a runaway, 150 lashes on 1 August.[4]

The relationship between whites and blacks was fraught but involved a significant degree of close interaction. During his first year in Jamaica, Thistlewood lived in a primarily black world. Between November 1750 and February 1751, he saw white people no more than three or four times.[5] On 8 January 1751, Thistlewood recorded that "Today first saw a white person since December 19th that I was at Black River." The forty slaves at Vineyard educated Thistlewood in Jamaican and African ways. Dick, the slave driver, introduced him to gungo peas (which were used in soup and served with rice) and slave medici-

Thistlewood's first post was at Vineyard Pen, marked on this 1763 map as on the southern edge of the Great Morass in southwest St. Elizabeth Parish, a few miles inland from the hamlet of Black River. From Thomas Craskell and James Simpson, *Map of the County of Cornwall, in the Island of Jamaica* (London, 1763).

nal remedies. Other slaves taught him how to cure sores and comfort irritated eyes. They told him about Jamaican plants and animals and adaptations of African recipes they had developed in enslavement. His diaries in the first year contain African and Creole words such as *calalu*, a vegetable stew; *pone*, cornmeal; *patu*, the Twi word for owl; and *tabrabrah*, a Coromantee, or Gold Coast, name for a type of rope dance. He heard African animal fables, such as how the crab got its shell, and learned of *duppys*, or ghosts, and *abarra*, evil spirits who lured individuals to their death by adopting the guises of friends and relatives. His slaves told him "if you hurt a Carrion Crow in her eyes (or a Yellow Snake) you will never be well until they are well or dead." He noted that to "drink grave water was the most solemn oath among Negroes" and began to distinguish between different types of African cultural practices. At Christmas, he allowed his slaves to celebrate and watched "Creolian, Congo and Coromantee etc. Musick and dancing." Six months later, on his departure for Egypt Plantation, a sugar estate of Dorrill's in Westmoreland, he threw a party for Marina, a house slave and his mistress, at which she got "very drunk." Thistlewood watched slaves singing and dancing in "Congo" style and marveled at one slave who could eat fire and strike "his naked arm many times with the edge of a bill, very hard, yet receive no harm."[6]

The day after Marina's party, Thistlewood also recorded in his diary, "Pro. Temp. a nocte Sup lect cum Marina," detailing in schoolboy Latin the last time he slept with his first Jamaican sexual conquest.[7] Thistlewood took full advantage of the sexual opportunities offered to white men. Living openly with slave or free mulatto concubines brought no social condemnation. White men were expected to have sex with black women, whether black women wanted sex or not. In his first year in the island—during which he slept with thirteen women on fifty-nine occasions—Thistlewood noted several prurient items of sexual curiosity. On 26 June 1750, he recorded an anecdote from Dorrill about a slave woman with a black lover and a white lover who had twins—one mulatto, one black. Three weeks later, the slave housekeeper at Vineyard borrowed his razor to shave her private parts, leaving Thistlewood to speculate that "some in Jamaica are very sensual." He learned from slave men how to make a powder that made men irresistible to women and that in Africa girls were not allowed to tickle their ears with a feather because it would arouse them. They also told him that "many a Negro woman [received] a beating from their husbands" when they drank too much cane juice because it made them appear as if they had just had sexual intercourse and that "Negro youths in this Country take unclarified Hoggs lard . . . to make their Member larger."[8]

Jamaica differed from Thistlewood's native Lincolnshire in both small and large ways. Thistlewood thought it interesting that "At dinner today, every Body took hold of the Table Cloth, held it up, Threw off the Crumbs and an Empty Plate, Jamaica Fashion." The heat, sunshine, and sudden tropical downpours were also outside his experience. Nevertheless, by the middle of what passed for a Jamaican winter, Thistlewood found himself "somewhat inur'd to the heat of the Country." A cold snap found people complaining of "the coldness and Sharpness of the North [wind] and asking one another the things to stand it" even though it was "hotter than our summer in England." Even more extraordinary was the tropical phenomenon of hurricanes. At midday on 11 September 1751, the wind, already fresh, became a gale. From 3:00 to 7:00 P.M., the hurricane raged. It "Blew the shingles off the Stables and boiling house" of Egypt, "burst open the great house windows that were secured by strong bars," and inundated the house with water. Trees were blown down everywhere, and the white people fled the great house and "shelter[ed] in the storehouse and hurricane house." The next day, Thistlewood surveyed the damage: "The boards, staves and shingles blown about as if they were feathers. Most of the new wharf washed away, vast wrecks of sea weeds drove a long way upon the land, a heavy iron roller case carried a long way from where it lay, and half buried in the sand." Thistlewood was half terrified and half excited about a physical event that made "all the lands look open and bare, and very ragged, [and] the woods appear like our woods in England in the fall of the leaf, when about half down."[9]

His fellow whites also piqued his curiosity. One of the first whites Thistle-wood met in Westmoreland was "old Mr. Jackson." Thomas Jackson was hardly a gentleman—he "goes without stockings or shoes, check shirt, coarse Jackett, Oznabrig Trousers, Sorry Hatt, wears his own hair"—yet he was a wealthy man, "worth £8–10,000." It was not difficult to make money in Jamaica's booming economy. Thomas Tomlinson, a servant, "expects to make £200–300 per annum by planting 4 to 5 acres on Mr. Dorrill's land by his leave." Abundant sexual opportunity, lavish hospitality, excellent shooting and fishing, and a remarkable egalitarianism accompanied whites' great wealth. Whites were given special legal advantages and were invited as a matter of course to the houses of leading citizens. The custos, or chief magistrate of Westmoreland, Colonel James Barclay, entertained Thistlewood within four months of his becoming an overseer at Egypt. Yet white supremacy was held precariously in a country where over 95 percent of the population on the rural western frontier was black. Whites acted brutally toward blacks because they knew only fierce, arbitrary, and instantaneous violence would keep blacks in check. Thistlewood knew blacks were prepared to turn the tables on their masters should the opportunity arise. On 17 July 1751, Thistlewood "heard a Shell Blown twice . . . as an Alarm." Dorrill—a man experienced in Jamaican mores—was highly agitated because he "greatly feared it was an insurrection of the Negroes, they being ripe for it, almost all over the island." Dorrill's agitation was "nought but a Silly Mistake," but white Jamaicans were correct in assuming that their slaves were "ripe for it." Two weeks earlier, Old Tom Williams had given "very plain discourse at Table" about the possibilities of a slave uprising (along with ribald tales of how he pleased his slave mistress).[10]

Africans were always prepared to resist enslavement. A Vineyard slave called Wannica told Thistlewood that in "the ship she was brought over in, it was agreed to rise but they were discovered first. The pickaninies [children] brought the men that were confined, knives, muskets & other weapons." Thistlewood found himself confronted at every turn by what he perceived as slave villainy. The second day he was at Vineyard, "Scipio's house was broke into and robb'd as supposed by Robin the runaway Negro." The robbers were, in fact, Vineyard slaves. Robin came to a bad end: he was hung for repeatedly running away, and his head was put on a pole and "Stuck . . . in the home pasture," where it stayed for four months. Thistlewood responded by whipping delinquents. In his year at Vineyard, he whipped nearly two-thirds of the men and half of the women.[11]

The Life of Thomas Thistlewood

This book is about how Thomas Thistlewood made sense of the strange environment he found himself in from April 1750 until his death at age sixty-five on 30 November 1786. Thistlewood is our main character, but the book is also about the society he lived in. I want to explore what it meant to be a white immigrant in a land characterized by extreme differences of wealth between the richest and the poorest members.[12] I am also interested in examining how Thistlewood operated in one of the most extensive slave societies that ever existed. Our perspective has to be largely that of Thistlewood. The source that we have, despite its remarkable depiction of the lives of illiterate if not inarticulate African-born and Jamaican-born slaves, reflects the prejudices and experiences of a white man in a black person's country. I make no apologies for the book's focus on Thistlewood. We need to know more about the foot soldiers of imperialism, especially the men involved at the most intimate level with slaves and slavery in the eighteenth-century British Empire.

Of course, to understand is in some ways to forgive. Forgiveness is especially easy when the person in need of forgiving produces the words that we rely on to construct a historical narrative. This account of Thistlewood's life and diaries is an empathetic one; it acknowledges the difficulties he was forced to labor under and the different context of an eighteenth-century world with values and experiences removed from our own. I hope, however, that empathy does not tend too much toward sympathy. Sympathy for the travails of a man living in the middle of a war zone (as Jamaica indubitably was in the eighteenth century) is constrained by the realization that the subject was definitely not on the side of the angels. Thistlewood was on the wrong side of history—he was a brutal slave owner, an occasional rapist and torturer, and a believer in the inherent inferiority of Africans.

Thistlewood's life can be recounted simply. It was not a life full of incident. He was born on 16 March 1721 in Tupholme, Lincolnshire, the second son of Robert Thistlewood, a tenant farmer for Robert Vyner. His father died on 18 December 1727, leaving Thomas £200 sterling to be paid when Thistlewood was twenty-one years old. Thus, from an early age, Thistlewood was in the uneasy position of being a fatherless second son with few prospects of obtaining land. Shortly after his mother's remarriage to Thomas Calverly on 27 September 1728, Thistlewood was sent to school in Ackworth in York, where he boarded with his stepuncle, Robert Calverly. Thistlewood received a good education for a person of his status, especially in mathematics and science. He continued his schooling until he was eighteen, when he was apprenticed to William Robson, a farmer in Waddingham, eleven miles due north of Lincoln. By this time, he had already established some of the habits he would keep throughout his life. He was interested in books and practical science, and he had begun a regular diary. He kept a diary on a semi-daily basis from 1741 onward.[13]

He was adrift in the world after his mother died at age forty-two on 7 October 1738. Thistlewood soon realized it was unlikely that he would become a tenant farmer as his father had been and as his brother was to become. He left Robson on 27 July 1740, explaining to him in a letter that he "cannot get money to pay you withal supplying [my] own wants & if I had staid with you till I was of age, I would owe you a great deal." Other factors played a part in his decision to leave. Thistlewood "had a mind to travell," and after leaving Robson, he journeyed south to Nottingham, Leicester, Stratford upon Avon, and Bristol. He returned to Robson's farm after the death of his stepfather on 19 November 1740 but never settled down. By 1743, he had entered into a partnership with his brother to be a tenant farmer for Robert Vyner, but he ended that partnership after less than a year. His wanderlust was strong now, as was his realization that he was unlikely to achieve his ambitions in Lincolnshire, or even England. His determination to leave may have been enhanced by events that occurred in late 1745. On 19 December 1745, Thistlewood was served a warrant for getting Anne Baldock pregnant on 1 August 1745 at a county fair. Baldock miscarried, but Thistlewood's reputation may have been damaged. On 7 March 1746, he left his family and Tupholme, taking with him £4.71 in ready money. He undertook a two-year journey to India via the Cape of Good Hope and Bahia, Brazil, on a ship belonging to the East India Company to sell English manufactures.

He returned to England on 27 August 1748, remaining in London until 6 October, then traveling to Lincolnshire. At loose ends, he alternated between the delights of London and the comfort of Tupholme and undertook an unsuccessful trip to the Low Countries in the summer of 1749 to sell goods he had brought back from India and Brazil. This was not a happy time for Thistlewood. He had no position and little chance of becoming a landed proprietor. Despite having torrid affairs with Elizabeth Toyne, the wife of his erstwhile employer, Thomas Toyne (Thistlewood related that on 21 October he had sex with "Mrs. T in the night 4 tempora" and on 28 October "Cum E.T.—cum illa in nocte quinque tempora") and another married woman, Elizabeth Toyne's friend, Jenny Cook, he had not found a suitable partner. He courted Bett Mitchell of Fulsby, noting on 5 March 1749 that she was the eleventh woman he had had sexual intercourse with, and they exchanged gifts to signal their intentions toward each other. But her parents turned Thistlewood down when he sought her hand in marriage. Mitchell's parents were right to do so: Thistlewood was twenty-eight years old and had little money and poor prospects.[14] Thistlewood was as low in spirits as at any other time in his life. He left Tupholme at the beginning of April for London. He had no job and was forced to rely on loans from his landlady. On 1 May, he recorded, "Took a walk in the long fields. Borrowed off Mrs. Gresham [his landlady] 5s. *Ecclesiastes* Chap. 7th. Verse 28th: which yet my soul seeketh but I find not: one man among a thousand I have found, but a woman among all these have I not found." In these low times, Jamaica was an appealing prospect. He departed for the island on 1 February 1750, arriving in Kingston on 24 April. He remained in Jamaica for the rest of his life.

It is his life in Jamaica that is of interest here. If his diaries had not been preserved, we would know little about him except for a few references in Jamaica's public records. Although he was an acquaintance of the wealthy sugar planter and historian William Beckford of Hertford and knew members of the prominent Ricketts family, he is not mentioned in Beckford's 1790 history of Jamaica or in the Ricketts family letters, the only other surviving written records of Westmoreland in Thistlewood's time.[15] The sole source that casts light on Thistlewood besides his diaries and associated writings is the collection of Edward Long's papers on Jamaica held in the British Library. Thistlewood wrote two letters on scientific and meteorological matters to Long, the scion of one of Jamaica's most distinguished families, owner of a considerable amount of Jamaican property, and author of the best contemporary history of Jamaica.[16] Thistlewood was not an important man, even if by the end of his life he had attained some small celebrity in his immediate neighborhood for the extent and quality of his garden and had become a justice of the peace. He did not mingle in the highest circles of Jamaica—Long never bothered to reply to Thistlewood's letters, for example—and had no descendants through whom his memory could be transmitted over time. His grave is not marked in the Savanna-la-Mar churchyard, and no trace of his house or property remains. His unusual name is not found in Jamaica today and is rare in Britain. If the name "Thistlewood" resonates at all, it does so in a way that would have displeased Thomas Thistlewood—the name became notorious in 1820 when his great nephew, Arthur Thistlewood, was executed for treason as the leader of the Cato Plot to assassinate the prime minister.[17]

Moving to Jamaica cured Thistlewood's wanderlust. He did not venture beyond western Jamaica in the thirty-seven years he lived in the island and seldom went more than a few miles from the southern Westmoreland town of Savanna-la-Mar. The only move he made after 1751 came in 1757 when he left for a year to take up an overseership at the Kendal estate, a sugar property belonging to John Parkinson located a few miles due north of Egypt in Hanover Parish. On 3 July 1766, he purchased a half-share of a 300-acre property a few miles northeast of Savanna-la-Mar. On 3 September 1767, he moved to this pen, which he named Breadnut Island. He described it in 1781, when he briefly considered selling it and returning to Britain, as containing 160 acres, of which between 60 and 70 acres were "Negro grounds and pastures, very clean; most of the rest is a rich open morass, great part of which in the dry season is good pasturage; it affords fish of various sorts, more especially mudfish, also crabs, and in the season plenty of wild fowl." From the highest point, where Thistlewood had built a house that had been destroyed in the hurricane of October 1780, "there is a prospect of the shipping in Savanna la Mar harbor, and the country all round."[18] Thistlewood developed Breadnut Island into a showpiece property, with one of the earliest and most spectacular gardens of western Jamaica.

Two great events intruded into this Arcadia (the original name of the 300-acre property was Paradise) between 1750 and 1786. Thistlewood provides us with vivid firsthand accounts of both events. In 1760, Thistlewood found himself in the middle of the greatest slave rebellion in the eighteenth-century British Empire, Tackey's revolt, in which slave rebels attempted to "extirpate the whites" and establish an African kingdom. Westmoreland bore the brunt of the rebel attacks, along with St. Mary's, and, as Thistlewood relates in his testimony about the revolt, the rebels came close to achieving their aims. At least 50 whites and perhaps 500 slaves lost their lives either in battle or in the grisly retributions that occurred after the rebels had been defeated. In terms of its shock to the imperial system, only the American Revolution surpassed Tackey's revolt in the eighteenth century.[19]

The second great event was the hurricane of October 1780. Hurricanes frightened white Jamaicans as much as slave rebellions. Thistlewood experienced his first hurricane as early as 1751, as we have seen. It terrified and excited him in almost equal measure. The hurricane of October 1780, however, was a different

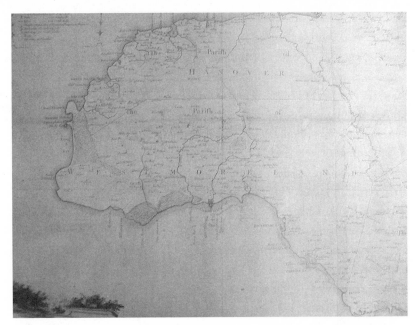

Between 1751 and 1767, Thistlewood was overseer at the Egypt estate in southern Westmoreland Parish, on the Cabaritta River, north of the main road heading west from Savanna-la-Mar. Breadnut Island, where he lived from 1767 until his death in 1786, is not marked on this 1763 map but was on the eastern side of the Cabaritta River, bordered on the north by Goodwin's land and on the east by the Kirkpatrick estate. From Thomas Craskell and James Simpson, *Map of the County of Cornwall, in the Island of Jamaica* (London, 1763).

matter. When Thistlewood compared the three hurricanes he had experienced (in 1751, 1780, and 1781), he ranked them on a scale of 1–10 as follows: "11th September, Violence or Force, NOT Velocity, say 6. 3rd October 1780, say 10. 1st August 1781, say 4."[20] The second hurricane was the most violent ever to strike the Caribbean in recorded history, and it made a direct hit on Westmoreland Parish. It devastated both the parish and Thistlewood, leaving "sad havoc all through the countryside." The loss of life was close to that in Tackey's revolt, and the physical destruction was considerably greater. At its height, the hurricane was "most tremendous, dreadful, awful & horrible. . . . [T]he elements of fire, air, water and earth seemed to be blended together . . . [and] it seemed as if a dissolution of nature was at hand." People could not stand upright in the force of the wind, and their clothes were torn from their bodies. "An old negroe man" who had "crept into an empty puncheon for shelter" was "carried over a high fence into a cane piece 2 or 3 hundred yards distance." The aftermath of the hurricane was as devastating as the hurricane itself; most trees were "blasted" and destroyed, and survivors were assailed by sickness that probably arose from lack of clean drinking water and the destruction of food supplies. Westmoreland bore "the appearance of the dreary mountains of Wales, in the winter season," with "not a blade of grass, nor leaf left or tree, shrub, or bush." Traveling to Savanna-la-Mar, Thistlewood found "the havock at the bay . . . past comprehension, an intolerable stench in the air, every thing rotting and such a great number of putrid carcasses laying unburied."[21] It also brought out the tensions in Jamaican society. Westmoreland whites feared that their slaves, "who were at that time exceeding turbulent & daring, well-knowing a number of Inhabitants had perished in the storm, and almost all our arms & ammunition destroyed," would take advantage of whites' desolation. Whites were "much afraid of the Negroes rising, they being very impudent."[22] Thistlewood's dwelling house had been destroyed, his prized garden had been flooded and ruined, virtually no trees remained upright, and he and his slaves faced the possibility of famine because of the scarcity of provisions. The British government, aware of the vast scale of destruction in its wealthiest colony, provided £40,000 sterling as a grant-in-aid.[23]

Thistlewood had his share of personal tragedies, such as the death by drowning of his nephew, John Thistlewood, who had come to Jamaica in 1764, on 30 March 1765 and the death of his twenty-year-old mulatto son, John (the product of a relationship with Phibbah, a Creole black house slave), on 7 September 1780. Moreover, the dismal demographic prospects afforded whites in Jamaica meant the frequent loss of friends and acquaintances. Life as a white man among brutalized slaves bent on revenge was also always dangerous. Thistlewood's stay in Jamaica was almost a very short one. On 27 December 1752, he barely escaped being murdered by a runaway slave named Congo Sam. But personal difficulties and setbacks were relatively rare. Thistlewood achieved much more in Jamaica than would have been possible in England. He spent the last twenty years of his life as an independent landed proprietor and died with a healthy estate worth £3,371.26 Jamaica currency or £2,408.04 sterling, including thirty-four slaves.

As well as securing moderate wealth, he gained some status within Westmoreland society. On 31 December 1769, he received a commission as a lieutenant at the Savanna-la-Mar fort with responsibility to "exercise the inferior Officers, Gunners and Soldiers thereof in arms" and hold them "in good order and discipline." Six years later, on 17 December 1775, he became a magistrate. This date marked the peak of Thistlewood's prosperity. He was comfortably well-off, respected, a figure of some consequence in his parish, and the owner of a sizable number of slaves and an attractive estate. He had achieved some measure of fame through his creation of a renowned garden. Moreover, he was in a stable relationship with a slave housekeeper, Phibbah, his partner since early 1754, even if domestic happiness did not preclude frequent philandering with numerous slave women. His position declined in the subsequent decade, but at his death on 30 November 1786 after a month-long illness, three months short of his sixty-sixth birthday, he could be satisfied that in coming to Jamaica thirty-seven years earlier he had made the right decision.

Jamaica in the Mid-Eighteenth Century

Thomas Thistlewood arrived in Jamaica at the beginning of a prolonged period of prosperity on the island. From the end of the War of the Austrian Succession in 1748 to the beginning of the American Revolution in 1776, Jamaica was the powerhouse of the British Empire. Growth began to falter only in the last decade of Thistlewood's life as Jamaica was adversely affected by the breakdown of trade with the rebelling North American colonies and as it was battered by a series of devastating hurricanes. Nevertheless, when Thistlewood died in 1786—two years before the advent of the abolitionist assault on slavery that would eventually alter everything for Jamaican slave owners—Jamaica was on the cusp of another sustained burst of economic growth. From the perspective of British politicians, Jamaica was the most valuable of all British colonies in the second half of the eighteenth century, the one whose loss could least be afforded.[24] From the perspective of the thousands of British immigrants who sought their fortune in Jamaica, Jamaica was the place par excellence where they could attain wealth and happiness—if they were fortunate enough to survive its dreadful mortality rate.

First settled by the English in 1655 as a consolation prize after their failure to take Hispaniola from the Spanish, Jamaica was the largest of the British West Indian islands. It lies about 90 miles south of Cuba and 1,000 miles west of Britain's other West Indian possessions. It is physiographically diverse, containing relatively high mountains, coastal plains, arid interiors, and swampy morasses. Temperatures and rainfall vary considerably depending on elevation and access to trade winds and coastal breezes, and variations in geological formation, soil types, and flora and fauna are equally pronounced in different regions and even within small districts. Although much of Jamaica's land was either too arid or too mountainous for effective cultivation, its size allowed for greater

A scene of industry from the beginning of Jamaica's greatest period of prosperity. Detail from map by Thomas Craskell and James Simpson, *Map of the County of Surrey, in the Island of Jamaica* (London, 1763).

agricultural exploitation than in any other British possession. By the middle of the eighteenth century, Jamaica was the largest producer of tropical goods in the British West Indies, accounting for 54 percent of tropical imports into Britain and approximately 13 percent of total imports into Britain.[25]

The importance of Jamaica in the empire was that it was "a Constant Mine, whence Britain draws prodigious riches."[26] Jamaican wealth advanced by leaps and bounds in the eighteenth century. In 1700, the total wealth of the island, as measured by wealth in inventories combined with estimates of real estate, was £2,217,662. By 1750, its wealth amounted to nearly £10 million, even though the white population had barely increased since 1690. Population was not much greater in 1774, but wealth had catapulted to £28,040,217, making Jamaica easily the wealthiest colony in British America and individual Jamaican whites the richest people in the British Empire.[27] Jamaican wealth was based on sugar and rum and trade with Spanish America. The overall value of Jamaican exports to Britain increased exponentially over the eighteenth century, with the greatest rate of growth occurring in the period when Thistlewood was living on the island. In 1730, Jamaica produced approximately 25,000 hogsheads of sugar and 7,000 puncheons of rum from 400 sugar plantations. A comprehensive study of

Jamaican trade statistics done by Governor Charles Knowles in 1754 confirmed a rapid increase in production, with sugar exports up 60 percent to 40,000 hogsheads. A survey of trade undertaken by Edward Long in 1768 indicated that sugar production had increased again by over 70 percent to 68,160 hogsheads from 651 sugar estates. By 1774, Jamaica exported goods worth £1,650,000 to Britain, of which sugar accounted for £1,188,330 and rum £213,568. The remaining goods comprised pimento, cotton, coffee, and logwood. By this year, 1,640,885.5 acres were cultivated of the nearly 4 million acres in the country. Of these, 160,000 were in sugarcane on sugar estates that together accounted for 500,000 acres. Internal trade, especially cattle breeding, was also significant.[28]

Jamaica's wealth accrued almost entirely to its white population. On the eve of the American Revolution, white Jamaicans were among the wealthiest subjects in the British Empire. In 1774, per capita white wealth was £2,201, with white men having average wealth amounting to £4,403. By contrast, wealth per free white was £42.1 sterling in England and Wales, £60.2 in the thirteen colonies, and just £38.2 in New England. The average white in Jamaica was 36.6 times as wealthy as the average white in the thirteen colonies, 52.3 times as wealthy as the average white in England and Wales, and 57.6 times as wealthy as the average white in New England. The richest Jamaicans had holdings that would have been emulated only by the wealthiest London merchants and English aristocrats.[29]

The largest component of individual and colonial wealth besides land was slaves. The Jamaican economy relied almost entirely on the labor of African slaves. Jamaicans had an insatiable appetite for acquiring slaves, few of whom survived long enough to establish a naturally reproducing slave population. As a result, white Jamaicans bought rather than bred their labor force and were the mainstays of the flourishing British slave trade. Between 1655 and 1808, 915,204 Africans landed in Jamaica. Of these, just over three-quarters (701,046) were retained in the island, amounting to one-third of retained slave imports shipped on all British carriers. The result was a slave population that grew dramatically, despite the fact that deaths constantly outnumbered births and despite exceptionally low female fertility. The number of slaves more than doubled between 1700 and 1750 to 120,000 and multiplied a further two and a half times to more than 300,000 by the end of the century. By the mid-eighteenth century, 26 percent of all black British Americans and 43 percent of all black British West Indians lived in Jamaica.[30]

Jamaica's slave population was large and distinctive. Africans failed to thrive due to poor diet, debilitating work regimes, and brutal treatment. The result

TABLE 1.1: Population in Jamaica, 1662–1788

Year	Total Population	Whites	Slaves	Free blacks
1662	4,207	3,653	554	0
1673	15,536	7,768	7,768	0
1693	48,000	7,365	40,635	0
1730	83,765	8,230	74,523	1,012
1752	ca. 120,000	ca. 10,000	ca. 110,000	NA
1774	209,617	12,737	192,787	4,093
1788	236,851	18,347	210,894	7,610

Sources: 1662: CO 1/15/192; 1673: Long Papers, Add. MSS 18273, BL; 1693: CO 137/2/97; 1730: CO 137/19 (pt. 2)/48; 1752–74: CO 137/70/94; 1788: CO 137/87.

was a slave population that remained between 75 and 80 percent African. It was a heterogeneous population, with slaves shipped to Jamaica from every slave-trading region of west and central Africa. In the third quarter of the eighteenth century, when Thistlewood was active in the slave market, the Bight of Biafra and the Gold Coast accounted for 63 percent of Africans imported into Jamaica, with just over 30 percent coming from the Bight of Benin, the Windward Coast, and west-central Africa. The process of sale and the dispersal of Africans from ship to plantation accentuated heterogeneity. The result was constant flux, disruption, and misery, especially for the approximately 60 percent of slaves laboring on sugar plantations, where the work regime was particularly brutal. Nevertheless, slaves did gain some measure of self-expression within an overall structure of fierce repression, social disruption, and constant uncertainty. They developed a rich cultural life, exemplified by their language, music, and religion. This culture helped mitigate the dehumanization inherent in their status and offered relief from the relentless torments they faced from their white overlords. They also established an alternative economic world through their efforts to grow food on provision grounds. Their economic endeavors allowed them to escape to some extent the perils of living close to subsistence.[31]

White immigration to Jamaica was also sizable—between 100,000 and 125,000 Europeans moved to Jamaica before 1776—but the health of the immigrants who moved to Jamaica in pursuit of Jamaica's legendary wealth was even worse than that of Africans. Whites suffered worse mortality rates than did blacks, despite slaves' debilitating work and punishment regimes. Every year between 1730 and 1770, between 1 in 8 and 1 in 12 whites died. Neither immigrant nor native-born whites were spared. Life expectancy at birth was under ten years, with a full third of infants born in Kingston in the second quarter of the eighteenth century dying before their first birthday and another third dying before the age of five. Those few native-born men and women who survived infancy and childhood to reach the age of twenty could expect to live another sixteen to eighteen years. Immigrants could expect to survive for twelve and a half years after arrival. Thistlewood thus was unusual in surviving the "seasoning" process after arrival, when morbidity and mortality were very high, and in living out close to a normal life span. The average immigrant was fortunate to live past age forty, with the average age at death of a sample of indentured servants arriving in Jamaica between 1719 and 1750 being thirty-three. Mortality rates began to improve after the end of the Seven Years' War but remained horrific right up to the end of slavery.[32]

White demographic failure prevented the establishment of a settler society. The average length of marriage in early Jamaica was astoundingly short—less than eight and a half years for marriages begun between the late seventeenth and mid-eighteenth centuries. Continuing high mortality among white settlers meant that white numbers could not be maintained by natural increase alone. White population hardly grew during the eighteenth century. As early as the 1670s, blacks formed a majority of the population, and the presence of a large black majority came to shape every aspect of society in Jamaica. During Thistlewood's time, whites accounted for between 6 and 8 percent of the total population. White Jamaicans came to depend on blacks for their economic well-being but feared being overwhelmed—both culturally and physically—by a numerically predominant black population that never assimilated fully to European ways.[33] Indeed, the enormous importation of Africans in the eighteenth century led to a rapid Africanization or re-Africanization of slave culture. The cultural gap between master and slave was probably never greater than in the decades on either side of mid-century. Whites were few in number, especially in rural areas such as Westmoreland where the proportion of slaves to whites was perhaps as high as 15 to 1, and tended to be recently arrived immigrants with little knowledge of their predominantly African-born charges and little interest in regulating slave cultural patterns. As a result, slaves were able to lead a quasi-autonomous existence, free from white surveillance, especially in their cultural and religious lives.[34]

The clear evidence of extensive Africanization in Jamaica and the failure of effective white settlement greatly alarmed contemporary commentators. White Jamaicans above all else wanted to transform Jamaica into a settled, improved, and civilized society. An "improved" society was, by definition, an English society. Jamaican patriots like Edward Long tried to claim that Jamaica was becoming increasingly English by mid-century as landscapes came to resemble those of England and as native-born whites began to adopt English manners of living. But to be English was to be white, and Jamaica was indubitably not white. Instead of becoming English, Jamaica, it could be argued, was retreating into African "barbarity." Evidence of the Africanization of European society was all around. Long lambasted white women for their overfamiliarity with slave servants. Women "bred up entirely in the sequestered country parts . . . are truly to be pitied" because their only examples of behavior came from blacks. As a result, a Jamaican woman's "speech is whining, languid, and childish" and "her ideas are narrowed to the ordinary subjects that pass before her, the business of the plantation, the tittle-tattle of the parish; the tricks, superstitions, diversions, and profligate discourses, of black servants, equally illiterate and unpolished." It was not entirely women's fault. Their menfolk had deserted them for the charms of "scheming black Jezebels." "In a place where so little restraint is laid on the passions," Long declared, "many are the men, of every rank, quality, and degree here, who would much rather riot in these goatish embraces, than share the pure and lawful bliss derived from matrimonial, mutual love." If white men did not marry but instead, like Thistlewood, rioted in "goatish embraces," then Africanization rather than Europeanization was the inevitable result, with dire consequences, Long believed, for the future of white dominion in Jamaica.[35]

Demographic disaster also influenced the character of white life. In particular, it heightened the already-strong impulses toward anarchic individualism inherent in the island since early settlement. Eighteenth-century Jamaica was a fast-living, intensely materialistic, and fiercely individualistic society. The white population was predominantly male (adult men outnumbered adult women by over 2 to 1), young (84 percent of adult men in Clarendon Parish in 1788 were between twenty-one and forty years old), and migrant.[36] Jamaica never made the demographic transition from an immigrant-dominated to a native-born-dominated society but resembled the heavily male, largely immigrant society of the seventeenth-century Chesapeake, in which the reckless and single-minded pursuit of individual gain was the central animating impulse and the chief social determinant.[37] Continuing high mortality and the transformations that living in a slave society induced were the other main influences on the character of white Jamaican life. They encouraged a resolve to live in the moment as well as a haughty independence, fierce egalitarianism, and intense racial consciousness.

White Jamaicans, Wealth, and Slavery

Migrants to Jamaica came principally to make money. The foremost characteristic of white Jamaicans, therefore, was an all-consuming ambition for wealth, an avaricious and aggrandizing self-interest. Jamaica was, as the early abolitionist James Ramsay lamented, a land devoted to "the Kingdom of I." Jamaicans sought the "allurements of profits" and "great and sudden fortunes," Long stated, "as if it were the only rational object of pursuit in this world." Moreover, in their "great haste to be rich," James Knight, writing in the 1740s, averred, they pursued private interests at the expense of the "generall good of the Country." That passion for wealth engendered an intense competitiveness and a desire for wild extravagance. Jamaicans were addicted to ostentatious display and devoted to luxury. They spent their money on lavish feasting, copious drinking, and all manner of sexual and sensuous delights. Jamaica was a gambler's paradise rather than a philosopher's retreat. "Careless of futurity," white Jamaicans showed little commitment to their native or adopted land, educating their children, if they had any, in England and caring little about developing and maintaining institutional structures. Everything was sacrificed on the altar of getting rich quickly. Jamaica was not a land of long-term planning. Its white citizens loved risk and hazard, their schemes were always vast but seldom well planned, and they "put no medium in being great and being undone." They were inordinate risk takers, but their passionate natures and fiery, restless tempers did not encourage a persevering spirit. One of the great themes of Jamaican history was the speed with which plans were made and begun, then laid aside in favor of fresh novelties. Excess and speculation rather than restraint and planning were their watchwords.[38]

But in order to achieve great riches, it was necessary to work hard. Establishing a sugar estate or other type of plantation was a time-consuming, expensive, and difficult undertaking. Involvement in commerce also required diligence and hard work. That so many Jamaicans achieved wealth suggests that they were industrious. Yet the means by which wealth was acquired—on the backs of overworked and badly treated slaves—militated against sustained economic success. Slavery itself was inherently dangerous. In their "rage to push on their estates," whites bought more and more blacks until the land was filled with a people they both despised and feared. Like children "playing with Edge-Tools, which they cannot manage," they exposed themselves to the constant risk that Jamaica would be "over-run and ruined by its own slaves." The likelihood of physical assault was not the only risk. Being a slave owner changed a white man's character. It might not be true that owning slaves transformed the "natural Disposition[s]" of Britons "from humanity into Barbarity," but it was undeniable that white Jamaicans treated their slaves with a brutality that demeaned them and disgraced the good name of a people who proudly declared that slavery was an un-British institution. Slavery was the very essence of barbarism, and the nature of slavery in Jamaica marked out its slave owners as barbarians. "No Country," Charles Leslie proclaimed, "excels them in a barbarous Treatment of Slaves, or in the cruel Methods they put them to death." An informed critic declared in 1746 that Jamaican slaves were the worst-treated slaves in any European colony and that nowhere else were slaves so completely at the mercy and caprice of their masters.[39]

Slavery not only made Britons brutal. It made them self-indulgent, indolent, and full of overbearing pride. Indolence, claimed contemporaries, was partly the result of the climate, which sapped the blood of people accustomed to more temperate climes, but mainly the result of having either from birth or from first arrival in the island a host of slaves who performed all menial tasks. In a society where being a worker meant being black and where blackness was a sign of ineradicable inferiority, working was a mark of servile status. Whites were expected to be lazy, listless, and self-indulgent in part because these were qualities to which no black person could aspire. Patrick Browne wrote soon after Thistlewood's arrival that white Jamaicans acquired an "aloofness" and "distant carriage" as a result of "the general obsequiousness of their numerous slaves and dependents, as well as from the necessity of keeping them at a distance."[40]

The ubiquity of slavery also made white Jamaicans intensely conscious of how disastrous it was to lose one's liberty. Few people evinced as much desire to uphold their independence. They gloried in being a turbulent people, "fond of opposition to their governors," as evidenced by a long series of disputes with metropolitan authority from the 1670s to the early 1760s. Their insistence on freedom was apparent in all areas of their lives. They were free from restraints of almost all kinds—legal, social, and religious. Plantations were almost autonomous kingdoms where masters were sovereign lords. White men extended that sovereignty outside the plantation. They took little heed, for example, of the doctrines of the church. Indeed, white Jamaicans were resolutely irreligious. Religion was "greatly neglected and disregarded," and "Church Doors are seldom opened." They were not much more observant of legal niceties. Although they prided themselves in living under British law and British legal and political institutions, white Jamaicans did not always use the law to solve personal disputes. Instead, they challenged each other to duels if they were gentlemen or resorted to fisticuffs if they were not. Soon after Thistlewood arrived in Jamaica, William Dorrill told him "that in this Country it is highly necessary for a Man to fight once or twice, to keep Cowards from putting upon him." White men were combative creatures, as hot-tempered as the climate was torrid. They were "liable to sudden transports of anger" and given to violence, although these outbursts were usually short-lived. Such combativeness was not surprising in a society in which slavery imbued slave owners with "something of a haughty Disposition" that "require[d] Submission" from all around them and in which every man insisted on being the "absolute master of himself and his actions."[41]

The ubiquity of slavery also put a premium on whiteness. The divisions in Jamaica were not so much between various classes of white men as between free and unfree, which meant, in practice, a division between white and black. Jamaican society was racially stratified rather than class stratified. The result was a blurring of boundaries between whites and an expansion of civil liberties for all white men. Jamaica's white population was more diverse than Britain's, but that diversity counted for little against the rigid divisions between whites and blacks. The danger that slaves posed to whites meant that all whites had to join together. This sense of racial solidarity greatly enhanced the power of poorer whites, who were more essential to the maintenance of white rule and the continuation of white prosperity than were poor whites in British North American or British society. Wealthy whites were forced to recognize poorer whites as their equals, at least insofar as they were white. Just as the presence of slavery increased white awareness of the value of independence, so too did intense racial consciousness advance white egalitarianism.[42]

Egalitarianism was an attractive feature of white life, especially for a comparatively poor man like Thistlewood. White Jamaicans' famed hospitality was also a positive aspect of Jamaican life. All commentators agreed that white Jamaicans were a particularly hospitable people who adored sociability, conducting their lives in a veritable whirl of visiting, playing games, attending parties, and entertaining. Knight rejoiced that "there is not more Hospitality, nor a more generous freedom shown to Strangers on any Part of the World. . . . [A] man may Travell from one Part of the Country to another and even around the Island with very little if any Expense. . . . He may with freedom go and dine, or lodge at the next Planters House and Persons of low rank and Condition are as cheerfully received and entertained by their Servants." Their entertainments were prolific, opulent, and fun. Unlike their seventeenth-century ancestors, who tried to live as in England, white Jamaicans in the eighteenth century adapted

English customs to tropical conditions. They were devoted to local and African-influenced delicacies such as pepper-pot and turtle soup, rum drinks, cassava bread, and tropical fruits and fishes, often devoured at that quintessentially West Indian social gathering, the barbecue. They wore lighter and brighter clothes than clothes worn in Britain and eschewed wigs. They dwelled in airy, spacious single-story houses where the furniture was limited but select and prided themselves on offering guests a magnificent table. White Jamaicans were attractive people, both in physique and in character. Leslie argued that "they seem perfectly polite and have a Delicacy of Behavior which is exceeding taking." While it was true that the warm climate made it hard for white Jamaicans to "forbear indulging themselves . . . in their Indolence," they were a naturally vivacious people with "a quick apprehension," "naturally strong passions," and "lively spirits" and unashamed extroverts who delighted in company and "social enjoyments" such as hunting, games, dancing, and music. Their "free and open dispositions" made them agreeable companions. Knight did not know of any "more Industrious, usefull, and beneficial Society to the nation" than these people, described by their greatest advocate, Long, as being "brave, good-natured, affable, generous . . . unsuspicious, lovers of freedom, tender fathers . . . and firm and sincere friends." Long also characterized them as "temperate, and sober . . . [and] humane and indulgent masters," but few others saw such qualities in them.[43]

Westmoreland Parish and the Jamaican Frontier

The area of the country that Thistlewood chose to live in had its own peculiarities. English settlement in Jamaica had concentrated in the southeastern parishes, especially around the principal towns of Port Royal in the seventeenth century and Kingston in the eighteenth century. The western and northern parishes were slow to develop, hindered by difficult geography, poor links to Kingston, and the long, successful resistance offered to white rule by independent blacks called Maroons who controlled the almost impenetrable Jamaican interior. In the first four decades of the eighteenth century, whites and Maroons were continually at war, with the Leeward Maroons under the command of their great leader, Cudjoe, blocking the attempts of whites to penetrate the interior and settle the fertile *poljes*, or wide valleys, of St. James and Westmoreland Parishes. The 443 whites and 7,137 slaves who resided in Westmoreland by 1730 feared constantly for their lives. The parish was not truly open for development until after 1739, when members of the Jamaican House of Assembly tired of their fruitless and expensive war with the Maroons and negotiated a peace treaty with Cudjoe and his followers. By this treaty, Cudjoe and his band were granted a large freehold property in the northwestern interior where they were to have almost sovereign rights and from which whites were excluded. They were also given rights to trade with whites. In return, Cudjoe promised to "cut, clear, and keep open large and convenient roads from Trelawney Town to Westmoreland and St. James's" and agreed to return runaways to their owners and assist whites in quelling local slave revolts. The presence of the Maroons gave Westmoreland peace and protection. They were very much part of the texture of Westmoreland life. Thistlewood noted in 1750 that he "met Colonel Cudjoe, one of his Wives, One of his Sons—a Lieutenant and other Attendants. He shook me by the hand and Begg'd a Dram of us, which we gave him. He had on a feather'd hatt, Sword at his Side, gun upon his Shoulder &tc Bare foot and Bare legg'd. Somewhat a Majestick look—he brought to my memory the picture of Robinson Crusoe." Six months later, at Vineyard, he met "Capt. Compoon" (Cudjoe's brother, Accompong), who also dressed distinctively (at least for a black man), wearing a "Ruffled Shirt, Blue Broad Cloth Coat, Scarlett Cuffs to his Sleeve, gold buttons . . . white Cap and Black Hatt, White linen Breeches puff'd at the knee."[44]

After 1739, settlement and production in Westmoreland proceeded apace. It was good planting ground. Governor Charles Knowles in 1754 described it as "tolerable even ground and what hills are in it are pretty easy of access and the soil fertile." By 1768, it contained 62 sugar estates and 96 other settlements (primarily cattle pens and estates producing cotton, ginger, and pimento), as well as 15,196 slaves and 13,750 head of cattle. It produced nearly 12 percent of Jamaica's sugar, despite having only 5 percent of Jamaica's white population and 8 percent of its slave population. Between 1730 and 1788, population and production expanded exponentially. The white population increased by 237 percent and the slave population by 145 percent, while sugar production increased from 5,450 hogsheads in 1739 to 8,000 hogsheads in 1768. Westmoreland's agricultural fertility and previously unexploited land made its residents very rich. The value of the average estate in Westmoreland between 1732 and 1786 was 42 percent higher than the value of the average estate in the island as a whole. A sample of 95 Westmoreland estates probated in this period reveals the average wealth to be £4,730.65, with the average slaveholder owning 58 slaves, of whom 31 were male. Thistlewood's estate placed him in the top third of probated estates. The largest estate belonged to Richard Beckford, the brother of London's Lord Mayor and father of the historian and acquaintance of Thistlewood, William Beckford of Hertford. Beckford owned a personal estate of £83,286.81 Jamaica currency (nearly £60,000 sterling), in addition to 9,242.5 acres. Four other men left estates of over £20,000 Jamaica currency, one of whom was William Dorrill, who died in 1754 with 2,787 acres and personal property worth £30,871.25 Jamaica currency, including 442 slaves. Westmoreland residents made their money primarily from agriculture: 63 percent of estates owned by men belonged to agriculturalists. Westmoreland did contain a small town, Savanna-la-Mar, but the main business of the parish was the production of plantation goods for sale in Britain.[45]

A "Marble Cover'd Book"

It was in this environment that Thistlewood sat down every day to write in his diary, tabulate daily rainfall and note weather conditions, copy passages from books he was reading, and, in 1764, compile an "account of the Game which I shot."[46] Some of the most basic facts about Thistlewood—such as what he looked like—are not known. Nevertheless, the cache of materials deposited in the Lincolnshire Archives through the generosity of their owner, John Monson, 11th Lord Monson, is remarkable, unparalleled for its insights into Caribbean life and slave society in the eighteenth-century British Atlantic world. No other source contains the wealth of information about slavery in the colonial period found in Thistlewood's diaries. The deposit amounts to 92 items, of which 37 are the journals of Thistlewood from 1748 to 1786 and 35 are weather reports from Egypt Plantation and Breadnut Island between 1752 and 1786. In addition, it contains the journal of Thistlewood's nephew, John, who lived with his uncle between 1764 and March 1765, nine commonplace books, two lists of books owned by Thistlewood, a volume entitled "Mr. Richard Beckford's Instructions," a book in which rules of war are set forth by Jamaica's governor in 1756 after martial law had been declared, a book of game shot in 1764, and a volume with a list of slaves and an account of their labor on the Egypt estate between 1758 and 1766.

The diaries interest us most. Each volume is a small book covered in paper with the year written on the front. Each journal spans one year and contains between 184 and 354 pages of closely written and occasionally faded handwriting, except for the first volume, which runs from 27 August 1748 to the end of 1750 and contains 535 pages. In total, the diaries include over 10,000 pages of daily entries covering 39 years, 37 of which were spent in Westmoreland Parish. Each page contains between 150 and 200 words, the total text running to perhaps 2 million words. Thistlewood was a remarkably diligent diary keeper, virtually never missing a day's entry. He wrote in a clear, if tiny, script, so readers have little difficulty in deciphering his handwriting, although on occasion it is too faint to discern. A few pages are too discolored to be properly transcribed. Nevertheless, the vast majority of the text is accessible. At times, it is difficult to distinguish between vowels, and some of Thistlewood's abbreviations are mystifying. Moreover, his spelling was less than perfect (though better than that of his nephew John, who had execrable spelling and even worse grammar), and he did not always care to make his entries grammatically perfect. In this book, I have modernized spelling and added punctuation if needed to clarify words and sentences. I have otherwise tried to leave direct quotes as Thistlewood wrote them.[47]

Our reading of the diaries must be mediated by our understanding of Thistlewood's strategies of inclusion and exclusion. He wrote the diaries to satisfy various needs arising from his personality. Although we can guess what that personality was like from reading his diaries, we have no other source by which we can validate our suppositions. Nor did Thistlewood provide us with much help in our effort to understand the underlying motivations behind why he wrote the diaries in the way he did. He did not tell us why he kept a diary so assiduously and what he gained from keeping such a detailed record of his life. Nor did he discuss why he wrote his diaries in the distinctive form he used. He wrote flat, serviceable prose in entries that are regular in form and consistent in the type of activities mentioned. Over time, the regularity of these entries meant that the overall length of each year's entries was remarkably similar. A typical entry contains details of his and his slaves' work routines; punishments he meted out; letters he wrote to other whites and which slaves delivered those letters; monies expended and on what; people he met and his interactions with them, including formulaic lists of his many sexual partners; illnesses he experienced and the remedies he tried (repeated bouts of venereal disease are the most memorable of these entries); books he read or borrowed; and items of curiosity he thought especially interesting and worthy of record. At the beginning and end of each year, he summarized the year's activities and analyzed his financial situation by listing his assets and liabilities. His diary was thus part account book, part aide-mémoire, and part recapitulation of a life as lived.

Here is an example of a typical day's entry, taken at random:

Friday 10th April 1761: Gave our Negroes today. Sent on board the Ruby Captain Sattie 5 tierces of sugar 5583 lbs Recpt Signed Wm Lindsay. Wrote to Mr. Thos Eddin, recd 100 yams. P. M. Cum Phibbah, Sup: Lect.

It was a slow day. This entry showed that he allowed his slaves to work for themselves rather than laboring in the fields, that he sent some sugar to Britain, that he transacted with a local merchant for some crops for his garden, and that he had sex with his mistress. In the same week, he noted that "Cyrus, Egypt, Susannah, Phillis and Abba in the hott house" recovering from illness, that he had given some trees to Dr. Gorse, that "Venus has got the Clap," that he had sex with Little Lydde (to whom he paid 2 bitts) and Little Mimber, and that he set his slaves to work fishing and planting. On Sunday, he "gave many Ticketts to our Negroes," presumably so they could go to markets or visit lovers or friends on nearby estates. On Monday, 13 April, he noted that "a Rebell Negroe [was] kill'd not far from Glasgow Estate lately (one off those who was at Mr. Thos: Torrent's) and the other took by his Negroes after a desperate engagement." This entry was the only one that week that ventured away from the commonplaces of ordinary life.

He does not appear to have reflected on how a reading of the diaries might make him appear to others. All of the textual evidence suggests that the diaries were intended for personal use only. An occasional entry indicates that he periodically returned to his diaries to read them and, if necessary, correct factual statements that he subsequently discovered to be wrong. But he does not seem to have shown his diaries to anyone else. The diaries are remarkably frank in their description of his sexual activities and the brutal methods he used to subdue and punish slaves. They contain no attempt at self-censorship and precious little self-justification. In this respect, the diaries present a warts-and-all portrait of an intelligent if not especially sensitive man unconcerned about the morality of his life and actions.

Thistlewood's Presentation of "Self"

The diaries' great strength and their principal weakness is their extreme lack of self-consciousness—they are a presentation but not an examination of self. Thistlewood appears to have kept a regular diary because he was an inveterate list maker and collector of facts. As a result, his diaries are diffuse, shapeless, and unremittingly concrete. They are not part of a polished autobiography, as are those of James Boswell, nor are they the raw material from which a later book can be created, as are the diaries of his Caribbean contemporary, John Stedman, whose *Narrative of a Five Years Expedition against the Revolted Negroes of Surinam* is based on his daily log. Nor were Thistlewood's diaries written to resolve problems of a pathological personality, as Kenneth Lockridge argues was true for William Byrd II of Virginia, or written as a form of emotional release and a justification for one's conduct against the opinion of a hostile outside world, as has been argued for Thistlewood's wealthy contemporary, Landon Carter of Sabine Hall, Virginia. If Thistlewood was concerned about creating in writing a coherent "self," as Patricia Mayer Spacks argues was usually true of eighteenth-century diary writers, then he was remarkably unreflective about the process of such self-creation. Thistlewood seems instead to have kept a diary "to keep a kind of time and motion study by which the individual records and judges his output day by day." What pervades the diaries is an overwhelming desire to maintain order, principally achieved through an obsessive fixation on facts. His diaries show Thistlewood's compulsive urge to find, generate, sift, handle, collect, and record factual impressions and were one way in which his passion for collecting facts and desire for routine and regularity could be advanced. His desire for self-improvement was intellectual and to an extent financial, without any hint of moral self-accounting. A deeply conservative man, he accepted the world as it was and himself as he was. This means that his diaries are remarkably honest and accurate, but it also means that we have little access to his inner life and the inner life of others. He seems to have had virtually no capacity for abstract analysis or self-analysis. His diaries exhibit, even for a pre-psychoanalytic age, extremely limited insights into what motivated his behavior, what fears and ambitions he might have had, and how he perceived his relationships with others.

It is instructive to compare Thistlewood's diaries with the famous diaries of his contemporary, James Boswell. Thistlewood and Boswell shared much in common, such as a thirst for sexual adventure and a love of learning. But Boswell's diaries are more revealing than Thistlewood's about his feelings, emotions, and attitudes toward others. His diaries demonstrate an acute self-consciousness, the diaries themselves being the embodiment of a lifetime's preoccupation with self-exploration. V. A. C. Gatrell has used Boswell's diaries to examine Boswell's sympathetic identification with others, exploring in detail his excursions to public hangings and in particular a seven-week obsession, recorded extensively in his journals, with the hanging of a condemned sheep-stealer, John Reid, in Edinburgh in 1774. Boswell recorded his own reactions to Reid's plight obsessively and narcissistically. On the night before Reid's execution, Boswell commented that "gloom came upon me." He noted, "I had by sympathy sucked the dismal ideas of John Reid's situation, and as spirits or strong substance of any kind, when transferred to another body of a more delicate nature, will have much more influence than on the body from which it is transferred, so I suffered much more than John did."[48] Thistlewood's dry retelling of occurrences shows no such self-consciousness.

Thistlewood's absence of self-scrutiny is most evident in his accounts of his many sexual encounters. His honesty about his sexual predations and his lack of concern about what these sexual acts implied about his life and character are extremely uncommon among writers of diaries.[49] He chronicled his sexual conquests in an evenhanded, regular, consistent way, listing each in an easily translated code. He described each sexual conquest as an event, concentrating on time, place, and person rather than on emotions. He always identified his partner by name, ethnic origin, or owner. He invariably mentioned the time at which the coupling took place and noted, often very precisely, where it occurred. The only variations were when the sexual position was unusual (he might note, "[S]tans! [Standing] backward," for example) or when the experience, from his point of view, was disappointing ("Sed non bene" [But not good] was an occasional laconic remark). He also noted whether other people were present and what payment, if any, he made to his sexual partner. Thus, after having sex with Rosanna "Sup Terr: hill Negroe gd" (on the ground on the hill of the Negro ground), he gave her a "Bitt" as payment.[50]

But even if his descriptions of his sexual actions can be relied on as to time, place, person, and frequency, his account of his sexual life is deeply unsatisfying. The problem is not that he was not representative of all white men—his comments on the sexual behavior of other men suggest that his sexual athleticism was more typical than extraordinary—but a question of balance. Thistlewood wrote of his sexual conquests solely as "acts," paying no attention to the emotional context within which such acts occurred. Moreover, he presented his many couplings solely from his own point of view. He never once displayed any interest in the feelings of his partner about the sex both had engaged in. Nor did he ever bother to explain how particular sexual encounters came to take place. His diaries in this respect are quite different from the much shorter diary of his nephew John. John was reticent about his sexual experiences. He does not mention keeping a slave mistress, though his uncle's diaries make it clear that he took up with a slave woman. Nevertheless, his diary crackles with sexual tension, as he debated whether he should enter into a sexual attachment. He also describes how some sexual encounters came about, relating that a "Negro wench came to persuade me if possible to lay with her" because she "wanted to have a child for her master" whom she feared to be impotent, adding that she "was a very likely wench of the Mandingo Countrey but speaks good English."[51] Thomas Thistlewood's account of his sexual behavior is fuller but less revealing. It is impossible to tell whether his sexual partners had sex with him willingly or whether he forced them. Thistlewood made no effort to stand back from his relentless compiling of facts about his sexual activity in order to draw meaning from them. His lack of concern about the wider meaning of his and others' lives is most apparent in the way in which he wrote about his relationship with Phibbah, his long-term mistress and a woman with whom he had a strong emotional attachment. Only once does he give a hint of his feelings toward Phibbah. In 1757, he left Egypt after a dispute with his employer. Phibbah "grieved much," leading Thistlewood to reflect that she was a "Poor girl" who was "in Miserable Slavery."[52] But this expression of feeling is unusual. Moments of reflection let alone emotion are so rare as to be remarkable and occurred only after transformative events in Thistlewood's life: his parting from Phibbah in 1757; the deaths of his nephew, his son, and his best friends; the slave revolt of 1760; and the 1780 hurricane.

A Representative Diary?

The deficiencies of the diaries as guides to eighteenth-century human behavior, however, cannot detract from the abundance of evidence they provide about what white and black Jamaicans did within their peculiar society. They are the richest source into either white or black society that I have come across in extensive archival investigations into Jamaican history. They offer a wealth of material about white society, slave interactions with their masters, and the manner of living in the eighteenth-century British tropical world. Their very richness makes them suspect: no one else kept a diary with the assiduousness of Thistlewood. Does this make Thistlewood unrepresentative? Is he an unusual man in an unusual society and thus not to be trusted? Of course, the very fact that Thistlewood kept a journal makes him curious. Just as Edward Long's intelligence and sophisticated understanding of history make his history not only one of the great historical works of his age but also the product of his particular brilliance and opinionated views, so too does the singularity of Thistlewood's diaries make him ipso facto unrepresentative. Diary keeping was not a normal preoccupation of white Jamaican men, and the type of person who keeps a diary — someone with a protobourgeois mentality, keen on accounting for time spent, and someone engaged in self-improvement[53]—does not fit with what we assume to be the quintessential eighteenth-century white Jamaican personality, in which self-indulgence and the lack of a persevering spirit were pre-eminent characteristics. As Alan Macfarlane has commented concerning another diary, if we used diaries on their own, we would receive a picture "biased toward the more methodical and the more introspective sides of life."[54]

Certainly Thistlewood was not the quintessential white Jamaican man. He was neither noticeably self-indulgent, except perhaps in his strong sexual appetite, nor conspicuously indolent and devoted to short-term pleasure. He seldom drank to excess, was careful about what he ate, and preferred his own company to the compulsive carousing that was common among white men. His slaves accurately summed up his personality as it appears in his diaries in the name they privately bestowed on him: "ABBAUMI APPEA i.e. No for Play." The name they called his subordinate, John Hartnole—Crakra Juba, or "Crazy Somebody"—was a much more typical moniker for a white Jamaican.[55] Being fascinated by books and an avid reader was also unusual. Few white Jamaicans read very much, at least if contemporary denigrations of the cultural ambience of Jamaica can be believed and if the absence of books in Jamaican inventories is a guide.[56]

Nevertheless, what distinguishes Thistlewood from other white Jamaican men is less significant than what connects him to them. Nothing in his diaries signifies that he was at odds with his neighbors in his behavior, personality, or values. He was not universally liked, which is not surprising given that he was prickly and highly conscious of his own dignity. He had several run-ins with authority figures, especially in his first years in the island, when his willingness to whip slaves first and ask questions later if he found them on his land created several powerful enemies among the owners of the slaves so treated. As an independent proprietor in the 1760s, he was prepared to openly insult one of the leading men of the parish when solicited for his political support. But his difficult personality did not prevent him from being recognized by other white men as an acceptable member of society and a man worthy of being included in significant social and political events in the parish. Wealthy white men invited him to dinner; he was made a lieutenant of the Savanna-la-Mar fort and a justice of the peace; and men of similar status to himself—tavern keepers, doctors, and slave overseers—appointed him as executor of their estates. By the time of his death, Thistlewood's position in Westmoreland Parish was clear. He was a respectable old settler, well-off without being wealthy, and a man of some local consequence as a justice and a vestryman. He had no wider fame, except perhaps in botany and horticulture. Like most white men in the parish, he made his living through planting and the ownership of slaves. He was skilled at both endeavors, as evidenced by the competition among planters to employ him as manager of their estates and slave forces. But he was not an extraordinary agriculturalist. He followed normal practices in cane cultivation and was not especially innovative as a pen keeper, though he had particular talents as a gardener. Thistlewood was nothing if not conventional, both in his behavior and in his views. Apart from exhibiting a strong dislike for Scotsmen, which may have been more pronounced than usual for white Jamaicans of English descent, he evinced no political or social opinion that marks him as unusual. He accepted the existing order as it was. He never questioned the morality of slavery, for example; the right of white men to dominate slaves, wives, and children; or, even in the American Revolution, the necessity of British sovereignty over its colonies. Nor he did he ever doubt that white men were bound to rule and that political and social authority should accrue to men who had the greatest social and economic standing in the community.

He was also very normal in what strikes modern readers as the most aberrant aspects of Jamaican life: his sexual, social, and physical relationships with slaves. Modern readers of Thistlewood's diaries—and I presume readers of this book —do not think well of Thistlewood because of the brutality of his behavior toward his slaves. His sexual appetite appears less that of a Caribbean Casanova than the unnatural and bestial longings of a quintessential sexual predator and rapist. His willingness to subject his slaves to horrific punishments, which included savage whippings of up to 350 lashes and sadistic tortures of his own invention, such as Derby's dose, in which a slave defecated into the mouth of another slave whose mouth was then wired shut, reveal Thistlewood as a brutal sociopath. It is hard to get past these aspects of Thistlewood's behavior in order to see him as he saw himself: a harbinger, in a modest way, of the Enlightenment in the Tropics; a scholar and perhaps a gentleman; a loyal friend and respectable imperial subject; and a man of principle and integrity.

A Violent Man in a Violent Age

As historians, it is not our responsibility to attribute retrospective blame. We do, however, need to explain why ordinary people such as Thistlewood acted in the ways they did—ways that dismayed contemporaries as much as they horrify us today. How could Thistlewood behave as he did toward his slaves and develop strategies of control that were designed to demean, demoralize, and traumatize them when in other situations and in relations with fellow whites, he adopted patterns of behavior that we associate with a man of intelligence and integrity? Why was his ethical behavior so strongly influenced by the situations in which he found himself? Thistlewood's behavior indicates a very strong sense of situational ethics, of having different codes of conduct for different circumstances. The conduct adopted depended on the race of the person involved. Although Thistlewood saw slaves as human beings and did not see them as biologically inferior in the manner of a scientific racist such as Long, he accepted common Jamaican understandings that whites could act toward blacks in any way they wanted with impunity. Whites had total license to behave toward slaves as they saw fit, with white juries excusing all white crimes toward blacks short of psychopathic serial murder. John Wright, who was convicted of murder after killing four partners, was the only white noted by Thistlewood in thirty-seven years of residence in Westmoreland who was punished for his ill treatment of slaves. Moreover, he was only "fated" when he murdered a mistress who was mulatto: perhaps if he had confined his killing solely to blacks, he would have been safe. In the end, he escaped hanging and died by shooting himself at sea, having been allowed to escape from jail on the condition that he left the country.[57]

That whites were free to act as they pleased toward blacks does not, however, explain why they were so brutal toward their slaves. White Jamaicans, as Charles Leslie noted, were notorious for their ill treatment of slaves.[58] One of the causes of that ill treatment arose from the almost complete absence of constraint over how that power was exercised. Psychological studies, notably the famous Milgram experiments on the makeup of authoritarian personalities, have confirmed the increased extent to which individuals are willing to abuse normal ethical standards when they are placed within institutional structures that allow normal ethical standards to be violated.[59] Studies of the Holocaust have revealed that extraordinary circumstances can encourage ordinary people to commit acts of unrestrained violence and evil.[60] Late-eighteenth-century commentators were similarly interested in the extraordinary circumstances that led white Jamaicans to treat their slaves so abominably. Some attributed white Jamaican brutality to the climate, arguing that the heat transformed the "natural Disposition" of Britons "from humanity into Barbarity." Others blamed the "Barbarity" on the way white Jamaicans were raised. "Bred for the most Part at the Breast of a Negro Slave; surrounded in their Infancy with a numerous retinue of these dark Attendants," white Jamaicans were, John Fothergill asserted, "habituated by Precept and Example, to Sensuality, and Despotism." They were used, in short, to "play the Mogul and *lord* it" over their slaves "without Controul." Not only did native-born whites take immense pride in the constant obsequiousness of their slaves; migrants also became quickly attuned to West Indian ways. "Like wax softened by heat," J. B. Moreton argued, men from other countries "melt into [Jamaican] manners and customs." He continued: "[M]en from their first entrance . . . are taught to practice severities to the slaves . . . so that in time their hearts become callous to all tender feelings which soften and dignify our nature; the most insignificant Connaught savage bumpkin, or silly Highland gauky, will soon learn to flog without mercy to shew his authority."[61]

Nevertheless, I would argue that the major impetus of white Jamaican "Barbarism" was the belief that slaves could only be controlled through severe force and were not entitled to the same treatment that was meted out to Englishmen. Jamaicans imagined that Africans were used to harsh treatment in their native land. They also thought them "a sort of beast, and without souls," "a set of vile beings, of a species different from ours." They believed Africans had "as great a Propensity to Subjection, as we have to command and love Slavery as naturally as we do Liberty."[62] Harsh measures were needed to control such "savage and uncivilized creatures." White Jamaicans believed in force because they were frightened. Jamaica was a society at war. Slaves had to be kept cowed through arbitrary, tyrannical, and brutal actions, supported at all times by the full weight of state authority. White Jamaicans developed a legal system and a social structure in which any brutality exercised by whites toward blacks could be excused by the fundamental necessity of keeping blacks subdued. Only in this way could white fears be assuaged. Such assumptions, of course, were a license for sadism and tyranny among all whites, not just those inclined to psychopathic behavior. Whites knew that they had the full support of the state and white public opinion for whatever they did toward slaves. As James Knight declared, "Whoever considers the Negroes Superiority in Number, the sullen, deceitfull, Refractory temper of most of them . . . and how much their Masters Interest depends on the Care, and Diligence of His Slaves must be Convinced, that there is an Absolute necessity of keeping a Vigilant Eye, and Strict hand over them."[63] Because white Jamaicans considered themselves at war, they convinced themselves that normal rules of behavior did not apply. This conviction was reinforced by their all-pervasive racism. As Long asserted, Africans were "men of so savage a disposition, as that they scarcely differ from the wild beasts of the wood in the ferocity of their manners"; thus they had to "be managed at first as if they were beasts; they must be tamed, before they can be treated like men."[64]

The ethos of Jamaican society was similar to that described by Primo Levi in his searing accounts of life in Auschwitz, a gray zone with moral rules peculiar to its own distorted social structure, a society with ill-defined and abnormal outlines in which oppressors and victims were both separate and joined together. As Levi observes, to understand the incredibly complicated internal structure and strange morality of such a society, one must understand how power operates when it is not constrained by moral considerations. Both the powerful and the powerless—the master and the slave—seek power in totalitarian societies, and power is "generously granted to those willing to pay homage to hierarchic authority." The immorality of societies based on the rightness of force alone makes the wielders of power themselves immoral, whether they are part of the oppressors' power structure, such as Thistlewood, or the oppressed, contaminated by the need to identify with, imitate, or emulate the oppressors.[65]

Outline of the Book

The operation of power in Jamaica is the principal theme of this book. The book is divided into two sections. In the first four chapters, including this introductory chapter, I examine Thistlewood as a white man trying to make his way in a new environment. I test what it meant to be a white immigrant in an economically, socially, and racially polarized society in which whites could attain great wealth (chapter 2), enjoy high status and a degree of equality with each other (chapter 3), and follow their "pursuit of happiness"—independence, individualism, and improvement in all its guises—as avidly as their contemporaries in mainland North America (chapter 4).[66] In the final four chapters, I consider Thistlewood's relations with his slaves and attempt to recover the lives of some of the slaves under his charge. In chapter 5, I analyze why whites were able to retain power in Jamaica despite being heavily outnumbered by a group of people with weapons of their own who were motivated by an all-consuming hatred of their oppressors. From an exploration of white-black interactions, I turn in chapter 6 to an examination of the structures within which Thistlewood's slaves lived and study in detail four male slaves' interactions with their master. For individual slaves, two countervailing principles operated in dealing with masters. On the one hand, proximity to a master spelled danger, assuring slaves of frequent punishment and constant changes in condition. On the other hand, only by getting close to masters could slaves escape from the debilitating grind of field work. In chapter 7, I examine female slaves' lives through the prism of resistance and assess whether this common paradigm in studies of slave societies can explain female slaves' behavior. The chapter concludes with an account of the life of Phibbah, Thistlewood's long-term mistress and the most extraordinary slave encountered in Thistlewood's diaries. Phibbah was Thistlewood's great support, an accommodator to slavery who could at times treat her fellow slaves with as much brutality as any white. Yet she was able to transcend slavery through her determined efforts to create a family estate for herself, her family, and her female friends. By accommodating herself to slavery and overcoming many of the obstacles that limited slaves' "pursuit of happiness," she forged the greatest challenge to Jamaica's slave system of any slave under Thistlewood's control. In the final chapter, I attempt to sum up the significance of Thistlewood and his diaries in the context of British American and Atlantic history.

The operation of power was complex in Jamaica. Whites had most of the power in society and exercised that power ruthlessly, but they did not hold a monopoly over power. Slaves possessed little power, but what they had, they used, sometimes to extraordinary effect. Masters did not always win; slaves did not always lose. But masters always had the upper hand, primarily because they controlled the coercive powers of the state. Slaves and masters negotiated relationships because masters could not force slaves to acquiesce to their authority unless slaves agreed, but the negotiations were wildly unequal, with slaves seldom having any choice but to accept the lot they were given. White Jamaicans were proud to live in a land of liberty, but that liberty was predicated upon the symbolic and real infliction of terror on slaves' bodies and minds. At bottom, Jamaica was an anarchic society, suffused with violence. Its pretensions to civility were mocked by the brutality with which whites alienated and traumatized the majority of the population. Thistlewood was a vital cog in that oppressive order. This book tells his story.

chapter Two

Mastery and Competency

Thistlewood Earns a Living

A moderate share of industry, with health, has laid the foundation of many a great fortune in Jamaica; this place is, therefore, justly an object of attention to those, whose slender patrimony, or indigent circumstances, render them unable to gain a competent provision in their native country. . . . They who arrive now have an advantage, unknown to our ancestors, of coming to an established society.—Edward Long, *History of Jamaica*

An English Migrant

On 1 February 1750, Thistlewood left for Jamaica on the *Flying Flamborough*. Apart from his books, his possessions were disappointingly meager. His twenties had been financially calamitous. He was not much richer in 1750 than he had been when he came of age in 1742, when his assets amounted to £205. His parlous economic position and poor prospects had doomed his attempt to marry Bett Mitchell, the daughter of a prosperous local farmer.[1] It was a good time to try his luck in Jamaica. Nevertheless, Thistlewood was not especially impecunious. Significantly, he came as a free migrant rather than an indentured servant, the condition of the majority of white migrants to Jamaica.[2] As a free migrant, he could do what he wanted when he arrived, a strong bargaining position in a land where whites could be certain of employment. Thistlewood came well prepared for the Tropics, even if some of the clothes in his ample trunk were better suited to a Lincolnshire winter than to Jamaican heat. He brought his bed and bedding, kitchen pewter, an assortment of personal household effects, and drawing instruments and a quadrant to enable him to pursue a trade as a surveyor. He also brought with him a library of approximately 100 books, 35 of which were listed in detail by title, author, and date of publication, suggesting that he had other ambitions related to the life of the mind besides making money.

Thistlewood never specified what drove him to Jamaica and what economic and social aspirations he had after he got there. Yet it is not difficult to tease out his aims from his behavior. First, he wanted a "competency," or sufficient income to provide for his needs and prevent him from falling into debt. Of course, what constituted a competency varied in the eighteenth century according to status, background, and capacity, but what Thistlewood regarded as a suitable competency seems clear. It meant having adequate money for his uncomplicated wants—enough money to purchase books, clothes, and scientific instruments from Britain; a handsome if not munificent income that allowed him to become a small landed proprietor; and wealth uncomplicated by high levels of indebtedness. Second, he wanted to establish himself on the land.[3] Thistlewood was a countryman at heart. Brought up as a farmer's son in a rural area of one of the least-populated regions of England, extensively trained in agriculture, and a keen follower of country pursuits such as hunting and fishing, he displayed little interest in city life, either in England or in Jamaica. He never visited Kingston, for example, after his initial arrival in 1750 and only sporadically went to Savanna-la-Mar, the only hamlet of any consequence in the heavily rural region of southwest Jamaica that Thistlewood settled in. Unable to become a landed proprietor in Lincolnshire like his father, stepfather, and brother, he achieved landed respectability in Jamaica. Possibly he would have been better off financially if he had remained an overseer since experienced and accomplished overseers could command very high wages, but owning land conferred social and personal benefits that a position as an employee could never offer. As writers of tracts promoting migration to the plantation colonies recognized, colonists did not seek material betterment as an end in itself. Rather, they wanted to use the wealth that residence in a slave society afforded as a means to become independent, masterless men. Jack Greene notes, "[T]he most powerful drive in the British-American colonizing process . . . was the drive for personal independence," by which colonists meant "freedom from the will of others . . . [and] a sovereignty of self in all public and private relations." Thomas Nairne and John Norris, authors of appeals for migrants to move to South Carolina, succinctly summed up the appeal of independence for eighteenth-century Britons. Free people wanted to escape working for wages, no matter how plentiful those wages were, because, Norris argued, "by Planting . . . on their own Land" they could "employ themselves very advantageously in their own Business." Nairne agreed: "How much better for Men to improve their own Lands, for the use of themselves, and Posterity; to sit under their own Vine, and eat the Fruits of their Labour," than to work for others. Nairne's vision was one that Thistlewood shared.[4] Third, Thistlewood craved recognition as a man of skill and intelligence. What renown Thistlewood had in mid-eighteenth-century Jamaica related to his expertise in horticulture and science. It was his gardening skill that distinguished him most in the small community in which he spent the majority of his life.

Thistlewood's Economic and Social Successes

Thistlewood achieved all of these aims during his lengthy residence in Westmoreland Parish. When he died in late 1786, he left a sizable estate that placed him comfortably within the ranks of the lesser landowners of the parish. Moreover, he had attained a satisfactory social position as a well-respected man in his neighborhood. He had been a justice of the peace for over a decade as well as a commissioned officer in the local militia. Although he was by no means a member of the Jamaican plantocracy, some of Jamaica's wealthiest and most cultivated men, such as the planter-historian William Beckford of Hertford Plantation, thought him worthy of their regard. In addition, he painstakingly developed a valuable property and outstanding garden in a picturesque spot in a tropical paradise. Thistlewood's gamble in coming to Jamaica had succeeded: he had achieved much more in his new home than he would have accomplished if he had remained in England.

Thistlewood's inventory of his personal estate—worth £3,371.26 Jamaica currency, or £2,408.04 sterling—indicates how well he had done. His landed property, which was relatively small, was not enumerated, but in 1789, his remaining executor, Charles Payne, sold his pen called Breadnut Island, containing 160 acres, for £600 currency—over twice what Thistlewood had paid for it when he purchased the property from Sarah Bennett in July 1765 but less than he would have received in the boom years before the American Revolution.[5] Altogether, he left an estate valued at over £3,000 sterling.[6] His wealth placed him in the top 20 percent of Jamaicans who left inventories between 1750 and 1787 and in the top 25 percent of inventoried residents of Westmoreland Parish. Since wealth was highly unequal, the top 10 percent of wealth holders possessing two-thirds of the total wealth, a better indication of Thistlewood's social position is that the value of his personal estate was almost equal to the value of the average inventoried estate in Jamaica from 1750 to 1787 and nearly three-quarters as large as the median inventoried estate of Westmoreland residents. Thistlewood was thus very much in the middling ranks of affluent white Jamaicans. He was comfortably above the mass of whites toiling for wages on plantations or in urban countinghouses, but he was not a plantocrat. He was a moderately prosperous planter, a reasonably successful figure in his local neighborhood but a negligible player in a wider arena. He had a typical and unremarkable estate, distinguished only by his extraordinarily large and well-documented collection of books and scientific instruments.[7]

But Thistlewood's estate was only ordinary in the context of the enormous wealth of mid- to late-eighteenth-century Jamaica. His estate would have been reckoned very large in most other areas of British America and would have been sizable in Britain. The average free white wealth holder in England and Wales owned property worth £210.50 (assuming a ratio of 1 wealth holder for every 5 free inhabitants). In the thirteen colonies, the comparable figure was £301. Thistlewood, therefore, was at least ten times as wealthy at his death as the average wealth holder in other parts of the British Empire.[8] Thistlewood was fortunate, or sensible, in choosing to migrate to Jamaica when the island was about to embark on a particularly prolonged period of prosperity. He was also wise to choose to set up residence in a society especially devoted to slavery. Slavery was the key to making money in Jamaica, as Thistlewood recognized. At the time of his death, he owned 34 slaves, worth over £1,500 currency, accounting for 44.2 percent of his total personal wealth and 38.8 percent of his total wealth. A slave force of 34 slaves was not large by Jamaican standards: the average sugar planter owned 204 slaves in the early 1770s.[9] But it was a very large slaveholding by the standards of British North America, where only the wealthiest Chesapeake planters owned more than 30 slaves.[10] It was Thistlewood's ownership of slaves that assured him of his competency and provided the backbone for his wealth and his pursuit of intellectual achievement.

A Land of Opportunity

The pursuit of money may not have been as great a driving force in Thistlewood's life as the quest for sexual gratification or the urge to broaden his mind through reading, but it was an important motivation nonetheless. Thistlewood was eager to maximize his moneymaking opportunities. He was careful about how the money he made was conserved and employed. His diaries also functioned as an account book—a means of keeping track of bills, monies received, and profits made or lost. A study of how Thistlewood acquired a competency helps answer several important questions: What economic and social possibilities existed in a mature plantation society for people who were not accomplished planters? Was Jamaica "the best poor man's country," as well as a prime destination for men of capital determined to make large fortunes? Did the development of a highly profitable sugar industry reduce opportunities for all but the very rich? Did slavery aid or retard economic opportunity for men arriving in Jamaica without property?

An analysis of Thistlewood's economic activities demonstrates that Jamaica was a land of opportunity for white men from all social conditions, whether native-born or migrant. Such a statement is contrary to a wide literature on eighteenth-century Caribbean society that presumes that the development of a mature sugar and slave economy militated against the interests of poorer white men.[11] But a reading of Thistlewood's diaries and associated writings shows that opportunities for white men in Jamaica abounded in the mid-eighteenth century. Adapting to Jamaica was not easy. Disease killed huge numbers of people, and the temptations of high living and luxury also led many white migrants to an early grave.[12] Moreover, not all whites found living among African slaves implacably opposed to white rule agreeable. Managing slaves was physically difficult and psychologically fraught. But if a migrant could cope with living in Jamaica's peculiar society—and Thistlewood was temperamentally suited to life in such an environment—then the possibilities for pecuniary advantage were

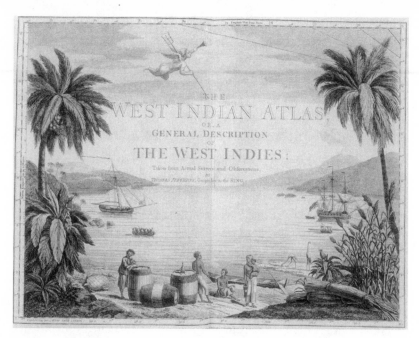

This typical West Indian scene depicts the quintessential features of eighteenth-century West Indian life: sugar and slaves in a transatlantic trading system. Title page, Thomas Jefferys, *The West Indian Atlas, or a General Description of the West Indies* (London, 1780). Courtesy of the John Carter Brown Library at Brown University.

great. The demand for white labor was virtually inexhaustible, and the island's wealth was legendary. Any man with a modicum of ambition and a measure of talent was in a very strong position to acquire a fortune superior to that possible anywhere else in Britain and its empire (save perhaps British India). If Jamaica was hell for the majority of its inhabitants—the Africans upon whose backs Jamaican wealth was created—then it was close to an earthly paradise for its small minority of white residents.

Thistlewood's thirty-seven years in Jamaica neatly span an important and distinct period in Jamaican history. He arrived when Jamaica was on the cusp of its most sustained period of prosperity, and he settled in a frontier region that was to be the engine driving economic growth. Thistlewood was well placed to take advantage of the multifarious opportunities available in this golden age of plantation production. He was a member of what Edward Gibbon Wakefield later described as the "uneasy classes" of England.[13] He was a second son in an age when most advantages in life accrued to eldest sons, and he was forced to make his own way in the world with little assistance from family or friends.

Nevertheless, he was well educated, an experienced agriculturalist (a rare skill for most migrants to Jamaica, who tended to have mercantile or trade origins),[14] and armed with useful letters of introduction from English notables. He could be assured of decent employment on arrival.

So it proved. Having sounded out longtime Jamaica residents about prospects in Jamaica, he introduced himself through Peter Collgrave's letter of recommendation to William Pullen, a Kingston merchant. Meeting with little encouragement, he headed to Savanna-la-Mar in Westmoreland Parish, where he handed Collgrave's letter to a wealthy sugar planter, William Dorrill. Thistlewood noted that he was "well-received," as was the case the next day when he visited another sugar planter, Thomas Storer, owner of the Belle Isle estate. Storer immediately offered him a job on his estate, promising that he could "succeed his overseer who leaves him in about two months."[15] Since Dorrill had already offered him a somewhat inferior position on his Salt River estate, Thistlewood was in the happy circumstance of being able to choose between several positions.

Thistlewood's plenitude of opportunities may have been related to the entrée that Collgrave's letter gave him, but it was more likely due to the chronic shortage of white labor in the island. Thistlewood quickly discovered that not everyone held Collgrave in high esteem. Within a week of arrival, he was informed that Collgrave had a reputation for excessive litigiousness.[16] Thistlewood would have probably done just as well searching for employment without any letter of introduction. As he was to discover in the next fifteen years, the plantation economy had an insatiable appetite for white plantation operatives. Few estates were able to obtain supplies of white labor sufficient to meet Jamaica's "deficiency" laws, which specified that every estate needed to employ a certain number of whites in proportion to the estate's slave population. In the first half of 1780, Westmoreland Parish collected £1,722.05 as a deficiency tax from estates with an insufficient number of whites. That year, there were 237 whites on 49 delinquent estates supervising 7,839 slaves, a ratio of 1 white for every 33 slaves.[17] The number of migrants entering Jamaica every year was neither large enough to meet plantation demand nor sufficient to replace whites who had died. Estates— especially sugar estates, where the work was demanding, slaves were numerous and especially difficult to manage, and mortality among both whites and blacks was extremely high—experienced rapid and continuing turnover of staff. On 9 April 1768, for example, Thistlewood recorded that since he had left Egypt in September 1767, eleven neighboring estates had hired new overseers.[18]

The result was that whites, especially whites who were skilled managers of slaves, could virtually demand their own price. Estate owners recognized this in the instructions they left attorneys for how white staff were to be treated. In 1754, Thistlewood copied instructions left by grandee Richard Beckford (the owner of over 900 slaves) to John Cope and his attorneys, Richard Lewing and Robert Mason. Beckford devoted considerable attention to the "care off White Servants," distinguishing their treatment from that of slaves. He noted that whites were "free men and have a right to ye Protection of ye Laws and are not to be Subjected to ye Will and Caprice of an Overseer." An overseer needed to "treat them with honesty and tenderness and Consider them a part of his Family." Beckford stressed the need for developing a familial relationship between whites further. Believing that "as Nothing Will Contribute more to Animate and Encourage them in ye discharge of their duty than ye Expectation of Reward and Preferment," he insisted that it be "an inviolable Rule" that his employees never "proffer a stranger to be Storekeeper or Distiller or Overseer whilst there is a Servant in my employ of sufficient Abilities to fill any Vacancy." White labor had to be cultivated—at almost any price.[19]

The certainty of employment encouraged Thistlewood to wait for nearly two months after arrival before deciding to accept an offer of work from Florentius Vassall, a wealthy sugar planter with a cattle pen in St. Elizabeth Parish. He turned down Storer's proposal on 9 June, believing that he "had better views which prevented me." Meanwhile, he canvassed Dorrill for advice about possible routes to riches. Some of the advice Dorrill offered was trite—he observed that "Advantageous acquaintance is oft contracted at Publick Schools" and said that "he buys when other people leave off"—but some was useful. Dorrill noted that planting grass and selling logwood were both "very profitable" and had low startup costs. For example, Dorrill had allowed Thomas Tomlinson, a man of similar condition to Thistlewood, to plant grass on four or five acres of Dorrill's land. Dorrill expected Tomlinson to clear £200 or £300 per annum. Hearing that Dorrill had contributed £140 to the cost of fitting out a privateer owned by Westmoreland Parish, Thistlewood briefly entertained the idea of becoming "a supercargo or factor in his sloop." But Thistlewood was most interested in becoming a surveyor. On 26 May, he noted that he "oft over-hear[d] gentlemen whom Mr. Dorrill mentions my Intent to be a Surveyor to say that it will be a very good thing for me, iff I understand but enough of figures for it, which gives me great hope." Thistlewood met a surveyor named William Wallace and began an association with James Crawford under Wallace's direction. All went well until 29 June when Thistlewood learned that Crawford "this morning wilfully threw himself into ye Sea by Wallace's and was drown'd, being so Mad that they could not hold him." Thistlewood was devastated, partly because "so straight a friendship [had] been Contracted between us, we being so much off a Temper as Seem'd to be one mind in two Separate Bodies," and partly because they "had form'd great hopes in ye Surveying Business that had ever been known in this Country." He believed that "we should have effected" such hopes if Crawford had lived, "but now my hopes are dead." On the same day that he learned of Crawford's suicide, Thistlewood agreed to become pen keeper for Vassall at Vineyard Pen in the plains of southwest St. Elizabeth for a wage of £50 per annum.[20]

Thistlewood was encouraged in his ambitions by the evidence he saw around him of ordinary men raised to extraordinary wealth. Social mobility was much greater than in England. When Dorrill informed him that "a Ratt catcher might have got an estate," Thistlewood thought it "very probable." He had already noted how wealthy Dorrill was and had met ordinary and uncouth men such as Thomas Jackson who were very prosperous. He may not have been able to aspire to the heights of wealth of absentee and London mayor William Beckford, but he could emulate Jackson and George Currie, a migrant from Newcastle upon Tyne. Currie started out very poor but by 1751 could treat Thistlewood to a fine meal and bring his indigent brothers over from Newcastle to "enjoy what he has got."[21]

Searching for a Good Overseer

Making money was open to all whites, whatever their origins, because the demand for white labor was virtually unlimited and the power of white labor over capital close to absolute. Thistlewood experienced for himself the effect of the scarcity of suitable white labor on wages. He never had to search for a job between 1750 and 1765, and his wages went up inexorably. His first wage, at Vineyard, was £50 per annum. In 1751, he accepted a position at Dorrill's sugar estate of Egypt for £60 a year, having turned down an offer from Wallace in August 1751 to assist him in surveying for £50 per annum the first year and £100 the second year and to "live as he lives." A major perk associated with any plantation job was free room and board; overseers in demand could insist on dining at the owner's table and could enjoy the same food and drink that wealthy planters feasted on. Thus, Thistlewood's expenses as an employee were minimal.

By 1754, Thistlewood's asking price had risen appreciably as planters tried to lure him away from Egypt. On 8 September, Philip Haughton, a fabulously wealthy planter from the northwestern parish of Hanover, offered him "£70 per Annum to goe live at his estate near Montego Bay to live and eat at his Table and have the liberty of killing fowls or Shoot when I pleased iff he was not upon the Estate etc." By relaying this generous offer to John Cope, Dorrill's successor as owner of the Egypt estate, Thistlewood gained a substantial increase in salary and better conditions. Cope promised Thistlewood £80 per annum and an incentive of 20 shillings a hogshead of sugar for every hogshead produced over 80. By 1756, the going rate for overseers had reached three figures. Thistlewood reported, "Mr. Jarrod has £100 per annum," as did Mr. Atkinson, the overseer for Jonathan Atkins.[22] Throughout 1756, he pestered Cope for a raise in salary, his mood not helped by the fact that Cope was well in arrears in paying him previous years' wages. Cope did little to meet his demands except to try to negotiate a deal whereby Thistlewood would act as Cope's clerk in his local magistracy and take all of the profits of the office. Thistlewood does not explain why he turned down this offer, but he was undoubtedly right to do so. Profits from office could be high, but they entailed much more risk, notably from debtors absconding without settling their debts, than the virtually risk-free position of being an overseer entailed. More significant, Thistlewood's profits depended on the capacities of Cope, and Thistlewood had good reason to doubt the abilities of his feckless and improvident employer. A much more attractive offer came from John Parkinson, the owner of Paul Island and Kendal sugar estates. Thistlewood was to live at Kendal, receive £100 per annum, "and afterwards to have my wages raised."[23] Tired of what he considered Cope's continual interference in his management of Egypt, Thistlewood accepted Parkinson's offer and left for Kendal in late June 1757. He stayed for a year, despite not liking the property and missing Phibbah, his long-time mistress, terribly.

Cope realized quickly what he had lost. Accomplished managers of slaves were not easy to find. By the end of 1757, he and John Dorwood tried to interest Thistlewood in accepting £200 per annum to manage the business of a wharf with five slaves that he himself would provide. He would have to feed himself, but Cope and Dorwood would cover the expense of feeding his slaves. Thistlewood was tempted but got cold feet after Christmas, so Cope proposed a new arrangement whereby Thistlewood would gain the half of the profits from the wharf that were due to Cope. Thistlewood "would not run the Risque" even after Cope agreed to throw in the use for life of some undeveloped land that Cope had patented. Dorwood also tried to lure Thistlewood away from Kendal, offering him £120 a year and "Salt Provisions." Thistlewood resisted this offer, as well as three proposals from Cope to return to Egypt. He relented only after Cope agreed to give him £120 per annum and an incentive payment of 20 shillings per hogshead of sugar for every hogshead made over 120. A significant factor in the protracted negotiations may also have been Cope's agreement to hire Thistlewood's slaves to work on the estate. Certainly he did not need to return to Egypt. At least three planters were willing to hire him besides Cope and Parkinson, who very much wanted to keep him in his employ. Offers continued to pour in even after he moved back to Egypt in 1758. In 1759, the wealthy planter Martin Williams sought him to work for his brother, George, at the Moreland estate. A year later, Parkinson tried to get Thistlewood back, promising that "he would make it worth my while." In 1761, Thistlewood was offered work by Bernard Senior, Parson William Ramsay, Susanna Elletson, and Parson Robert Atkins. The latter, the rector of Kingston, with a yearly clerical income of over £1,000 in addition to the fortune of his wife, the wealthy widow of a Westmoreland planter, offered him on 5 October 1761 the best deal yet— £160 per annum, the hiring of his slaves, and the promise of being made Atkins's attorney at a salary of £200 per annum after Atkins left the island in 1763. By 1767, as he was preparing to leave waged employment behind, he heard that the attorney of William Beckford was willing to hire him "at any rate." One presumes that if he had remained a plantation employee and moved to a leading estate, he would have been able to command a yearly wage of over £200; in 1779, he reported that an overseer on Robert Woolery's Midgeham estate was hired at the remarkable rate of £300 per annum. Nine years earlier, he related that his friend and his former underling, Harry Weech and Billy Foote, "both ignorant of planting," had been given "the attorneyships of Lincoln and Petersfield said to be worth £300 pr: ann."[24]

Thistlewood's rapid rise up the plantation ladder and continual job offers from leading planters in the district illustrate the extent to which servants were in a stronger position than masters in the Jamaican economy. Planters desperately needed white workers and were forced to pay market rates in a market where demand for white labor was unlimited. Moreover, planters were obliged to pay employees in cash. Since planters often lived on credit and found cash difficult to come by, meeting these demands placed them under significant financial strain. Thistlewood's nephew John thought his uncle was so vital to Cope's enterprise that if he left "it will be Mr. Cope ruin for all his Creditors will sue him Emediately."[25] As Cope discovered, an employer had relatively little leverage over an employee: white men could always find new positions if they were unhappy. Masters would then be forced to employ any available white man. Many potential employees were highly unsatisfactory—they might be drunkards, sexual predators, or poor managers of slaves with little to no work ethic. In 1760, for example, Thistlewood received instructions from Cope to employ Walter Perry, who had previously been at the Salt River estate. Perry was most unsatisfactory. The first night he was at Egypt, he proved "very Troublesome in [fellow servant John Grove's] house," and Thistlewood was "obliged to get up and have him moved to the Cookhouse." Nine days later, he discharged Perry. A week later, Perry returned, "begg'd hard," and was rehired for £25 per annum. Within a month, Perry was again causing trouble. He "made such a Noise at Night I could not rest, nor would he hold his Tongue for all I could say to him." Perry ended up in the hothouse, where sick slaves were tended. The last straw came a day later. Thistlewood found Perry "long dead drunk last night on the Floor [of] John's house Says he has lost all but 2 Bitts out of the one pound Twelve and sixpence paid him yesterday by Mr. Cope, this Forenoon [4 December 1760] he March's." But the demand for labor was so great that even a manifestly unsuitable employee such as Perry was able to get another position the day after his dismissal.[26]

Asset-Rich but Cash-Poor

In British North American plantation societies, wealthy planters were able to cement community relations by binding less wealthy men to their interest with small but important loans. In Jamaica, however, it was the master who was financially obligated to the servant.[27] By mid-century, liquidity was a significant problem for planters. Jamaica was short of working capital, and planters operated in an interlocking web of credit and debt in which cash changed hands infrequently.[28] But employees insisted on negotiating wages that were paid mostly in cash rather than in kind. The result was that most planters—asset-rich but cash-poor—found it difficult to meet their wage bills. Cope, for example, was always short of money, in part due to improvidence and incompetence but also due to the exigencies of plantation management.

Jamaican inventories reveal numerous examples of bookkeepers and planters who died with few possessions except for large debts owed to them by their employers. Joseph Reeves, a bookkeeper in Hanover Parish, for example, died in 1753, leaving an estate of £382, which included a horse and a slave. The majority of the estate, however, was made up of debts, presumably from his employers. Montague James, a wealthy sugar planter, owed Reeves £260, and Thomas Torrent and William Penny each owed him £50. Darby Morgan's inventory dates from the same year. He was more established than Reeves—a planter rather than a bookkeeper—and died with a personal estate of £960 that included seven slaves. Nevertheless, much of the estate was made up of debts, including £403 owed to him by Isaac Knott.[29] If Thistlewood had died in the 1750s, his inventory would have been similar. All three of his employers—Dorrill, Cope, and Parkinson—were slow to forward him his wages. In 1756, Thistlewood noted that he was due £157.01 from Dorrill's estate—amounting to nearly two years' salary.[30] When he left Cope's employ in June 1757, Cope owed him £92.47, and a further £15.63 was due from Dorrill's estate. At the beginning of 1761, Cope owed Thistlewood £329, which he managed to reduce during the year to £15.61. But by January 1764, Cope's liability to Thistlewood had risen again to over £400. Cope did not manage to wipe the debt clean until October 1770, three years after Thistlewood's departure from his employ.

Cope's inability to pay Thistlewood's wages was a constant source of friction between the two men. The difficulty was mostly Cope's because Thistlewood could always rightfully claim the debts owed to him if he decided to leave (as he did in 1757) and Cope would have to pay. Cope needed to promise ever-larger salaries in order to keep his overseer and boosted Thistlewood's income, and the size of Cope's debt, by agreeing to hire Thistlewood's slaves. But Cope did not have the ready cash to meet his obligations. On 23 June 1764, he was reduced to begging Thistlewood to stay, even though he "could not pay me till next year."[31] The solution was to pay in kind: Thistlewood was able to export a share of Egypt's rum production in lieu of wages. More important, Cope stood bond when Thistlewood tried to purchase slaves. Merchants hesitated to lend to landless servants but were willing to lend on the security of a sugar estate, even one that was heavily mortgaged. Thistlewood purchased his first slave, Lincoln, in 1756 with Cope's help. He did not need Cope's security in 1758 when he bought three slaves from Parkinson, his employer at Kendal, but he did force Cope to pay for the slaves in lieu of wages. Cope paid for sixteen more slaves in two separate purchases in 1761 and 1765. Significantly, Cope paid for Thistlewood's slaves on Thistlewood's terms, retaining no interest in the purchased slaves whatsoever. He also helped Thistlewood secure a commission in the militia and paid for the manumission of Thistlewood's son, John.[32]

A Difficult Servant

Thistlewood faced other problems with his employers besides getting them to pay wages. He was a prickly, difficult man, conscious of his dignity and well aware of his worth. He demanded that his employers recognize his abilities, allow him considerable independence, and leave him alone to manage as he saw fit. This attitude sometimes caused problems, especially in his first years in Westmoreland, when he was relatively unknown. Jamaican planters were proud and feisty, quick to take offense at perceived slights, and they were accustomed to having their orders obeyed at all times. The imperiousness and self-importance they derived from commanding dependent slaves were transferred to their dealings with their white servants, with unfortunate results. Thistlewood found this out soon after taking up his first position, at Vineyard Pen. When he wrote a letter to Florentius Vassall about "the hardships of my living" and "my ill-usage since I had been in his Service," Vassall exploded in anger, declaring that "if he should ever receive such another letter from me as my last, he would make the Blood flow about my face." Thistlewood, characteristically, did not back down: "I answered he must not want for another but do it now if he thought proper." Vassall responded by instructing his slave driver "to obey Mr. Mordiner in every thing as himself and look upon him as his Master." Thomas Mordiner also worked at Vineyard. The insult quickly led to Thistlewood seeking another position, a decision that he was unwilling to change even when Vassall turned "very good Tempered and Compliant."[33]

Thistlewood was not a man to be trifled with. Within a month of becoming overseer at Egypt, he ordered Theodore Stone, who would later be the Westmoreland representative in the assembly, to stop shooting on the estate without permission. A few months later, he engaged in a heated dispute with wealthy planter Jacob Ricketts about whether Thistlewood could whip Ricketts's slaves if they wandered onto Egypt. Thistlewood stood his ground, as he did two years later in a similar dispute with the leading man in the parish, Colonel James Barclay, over Thistlewood's right to whip another man's slaves. His neighbors soon learned to leave Thistlewood alone.[34]

Disputes with neighbors could be resolved; difficulties with employers were more intractable. Thistlewood was never entirely satisfied with his job at Egypt. The wages were relatively low, the work was hard, and the management style of the owners left much to be desired. As early as 11 August 1752, he expressed his dissatisfaction to Dorrill. Dorrill was sympathetic. He "did not desire me to stay against my will," but he would not "turn me away" unless Thistlewood wanted to go. The same scenario recurred on 13 March 1754, with Dorrill giving "his approbation but not his Consent" to Thistlewood leaving "the Care and management off this plantation." Dorrill's conciliatory style encouraged Thistlewood to remain. He was less happy in the employ of Dorrill's son-in-law, John Cope. Thistlewood's disdain for Cope—a feckless man devoted to drink and, according to Thistlewood, sex with prepubescent black girls—is apparent throughout his diaries. Cope's personal weaknesses did not worry Thistlewood unduly, but his perennial difficulties with money and his deficiencies as a plantation owner were of more moment. Cope was not up to the task of managing a sugar estate. He was able to survive in the halcyon days of economic boom in the 1760s and 1770s, although he had a close call in 1765 when he escaped being arraigned for debt only by traveling to Kingston with £1,900 in cash to settle his accounts and he had to sell Paradise Pen in 1774 for £10,500, far less than the £19,508 he had valued it at on 21 December 1766. But the natural disasters and economic hardships of the 1780s led to his complete failure. Even before the 1780 hurricane, Cope was in trouble. On 22 January 1770, Thistlewood reported that Cope had signed a fifth mortgage on Egypt. By March 1780, Cope was trying to sell Egypt, despite the fact that his wife (from whom Cope had derived his right to the property) was "exceedingly averse" to the sale. Egypt was finally sold on 6 July 1784 at auction for a mere £8,300, a humiliating public embarrassment for the custos of the parish. When Cope died on 1 March 1792, his inventory amounted to just £3,150.93, £220.33 less than that of his erstwhile employee at his death.[35]

Thistlewood continually quarreled with Cope over money, conditions, and his interference with Thistlewood's management. Thistlewood's principal complaints were that Cope undermined his authority over white servants, especially by being partial, in Thistlewood's view, to William Crookshanks, whom Thistlewood had little time for,[36] and that he gave Phibbah "no Time." These complaints led him to write to Vassall in 1759 to inquire whether Vassall had a position open, even though he professed to have "a great dislike for often changing estates."[37] By 1760, Cope had heard of Thistlewood's dissatisfaction and summoned him to Savanna-la-Mar. Cope informed him that "he had hired another Overseer, and would bring him tomorrow fortnight." No new overseer was ever sent. Thistlewood's resentment festered. By 1761, he again thought of leaving Cope. His friend, Samuel Hayward, told him that "he thinks Mr. Cope's affairs desperate and wishes I had what was due to me." Parson Ramsay, who was eager to employ Thistlewood, urged him to leave Cope. Matters came to a head early in 1763 over a dispute concerning two puncheons belonging to Thistlewood that Cope had returned as under proof along with a "chiding letter." Thistlewood exploded. "Sir," he wrote Cope, "I have often thought you Certainly make it your Study how to lay this Estate under the greatest Inconveniences," as his return of rum that "was better than common market proof" demonstrated. He concluded with a flourish: "I have never expected better Treatment from you Whilst in your Service." Later in 1763, Thistlewood again had reason to be angry with Cope when Mr. Moffat, a slave dealer, refused to accept Cope's bond as payment for newly arrived Africans.[38] Thistlewood began preparing in earnest to leave Egypt and to set up for himself. On 12 March 1766, he settled his accounts with Cope (although Cope still owed him a considerable sum) and noted that "after this day I take my Negroes away and prepare to leave the place my Self as soon as convenient." Two months later, he started sending his slaves to work on his new property. He left Cope for good in September 1767. Even after he left Cope's employ, he fell victim to his former employer's caprices. On 16 September 1768, he rode to Egypt to meet with Molly Cope, who insisted that Thistlewood pay "£18 ready money to her for a year's wages for Phibbah's hire although it will not be due till the 16th day of November and Mr. Cope still greatly in my debt." For Thistlewood, this was further proof of Cope's "strange meanness—but Mr. Cope is capable of any meanness whatever."

Thistlewood and White Labor

Thistlewood was no doubt pleased to leave the employment of a man he did not respect and to be free from the burden of supervising white drivers, distillers, and tradesmen. White men employed on sugar plantations were a motley crew. Turnover was constant. Between 16 April 1759 and 27 July 1764, for example, eighteen white men worked under Thistlewood at Egypt. Only John Groves, who panicked in the tumult of Tackey's revolt and thus lost Thistlewood's confidence, stayed for longer than a year. Most of the rest lasted for less than three months. Several, such as William Deacon, who was employed between 11 and 16 June 1761, stayed for only a few days. The perpetual turnover meant that Thistlewood often had to cope without white assistance, as he did between 21 December 1762 and 10 March 1763. Quality was an even greater concern than turnover. Even if we accept that Thistlewood was not an impartial judge of the abilities of his underlings, it is hard to deny that several of the white men employed at Egypt were less than ideal. Walter Perry, John Burgess, Thomas Mackenzie, and Patrick May were all dismissed for drunkenness. May's discharge was typical. On 22 May 1763, he went to Savanna-la-Mar and returned "sometime in the Night in Liqr." He picked a fight with Thistlewood's slave, Nanny, "whom he kept," and "Shot at her with Small Shot, one of Which Struck her head near the Top and the others her Ankle, both these Shots seem to be lodged." The next day, Thistlewood "told him to go about his business and he went."[39] James Rogers also drank heavily but was dismissed for beating slaves with too much gusto, even by Thistlewood's standards. A month after his dismissal, Thistlewood reported: "James Rogers has been hired to live upon Quasheba's

Mountain and has Chop't Some Negroes sadly, the Constable is after him."[40] Groves also departed "because he might not flog the Negroes as he pleased; very Stubborn and resolute." His next employment ended for the same reason: "I hear John Groves lived a little while (a week or ten days) with Mr. McDonald at Roaring River, but was discharged for beating the Negroes impudently in the Boiling house."[41] Robert Gibbs, a Barbadian and "a Worthless Fellow," was dismissed for continual indolence, Thomas Beard was discharged for frequently absenting himself from work, and Richard Lloyd decided that he preferred to be a privateer rather than a slave driver. Those servants who were not dismissed for misconduct were likely to sicken or die. John Orman, Christopher White, and, most tragically (for he probably would have become Thistlewood's heir), John Thistlewood all died from disease or accident while in service.

The poor quality of the lowliest white plantation workers can be seen less in those who were dismissed than in those who were considered satisfactory. Thistlewood had two employees whom he gave good references when they left Egypt. Henry McCormick stayed the longest. He arrived on 27 July 1764 and departed on 12 August 1766 because he did "Not Choose to Stay under Mr. hartnole [Thistlewood's successor as overseer at Egypt]." Thistlewood "gave him a Character thus!," declaring that in his two years at Egypt "he has behaved very well last Crop he was in the Still house and was very Carefull: he now leaves Egypt of his own desire." But in November 1764, both John Thistlewood and Thomas Thistlewood noticed that he entertained "two white ladies" from Savanna-la-Mar who "staid all night with him," and on 8 January 1766, Thistlewood reported that "harry McCormack was drunk this Morning, tumbled out off the Cart and the Wheels run over him—badly bruised." Six months later, Thistlewood had to reprimand McCormick "for encouraging mean white people to come to the still house to him" and for "frequenting the Negroe houses in the Night etc." McCormick's amorous proclivities may have hastened his end. On 9 April 1768, Thistlewood repeated "a report that henry McCormick is killed by a tree falling upon him" and implied that it was not an accident: "ye Negroes who were felling ye tree" and who were now runaways had "murdered him for meddling with their women."[42] Henry Weech, a native Jamaican, became a close friend of Thistlewood's after serving under him for eighteen months after Thistlewood's return from Kendal and then becoming the overseer of Cope's other sugar estate, Paradise, in 17 April 1759. Yet, by his own testimony, he was capable of horrific brutality, claiming in 1765 that he had savagely mutilated the face of his mulatto sweetheart "in Jealousy" at her supposed infidelity with a black man. At the time, Weech kept two mulatto sisters and a white woman. He died eight months later, on 13 August 1766, at age thirty, from cirrhosis of the liver.[43]

Thistlewood as Slave Owner

Why, then, did Thistlewood stay at Egypt so long? During Thistlewood's second stint at Egypt, eight overseers came and went from Cope's Paradise estate. Given Cope's capriciousness, the inadequacy of most white plantation operatives, the arduousness of making sugar, and the unremitting hostility of slaves enmeshed in the hellish conditions of the mid-eighteenth-century sugar system, it is understandable that few white men were able to stomach being an overseer for long. Certainly Thistlewood always had other options. With his education, he could have taken up school mastering, as his friend William Barnet did. A more profitable option would have been to emulate his closest friend of his early days in Westmoreland, Thomas Emotson, and become a tavern keeper. Emotson claimed in 1760 that he cleared £500 per annum from this occupation.[44] He could have returned to his initial dream of surveying, having been approached in 1753 by Robert Brown of St. Elizabeth about forming a surveying partnership. He could have tried his luck in another country—he was tempted to cut logwood in Honduras, made favorable comments about trading possibilities in Surinam, and noted the delights of Pennsylvania. Indeed, before accepting Dorrill's offer at Egypt in September 1751, he had decided that if no good offer came his way, "I should have gone to Hispaniola with Captain Riviere de la Bruce, to have learnt to make Indico."[45]

Thistlewood, as was his usual practice, did not explain why he stayed or why he chose to become a pen keeper after leaving Cope's employ. But it seems likely that he had an ambition to become a landowner from early in his time in Jamaica. On 26 February 1751, he noted that "[t]he governor now proposes to grant any person an Order for land, except that they will take the oath, they have slaves and no land to work them on." A month later, he visited George Currie, who was some sort of land agent for the Jamaican government, and was told "the way to procure an order for land is to bribe ye governors secretary with a doubloon." A major inducement for his return to Egypt in 1758 was Cope's promise to give him land—a promise that, like so many of Cope's promises, came to nothing. The key to becoming a landowner was to save money for its purchase and, more important, to buy slaves to work on the land. Thistlewood remained as an overseer for so long because it afforded him the best opportunity to buy slaves, his principal financial ambition in the 1750s and 1760s. Being an overseer was often disagreeable, to be sure, but it was virtually risk-free and provided a steady income.

Slaves were the key to Thistlewood's prosperity. Slaves were highly desirable forms of property for three reasons. First, and most obvious, slaves could be used to produce income as workers. The great majority of slaves in eighteenth-century Jamaica were productive workers. At least three-quarters of all slaves could be employed in some way. On the well-documented York estate in Trelawney Parish in northwest Jamaica, 68 percent of slaves in 1778 were between the ages of fifteen and forty-four, with fewer than 15 percent being young children or superannuated adults.[46] Thistlewood's slaves tended to be productive adults. At his death, only eight of thirty-four slaves were children too young to be put to productive use. The proportion that was productive was higher when he was building his slave force in the 1760s. In the early 1760s, for example, only one of fourteen slaves owned by Thistlewood could not be put to work. Moreover, one did not need to own property to be able to earn income from one's slaves. The demand for slave labor, especially on sugar estates, where the need for healthy slaves was always acute, was as great as for white labor.

Second, slaves were a valuable investment that appreciated considerably over time. Slave prices skyrocketed during Thistlewood's time in Jamaica. In 1756, Thistlewood bought his first slave, Lincoln, a sixteen-year-old Ibo, for £43. Within a couple of years, the asking price for similarly aged male slaves had risen to £50. By 1762, Thistlewood paid as much for a nine- or ten-year-old girl as he had paid for Lincoln. In 1765, a man-boy fetched a price of £54. By the early 1770s, when the slave trade was at its height and the sugar economy was flourishing, slave merchants could get "£60 for the Women and £52 and duty for girls not 10 years old."[47] In 1775, one slave dealer insisted on £59 plus duty for any slave. He, too, was able to get his price. Slave buyers were willing to pay such inflated prices because they could be assured that the slaves they bought would rapidly appreciate in value. Acclimatized slaves were considerably more valuable than new and unseasoned Africans. In 1773, Thistlewood, as executor of his partner Samuel Say's estate, arranged for the sale of Say's thirty slaves at auction. Thistlewood insisted on strict terms: cash or bills of exchange only, with a deduction of 6 percent "for prompt payment." All of the slaves were sold and fetched a total price of £2,216.28. The average price was an impressive £73.94, with skilled slaves bringing extraordinary prices. Colin, a driver, and Fanny, a field worker bought by Thistlewood, each went for £85; Doll was sold for £101.03; Quacco, a carpenter and sawyer, was bought for

£100; Alexis fetched £111; and Carrydom, a mason, was sold for the top price of the day of £171. Eleven years later, Thistlewood bargained equally successfully with Julines Herring in regard to his deceased friend Samuel Hayward's highly productive slave force, receiving £5,200 for fifty-two adults and one child—an average of £100 per slave.

Inventories bear out the value of buying slaves as an investment. Between 1739 and 1775, the average price of a slave jumped by 145 percent, reflecting less a shortage of supply than the robustness of the Jamaican economy in this period.[48] A slave that survived "seasoning" was thus a rapidly appreciating asset. The biggest risk was that slaves would die before they had earned enough to recoup their purchase price. Owners of sugar estates could count on nearly a third of their slaves dying before they were "seasoned" (a process that could take two to three years).[49] Buying slaves could be financially disastrous. Thistlewood recounted in 1784 that Sir James Richardson, who ate bread and cheese with Thistlewood and whom Thistlewood thought "a sensible man," had lost 141 of the 190 slaves he had bought in the last fourteen years, "such bad luck has he!"[50] Although Thistlewood was either a much better manager of slaves or more fortunate than Richardson, he had his share of bad luck as well. On 17 August 1773, he listed his losses in the last month. They included two hogs, a young calf and a steer worth £11.50, two suckling children—Phoebe's child and Nanny's child, each worth £5—and Abba's Neptune, a boy near the age of seven valued at £35. Thistlewood resigned himself to fate: "God's will be done."[51]

He could afford to be equable about his losses because they were rare. Thistlewood did remarkably well with his slave purchases, possibly because he took considerable care in choosing the slaves he purchased. He preferred men-boys and girls, "none exceeding 16 or 18 years old, as full grown men and women seldom turn out well," and noted that he had "observed that many new Negroes, who are bought fat and sleek from aboard the ship, soon fall away much in a plantation, whereas those which are in a moderate condition hold their flesh better and are commonly hardier." In addition, "Those whose lips are pale, or whites of their eyes yellowish, [are] seldom healthful."[52] Only three slaves of the twenty-seven he bought between 1756 and 1778 died within three years of their purchase. Four slaves caused him so much trouble that he sold them, although only Simon, whom he bought for £51 in 1758 and sold three years later for £35, lost him money. The other three troublesome slaves, all women, were each sold for £40 after having served him for six, thirteen, and twenty-two years, respectively, and having cost him £131.50 to purchase. In sum, of the slaves

Thistlewood purchased, sixteen stayed with him until his death, seven prede-ceased him, and four were sold. In addition, he gained fourteen children from the reproduction of his slave women and had the use of Bess (whom he counted as part of his property although she was a gift from Sarah Bennett, a free col-ored woman, in 1765 to Thistlewood's mistress, Phibbah) and Bess's two chil-dren. From these slaves, he received 500 years of service. Seventeen slaves la-bored in his service for over 20 years apiece, with the first slave that he bought, Lincoln, serving him for nearly 31 years.

If we assume, based on calculations made by Barry Higman for Jamaica in the early nineteenth century, that the average production per slave was at least £10 per annum and note that the amount his slaves were worth in 1786 (£1,505) was virtually identical to the amount he spent buying slaves (£1,503.26), then This-tlewood would have derived £5,000 profit from his slaves between 1756 and 1786. We reach similar conclusions if we follow the method advocated by Rich-ard Sheridan for estimating rates of return for slaves in Jamaica between 1765 and 1775. Sheridan computed the average return per annum at between 6 and 11 percent, depending on how long the slave had been in service. Using Sheri-dan's estimates, we can calculate that Thistlewood grossed £4,958.40 from his slaves between 1756 and 1786, assuming a capital value of £80 for prime male hands and £70 for prime female hands. Most of his slaves more than paid for their purchase price, with Lincoln providing Thistlewood with 623 percent of his purchase price and fourteen slaves providing Thistlewood with between 300 and 470 percent of their purchase price. Thistlewood lost money on only five slaves, most notably Syphox and Bristol, adult males purchased for £56 and £54, respectively, in 1765 who both died within a year of purchase.[53] Against this sum, we need to place the costs of maintenance. These costs were minimal since his slaves provided most of their own food, except in the aftermath of the great hurricane of 1780, when supplies were very short and Thistlewood had to spend considerable sums on imported foodstuffs. Thistlewood supplied cloth-ing and paid a few pounds a year for a doctor. Masters were supposed to pro-vide slaves with coarse linen shirts, caps, jackets, blankets, and petticoats or trousers, according to the sex, but commonly they provided only breeches for men and a single petticoat for women. Masters seldom gave slaves more than five yards of cloth a year and almost never gave them shoes or stockings.[54] Thistlewood does not detail the costs of maintaining his slaves, but the total was unlikely to have been more than £20 to £30 per annum and was less when he was an overseer at Egypt and the care and feeding of his slaves was covered in his overseer's contract. Douglas Hall estimates that in 1772 the cost of maintaining twenty-four slaves was approximately £27–28, implying a net return of over £200 if slave productivity was at least £10 per slave per annum.[55]

Third, the demand for slaves was so high that a slave owner could always be certain of selling his slaves quickly, even when he was unable to sell anything else. Thistlewood was in general a buyer rather than a seller of slaves. He only sold slaves he considered more trouble than they were worth. Nevertheless, he knew he could sell his slaves whenever he wanted, in contrast to his landed property, which he was unable to sell when he put it on the market in 1781. Samuel Say's slaves were sold and divided up without any difficulty when Thistlewood was charged with selling them as Say's executor. Significantly, nine different owners bought Thistlewood's thirty slaves after his death. Unlike land, which was seldom divided, slave forces were inherently dividable. The result was that a landowner short of cash could easily sell one or two slaves without having to liquidate all of his holdings. The salability of slaves can be seen in cases in which marshals seized slaves in lieu of payment of debt or debtors fled the country, taking their slaves with them.[56] Moreover, a landowner could rely on getting cash or short terms of credit for his slaves. Whereas property could be paid off over six or seven years, slaves had to be paid for in no more than three years. For white Jamaicans wanting to return home, the certainty of payment for slaves and the relatively strict credit terms were a decided bonus since getting money out of mid- to late-eighteenth-century Jamaica could be protracted and cumbersome.[57]

Thistlewood's fortune was built firmly on the backs of his slaves. After 1768, he called himself a pen keeper, but a more accurate description would be "slave owner." The great majority of his income was derived not from his pen-keeping activities but from hiring out slaves to work on neighboring sugar estates or to build public works, such as bridges, for the parish. At the end of every year, Thistlewood tried to account for his annual income. Table 2.1 details the composition of his personal estate between 1756 and 1786, and Table 2.2 outlines the makeup of his income between 1767 and 1786. Table 2.2 is an incomplete summary, however, since Thistlewood did not include all of the money he received for the sale of livestock, money he received for the sale of logwood cut on his estate, money he made from casual jobs such as surveying, or the substantial sums his slaves earned for him through independent labor. He lists the amount he earned from hiring out his slaves for eleven years between 1768 and 1779. In those years, his average earnings from slave hiring were £172.54 and the average percentage of his income that was derived from slave hiring was 77 percent.

If we assume that he maintained such earnings throughout his twenty years on the pen and that he made no money from his slaves in the year of the 1780 hurricane, then his total earnings from slave hiring between 1767 and 1786 would come to £3,163.23. This sum would have amounted to 57 percent of his total income from the pen, with the overall percentage lower than the percentage in most years because he received very large sums in 1784 and 1785 for the sale of logwood. Most of the money received for slave hiring came from local sugar planters needing extra labor. In 1771, for example, Thistlewood earned £182.75 for 1,949.5 days of slave labor on the Friendship sugar estate and £36.28 for 387 days of work in the sugar harvest on the Masemure estate. He also received in that year £191.93 for slaves owned by Samuel Hayward who worked 2,047.5 days on the Friendship estate.[58] A comment Thistlewood made about Hayward suggests that the sums Thistlewood received from slave hiring were not exceptionally lucrative. Thistlewood thought that "Mr. haywards negroes 45 to 51 workers have earned him £1401 some odd shillings the last year, on different estates, he asks so much for them." Even if this was for two years, the sums quoted imply a return per slave of over £27 per annum.[59]

Thistlewood Becomes a Pen Keeper

The large sums that Thistlewood received from slave hiring suggest that he would have been better off remaining as an overseer, supplementing his wages by hiring out slaves and investing the proceeds in new slaves. If he had taken up Parson Atkins's offer of an attorneyship at £200 per annum, his total income would have averaged nearly £400 a year. Instead, his annual income as a pen keeper was between £275 and £300.[60] Becoming the manager of a sugar estate, especially a large one owned by an absentee landlord, was a profitable alternative to striking out on one's own. Robert Mason, William Beckford's Jamaican sugar manager, was reckoned in 1762 to have an annual income of £2,500.[61] Such wealth was exceptional; it provided Mason with an income larger than that of most sugar planters and equal to that of a prominent merchant or attorney. Moreover, it was secure income, earned without undertaking the risks that owning landed property entailed. Many white Jamaicans combined "jobbing" (slave hiring) with plantation employment. A census of St. James taken in 1774 lists 38 "jobbers" (out of a total of 221 slave owners) who owned 1,504 slaves— nearly 40 slaves each and 9 percent of the slaves in the parish.[62] Thistlewood's partner at Breadnut Island Pen, Samuel Say, for example, accepted an offer of an overseership from Martin Williams of the Old Hope estate in April 1770 and

TABLE 2.1: Summary of Thistlewood's Personal Estate, 1756–1764, 1766–1786

Year	Slaves	Horses	Cattle	Sheep	Cash	Credits	Debts
1756	1						
1757	1						
1758	1	1			10.41	149.56	14.94
1759	4	1	1		Very little	163.47	52.67
1760	4	1				197.26	120.46
1761	4	1			12.66	397.34	15.13
1762	14	1			58.72	8.40	16.92
1763	14	1			42.38		
1764	14	1			25.84	416.00+	None
1766	25	2			34.75	ca. 500.00	287.00
1767	28	2				489.07+	228.22
1768	27	2			32.06	200–300.00	79.00
1769	26	2			12.26	150.66+	33.16
1770	26				56.86	89.44	37.11
1771	25				22.57	127.81	95.61
1772	24				78.56	100.21	9.78
1773	27				40–50.00	76.44	15.16
1774	28	4	9	30	43.14	216.11	34.00
1775	29	3	15	27	146.96	301.25	20.00
1776	28	2	22	38	140.04	305.05	33.00
1777	29	3	28	45	212.83	62.30	ca. 20.00
1778	28	3	29	59	456.44	249.72	18.00+
1779	32	5	25	71	184.00	151.53+	18.00+
1780	32	7	26	72	306.54	253.04	50.00+
1781	32	4	25	68	458.93	37.00	Very little
1782	33	5	31	83	None		
1783	34	5	29	98	1,125.41	108.08	None
1784	32	4		121	861.93	221.00	18.00+
1785	32	4	6	136	957.20	759.92	18.00+
1786	34	4	9	136	136.00	402.72	18.00

Source: Start of year summaries, Thistlewood diaries, 1756–64, 1766–86.

Note: "Credits" means monies other people owed to Thistlewood (in pounds Jamaican currency); "Debts" means monies Thistlewood owed to others.

became an absentee pen keeper, leaving his pen in the hands of his black mistress, Vine. When he died in December 1772 at age forty-three (eight years younger than Thistlewood), he owned three more slaves than Thistlewood, and his slaves and land sold for £2,988.48. His total personal estate was valued at £5,470.05, with land worth nearly £2,000.[63] Thistlewood could easily have

TABLE 2.2: Composition of Thistlewood's Income, 1767–1786

Year	Produce	Slave Hiring	Cattle	Logwood
1767	6.63		14.00	
1768	23.50	109.43		19.60
1769	25.88			
1770	33.50	109.37		
1771	29.16	219.00		
1772	47.13	160.37		
1773	39.38	216.00	60.00	
1774	61.68	196.66		
1775	54.66	192.17	53.00	
1776	50.83	246.01		
1777	48.05	168.01		
1778	7.68	70.00		
1779	60.28	210.85		
1780	None	None	64.00	
1781	39.78			
1782	41.13			
1783	63.91		221.00	
1784	50.41			ca. 500.00
1785	61.38			ca. 700.00
1786	55.78			

Source: End of year summaries, Thistlewood diaries, 1767–86.

Note: Figures are in pounds Jamaican currency.

taken this route: he had been told that Mason was "willing to hire him at any rate to live upon Bluefields estate." As Mason's protégé, he would have had a very good chance of entering into the plantation elite, comprised of attorneys with several estates under their care.[64] But Thistlewood did not pursue the matter. He had already made his intentions clear after Say's death when he turned down Williams's proposal that he replace Say at Old Hope.

Thistlewood was not governed by money alone. By the 1760s, he had tired of wage dependency, no matter how high the wage. He desired the independence that in the eighteenth century came only from owning your own land. Becoming a pen keeper did not maximize Thistlewood's earning capacities, but it greatly enhanced his social position. It was only after he became a pen keeper that he was invited to become a justice of the peace and a lieutenant of Savanna-la-Mar fort. Owning land, in short, allowed him to become a gentleman of some standing in his community. The local plantocracy visited him with some regularity.

On 15 March 1775, for example, he entertained John Cope, custos of the parish; Richard Vassall, from a wealthy St. Elizabeth family; and William Blake, soon to be a representative in the Jamaican House of Assembly for Westmoreland, at a lavish feast at his house. On 11 June 1778, he ventured to Hertford Pen, the seat of William Beckford, on business and was invited to stay all day. He "Played at billiards" and cricket and "Looked over many Folio Volumes of excellent plates of the Ruins of Rome" and then dined in the company of several leading planters. Beckford was so impressed by Thistlewood's company that the next month he sent him six engravings depicting views of rivers and the Beckford properties. The most vivid indication of how far Thistlewood had risen socially since his first arrival was Florentius Vassall's cultivation of his friendship in the 1770s. In 1751, Vassall had threatened to make Thistlewood's "Blood flow about [his] face" for his impudence. In 1778, he received him very warmly at his estate of Sweet River and conversed with him at length on politics, trade, and botany. The next day, he sent Thistlewood "an excellent piece of Cheshire cheese." Even more generously, Thistlewood noted that Vassall offered him land "for a plantane walk upon his mountain or land to settle upon my life, free of quitrents." On this land, Thistlewood could "have the liberty to develop a garden at Sweet River, friendship or Greenwich, call it and use it as my own etc." When Vassall died four months later, Thistlewood joined seven other pallbearers, all wealthy planters, to mourn the elderly grandee's death.[65]

Vassall's change of heart toward Thistlewood resulted from their shared interest in horticulture. Thistlewood's garden did the most to define his position in Westmoreland society. It provided him with a small income—sales of produce averaged £40.04 per annum over twenty years—and, more important, it gave him a measure of local renown and allowed him to pursue his intellectual yearnings. Thistlewood gravitated socially toward the few white Jamaicans who were interested in reading and science. His intellectual and social aspirations were directed toward developing one of the best private gardens in western Jamaica. By 1775, he had transformed his Breadnut Island property from a semi-ruinate piece of marginal land into a productive garden and a horticultural showpiece—the first place that residents went to buy seeds and vegetables. His gardening skills gave him entrée into a grander world, with wealthy planters like Vassall and William Henry Ricketts courting him, and cemented friendships with other Jamaicans of an intellectual bent, such as Ricketts and Robert Pinkney, a medical botanist. They even gave him a connection to the highest reaches of Jamaican society. On 29 March 1772, Cope entertained the Jamaican governor at a dinner. Thistlewood supplied the food, including game and "10 large broccoli, about 3 quarts of English peas in the pods, and a large calabash full of asparagus; also 4 ripe figs, 3 sweet limes, and flowers." The governor was so impressed that, according to Thistlewood's friend Harry Weech, he and his wife "several times expressed a great desire to come and see my garden, but were prevented by Mr. Haughton's representing the road to be so very rocky and bad." The importance that Thistlewood attached to horticulture can be seen in his will, in which the only two bequests he made to friends were to Henry Hewitt of London, who supplied him with seeds, and Francis Scott, a gardener from Northumberland who migrated to Jamaica in 1771 and was instrumental in Thistlewood's successful planting of asparagus. Both received £50 sterling.[66]

The intellectual satisfaction and social prestige that Thistlewood derived from gardening explain why he did not seek to become a sugar planter. Substantial fortunes could be gained from planting sugar. Sugar planters were the wealthiest men in Jamaica. Only the largest Kingston merchants—involved indirectly in the production of sugar through marketing—could match their fortunes. The average sugar planter had personal wealth over three times and total wealth nearly five times as great as Thistlewood's. Edward Long estimated in 1768 that the total wealth of the average sugar planter amounted to £19,027 sterling (£26,638 Jamaica currency), of which personalty accounted for £9,064. Inventories bear out the accuracy of Long's estimate. Richard Sheridan calculates that sugar planters left a median personal estate of £9,361 in the early 1770s. Cope's valuation of his Paradise sugar estate in 1766 at £13,934 sterling approximates such estimates.[67] The wealthiest sugar planters far surpassed such levels of wealth. Richard Beckford died in 1756 with 910 slaves and an estate of £59,490.44 sterling. His absentee brother, William, was even richer, reckoned by Thistlewood to have 2,200 slaves, as was Charles Price, "Said to be as rich a Man as William Beckford, for possessions but in debt."[68] Sir Simon Clarke, the son of a baronet transported to Jamaica in the 1720s for highway robbery, was richer still. Thistlewood noted at his death in 1777 that Clarke was "Said to be worth half a Million," a figure likely to be accurate given that his inventoried personal estate came to £269,592.32.[69] The Beckfords and Clarke inherited large properties, but it was also possible for men from humbler backgrounds to acquire great wealth from sugar. Thistlewood commented in 1765 that "old Philip Haughton died worth 400 thousand pounds currency had 70 thousd: Sterling in the Bank at home (yet about 20 years ago worth about 10 thousand currency)."[70] John Tharp, with whom Thistlewood negotiated over the sale of Samuel Hayward's slaves and whom he noted bought "430 Negroes from a gentleman in Carpenter's Mountain at £50 per head, all Creoles," was the son of a Hanover planter who died in 1754, leaving £11,690.87, including 154 slaves. He became the largest slave owner ever known in Jamaica and at his death in 1805 had gathered a personal estate worth over £362,000, with 2,990 slaves.[71]

Nevertheless, the costs of entering the sugar trade were formidable. Sugar production entailed elaborate processing, requiring a substantial investment in mills and boiling houses. It needed abundant labor and sufficient land not only to grow sugarcane but also to feed and house slaves. All of this required a substantial capital outlay. Moreover, making sugar was difficult, as Thistlewood well knew from his many years laboring on an estate on poor sugar land. As Samuel Martin of Antigua espoused in his highly regarded 1754 tract, *An Essay On Plantership*, the planter must be "adept in figures, and all the arts of economy, something of an architect, and well-skilled in mechanics," as well as being an expert sugar boiler and distiller, an astute manager of both white servants and black slaves, and "a very skilled husbandman."[72] Sugar planting promised enormous returns, with an annual rate of return of nearly 14 percent in Jamaica in the 1750s (and probably more in frontier areas such as Westmoreland), but it entailed enormous risks.[73] For every John Tharp, who turned a moderate patrimony into a great fortune, there was a John Williams, the proprietor of the Old Hope estate, who died in jail, having inherited 357 slaves from his parents but having "spent and made away with since he commenced . . . £53,000."[74] Thistlewood's observations of Cope's deficiencies and consequent difficulties disillusioned him about the joys of sugar planting. His aside of 15 May 1779 sums up perfectly why he never ventured into sugar: "To be the owner of a sugar works is to have external dignity for inward or external grief."

Achieving a Competency

Besides the difficulties faced by sugar planters, one universal difficulty was securing debts. Thistlewood was careful not to become indebted—the example of the improvident John Cope was a lesson in the folly of excessive indebtedness. In the twenty-six years Thistlewood detailed his credits and debts, his average indebtedness was just £43.24, or a little over 1 percent of his total wealth. The substantial costs of buying slaves and establishing himself on the pen led to increased debt of more than £120 in 1760 and over £200 in 1766 and 1767. In the last fifteen years of his life, he owed very little—just over £18 on average per annum. When he died in 1786, Thistlewood's only debt was the annual payment of £18 that he owed to Cope for the hire of Phibbah. Thistlewood achieved the financial independence so desired by eighteenth-century men. Not all white

Jamaicans, unfortunately, were as financially prudent. Before the American Revolution, Jamaica's general prosperity allowed debtors some relief, but even then, indebtedness and litigiousness over debt were endemic. By the 1780s, after a series of devastating hurricanes and a decline in profitability due to the effects of the Revolutionary War, debt was becoming a major problem for extravagant or unlucky planters. In 1780, Thistlewood reported that his attorney, John Rodon, a leading lawyer in the capital, St. Jago de la Vega, had earned the extraordinary sum of £20,000 in the last year "but that he only received 15 hundrd: the rest booked." By 1786, a large number of Westmoreland sugar estates were in severe difficulty. Thistlewood listed twenty-four estates that he thought "likely to change masters," noting that "Egypt and Paradise already have." A few people found the situation so desperate that they absconded. It was not a fate that Thistlewood had to face, but he did have to take legal action against several nonpayers in the 1780s. On 24 October 1782, he initiated a suit against the attorney of William Beckford of Hertford for £206.91 for slave labor, which he won. Beckford's attorney paid up two months later.[75]

The major problems that Thistlewood faced, however, were not man-made. The greatest crisis—and the only one that led him to despair—was the devastating hurricane that flattened Westmoreland on 3 October 1780. The hurricane destroyed Thistlewood's house, wrecked his garden and property, and caused "Sad havoc all through the countryside." It was the greatest natural disaster to strike Jamaica since the Port Royal earthquake of 1692. The hurricane caused thousands of pounds worth of damage in both Jamaica and Barbados, prompting Parliament to offer relief of £40,000 sterling to Jamaica and £80,000 sterling to Barbados—the first relief granted by Parliament for a natural disaster in British America since a much smaller grant to South Carolina in 1740. Thistlewood calculated his damages at £1,000, not counting his loss of income—he made no money at all in 1780. The parliamentary relief went only a little way toward covering such losses. On 9 January 1782, Thistlewood sold his share of the aid to a local bookkeeper "for . . . £140 2d."

Thistlewood's diary entries for late 1780 and early 1781 bear testimony to the physical devastation of the hurricane and the depression that gripped him. It appeared that all his hard work had come to naught. He confided to his diary that "Mr. James Robertson declares he is afraid to fall asleep, as such dreadful hurricanes and confusion present themselves to him, as far exceed the real one. Just so with myself and several others, the nerves so affected." He went about repairing his house and garden, but his heart was not in it. He commented in a lengthy description of the hurricane appended to the end of the entries for

1780: "The hurricane has made every body look ten years older than they did before, and the healthiest show a great dejection in their countenances—nothing looks pleasant or agreeable since." It was, indeed, "as iff a dissolution of nature was at hand." Thistlewood was so low that he contemplated giving up his estate. He placed an ad in the "Montego bay paper" for the sale of his pen of 160 acres and "26 or 28 Negroes, 15 of which are field Negroes, the rest fishermen, house Negroes, watchmen and children. Likewise 25 head of horned cattle & about 60 sheep." The extent of the devastation of the hurricane was clear: "There is only the ruins of a dwelling house at present, but the proprietor has already collected a sufficient quantity of stone upon a very eligible spot, for building a dwelling place." Thistlewood declared that he wanted to sell solely because "of his ill state of health requiring him to leave the island." Despite the property's many attractions, including "a prospect of the shipping in Savanna la Mar and the country all around," Thistlewood got no offers. He soon regained his customary optimism and let the matter of selling drop, at least until very shortly before his death, when he put a deposit on a smaller property.[76]

Thistlewood was right to continue in his optimism. Jamaica had been good to him. His first twenty-nine years in England had not allowed him to fulfill either his financial or his intellectual goals. By contrast, his thirty-seven years in Jamaica had allowed him to achieve his ambitions. He had gained a comfortable competency as a pen keeper and slave owner. He had become a landowner with minimal debts and maximum independence. Most important, he had achieved "mastery" as a horticulturist and amateur scientist. If he had stayed in England, it is unlikely that he would have amounted to anything. Thistlewood found that a plantation society based on African slavery afforded manifold opportunities for a man of talent and determination. By the time he died, he was a wealthy man and a respectable member of local society.

For whites, therefore, Jamaica was a land of opportunity. If one was willing to gamble that one would not die young, then Jamaica provided a white man with all that he needed: material prosperity, social advancement, and even intellectual achievement. Thistlewood was fortunate to arrive when he did. But he showed admirable qualities of persistence, steadfastness, and mental and physical toughness. It is not surprising that he did well. His success, however, did not come entirely unaided. Crucial to Thistlewood's success was the labor of African slaves, those he managed and especially those he owned. As Barbara Solow has argued, it was slavery that ensured colonial economic growth: those areas that had slaves prospered, those that were too poor to be able to exploit slaves languished.[77] Thistlewood's experience in Jamaica demonstrated the proof of this obvious but often unexplored contention. Thistlewood did well in Jamaica because he had abundant slaves to work for him. Slaves gained for white Jamaicans their much-vaunted wealth. Slaves were also crucial in ensuring white happiness. Thistlewood's intellectual pretensions were underwritten by his slaves' labor in forming and tending his garden. Slave women, especially his mistress, Phibbah, satisfied his sexual and emotional needs. Moreover, his idea of himself as a landed gentleman was inconceivable without owning and using slave labor. Nevertheless, white Jamaicans' dependence on slavery and slaves rendered them open to all sorts of dangers. In their "rage to push on their estates," white Jamaicans were indeed "playing with Edge-Tools."[78] Slaves made white Jamaicans such as Thistlewood wealthy and comfortable. They also made them ever fearful and uncertain. Their mastery was founded, at bottom, on an acute dependence—a dependence that was to be brutally exposed two years' after Thistlewood's death when the reality of the abolitionist threat to Jamaican slavery suddenly became clear.

chapter Three

Cowskin Heroes

Thistlewood, Slavery, and White Egalitarianism

The natural consequence of the order of things which prevails here, is, that all those titles of honour which are elsewhere the *pabula* of emulation, of rivalry and of discord; which inspire so much pride, and create so many claims in some; so much ambition and envy in others; shrink to nothing, and entirely disappear before the sole title of WHITE. It is by your skin, however branded it may be, and not by your parchment, however worm-eaten, that your pretensions to gentility are judged.—Francis Alexander Stanilaus, Baron de Wimpffen, *A Voyage to Saint Domingue, in the Years 1788, 1789, and 1790*

"Never Had Such a Sett-down Before"

Thistlewood had ambivalent, sometimes uneasy, relations with the leading planters of Westmoreland Parish. He gives little hint of his political philosophy in his diaries or his commonplace books, but he was partial to men with ordinary backgrounds like himself and suspicious of the high and mighty. Several times he went out of his way to aid poor but respectable whites (he had little sympathy for "mean white people").[1] As a magistrate, for example, he intervened on behalf of indentured servants against their wealthy employers. On 16 July 1777, he adjudicated in a case in which William Boddington brought Archibald McNillage, an indentured servant, to court "for drunkenness, refusing to work etc." Thistlewood thought McNillage "sickly ill used." He and his fellow magistrates ordered Boddington to pay McNillage wages of £27.20. Thistlewood and William Bossley (a magistrate who was so incensed by Boddington's treatment of McNillage that he wanted to send a complaint to the attorney general when McNillage died in August 1777) had both been servants on sugar estates and felt sympathy for someone who started out in Jamaica under similar circumstances.[2]

Thistlewood was concerned about McNillage because he was acutely sensitive to condescension from above. He was unwilling to defer to his superiors when he thought them arrogant, conceited, or insufficiently appreciative of his merits and position. His first years in Westmoreland, during which he was a person of no importance in the parish, were marked by numerous run-ins with people in authority, as noted in chapter 2.[3] Thistlewood insisted that others recognize him as a person of account. He was very sensitive to perceived slights and snubs. In a telling episode in 1766, he deliberately insulted a leading man in the parish. On election day, Thistlewood had gathered with other voters at the courthouse in Savanna-la-Mar, where he encountered William Lewis, custos of the parish, who offered to shake Thistlewood's hand. Thistlewood, however, withdrew his hand because he "did not know him, as he had never deign'd to take the least Notice of me before this Minute, altho' I have resided 15 or 16 years in this Parish." Thistlewood wrote in his diary that Lewis was astounded and "affronted for which I did not care" and "threatened to be even with me Which I did not Note at all." Three days later, Thistlewood recorded, with some satisfaction, that Lewis had "declared he never had such a Sett-down before, as I gave him last Friday." Six months later, Thistlewood expostulated about his treatment at William Witter's property, Dean's Valley, where he had spent the evening as a member of a group sent to recapture runaway slaves.

Thistlewood and his fellow militia members "were not admitted to the presence of Mr. Witter (he being a patrician, a great Scoundrel and Coward)." Instead, "we Plebeans" were fobbed off with "4 plantanes and a little bit of Stinking pork for all our dinners which came from Mr. Cargill who sits very great in the Back piazza." As a result, "everyone off our party [was] greatly dissatisfied with their usage." Witter had committed one of the greatest sins of Jamaican life —he had ignored the common understanding that white men were entitled to abundant hospitality when they visited great estates, regardless of their social condition. Thistlewood felt entitled to complain.[4]

Thistlewood's behavior in these episodes could be interpreted in three ways. First, it shows that he was prickly, conscious of his own dignity, and insistent that others recognize his merits. Thistlewood was not an easygoing man with convivial habits. He was often uneasy with other whites because he preferred his own company. Lewis was not the only man whose hand Thistlewood refused to shake. On 15 February 1755, Thistlewood noted that "young Russell . . . would gladly have Quarrell'd with me because I refused him my hand." On at least two occasions, Thistlewood declined to take up invitations to join local clubs frequented by whites.[5] He chose to stay home and read or write in his diaries. Yet, though solitary, he was not a loner. His diaries detail frequent mingling with other whites and close friendships with several men and at least one white woman, Hannah Blake. Nothing in his diaries suggests that he was misanthropic or that he had particular difficulties dealing with other people. Certainly he often displayed an easy familiarity with people of higher status than himself. His distaste for Lewis's and Witter's pretensions was clearly not founded on a general disdain for men of high status.

Second, Thistlewood's occasional antipathy toward those who were nominally his superiors could be a sign of an incipient class conflict between wealthy whites and poor whites, but external evidence does not support such an interpretation. Observers commented that class seldom divided white Jamaicans, even if the differences between whites from various social strata were clear. Edward Long—no fan of democracy but an astute observer of white Jamaican society—argued that there were no distinctions among whites besides those between good and bad citizens.[6] Nevertheless, Jamaica was not an egalitarian society, and the eighteenth century was not an egalitarian age. The dominant social ethos and cultural metaphor of eighteenth-century Anglo-America was patriarchalism, an ideology based on the theory of the Great Chain of Being in which the ideal society was one that had an organic social hierarchy in which subordination was both normal and normative.[7] Thistlewood shared this understanding of the ideal social order. Jamaica was a "deferential community," in Walter Bagehot's sense of the word. It was a polity that was consensual in its social and political relations but hierarchical in its distribution of power and authority, even if, as in all of Anglo-America, deference did not arise from class prerogative or class privilege alone but from a popular base of consent among ordinary white men.[8]

One reason why Thistlewood never questioned the propriety of slavery was because he accepted that in any society some people were bound to rule and others were bound to serve. He believed that government should be reserved for enlightened and capable men—gentlemen of ability and fortune—and that subordination of others was not only inevitable but also necessary and desirable. His antagonism toward certain members of the Jamaican elite did not mean that he doubted the right of the rich and wellborn to be the rulers of society. He praised individual members of the elite explicitly on several occasions and implicitly accepted their right to political and social dominance. When Theodore Stone, a longtime assemblyman from a well-established and wealthy Westmoreland family, died in 1770, Thistlewood eulogized him effusively, stating that his death was "a great loss to the parish in general and to Savanna in particular, as he had their interests greatly at heart." In 1785, he noted that Hugh Lewis (a relative of William Lewis, whom Thistlewood had offended in 1765) had been "an excellent councillor" and that his death was "much lamented."[9] Only members of the wealthy planter elite aspired to be assemblymen, and Thistlewood expected nothing else, never commenting that a representative other than a wealthy gentleman might be appropriate. Despite his reservations about John Cope as an employer, he voted for him as an assemblyman. Thistlewood accepted the inevitability and desirability of hierarchy and the right of the wellborn to control the rest of society in the same way that he accepted the inevitability and rightness of enslaving Africans.[10]

Yet although white Jamaicans accepted inequality as an essential characteristic of a functioning society, they insisted that each white man have a high degree of personal independence. If inequality between free and unfree people was the glue that held Jamaican society together, the equality of independent white men was the oil that promoted the smooth running of that society. White Jamaicans recognized that there was an intimate connection between slavery and freedom.[11] The more slavery was mandated as necessary for the subjugation of racial inferiors, the more white Jamaicans believed it was necessary for white men to promote liberty and independence among themselves. Thistlewood's resentment toward William Lewis and William Witter arose out of an ideological milieu in which slavery created conditions of relative equality between whites. Thistlewood, like other white Jamaicans, evinced an exaggerated spirit of liberty and independence and was fiercely concerned about his own rights and privileges in a society that was committed to massive inequalities not only between whites and blacks but also between various groups of whites. It is this third interpretation—ideological egalitarianism within structural inequality—that best explains Thistlewood's relationship with other whites in Jamaica. The contradictions between supporting an ideological commitment to white equality and condoning social structures that were heavily inegalitarian created tensions between supposedly equal white men, tensions that were enhanced by white Jamaicans' professed and spirited devotion to their own independence at a time when that independence was severely compromised by their dependence on slavery.

A "High Spirit of Independence"

White West Indians' jealous regard of their corporate and individual rights resonates throughout seventeenth- and eighteenth-century Caribbean history. In the political realm, Jamaicans were especially zealous defenders of their rights as Englishmen against what they considered the tyrannical incursions of the British crown. They reveled in metropolitan accusations that they were people of an "ungovernable Spirit," a people of "perversity and futility" whose "darling passion" was "Contention."[12] In their personal lives, white Jamaicans also demonstrated a love of freedom and impatience with insubordination. The Reverend Richard Renny, writing in 1807, believed that white Jamaicans' "high spirit of independence" was apparent in their very appearance. White Jamaicans, he asserted, had "No tremulousness of voice, no cringing tone of submission, no disgraceful flexibility of body [and] no unqualified humbleness of countenance." They spoke "what they think, without fear or reserve," and prided themselves that "No people were more free than themselves or more watchful of their freedoms." "They pay the most vigilant attention to every circumstance," Renny concluded, "which can encroach upon their liberty."[13]

In other slave societies, such contumacious behavior by white slaveholders was attributed to their wealth, their virtue as people of the soil, and high levels of white property ownership. David Ramsay, the historian of colonial South Carolina, attributed South Carolinians' love of liberty to the limited progress of luxury among "contented unaspiring farmers" who "settled on lands" of their own where they were "both farmer[s] and landlord[s]." Because the farmer "had no superior to whom he was obliged to look up . . . he soon became independent"; "At liberty to act and think as his inclination prompted, he disdained the ideas of dependence and subjection."[14] West Indians were more honest about why they venerated freedom so strongly. Bryan Edwards, the distinguished historian and longtime resident of Jamaica, had a particularly acute understanding of the causes and effects of white Jamaicans' love of liberty. Like Renny, he noted that "a marked and predominant character to all the white residents" was "an independent spirit and a display of conscious equality throughout all ranks and conditions." Such "conscious equality" was noticeably different in "the countries of Europe," where "men in the lower orders of life" seldom considered themselves to be "nearly on a level with the richest." In the West Indies, by contrast, "the poorest white person . . . approaches his employer with an extended hand." The origins of such "conscious equality" were not difficult to find, Edwards believed. They arose "from the pre-eminence and distinction which are necessarily attached even to the complexion of a white Man, in a country where the complexion, generally speaking, distinguishes freedom from slavery." Whites were equal because they were equally dependent on each other for protection from their slaves. Egalitarianism, therefore, was born out of fear. Edwards stated: "Fear—that absolute coercion that supersedes all questions of right—is the leading principle upon which all governments in slave societies are supported."[15]

This equality, in Edwards's view, had mainly beneficial consequences. Of course, because they had slaves, whites were guilty of "an ostentatious pride and a ridiculous affectation of splendour." But in general, the relative equality of all whites "awakens the laudable propensities of our nature—frankness, sociability, benevolence and generosity."[16] Patrick Browne, in his natural history of Jamaica, agreed. He thought the "general obsequiousness of numerous slaves and dependents" made whites "Remarkably fond of grandeur and distinctiveness," but with a "free and open disposition" that allowed them to be "friendly . . . [and] honest in their dealings and punctual."[17]

Not every commentator was convinced that the "conscious equality" of whites was beneficial. William Beckford of Hertford Pen bemoaned "the levelling principle that obtains among the white people of Jamaica." Not only did it "entrench upon the duties of society"; it "annihilate[d] the bonds of power and the good effects of subordination," which were vital in a society based resolutely on slavery. Beckford argued that unrestrained power over slaves led to tyranny. In Europe, "the chain of subordination that descends from link to link . . . preserves the strength of the whole . . . [while] giv[ing] ease and motion to some particular parts, and which, without constraint, ensures obedience." European adherence to the principles of the Great Chain of Being provided solidity and stability. Conversely, the "levelling principle" between whites in Jamaica and the great gulf that existed between independent whites and dependent slaves, who were "thrown at a distance from the ideas of equality," exacerbated white tendencies toward tyranny. "The weight of command does not descend by perceptible degrees," Beckford argued, "but falls at once to crush the timid, and to confound the bold; although the inflictor of punishment may not be possessed of more reason, or more sense, than the unhappy wretch who suffers and who, as he cannot resist, is obliged to succumb."[18]

Egalitarian Tyranny

Beckford raised an important paradox central to understanding white Jamaican society. The white Jamaican male was an egalitarian tyrant, determined to defend his own liberties while at the same time trampling on the freedoms of blacks. The political and social atmosphere of Jamaica in Thistlewood's time exhibited a complex and combustible blend of ostensible equality and demonstrable elements of social deference and hierarchy, all predicated on a fierce and all-encompassing commitment to chattel slavery. The fabric of white society was influenced by the predominant role of slavery as an institution in Jamaican life. In effect, the independence of white men was based on their absolute dependence on slavery as a social system. White Jamaicans were committed both to egalitarianism and to tyranny; they placed the highest value on independence at the same time that their reliance on slavery made their dependent character ever more manifest.

The paradoxical effects of white Jamaicans' absolute commitment to the maintenance of slavery and white supremacy were politically important. As Jack Greene has shown, white Jamaicans' dependence on slaves fatally undermined their ability to secure the "true liberties" that they insisted on protecting in their many disputes with metropolitan government. By the 1760s and 1770s, they were questioning whether the deep entrenchment of chattel slavery in their society had transformed the identity of a settler population previously accustomed to asserting "a manly resolution and constancy" in defense of their privileges by reducing them to dependence on Britain, a dependence "incompatible with their claims to identity as free-born Britons."[19]

Wealthy whites also relied on the support of less well-off whites. In societies where the proportion of whites was greater than in Jamaica, wealthy whites sustained a commonality of interest with poorer whites through clever manipulation of shared patriarchal ideals and a common commitment to the institution of slavery. In the Chesapeake, South Carolina, and Britain, the relationship between rich and poor whites was based not on "conscious equality" but on well-developed patron-client interactions, deference, and, most important, the elite's constant attention to poorer whites' interests.[20] In these societies and in Britain, slavery supported the traditional social order, an order in which virtually all relationships were regarded as patriarchal or familial.[21] Even if patriarchs in these societies were "anxious" about how to maintain their authority and even if the limits of deference among the poorer sort were significant, the metaphors of patriarchy—employed to express and naturalize unequal social relations of every kind—operated to enhance planter authority to an extraordinary degree.[22]

Jamaican planter authority was not quite so untrammeled. The particular social conditions of mid-eighteenth-century Jamaica meant that wealthy whites relied on both the ideological and practical support of poorer whites. The "conscious equality" that distinguished West Indian whites was rooted in a degree of real equality that was not replicated in British North American colonies. The "pre-eminence and distinction" that went along with a white "complexion" was heightened by the fact that white complexions were so rare. Poor whites had to be feted and treated with care because there were so few whites and so many slaves. In addition, over 80 percent of whites leaving inventories in the mid-eighteenth century and close to 100 percent of men who had resided in Jamaica for some time were slave owners and thus as much masters as wealthy sugar planters.[23] Recently arrived whites and poorer whites exerted a financial leverage over other whites, given indebted planters' need to pay white plantation operatives high cash wages. The paucity of whites also meant that wealthy planters could not monopolize the higher offices and reserve for themselves the advantages of being thought public-spirited. In the American South, a small group of interrelated gentry families justified their monopoly of political office by drawing on a widely shared faith in stewardship and a belief that government was the responsibility of enlightened and capable men. They could fill all political offices from within their own numbers and gained respect because they worked assiduously and selflessly (in least in their own eyes) to further the public good. As Lieutenant Governor William Gooch of Virginia argued in the early 1730s, the middling and lower ranks of white men did not need to do anything in politics except mind their own business, shun those "given to Noise and Violence," and "Submit . . . to every Law."[24] In Jamaica, wealthy whites were not numerous enough to fill all of the offices necessary to maintain planter authority. Wealthy planters were able to maintain their dominance in the Jamaican House of Assembly and Council. But at lower levels—positions such as justices of the peace, militia officers, and vestrymen—political participation had to be extended below the ranks of the wellborn and the wealthy.

Thistlewood's Political Career

Thistlewood's career illustrates how ordinary whites were included in local power structures. He was neither rich nor wellborn. Yet from an early stage he was invited to take up significant political duties. He achieved a degree of local political prominence that would have been impossible not only in his native England but also in any British North American colony. Within eighteen months of arrival, he was appointed "surveyor of the highway, from the River Styx" to Colonel James Barclay's gate. By 1755, he had been appointed a way warden, and two years later, he was promoted to be "Clerk of Mr. Cope's Company" in the Westmoreland militia. He also served on local juries, his first appearance occurring in September 1758, when he served at an inquest.[25] He was on a first-name basis with members of the Westmoreland plantocracy, with whom he occasionally socialized. By January 1752, less than two years after he had moved to Jamaica, he had been invited to dinner with Barclay, the custos of the parish. He increasingly attended dinners at the homes of the plantocracy or entertained them in his home. In 1760, for example, he gave a dinner for "Brigadier Norwood Witter, Major John Cope, Mr. David Lopez, Mr. Murdock McLeod, and Mr. John Hutt." After Thistlewood bought Breadnut Island Pen in 1767, dinners with the elite became more frequent. In March 1775, for example, Thistlewood dined with wealthy planters four times in two weeks.[26]

Becoming a landed proprietor was the most significant event in Thistlewood's steady rise in the Westmoreland social and political hierarchy. Before purchasing property, he had served his parish in mainly lowly capacities. After 1767, his status was greatly enhanced. His former employer and debtor, John Cope, promised him early in 1767 a commission as a lieutenant of the new fort being built at Savanna-la-Mar, an appointment that finally came to fruition in 1769. In 1775, Cope, now custos but financially indebted to Thistlewood, offered to appoint Thistlewood justice of the peace, an honor he eagerly accepted, even though it cost him £71, which Thistlewood thought "an incredible price indeed!" At the end of the year, he proudly wrote the details of his commission in his diary, documenting this recognition that he was indeed a man of substance. He first sat a month later (although he had sat without commission earlier in the year) and continued to act as a magistrate until shortly before his death. At his death, his name was accompanied by "J.P." in the parish register. He had achieved a great deal, becoming a man of substance in his adopted community. What his ex-countrymen in Tupholme, Lincolnshire, would have thought of Thistlewood's elevation, having last noticed him when he was summoned to court to account for a miscarried bastard child, can only be imagined.[27]

Advancing such a seemingly lowly person up the ranks made sense in a society desperately short of men able to serve in the public realm. First, allowing poorer men to achieve office and position meant that hard-pressed employers such as Cope could assuage the employees to whom they owed money. Cope was able to use his position as custos to provide patronage for Thistlewood. He did this by securing him militia commissions and magistracies, getting him released from onerous jury service, and excusing him from marching with the militia. Thus, on 3 October 1761, Thistlewood wrote that Cope had promised to "get me a Commission to be superceded in order that I might be quiet in regard to the Militia." Three years later, Thistlewood was summoned to be "on the jury but excused by Cope."[28] Second, wealthy planters needed the support of people like Thistlewood at election time. Elections in Westmoreland were frequent and closely contested. In 1754, Thistlewood noted that four men competed to become assemblyman (two were elected for the parish), with the closest loser failing by only five votes. Thistlewood could not vote at that election because he owned no property in the parish, but he voted regularly thereafter. Candidates solicited hard for votes: in 1756, Thistlewood noted, "there has been making interest for Kit Senior to be elected for this Parish." In 1768, Theodore Stone solicited his vote. Stone met with a better response than did William Lewis, whose hand Thistlewood refused to shake. Thistlewood believed that Stone worked hard for local interests. At the election in October, he voted for Stone and Cope, both of whom were elected.[29]

Thistlewood listed the results of nine elections. The only uncontested one was in 1770, when Stone and Hugh White—both highly respected local planters—became assemblymen. All of the others were contested, often vigorously. In 1771, Edward Bullock, "a famous councillor at Law" and, like Thistlewood, a migrant, "was put up as a Member for this parish in lieu of young Mr. [William] Lewis who has resigned to please his grandfather dr. Gregory and to keep out Mr. Edward Woolery." Thistlewood voted for Bullock, but his candidate was unsuccessful (losing by "45 to few more than 20") because, according to Thistlewood, "the Creoles . . . [were] very hot in Edward Woolery's Interest, to screen him from a gaol," and had persuaded Scottish residents to vote for him. The election of 1781 was even more contentious. The first election in February resulted in Cope being decisively rejected by electors in favor of George Crawford Ricketts and John Lewis. Both Ricketts and Lewis were wealthy planters, but as custos and theoretically the leading man of the parish, Cope would have expected to have his social authority validated by election. Cope demanded and got a recount, arguing that several electors did not meet necessary residence requirements. In a reelection in April, Cope comfortably reversed the previous result, securing 60 votes to 62 for Ricketts, 47 for John Lewis, and 27 for William Blake.[30]

Thistlewood commented after the 1781 reelection that "there are about 170 persons who have votes in this parish." Since each elector could vote for two assemblymen, the returns indicate that a minimum of 98 voters, or 58 percent of the electorate, voted in 1781. A higher percentage of eligible men voted in Westmoreland than in Virginia, where around 40 percent voted in the mid-eighteenth century, let alone in New York, Pennsylvania, New England, and South Carolina, where voting percentages sometimes sank below 25 percent.[31] This suggests a widespread popular interest among white Jamaicans in assembly elections. Moreover, the results were close enough that every vote had to be courted—not just at election time but, as William Lewis discovered in 1766, before elections as well. Thistlewood expected rich planters to cultivate his interest in politics just as they pursued him when they wanted him to work for them. Candidates feted electors at election time, plying them with liquor and food. Thistlewood describes an election held in 1768 in which there was "a surprising quantity of victuals, and a vast many people." Candidates were expected to treat their voters handsomely at local taverns. Thistlewood reported that his friend Thomas Emotson lamented in 1766 that "he has been dunning Mr. Crawford for his treat on the Election day £16 but Can't get it."[32]

The Cult of Hospitality

White unity was fostered by an all-embracing cult of hospitality—whites prided themselves on their open dispositions and their generosity toward other whites. Every commentator on white society in Jamaica noted that white Jamaicans were famed for their hospitality. James Knight, who wrote an unpublished history in the 1740s, can speak for a multitude of writers: "It must in Justice and Honour to them be observed, there is not more Hospitality, nor a more generous Freedom shown to Strangers in any Part of the World, for any Person who appears like a Gentleman and behaves himself Well, is Sure of a Welcome to their Houses and the best Entertainment they can Afford . . . [while] Persons of low rank and Condition are as cheerfully received and entertained by their Servants."[33] As Knight argued, gentlemen were not the only ones who benefited from whites' presumption of hospitality. "Even vagrants," William Beckford commented, with less enthusiasm than Knight, "are seldom refused protection and food."[34]

The importance of hospitality as a value uniting whites and separating even the meanest white from blacks and coloreds is a constant theme throughout Thistlewood's diaries. The most noticeable characteristic of white hospitality was the extraordinary welcome that whites extended to strangers. Thistlewood benefited from this generosity when he first arrived in Westmoreland and "walked to William Dorrill's Esq," where he "was well rec'd." Dorrill—who did not know Thistlewood—invited him to stay for a meal, provided him with a horse, let him remain on his plantation, offered him a job, and introduced him to other members of the Westmoreland plantocracy.[35]

The contrast between how Dorrill behaved toward whites and how he behaved toward blacks was so great that it was bound to have made an impression. Thistlewood learned the lesson well. Although temperamentally a solitary person and not always eager to endure the inconvenience of entertaining strangers, he followed the general practice of offering hospitality to traveling whites. In the first four months of 1752, for example, Thistlewood welcomed five "poor white men." In January, "a pretty well dress'd man, whose horse was Wearied . . . begged a Nights lodging and refreshments for his horse." Thistlewood "Lett him lay in the hammock in the hall." Such hospitality was extended to him as well on the rare occasions that he left Westmoreland. Seeking employment in April 1754, he traveled "to the northside," where he found favor at a number of great houses and met planters "glad to see me."[36]

When Thistlewood first arrived in the island, he spent much of his time alone or in the company of slaves. The loneliness of new migrants on isolated plantations was a well-worn theme in Jamaican writing. In the early nineteenth century, John Stewart noted that newly arrived bookkeepers had the least-enviable situation in the country, a bookkeeper being "a sort of voluntary slave, who condemns himself for a term of years on a paltry salary, seldom more than Sufficient to support him decently in clothes, to a dull, cheerless, drudging life, in hopes he will one day become an overseer." If he "has no acquaintance with any decent white families in the neighborhood (which is generally the case), he is totally precluded from all intercourse with virtuous female society" and instead "finds himself placed in a line of life where, to his first conception, everything wears the appearance of barbarity and slavish oppression."[37]

Over time this isolation lessened. Thistlewood was a private man who was not especially sociable. But by the time he became a landed proprietor, he entertained other whites frequently at his house and was often invited to gatherings. If we examine his social activities between January and July 1775—a normal half-year in his life, albeit one when he was at the peak of his prosperity in Westmoreland—we find him involved in a constant round of socializing. He either dined out or invited friends to his home on 73 occasions. He had people share breakfast with him on 3 occasions and breakfasted elsewhere twice. He participated in 17 tea parties, had people dine with him on 18 occasions, and dined with others 33 times. He was invited to dinner at 11 places, including the Bluecastle, Paul Island, and Retrieve estates. He dined with Savanna-la-Mar attorney Jeremiah Meyler and spent evenings with his friends Samuel Hayward (his most frequent dining companion), Richard Dobson, and John Chambers.

Generally, Thistlewood preferred to dine quietly with just one other person, usually a male friend such as Hayward. But he also visited local white women, as on 25 January 1775, when he had "tea with Mrs. North." He shared the company of white women on 11 occasions in 1775. Nevertheless, a fixed division between whites and free blacks or coloreds existed: Thistlewood never entertained or was entertained by freed blacks, despite the presence of his long-term mistress, Phibbah, and his close friendship with Phibbah's friend and his partner Samuel Say's mistress, Vine. On four occasions, he dined with large groups of men and women, including two gatherings where white families were entertained. On 20 April, for example, he "dined and drank tea with Mr. Chambers." Present were "Mr. and Mrs. Chambers and family, Capt. Richardson Capt. hore Mr. hayward Mr. Dobson dr. Allwood James Wade and dr. Rook." On 21 March, he was invited to Cope's Paradise estate. The families of William Blake and Florentius Vassall joined the Cope family as guests, along with Thistlewood and a visiting ship captain. After dinner, Westmoreland grandees William Beckford and his wife and Mr. Bellamy joined the group to drink tea. That Thistlewood was invited to such an event shows the extent of his social acceptance in Westmoreland. In the 1780s, his friendship with Hannah Blake, a wealthy widow, led to his participation in social occasions dominated by women. In February 1780, for example, Thistlewood dined with Blake at Southfields in the company of one other man and four women. He repeated the visit in June, when, once again, females outnumbered males.[38]

Nevertheless, men usually predominated at the dinners and entertainments that Thistlewood attended or gave himself. Male dominance at social occasions is not surprising given Thistlewood's bachelor status (having a black mistress did not count as being attached) and given the numerical predominance of single white men in rural Jamaican parishes. No demographic analysis of Westmoreland Parish exists, but a breakdown of the population by age and sex for another rural parish, Clarendon, in 1788 suggests that white women were very much in the minority. In Clarendon, nearly half of the population were adult males, and the ratio of adult men to adult women was 3.1 to 1.[39] Thistlewood did not invite a single woman to dine at his residence. Instead, the three large dinners he gave in 1775 were exclusively male events. On 6 January 1775, he entertained Samuel Hayward, John Chambers, Richard Dobson, and Hugh Duncan at dinner. Dobson returned to his next dinner on 9 March 1775, along with Cope, Captain Parker, Captain Jesse Curling, and Captain Samuel Mason. On 15 March 1775, Thistlewood again invited only men to dinner, this time entertaining four members of the local plantocracy: John Cope, Richard Vassall, William Blake, and Nicholas Blake.

By 1775, Thistlewood was fifty-four years old. His entertaining was restrained and convivial rather than wild and uproarious. After he had become a landowner, he had begun to entertain his neighbors at large feasts. In October 1768, for example, he fed eight men "roast beef, crabs, shrimps, roast teal, boiled pudding roast papaya cheese punch grog porter French brandie." For Christmas that year, he invited four male friends to dine on "stewed mudfish, and pickled crabs, stewed hogshead, fryed liver etc quarter of roast pork with papah sauce & fresh potatoes, bread roast yam, & plantains boiled pudding very good cheese, marshmelon, watermelon, oranges, French Brandy . . . punch and porter." Fourteen months later, seven men "dined with me" on "a fine roast goose with papah sauce, stewed fish, a roast coot & 2 roast plover, boiled pudding, cheese etc grog, punch & porter."[40] Early on, restraint was less notable. Thistlewood was not a notorious carouser and hell-raiser, but many other Jamaican men were. His diary suggests that white Jamaican men's reputation as hard-drinking fornicators was well deserved. Many social occasions degenerated into wild debauches. In March 1755, for example, Thistlewood told of an evening during which Cope and five other men were "heartily drunk" and gang-raped Eve, a house servant. Six years later, Cope and two of his friends again "got very drunk; disturbed. me sadly in the night," seeking out slave women to sleep with. In 1756, "Dr. Micham dined and supp'd here got very drunk took a Pistol out off his Kitt to Mr. Cope etc they quarrelled Dr. Micham walked home." Court days were especially likely to occasion drinking bouts. In 1758, Thistlewood and his fellow jurors "played at Cards etc and all got well in liquor with drinking forfeits etc don't know how I got to Bed Scarce." Thistlewood was wary of court days ever after. In 1778, he refused an invitation from Mr. Wardlow, who wanted to "treat the Bench with a dinner," because he "suspected hard drinking."[41]

Jamaican Patriarchy

The debauches that many white men loved gave a particular tone to eighteenth-century white Jamaican society. Patriarchalism was the dominant ideology and the prevailing ethos governing white relations with blacks, as in the rest of Britain's eighteenth-century American empire. But patriarchy was different in Jamaica, primarily because of the peculiarities of white demography and the urgent necessity that whites demonstrate their mastery over blacks. The majority of the white population were recently arrived young men from Britain seeking their fortunes. They had to acquire these fortunes from the hard work of brutalized African slaves. Whites understood from the start that the only way to control their slaves was to foster white unity and maintain a sense that all whites were involved in the same enterprise of survival. At the same time, slaves had to be ruthlessly and brutally kept in their place. The result was that society was governed by an implicit assumption that all white men were to a significant extent equal, at least insofar as they could treat dependents, especially slaves, any way they liked. Generally, the methods employed by white men to cow dependent slaves involved making them afraid through the constant and arbitrary application of raw power.

Westmoreland was a remarkably underinstitutionalized frontier society, even by the standards of plantation America. Authority was maintained mostly by brute force. Unlike in North America, the savagery of white relations with blacks did not lesson over time. In British North American plantation societies, the raw savagery so evident in white Jamaican dealings with slaves diminished over the eighteenth century. By the latter half of the eighteenth century, the dominion of white men over slaves, women, and children was checked, and its most poisonous effects were mitigated. Women and slaves won limited advances in individual rights, especially after the American Revolution; the state assumed some responsibility for supervising household relations; and, most important, the growing importance of stewardship or paternalism as a governing value for household heads softened the North American patriarch's overt brutality toward dependents.[42] In North America, patriarchalism gradually metamorphosed into paternalism. Patriarchal masters stressed obedience to authority and resorted to violence when that authority was questioned. But they seldom deluded themselves that slaves and other dependents were content. Paternal masters, on the other hand, treated dependents better but expected them, in turn, to be grateful for this benevolence. Under paternalism, masters' violence was less openly countenanced and more often condemned as counterproductive and regressive.[43]

This shift from patriarchalism to paternalism never occurred in Jamaica. It remained a patriarchal rather than a paternal society throughout the eighteenth century. Moreover, it remained a society with a particular variant of patriarchalism, derived from its peculiar demography and unusual social relationships. Patriarchalism was very raw in Jamaica. White men there were less concerned than white men elsewhere in the British world with making sure that their authority was tempered by an understanding that patriarchs had to recognize mutual obligations between household heads and dependents. Jamaican men refused to accept any constraints on their freedom to act as they chose, least of all constraints placed on them by dependents. Patriarchy was not shaped by concepts of stewardship but was "the manifestation and institutionalisation" of raw male dominance, with scant regard to the duties men owed to others.[44] What made Jamaican patriarchalism unique was that white male dominance could be exerted only over women, children, and slaves. It could not be exercised over independent white men. Thus, patriarchy in Jamaica was Janus-faced. It looked backward to ancient notions of patriarchy that assumed that dominant men could do whatever they pleased to inferiors. But patriarchal assumptions were not predicated on an all-embracing, hierarchal chain of subordination that linked all people in a vertical line of authority. White Jamaican men's patriarchal assumptions instead were based on a fundamental equality between white men. In this respect, white Jamaican men looked forward to the ways in which power was negotiated between independent men in slave societies in a democratic age. In democratic slave societies such as nineteenth-century South Carolina, a common commitment to white supremacy and patriarchal governance created "Herrenvolk democracies," or what Stephanie McCurry argues is better described as "republican democracies," that forced the ruling planting elite to pay at least symbolic and often real attention to the will of the electorate.[45] To some extent, the political culture of Jamaica in the eighteenth century foreshadowed that of South Carolina three-quarters of a century later.

Herrenvolk Egalitarianism?

The combination of Jamaica's culture of hospitality, the demand for white employees, the need for whites to join together to prevent or counter slave opposition, and the increasingly rigid divisions between whites and blacks operated to increase the extent to which whites were forced to mix with each other. Jamaica's peculiar social conditions meant that there was a constant intercourse between whites at all social levels. Even though whites recognized the need to keep separate ranks of society distinct and even though they were imbued, as slaveholders and eighteenth-century Englishmen, with a firm desire to maintain hierarchical relationships, the reality of life in Jamaica meant that whites of all conditions mingled with each other in a spirit of "conscious equality." This "Herrenvolk egalitarianism" was distasteful to men such as the early abolitionist and good conservative James Ramsay, who feared the tyrannical impulses implicit in contractual societies in which the interests of the individual were given priority over those of the community. Ramsay believed that in order "to support their opinion of every man's right to the kingdom of I they are obliged wholly to dissolve society and reduce men to that savage state, where such equality only can take place." "[S]ociety cannot be maintained," he asserted, "but by the inequality of condition and various ranks arising from the social compact."[46] It was also a somewhat artificial egalitarianism since in practice it shored up the power of elite planters. The historical experience of slave societies, Jamaica being no exception, was that slavery rarely promoted a truly egalitarian order, even in avowedly democratic polities. Great planter dominance in Jamaica was never tested by poorer whites throughout the period of slavery; the challenges, when they came, emerged from the metropolitan center and, eventually, in 1865, from the freed black peasantry.[47]

Whites were accorded special privileges in eighteenth-century Jamaica, even when they were ostensibly servants. Richard Beckford's instructions to his attorneys, discussed in chapter 2, distinguished between how whites were to be treated and "the unhappy Situation of a Slave." White servants ought to be treated by an overseer as "part of his family"—a telling phrase in an age imbued with patriarchal doctrines, stressing the common links between whites in a racially divided society. Whites, even those who "become a burthen to [their masters] and a Nuisance to society by their debauchery and ill-example," were still "free men and have a right to the Protections of the laws and are not to be subject to the will and caprice of an overseer."[48]

Thistlewood was careful to follow such advice. He was never violent toward fellow whites, despite considerable provocation. In 1757, his white subordinate, Thomas Fewkes, became "very abusive" and "Swore he would Set Fire to the Plantation, great House and that he would see my heart's blood in the Morning." Thistlewood did not respond. The next morning, Fewkes continued his verbal onslaught. Thistlewood feared for his safety. He put Fewkes "in the Bilboes [stocks] his insolence was so great." He was careful, however, not to use force. He knew that he could not arbitrarily exercise authority over a white man. He went to some effort to obtain a warrant against Fewkes so that he could dismiss him legitimately and rode to Colonel Jacob Ricketts's house to seek advice. Ricketts told him to take Fewkes "down to the Bay" two days hence so that Ricketts and fellow magistrate William Lewis could adjudicate what to do. Thistlewood was not satisfied with such a delay and with the possibility that Fewkes would not be punished (we have already seen his disdain for Lewis). He rode to five other magistrates seeking a warrant but met with no success. The next day, after persuading a magistrate to grant him a warrant, he rode to Savanna-la-Mar and gave the warrant plus "two Bitts" to a constable, who accompanied him back to Egypt Plantation. There, he "served the warrant upon Thomas in the Bilboes, let him out and discharged him [from] the plantation: the Constable Commanded Samuel Mathews in the King's name, to Aid and Assist him." The affair, however, was not finished: Thistlewood accompanied Fewkes to Colonel Barclay's house, which they left because "Thomas could not get Security sufficient," then to the house of Mr. Bosley, who could not help him, and finally to the plantation of Colonel Ricketts (all on foot because "Mr. Cope would not let Thomas have a Mule"), "whereupon Thomas submitting himself in an extraordinary manner and desiring the gentleman to forgive him etc I forgave him, upon Paying the Charges." The next day, Thomas left the Egypt estate, although Thistlewood had "detained his gun and Cutlass by Mr. Cope's order."[49] Thistlewood had gone to extraordinary efforts to rid himself of a troublesome servant while allowing that servant the full protection of the law. Perhaps it was because of the care he took to follow proper procedures that he was so angry as a magistrate in 1777 at a white overseer who had mistreated a servant.

The spirit of "conscious equality" between white men was tested by the various prejudices and inherited presuppositions about rank and position that white Jamaicans brought with them from Britain. Equality coexisted with hierarchy and rank, leading to tensions and complex relations between white men. Jamaicans were well aware of differences in rank. The elite may have dined and socialized with Thistlewood. They may have sought his opinion and solicited his vote. But they did not consider him their equal, even if they relied on him more than he needed them. The distinction between Thistlewood and the planter elite was especially apparent when Thistlewood was a servant. Two weeks before Christmas of 1760, Cope entertained the leading men of the parish, including James Barclay, Theodore Stone, and "young Mr. Vassall," at Egypt great house. Thistlewood noted that "I eat in my own house no Chair or Convenience for me in the gt: House."[50] Thistlewood never reached the highest ranks of Jamaican society. He was never invited, for example, to meet governors on their several trips to the parish or attend the lavish balls that accompanied such visits. He could only repeat gossip about the balls, noting in 1767, for example, that he had heard that "Theo Stone and Mrs. Vassal, old Flor[entius]'s wife, wear the richest dres[s] of all the gentlemen & ladies at the governor's ball, on the King's birthday."[51] Thistlewood was never quite a gentleman, despite his frequent mingling with ladies and gentlemen and even if some of the supposed gentlemen lacked genteel refinement, such as the elderly Creole planter, Tom Williams, who Thistlewood noted in 1752 wore nothing at home "but a shirt, and fans himself with the fore lap before his daughter." Wealthy planters sometimes found it difficult to reconcile their own status as gentlemen who must be obeyed in all things with the demands of white tribal unity that required them to treat social inferiors as equals. William Lewis, whom Thistlewood offended so mortally on Election Day, clearly found dealing with inferiors difficult. A year after Thistlewood snubbed him, he got into an argument with John Underwood, a man of similar status to Thistlewood. Underwood, Lewis claimed, had voted when the magistrates were not present, thus offending the honor of the bench, yet he had the audacity to still "walk this piazza." "Such vermin as you," he expostulated, "ought to be drove out of ye parish."[52]

Thistlewood never experienced such obvious social disdain. Generally, wealthy planters took pains to court him. When he did enter into disputes with other white men, it was invariably a contest between relative equals. In 1771, for example, he was involved in a bitter argument with George Robert Goodin, a wealthy neighbor, over Thistlewood's request for access to logwood on Goodin's estate. Goodin had been incensed that Thistlewood's slaves had used his property to catch fish. He was in no mood to help his neighbor, writing to "Mr. Thistlewood" that although "I ever had the Utmost pleasure in Obliging whenever in my power," he now shared "an equal Enjoyment in the Contrary" and refused Thistlewood the logwood "for that Man diverted off Neighborly Friendship has no right to ask Favours and consequently to expect their being granted." Significantly, Goodin couched his objections not in terms of his own rights but in terms of Thistlewood's deficiencies as a good neighbor.[53]

"I Would Not Take His Word for a Straw"

Thistlewood's touchy insistence that he be granted his rights and accorded full respect spilled over into his dealings with public officials. His respect for their authority was limited. In 1768–69, he was engaged in a fierce dispute with John Fitzgerald about logwood that Fitzgerald had cut on his land. When Thistlewood attempted to serve Fitzgerald with "a bill of parcels" for Thistlewood's loss, Fitzgerald "pushed it away and told me I might wipe my arse with it." It took Thistlewood over a year to recover the £24.23 Fitzgerald owed, including £1 for the delay. The deputy marshal, William Barnes, was less than helpful, in Thistlewood's opinion, in following up Thistlewood's action. Barnes was "in awe" of local judges and attorneys, but Thistlewood was not deterred. After Barnes "had a few words about Fitzgerald's debt to me," Thistlewood declared that "I would not take his word for a straw, which moved him a great deal." He approved, therefore, of his friend Samuel Hayward's plan to expose Barnes's "villainy"—a plan that resulted in Barnes proffering Hayward "a written challenge."[54] Marshals were feared and disliked by white Jamaicans, primarily because they seized property as satisfaction of debts. When they were reprimanded, Thistlewood was pleased. In 1768, Zachary Bayley, a merchant prince from Kingston, arrived in Savanna-la-Mar to suspend the chief collector of taxes. The suspension—lifted six months later—caused "great joy at Sav la Mar." Thistlewood supported several efforts to weaken the power of marshals. In 1770, for example, he "signed a petition for a law to make it a felony against the deputy marshal to return satisfied without paying money immediately into the provost marshall's office."[55]

Ethnic divisions were more noticeable than social and class divisions. Whites were divided into immigrants and Creoles and into Englishmen and non-Englishmen. Hostility between immigrants and Creoles was limited, in part because a large percentage of the population were immigrants. Thistlewood notes only one instance of antagonism between the two groups—the contested election of 1771 when what Thistlewood considered an unholy alliance between Creoles and Scots defeated Edward Bullock, "a famous Councillor of Law."[56] More significant divisions were between ethnic Englishmen and Scots and Jews. Unlike other Jamaicans who were almost as fiercely anti-Semitic as they were racist, such as Edward Long, Thistlewood was more contemptuous of Scotsmen than he was of Jews. By the mid-eighteenth century, North Britons comprised an increasing proportion of Jamaican whites. Contemporary estimates suggest that by the American Revolution one-third of the white population were Scots.[57] Successful and clannish, they provoked resentment among English settlers. In 1762, Thistlewood quoted approvingly an anti-Scottish saying of "old Tom Williams off the old hope" that "a Scotchman, like a Fly was in every one's dish, like a Rat to be found in every hole and Corner, and like a Fart never return'd to whence they came." Thistlewood was convinced that Scots stuck together and looked after their own. He concurred with the sentiments of a white man "hang'd at Sav la Mar for killing a Sailor at Lucea" who "made many bitter speeches against the Scotch" that Thistlewood thought "not at all agreeable to them: being pretty near the Truth." Two years later, he opined that a slave was acquitted despite being "an impudent audacious fellow & great Villain" because "no trouble [was] Spared by the No: Britons to save him." The news that a Scot had superseded the secretary of the island led him to proclaim, "No Englishman will be permitted to hold a place under them."[58]

He was more curious than hostile toward Jews (and said nothing at all, positive or negative, about the Irish). He came across relatively few Jews in Westmoreland, since the majority were concentrated in the towns of Kingston and Savanna-la-Mar.[59] His first mention of Jews was of "Jewish strangers" in 1756. Thistlewood listed at length what was "strange" about them—they "can't eat custard or pudding after meat etc their Roast Meat Basted with oil." Most of his mentions of Jews were favorable, although he did think a petition he signed in 1775 to prevent Jews from escaping paying deficiency taxes on property was "very just." Individual Jews were "very agreeable and Cheerful" and "bore a good Character." Nevertheless, he recognized that Jews fitted imperfectly into white society and suspected that, like the Scots, they were excessively clannish. On the day of the disastrous hurricane of 1780, Thistlewood recounted an anecdote told to him by William Antrobus. Antrobus had sought shelter in the house of Abraham Lopez, where he "heard the Jews, especially little humpback Moses Lopez praying o lord deliver thy children people of Israel from this storm, protect us thy chosen people & us only o Lord. Mrs. Bullman & others opine the same."[60]

Thus, divisions within white society did exist. What is notable, however, is the extent to which white solidarity tested inherited assumptions about people's place in society. Elite men were unable to separate themselves from the rest of white society. In part, the relative lack of distinction between white men arose from the unimpressive genealogies of even the leading men in the island. The popular notion of Jamaica in England from the late seventeenth century onward was that the island was the refuge of scoundrels and wastrels. Edward Ward, a turn-of-the-century scribbler who wrote scurrilous texts about the colonies, probably without visiting them, derided Jamaica as "The Receptacle of Vagabonds, the Sanctuary of Bankrupts, and a Closestool for the Purges of our Prisons." James White, a discontented clergyman, wrote twenty years later that almost all of the leading men were from humble origins: Peter Beckford, for example, the founder of the massive Beckford fortune, was the son of an illiterate horse trader. "All new Gov's," he declared, "turn out whom they please and make others [officers] and so our tavern keepers, taylors, carpenters, joyners, are infallibly colonels, JPs as soon as they purchase plantations and our Printer in his papers, Styles them everyman Esq and each Colonel Honourable." The anonymous author of a 1714 tract on the troubles of Jamaica wrote in a similar vein that "Gentlemen of very liberal Education, some even at Universities," found themselves supplanted in the governor's affections by men "sprung up as suddenly, in one Night's time, as Mushrooms out of a Dunghill," men characterized by "profound ignorance, accompanied by vast Impudence," by "stupid, blind, indolent, and implicite Acquiescence," or by "a crafty, active, knavish Genius, blended with Lewdness, Atheism, and Irreligion," all "varnished over with a servile, fawning, seeming Obsequiousness."[61] Such animadversions were unfair since the social origins of white settlers were no less undistinguished than those of settlers elsewhere in British America and since for every person of low repute who became wealthy, there was a great planter who came from respectable stock.[62]

Equality and Slavery

A more important source of white egalitarianism came from the "reciprocal dependence and respect" that being members of a greatly outnumbered minority among a hostile majority engendered. Slavery bred "an ostentatious pride and a ridiculous affectation of splendour," but it also contributed to "an impatience of subordination." The ubiquity of white slaveholding meant that "men accustomed to be looked upon as a superior race of beings to slaves submit with reluctance, if they submit at all, to be treated as if they enjoyed no will of their own."[63] Moreover, the ubiquity of white slaveholding diminished the authority of the wealthiest whites by extending the habits of command well down the ranks of white society. When almost all whites commanded slaves—Thistlewood was in charge of forty-two slaves within weeks of arriving in Westmore-land and eighty-nine slaves within eighteen months of arrival—"mastery" was a universal characteristic of whiteness. Poorer whites found it difficult to defer to richer whites when they themselves were absolute masters in their own house-holds, with almost complete control over the lives of adult men and women. Being a "master" in a patriarchal society meant that poorer whites appropriated the language and behavior of patriarchs, even when they were themselves os-tensibly dependents. A master in eighteenth-century parlance was someone who ruled or governed, a "Possessor," "One uncontrouled," someone with ser-vants who acted "with the power of governing."[64] By this standard, Thistle-wood was a master almost on arrival and, as a master, in certain respects was equal to his social superiors.

It has been argued that in some slave societies, notably the antebellum Amer-ican South, the acquiescence of yeomen was obtained by exploiting white fears of black violence and insinuating that those fears would be assuaged only if the most dominant slaveholders—those with special "knowledge" of slaves and special control over slave behavior—were allowed to make the rules about how slaves were to be treated. As long as dominant planters demonstrated to yeo-men that they could control slave conduct, nonslaveholders were willing to de-fer to their authority, at least in regard to slavery.[65] Such strategies did not work when over 80 percent of white men owned slaves and an even greater per-centage had de facto authority over slaves. They also did not work when, as in eighteenth-century Jamaica, planters' control over slaves was tentative, their authority over slaves was constantly being challenged, often violently, by slave rebels, and white dominance was only maintained through internal help from white militias and British troops.[66] In addition, the line between black and white was so clearly demarcated and the "naturalness" of white superiority was so ob-vious that few poor whites felt constrained by the fear that their actions might undermine the basic fabric of race relations. Indeed, slavery exacerbated the lack of deference that poorer men displayed toward richer men. The presence of black slaves "served as omnipresent reminders to independent men of pre-cisely how valuable their independence was" and was "a powerful preventive to their giving unreserved deference to people and institutions in authority."[67]

The spread of mastery throughout white society created tensions as well as providing a basis for white egalitarianism. Relations between independent white men and their white employees were contradictory and ambiguous. Patriarchal metaphors or taxonomies compared political society to "a large and well-regulated Family, in which all the officers and servants, and even the domestic animals, are subservient to each other in a proper subordination."[68] "Proper subordination" did not work well among men who were unwilling to accept subordination, were determined to show manly independence, and insisted on the assertion of self at every opportunity. Poor white men challenged rich white men constantly, especially over slavery. Thistlewood was no exception. His altercations with Vassall and other local planters over how slaves should be treated were typical. Even more characteristic were disputes between Thistlewood and local planters over how Thistlewood dealt with slaves, especially in his first years in the island, when he was a servant of low status not properly integrated into local society. Thistlewood maintained a strict authority from the start on his plantations, not hesitating to punish other men's slaves for violations of plantation discipline on his land. As Thistlewood became more established — and as his reputation for being a man who would not back down grew — his difficulties with other slave owners diminished. But disputes between Thistlewood and other white men over who should punish slaves never entirely stopped, even after he moved to Breadnut Island as a landed proprietor. In 1768, two slaves told Thistlewood that "somebody was cutting wood on my land." Thistlewood "immediately took my gun" and found "Quashie belonging to mcLeod etc runaway" and Cyrus, belonging to Mr. Lapley, "felling a large white wood." Thistlewood "fired a couple of ball[s] among the tree[s]" over Quashie's head and took Cyrus into custody. Their owners were furious, confronting Thistlewood at his friend Samuel Hayward's house, "where we had words and ill language etc etc."[69]

What is significant about these battles of will between Thistlewood and great planters is that Thistlewood always succeeded in forcing the ostensibly superior man to back down. He won because he was a master even when he was a servant and because mastery justified the use of power. Because he repeatedly demonstrated his willingness to act the part of a master, or patriarch, it was logical for Thistlewood to be considered, after he became an independent proprietor, someone suitable to govern the parish. He became an officer in the militia within three years and a justice of the peace within seven years of settling on Breadnut Island Pen. He had already established himself as an important member of the community and, more important, had shown through his firm dealings with his slaves that he understood the nature of power and authority in a colonial plantation society. Before he joined the chief local governing body, he was dismissive of how it operated. On 19 March 1772, he expostulated that he did not bother to go to choose churchwardens "as it is all a Farce, for at all vestries the Justices carry all as they please. Owing to their numbers." But when he became a justice, he changed his views. On several occasions, he nominated people to serve as vestrymen. On 20 January 1784, for example, Thistlewood put up Julines Herring and Hugh Wilson for election. Both were elected.

Thistlewood and the Wider World

Thistlewood's political horizons did not extend very far. He was not very interested in politics. He owned very few standard political texts in his extensive library, with Montesquieu's *Spirit of the Laws* the only work of political philosophy to stand out. He did note in his diary that he had read Bolingbroke and included transcriptions from Bolingbroke as well as Montaigne in his commonplace book. As a justice and vestryman, however, he gave more weight to local issues than to larger political considerations. Overall, he made reference to wider political affairs just eighty-five times in thirty-seven years, of which eleven came in a three-month period in 1782 when the French seemed likely to overpower the British in the Caribbean before being halted by Admiral George Rodney at the Battle of the Saintes. He hardly mentioned the two great events that occurred during his time in Jamaica: the Seven Years' War (nine references) and the American Revolution (ten references). When he did note these conflagrations, his references were idiosyncratic and were focused very much on the Caribbean. In 1762, for example, he wrote a long extract on the fall of Havana. The American Revolution worried him only insofar as it increased piracy on the seas and opened up Jamaica to French or Spanish invasion. Unlike North America, which had been freed from the fear of invasion by Britain's victories in the late 1750s and early 1760s, the British West Indies always faced the possibility of being overwhelmed by a foreign power. During the American Revolution, that fear became real. The reduced number of British forces in the British West Indies and the overstretched British navy left Britain's valuable sugar colonies vulnerable to assault, especially from the French. In 1778 and 1779, the French invaded and occupied Dominica, St. Vincent, and Grenada and, in early 1782, conquered St. Kitts. The French naval commander, Admiral d'Estaing, boasted that he did not intend to leave George III enough sugar "to sweeten his tea for breakfast." In 1782, Jamaica itself was directly threatened, with the French commander Admiral François de Grasse planning to join the Spanish fleet in a grand attack on the island, reportedly carrying with him "50,000 pairs of handcuffs, and fetters . . . intended to confine the negroes."[70] The threat of invasion greatly worried Thistlewood. He made twenty-two references to possible invasion in 1762 and 1782. Indeed, he was more concerned about foreign invasion than he was about internal revolt from Jamaica's "intestinal" enemies, rebel slaves. He noted his concern about slave revolt on only three occasions: in 1776, when there was a rebellion in nearby Hanover Parish; in 1780, following the aftermath of the great hurricane when slaves looted Savanna-la-Mar; and in 1760, when he was caught up in Tackey's rebellion.

Thistlewood was instinctively patriotic. British victories at Cape Breton and St. George in West Africa in 1758 were noted in the diaries with triumphal exclamation marks. In the American Revolution, Thistlewood sided with the British rather than with the Americans. Soon after hearing about the Declaration of Independence, he quoted approvingly "John hartnole's wish to the No: Americans. Cobweb Breeches, hedgehog Saddles, Jolting horses, Strong Roads & tedious Marches, to the Enemies of Old England." In 1780, he attended a quarter session and noted that "almost everybody drunk last night at the bay upon the news of Charlestown being taken, firing off great guns, muskets." Not everybody shared his patriotism. His friend Samuel Hayward had his house "pelted with brickbats because he did not put up candles" to celebrate the fall of Charleston. Florentius Vassall was also inclined to support the American side. He desired that "the North Americans might beat the English else they will be enslaved & ruled with a rod of iron, and next us." He foresaw British defeat "as the Americans will never bear it long, as what army we can keep there will never be able to keep in awe on extent of 2 thousand miles" of American territory.[71]

But most political events passed him by. He noted in 1751 that he had heard that Frederick, Prince of Wales, was dead, but it was of interest mainly because of the nearly three-month delay in receiving the news. He did not note the accession of George III in 1760 or the transit of British prime ministers. He was similarly uninvolved in Jamaican politics. The two privilege controversies between Governor Charles Knowles and the assembly in the 1750s and between Governor William Lyttleton and the house in the 1760s largely escaped his comment, with just one reference to the former and three to the latter.[72] He also ignored metropolitan movements to abolish the slave trade. In 1785, Thistlewood noted that "mr. barker lent me a Treatise, or an Essay on the Treatment or Conversion of African Slaves, by the Revd James Ramsay MA," but, disappointingly, given the relevance of the thoughts of a West Indian on an early abolitionist tract, he made no comment on what Ramsay had written in either his commonplace books or his diaries.[73]

What concerned Thistlewood were local and parish matters. His only direct involvement in wider politics arose out of local complaints. In 1763, he felt moved to write a letter to the governor "concerning my being served with a Copios and forced to pay £5 15 shillings unjustly." The result was a stiff admonishment of the Westmoreland deputy marshal by Jamaica's provost marshal. In 1778, he supported a variety of suggestions put forward by electors to their representatives to build a new gaol, block plans to move the county courts from Savanna-la-Mar, and enact legislation designed to force absentees to pay high taxes on uncultivated land. A year later, he was appointed as a member of the committee of the vestry to draw up instructions as to how local assemblymen should vote and presented a plan for a tax on land that he proudly commented "was universally approved of." His predisposition toward local inhabitants and hostility toward absentees were further shown in his support of a justices' decision in 1782 to take away militia commissions from those who left the island without the governor's leave. His greatest passions were stirred in the aftermath of the hurricane of 1780, when he analyzed at length the division of parliamentary relief monies. Beside several undeserving names, he wrote derogatory comments such as "shamefull!," "for what reason?," "for what?," and "a bankrupt."[74]

The Importance of Order

The primary local concerns revolved around issues of order and were dealt with by the local courts. Thistlewood took his duties as juryman, vestryman, and justice seriously. His diaries detail numerous trips he took to town to take part in court proceedings. The brief of the local court was wide, but in practice the majority of the court's time was spent on three activities: adjudicating in quarrels between whites over money; controlling the overexuberance of white men in their relations with other white men; and cowing and disciplining slaves, using the full panoply of state instruments of terror. The proceedings of the last day of 1768 were typical. Thistlewood was on the jury all day and "did a great deal of business: eg Mr. Thos Townsend recovered 2 negroes, mr. bucknor payment for 47 mahogany plank cutt off his land without his leave, dr. roach above £100 due to him."[75]

Courts performed a variety of functions in eighteenth-century plantation societies. They affirmed the social hierarchy and in particular assured the social and political dominance of whites over blacks.[76] Whites went to court to settle debts, "do business," drink, and exchange gossip—on the court day noted above, for example, Thistlewood was told by two men, both under thirty years old, that one had had the clap seventeen times and the other had had it fourteen times. But court day was as important symbolically as it was practically. It enabled Westmoreland whites to display "the codes by which those who share in the culture convey[ed] meanings and significance to each other."[77] What court day reinforced above all was the notion that whites needed to be ever vigilant against slaves. An important part of the business of the court was trying and punishing slaves, a practice first developed in Barbados in 1661 and subsequently adopted as part of the slave codes of Jamaica, South Carolina, and other West Indian and North American slave societies.[78] Of course, such slave courts were hardly necessary. Whites were perfectly capable of punishing slaves themselves. In practice, no limit to their authority existed.[79] Thistlewood exerted almost absolute control over his slave charges. His only active involvement in disciplining slaves through the use of state authority came in 1752, when he was attacked by a runaway slave, Congo Sam, and sent him to the local magistrates, hoping (in vain, as it turned out) for a severe punishment, and in 1765, when he hauled a persistent runaway from Egypt Plantation, Plato, into court. Plato was "Sentenced to have 100 lashes at 4 difft places on the Bay (25 at each place) and to have his right Ear cut off, which was immediately executed."[80] Yet the courts served a useful purpose. They demonstrated to both whites and blacks how determined whites were to maintain their authority and to use whatever means were necessary to keep blacks under control. Courts were also useful in educating whites in the proper behavior of slaves and in implicating all whites in extensive community coercion of slaves. Legal action involving slaves was important symbolically: it was the "code" that taught whites modes of behavior toward slaves and imparted meaning about what constituted improper slave behavior and proper slave punishment.[81]

Punishing slaves and regulating slave behavior took up a substantial portion of court time. In 1762, for example, Thistlewood was summoned to the grand jury to decide two cases involving blacks, including the prosecution of a free colored woman for "making Mulatto Balls" (dances for the free colored population). Juries made a point of authorizing barbarous public punishments for slaves found guilty of serious infractions. On 3 May 1775, two magistrates, three freeholders, including Thistlewood, and a prefector met and "Tryed Negro Man Fuller from Salt River Estate for running away for 9 months. Condemned him to have 39 lashes, have Ears Cut off, then 39 lashes again at gallows." A year later, the court acquitted "a runaway Negroe belonging to Mr. Beckford" because he had "not been three years in the country." Nevertheless, the slave was punished: "dr. Panton ordered him 39 lashes under the gallows." In 1786, Thistlewood noted approvingly that "the bloody minded villain Plato was burnt today," after having terrorized Westmoreland for several years. Four months before Thistlewood's death, he and William Antrobus sat as magistrates and condemned a slave of William Beckford's to "100 lashes under the gallows and to have both Ears cut off" for stealing cattle.[82]

Courts thus provided a very public demonstration of white power over blacks and a symbol of white supremacy. The privileges of whiteness were reinforced at every turn, and the necessity of white unity was hammered home through white imposition of terror on slaves. In the aftermath of the failed slave rebellion in Hanover in 1776, for example, Westmoreland held "a meeting off the Justices and Vestry today regarding the discoveries of the Negroe's design, lately come to light in Hanover, by a white Person's accidentally overhearing their discourse. Resolved to be on our guard and to inspect their behaviour Narrowly." White tribal unity was enhanced by lenient treatment of masters brought before the court for excessive brutality toward slaves. Thistlewood took part in several inquests into the deaths of slaves caused by white violence. He was summoned to the Ridgeland estate "to appear as a juror upon an inquest off a Negroe Man." John Richie, a bookkeeper, had shot the slave. The jurors found Richie guilty of manslaughter, "for he pretended that the Negroe was impudent, and he striking him with the gun, She went off and shot him." Richie suffered no punishment—by the time of the inquest, he had left the estate. An even more blatant pardoning of a white man for excessive brutality came at an inquest at Kirkpatrick Pen in 1771. Quashie, "a most perverse, ill minded negroe," had died a month after being given a severe flogging by the owner, George Lesley. The slave's supposed character flaws were sufficient to sanction murder: the five assessors brought in a verdict of "natural death."[83]

The Limits of White Power

Yet mastery had its limits. White equality was predicated on black inferiority. Masters of subordinate blacks were all equal, despite differences in rank and wealth, because they were able to exert control over others. That exertion of control was necessary because otherwise, as whites very well knew, their slaves would overrun them. An elite unified by color and, as Bryan Edwards recognized, by fear kept slaves in a state of servility through the use of terror. The structures of chattel bondage and white supremacy were intimately intertwined. African slavery was not only one of many forms of demarcation between superiors and subordinates in a world marked by complex hierarchies but also the foundation on which social order rested.[84] But although slavery unified whites and made their society remarkably egalitarian, it also divided them. The easy equation of white superiority and black inferiority was complicated and contradicted by the reality of slavery, in which power was continually negotiated and renegotiated between individuals, each striving for advantage. Because slavery was such a personal, intimate institution, slaves had ways in which they could use white supremacy to their own advantage and weaken whites' tribal unity.

Slaves' ability to crease the supposedly smooth fabric of white solidarity was most apparent in sexual matters. Edward Long was right to lament that white Jamaican men's infatuation with their colored mistresses opened up a fissure between the races that black women were able to exploit. We can see how sexual involvement with blacks could weaken relations between whites by looking at the love life of Thistlewood's subordinate at Egypt Plantation in 1754, William Crookshanks. Like Thistlewood, Crookshanks partook freely of the sexual delights available to young white men in Jamaica. Within a month of arrival, he had contracted his first bout of venereal disease. Like Thistlewood, he soon became drawn to one slave, Myrtilla, who belonged to Elizabeth Mould, the colored mistress of the late William Dorrill, and William Mould, a "blue-coat" boy[85] who married her after Dorrill's death. Myrtilla miscarried a child in mid-February 1755 that Crookshanks thought was his but that Thistlewood unkindly attributed to a slave, Salt River Quaw. Thistlewood had an uneasy relationship with Crookshanks, especially after Crookshanks verbally abused Thistlewood's mistress, Phibbah, "in a strange Billingsgate language . . . [which] she answer'd pretty well." Crookshanks was "affronted," probably because Thistlewood took Phibbah's side. Thistlewood was also dismissive of what he considered Crookshanks's coddling of Myrtilla, whom he considered a malingerer. Crookshanks, he believed, had allowed his passion for his slave to get in the way of his financial interests and, more important, his relationships with other whites. Crookshanks's love for Myrtilla eventually led to his downfall. William and Elizabeth Mould agreed to let Crookshanks hire Myrtilla for a year (a bad bargain since it cost him £20 and Myrtilla earned him just £15.75). In 1756, however, they insisted on reclaiming their property when the year's lease was up. Moreover, they punished Myrtilla for her infractions by putting her head in a yoke. Crookshanks was distraught and made what Thistlewood described as "an extraordinary scene," hysterically abusing the Moulds before abjectly repenting, dropping to his knees, and "begging their pardons etc."[86] Crookshanks had damaged his position in white society by showing excessive concern for a slave and questioning the authority of whites over their slave property. He eventually left the island for the Mosquito Coast, where, to Thistlewood's evident satisfaction, he did not prosper and eventually perished.[87]

White egalitarianism was based on the subordination of slaves, but it could founder on an equally important assumption that undergirded Jamaican white society: that a master had absolute rights over his slaves. As we have seen, Thistlewood's principal difficulties with his white neighbors came when he usurped a master's right to punish his own slaves. In the end, however, even property rights over slaves had to bow to white supremacy as the sine qua non of white Jamaican existence. Although Thistlewood's wealthy neighbors fumed about his cavalier punishments of their slaves, they were forced to accept his actions because Thistlewood as a white man had rights over and above those of black slaves. Thistlewood was similarly powerless to control how whites under his power acted toward slaves. When he remonstrated with two servants at Egypt about the ferocity of their beatings of slaves, both left the estate. Another servant "Quarrell'd with my Nanny whom he kept, and Shot at her with Small shot," which "seem to be lodged." The best that Thistlewood could do was "to tell him to be about his business." When drunken strangers attempted to rape a slave and set fire to both her and her hut, Thistlewood was able to force them off the property but could take no action against them.[88] Thistlewood knew very well that trying to get whites punished for acts against slaves was nearly impossible. Thistlewood was unable to gain recompense for the "wanton" shooting of Humphrey—"a Stout hopefull young Fellow, [who had] begun to Understand his Business"—by whites and colored men in a canoe in 1764 because a white man took responsibility for the killing when the matter came to court. Thistlewood reported in 1761 that one of his friends, John Cunningham, "Shott a Free Negro, Free Dick of Corowina," with complete impunity—the matter did not even get to court. Even freedom was not sufficient to protect blacks from whites. The result was a white people remarkable for its truculence, arrogance, and brutal exercise of tyranny. As J. B. Moreton wrote at the end of the eighteenth century, "the most insignificant Connaught savage bumpkin, or savage Highland gawky" learned on arrival in Jamaica "to flog without mercy" to "shew [his] authority." These white immigrants became slave owners "and cowskin heroes . . . proud, insolent, and haughty." "The pre-eminence and distinction which are necessarily attached even to the complexion of a white Man" in Jamaica encouraged these "cowskin heroes" to become egalitarian tyrants. The brutality of their slave system and the utter degradation and helplessness of their slaves were not aberrations but preconditions supporting Jamaica's remarkable equality between whites. Thistlewood's touchiness about insults, his considerable self-regard, his readiness to confront his superiors about injustice, and the love of liberty he shared with other white Jamaicans were not surprising in a society in which the ubiquity of slavery had given special importance to the privileges afforded men of white complexion, "in a country where the complexion, generally speaking, distinguishes freedom from slavery."[89]

chapter four

In the Scientific Manner

*Thistlewood and the Practical Enlightenment
in a Slavery Regime*

The Negroes of the French colonies are bound by the penal Code, and
judged according to criminal regulations; the Edict of 1685 regulates the
punishment that their masters can inflict upon them, and establishes a kind
of ration between offence and punishment; but that does not stop Negroes
from dying daily in chains, or under the whip; from being starved, smoth-
ered, burned without ceremony: so much cruelty always remains unpunished,
and those who exercise it are ordinarily scoundrels or persons born in the
gutter of European cities; the vilest men are the most barbarous.—Michel-
René Hilliard d'Auberteuil, *Considérations sur l'etat present de la colonie
française de Saint-Domingue*

"A Good Natural Philosopher"

On 12 May 1768, Thistlewood was told disturbing news by Samuel Hayward, his closest friend. Hayward had seen a recent Kingston paper that related, as Thistlewood put it, that "My dear friend Dr. Anthony Robinson is dead." Thistlewood was devastated. That night he could not sleep, being "so much concerned about dr. Robinson." The next morning, he "walked out alone and wept bitterly." He pretended that he "still continued usually as before," but Robinson's death was a great blow. In Robinson, Thistlewood had found a soul mate, someone living in the distant margins of empire that shared Thistlewood's passion for botany and horticulture. Robinson was the embodiment of the Enlightenment in the Tropics, "a good natural philosopher and the greatest botanist that ever was in Jamaica, his genius perfectly adapted to examining plants."[1]

Thistlewood poured out his heart in a long encomium to "the most agreeable companion I was acquainted with." His entry of 12 May 1768 is one of the few passages in his diaries that reveal much about his motivations and ambitions. He had not seen Robinson for nearly five years and could hardly consider himself much more than an acquaintance. But when Robinson had briefly lived in the parish in 1761 and 1762, Thistlewood had established a bond with him. Robinson "spent a good deal of his time at Egypt with me and I was never happier than in his company." He taught Thistlewood how to draw birds and plants in the scientific manner since he could draw "ye life, plants or animals exceedingly well." Thistlewood responded enthusiastically, giving detailed descriptions of birds he had shot and plants he encountered, including a man-o'-war bird, a "Female Carpenter Coot, [a] Flower off the Bladder Kitima, [and a] Flower off a Sort off Water Lilie." The two men exchanged views about natural history. Robinson had been appointed by the governor on a salary of £200 to collect curiosities for the Royal Society and was very well read—"he had Linneaus almost by heart, [and] was well acquainted with the work of Sloan, Ratesby, Edwards, hill, miller, gerrard, Parkinson etc." Thus, when he told Thistlewood that "Brown's history of Jamaica is a good performance, he having examin'd a great deal off the plants etc and compared them," Thistlewood was impressed enough to purchase, at considerable cost, Patrick Browne's 1754 natural history of Jamaica. Robinson was more than just a friend. He was an intellectual companion; his "enquiries were not for curiosity alone. He endeavored to search for such properties in plants as might render them serviceable to mankind." His scientific skills had not made him rich: despite being a favorite of two governors, Edward Long, and the two richest men in the island, Henry Dawkins and Charles Price, he "had no great success on acquiring a fortune." Nevertheless, he died, according to Thistlewood, "greatly admired and beloved."[2]

Thistlewood's lengthy tribute to Robinson is remarkable in two respects. First, it demonstrates his ambition to transform himself into a learned Enlightenment gentleman. Second, it suggests that Jamaica was not quite a cultural wasteland. Westmoreland Parish did not have the cultural riches of London, or even of the English provinces, but it was not entirely intellectually bereft. Planters read books, went to plays and musical events, and participated in a limited fashion in the great flowering of interest in science and nature that characterized the Enlightenment. Just as in provincial Britain, some residents of the most distant colonial frontiers sought to advance civilization and the civilizing impulse.

A Civilized Place or a Barbarous Outpost?

Yet Westmoreland was not a civilized place. Examples of cruelty abound in Thistlewood's diaries. Jamaicans were notorious for their savage punishment of slaves. As Charles Leslie noted in 1740, "No Country exceeds them in a barbarous Treatment of Slaves, or in the cruel Methods they put them to death."[3] The contrast between the progressive society that some white Jamaicans tried to create for themselves and the regressive and retributive society that existed for blacks was everywhere apparent. On the very day that Savanna-la-Mar became a free port, showing the extent to which it had established itself as a commercial community (which Scottish Enlightenment writers thought was the final passage in the natural development of society), "a stout negroe man" and "resolute rebel" was "gibbeted Alive in the Square before the long Stores."[4] When Thistlewood first met Robinson in the spring of 1761, his parish was recovering from the aftermath of Tackey's revolt and white fury against black rebels was being expressed in a series of sickening public displays of retribution. As Bryan Edwards later wrote, "[I]t was thought necessary to make a few terrible examples of some of the most guilty of the captives." Over 100 rebels were executed, and perhaps 500 were transported off the island to Honduras. The ringleaders were gibbeted alive, such as "Capt. Forest's Goliath and Davie," or, like "Mr. Crawford's Tackie" and Cardiff, "Condemned and Burnt by a Slow Fire." William Grove's Apongo or Wager, a remarkable man whom Thistlewood considered "the King of the Rebels," and "Campbell Addison's Cuffee" were condemned to "hang in Chains 3 days then be took down and burnt." Four months after Thistlewood and Robinson amused themselves by "drawing

Birds, plants etc," Thistlewood allowed one of Egypt's slaves to give "Witness against Allen's Quamina: he is to be hang'd at the estate, his head Cutt off, and Body Burnt."[5] The death and mutilation of blacks were routine. In Savanna-la-Mar, the heads of hung or burned slaves were displayed on poles to remind others of the punishment of their crimes. Less than a fortnight after learning of Robinson's death and while he was still grieving over the loss "of my friend dr: A.R.," Thistlewood went to Savanna-la-Mar to post letters home and talk with the comptroller, also named Robinson, about rose plants. On the way home, he casually noted that "they were hanging two rebel Negroes."[6]

Thistlewood was a brutal, sadistic master who controlled his slaves through the use of extreme violence and arbitrary and cruel tyranny. He demonstrated his power and toughness daily through acts of violence intended to humiliate as much as to punish. A favorite punishment in 1756 was what he called "Derby's dose," in which a runaway slave was flogged, "salt pickle, lime juice & bird pepper" were rubbed into the open wounds, and then another slave defecated in his mouth. He was "immediately put in a gag whilst his mouth was full" and made to wear the gag for "4 or 5 hours." Another variation was to have a slave "piss in his eyes & mouth" or to rub molasses on a runaway slave and expose him "naked to the flies all day and to the mosquitoes all night, without fire."[7] Floggings were routine and ferocious. Three months after becoming an overseer, for example, Thistlewood gave "old Titus" fifty lashes for helping a runaway and, after he "confess'd to have satt and eat with [the runaway slave, Robin] several times," gave him "a hundred more . . . for which piece of villainy."[8] At Egypt, Thistlewood whipped a slave on average more than once a week. In 1756, he gave slaves 57 whippings, gagged 4 slaves without whipping them, and put 11 slaves in stocks overnight. Given that the slave population at Egypt was 60 adults in 1751, each slave—especially male slaves, who were punished more frequently than women,—might expect to be physically punished at least once a year.

Thistlewood's eagerness to participate in Enlightenment discourse and his willingness to treat his slaves savagely point to a contradiction that needs explaining. How could an Enlightenment man also be a cruel tyrant? Thistlewood's behavior does not fit our understanding of changes in the intellectual discourse concerning the use of violence in the second half of the eighteenth century. Order and civilization were increasingly linked in bourgeois Western thought. The modern civilized personality developed from the slow elaboration of rules about conduct that emphasized emotional self-restraint.[9] As this new intellectual order emerged, people who patterned their behavior on these rules of conduct gradually came to eschew personal violence and envision punishment in new ways. It became less personal and more bureaucratic, less often directed by strong-willed individuals and more often exercised by a powerful state. Harsh and arbitrary corporal punishment exercised by hot-blooded and emotionally unrestrained masters on the bodies of suffering slaves did not fit this new conception of discipline.[10] The deepening value attached to sympathy, moreover, encouraged an emotional response to personal suffering.[11] Slaves received increasing sympathy, especially as abolitionists highlighted slavery's cruelties and illuminated its deviations from bourgeois conceptions of civility and respectability. Slavery became emblematic of antimodernity, and slaves became exemplary victims of barbarity.[12]

Thistlewood did not take part in this developing discourse. He expressed no discomfort over the existence of slavery, nor was he concerned about his actions as a slave overseer and slave owner. Unlike Zachary Macaulay, a later migrant to Jamaica who was so shocked after he began work supervising slaves by the casual promiscuity between white men and their slaves and the pervasive violence that permeated white dealings with slaves that he became a fierce abolitionist campaigner,[13] Thistlewood never doubted, even on first arrival, that violence was essential to the maintenance of the slave system. What we perceive as a problem—the contradiction between Thistlewood's modernity and his ready acceptance of violence as a way of dealing with slaves—was not a problem for Thistlewood or white Jamaicans and Britons generally in the eighteenth century. It is true that by the late eighteenth century educated Britons started to see violence, especially casual violence directed against children and animals, as regressive. Nevertheless, traditional understandings that children, wives, servants, and social inferiors needed to be disciplined with violence were widely held. Masters at prestigious boarding schools flogged the children of the elite with gusto. The army was notoriously violent—an average soldier serving in the British Army in the Seven Years' War could expect to see a flogging of 50 to 100 lashes every day or two, a flogging of 300 to 1,000 lashes once or twice a week, and an execution at least once a month.[14] Moreover, just at the time when humanitarianism was beginning to flourish in the second half of the eighteenth century, the English state embarked on a rapid expansion in the numbers of men and women publicly hung. Approximately 7,000 people were hung in England and Wales between 1770 and 1830, suffering slow and painful deaths in front of crowds that sometimes reached 100,000 people. It may not be true that the English were an especially callous people who "had not yet learned to dislike the sight of pain inflicted," but they were clearly not a people opposed to violence.[15] Nor were they predisposed to oppose slavery. Until 1750, antislavery sentiment was close to nonexistent. Most writers on imperial topics saw the slave trade as integral to the triumph of Britain's commercial economy and saw slavery itself as mainly beneficial to a savage race living under tyrannical conditions in Africa.[16]

In Thistlewood's lifetime, one could combine a belief in progress and modernity with a traditional belief in the necessity of state and private violence without diminishing either belief. One could also believe in the morality of keeping Africans in enslavement without inspiring condemnation or being thought logically inconsistent. But by the time of Thistlewood's death in 1786, an ideological shift of some importance was occurring. Après Thistlewood came the deluge. Jamaican slaveholders were assaulted by an abolitionist onslaught they had not anticipated. All of a sudden, Jamaican slave owners became vivid symbols of a retrogressive culture to a disapproving metropolitan audience.[17] The next generation of Jamaican slaveholders were forced to think more systematically about the violence that governed relations between masters and slaves. Given what came afterward, therefore, it is instructive to examine how an ordinary man who accepted the prevailing Enlightenment orthodoxies of his time could consider himself progressive while accepting notions that were seen very shortly after his death as emblematic of what metropolitan Enlightenment thinkers most wanted to eradicate. The key to resolving this problem—a problem that Thistlewood would not have recognized—is to understand why Thistlewood had such a sympathetic identification with Anthony Robinson but had no similar identification with the slaves with whom he spent the majority of his life. In the end, it was his acceptance of white assumptions that slaves should be treated as a species of humanity toward whom normal rules of humanitarianism, liberty, and justice need not apply that indubitably shaped his intellectual horizons.

The Republic of Letters in the Tropics

Thistlewood fits within what Robert Darnton calls the "petit Enlightenment" formed by the extraordinary proliferation of books from the early eighteenth century onward. Ordinary men and women were transformed in the eighteenth century by their exhilarating exposure to a burgeoning print culture. They formed societies of voracious and often indiscriminate readers, participating in an explosion of print whereby they were given access to a metropolitan culture from which those still confined to oral culture were excluded.[18] Thistlewood was one of these ordinary people whose lives were revolutionized by reading.

His continual consumption of books gave him admission into the cultural magic circle of the British Enlightenment, even if he resided at the farthest reaches of that circle. His avocation as a reader, as much as his identity as a slave owner, was key to his character, setting him apart from most whites and all black Jamaicans.[19]

Although he gives us few clues about when and how he read books and seldom reflected on what he read, the numerous entries in his diaries about the books he received, his laborious copying of passages from the books he was reading in his commonplace books, and his several lists of the books he owned point to the central importance of books and reading in his life. He began reading early. An eighteen-page quarto volume dating from around 1745 contains lists of books that Thistlewood had purchased (or that had been purchased for him) since childhood. The first entry, for 16 March 1730, when Thistlewood was approaching his ninth birthday, notes maps of Lincolnshire and Yorkshire, magazines, songs, *Robinson Crusoe*, and a Bible. By his late teens, Thistlewood owned ninety books. He bought between fifteen and forty new books per annum between 1739 and 1745, favoring books on poetry, translations of the classics, almanacs, sporting books, and popular magazines, such as *The Spectator*.[20]

He continued reading and purchasing books in Jamaica. Among the few possessions he brought with him on the *Flying Flamborough* were seventy-five books in two sea chests. Included among these books were standard works such as *Paradise Lost* and *An Essay on Man* and the works of Chaucer, as well as books on medicine, surveying, navigation, geography, and history and quintessential Enlightenment texts such as Addison's *Cato*, *The Tatler*, *The Spectator*, and Samuel Butler's *Hudibras*. He brought a Bible and the Book of Common Prayer, but religious books were poorly represented. He also took with him several risqué books, such as *Onania, or the heinous sin of self-pollution* and *Satan's harvest home, or the present state of whorecraft, adultery, fornication, procuring, pimping etc.*[21] These books formed the core of what was to become an impressive library, mostly bought from London suppliers, that at its peak in the late 1770s may have included over 1,000 volumes. The library was culled between the 1770s and his death by sale, by donation, and as a result of the devastation of the hurricane of 1780. In that year, Thistlewood threw away hundreds of ruined books, papers, maps, and documents and gave over 100 slightly damaged books to Hugh Wilson.[22] Nevertheless, at his death in 1786, Thistlewood had built up his library again to 262 titles that were valued in his inventory at £163.50, including the collected works of Voltaire, which were valued at £25.11.[23] It was not the largest or most impressive library in Jamaica—Nicholas Bourke, for example, the legislator and author of *The Privileges of the Island of Jamaica Vindicated* (1765), a searing and learned defense of assembly privileges from executive incursion, left a library of 440 volumes at his death in 1771—but it was remarkable for a man of middling status.[24]

Almost all of Thistlewood's books were obtained from his merchant supplier, Henry Hewitt of Old Brompton Road, Kensington, London.[25] Only occasionally did he purchase books in Jamaica. In 1756, for example, he bought the *Laws of Jamaica* for £4.75.[26] Generally, however, he received a chest of books from London nearly every year. At the end of 1758, he listed the books he had received from Hewitt. They included histories, a poem on religion, books on science and math, a dictionary, a treatise on gardening and husbandry, and the political economy of Sir Josiah Child and Joshua Gee on trade. In total, he acquired seventeen books, each of which he carefully listed by title, edition, and year of publication. On 29 June 1761, he listed sixteen books and magazines he had received on 9 April from Hewitt, including works of literature, general histories of Europe, Patrick Browne's handsomely illustrated 1756 natural history of Jamaica, an almanac, and Owen's *Weekly Journal and Chronicle*. In 1765, he received a chest containing twenty books, and in 1766, he bought seven titles, among which were the expensive works of Voltaire. His book purchasing increased as he became more prosperous. The list of books he received on 11 April 1771, shipped on the *Henry*, took up three full pages of his diary. He noted on 9 March 1774 he had received, among other books, an account of Cook's voyages on *The Endeavour*, the *Letters of Junius*, and *The Art of planting and cultivating the Vine*. In addition, he was sent a "Nautical Almanac, Covent Garden Magazine, London newspapers etc." In 1779, another bumper crop arrived, including more of Cook's voyages, William Robertson's *History of America*, and Bryan Edwards's *Jamaica, a poem in three parts*, written in the island in 1776. In 1780, an even larger chest of books arrived. The disaster of the hurricane of 1780 slowed down his book purchasing for a year or so, but by the mid-1780s, he had returned to his old pattern of receiving a chest of books from London every year. His last shipment arrived on the *Westmoreland* on 21 December 1785. As usual, it included some expensive purchases, such as the *Encyclopaedia Britannica*, valued a year later at £10.50. Once again, he had books on Cook's voyages, as well as Henry Swinburne's *Travels*, *Memorials of Human Superstition*, magazines, and novels.[27]

Thistlewood's delight in books and reading gave him entrée into a circle of similarly inclined white Jamaicans. Thistlewood not only bought books but also exchanged them with others. On 4 August 1755, for example, Thistlewood noted that he "dined at Mr. Barnet's" in Savanna-la-Mar and that he had "lent him Bacon's *Silva Silvarum*." In return, he received "the 1st and 2d vol: of Plutarch's *Lives* translated from the Greek (a very neat Set, with Copper Plates) Small 12 mo London 1749." A mutual interest in books led to "a great deal of improving discourse with Mr. Barnet." At times, Thistlewood and his friends borrowed from each other so frequently that it is hard to imagine that they had the time to actually read what they borrowed. In April 1756, for example, Thistlewood borrowed the first volume of Camden's *Britannia* from his fellow former servant and now landowner, William Mould; was lent John Hawksworth's *The Adventurer* and the *Letters of Bolingbroke* by John Cope (which he considered "very fine and instructive"); and "had the Reading of the history of the Pirates (belonging to Mr. Jarrod)," which he "returned . . . to William Crookshanks." A month later, Thomas Emotson lent him John Locke's *Essay Concerning Human Understanding*.[28] His diaries list thirty-six people from whom he borrowed books. He occasionally borrowed books from wealthy planters, such as Cope and Nicholas Blake, and borrowed even more rarely from his social inferiors, such as an unnamed wheelwright on 30 August 1755. He borrowed books mostly from men but did lend his precious works of Voltaire to Mrs. Cope and her daughter, Hannah, and borrowed books from Hannah Blake, Bessie Brown, and Harry Weech's wife.

The primary members of Thistlewood's book circle were men similar to himself: small planters and minor professionals. Thistlewood exchanged books most often with his close friend Samuel Hayward, his neighbor and fellow landowner Samuel Say, and Savanna-la-Mar lawyer Robert Chambers. He also exchanged books with William Pommells and Richard Panton. Hayward and Thistlewood were particularly active, exchanging books every three or four months. Thistlewood tended to give Hayward books relating to science and husbandry, and Hayward gave Thistlewood novels, plays, and philosophies. In 1762, Hayward borrowed books from Thistlewood on seven occasions, and Thistlewood borrowed books from Hayward three times. In 1765, they each borrowed books from the other on four occasions. In 1767, Thistlewood borrowed books from Hayward four times, and Hayward borrowed from Thistlewood once, and in 1770, the respective figures were five and three. All in all, in the 1760s and 1770s, Thistlewood exchanged books between once and twice a month. He usually had books lent out to friends—a fact solemnly recorded in his annual accounts, in which he customarily listed people who had not yet returned books. On 1 January 1771, for example, he noted that Hayward had his *Laws of Jamaica* and that Thomas King, Emotson, Say, and Robinson each had books outstanding.

Exchanging books was a significant form of social intercourse between whites of similar social status in sparsely populated rural areas. In effect, whites with a love of reading formed their own informal circulating libraries. Books could pass through several hands before returning to their owners, as *The history of the pyrates* clearly had done in 1756. Borrowing books from like-minded friends was one way, of course, in which moderately prosperous readers distant from the centers of book publishing could keep up to date without having to undertake the laborious and expensive process of ordering books from Britain. It was through books, especially those dealing with botany, that Thistlewood cemented his most intense friendships. Pommells recognized that a mutual love of reading had connected him with Thistlewood by leaving him in his will a parcel of books and "sundry papers."[29] Significantly, three of the men he exchanged books with regularly—Pommells, Hayward, and Say—made him executor of their estates.

Thistlewood, however, provides little help in explaining the contexts within which white Jamaicans exchanged books. He was more concerned with listing books than with discussing them, both in his diaries and in his commonplace books. He recorded only five comments in his diaries about the quality of the works he read. Four of these comments, moreover, concerned works relating to Jamaica—the only exception being his remarks on Bolingbroke's letters. In 1757, he related the views of his surveyor friend, William Wallace, about Charles Leslie's *A new and exact account of Jamaica*, published in 1740. Wallace was dismissive about the work's accuracy, claiming that Leslie, who had been a fellow servant, "wrote before he had been a year in the Island and [was] not well informed." Wallace believed that Leslie "had a good deal of impudence."[30] On 3 January 1775, he reported the observation of Captain Charles Sattie that Edward Long's acclaimed two-volume history of Jamaica was "very dry." Finally, he added to a note that he had read Matthew Lewis's *Oration in Praise of General Guise* that Lewis was the brother of Billy Lewis of Westmoreland Parish, that his work was "ingenious and well wrote," and that he "is s[ai]d to be very clever."[31] Otherwise, he was remarkably silent about what he thought about the books he read, even when he was reading works of obvious power and influence. He made no comment, for example, about what he thought of Adam Smith's *Wealth of Nations* or Edward Gibbon's *History of the Decline and Fall of the Roman Empire* when he read them in 1777 soon after their publication.

Thistlewood's commonplace books are only slightly more revealing than his diaries about the meanings he got from books. Unlike English contemporaries such as Anna Larpent, who not only recorded everything she read but also described how she read and what she thought about the books she read, Thistlewood merely listed the books he owned or had been given and transcribed passages, often lengthy, that struck him as interesting or noteworthy (almost always without accompanying comment).[32] His only mention in his diaries of his reading habits merely states that on 23 October 1756 he "Staid at home . . . transcribing out of Martin's Philosophy of Grammar." It was the book as object as much as the contents of the book that most impressed Thistlewood. He carefully noted the full details of publication of many of his books in his diaries and almost always included publication information with transcriptions in his commonplace books. His catalog of his library suggests that he took great pleasure in arranging and rearranging his books, either by himself or with the assistance of his slaves. He also noted, in about one of every thirty entries, when someone praised a book that he owned. One of the first things he did when he moved to Breadnut Island in 1767 was to create a place to store his library. Two days before taking possession of the pen and before any of his other belongings had been sent to his new dwelling, he "carried my Book-case, in the battoe to the Pen" with "the books in baskets upon Negroes heads." He immediately "put up all safe, except Human Prudence, which Mirtilla let fall in the dirt by accident, but not much hurt."[33] Books evidently meant a great deal to him, as did the presentation of his library. On 6 September 1777, for example, he noted that he "had finished cleaning my library."

We do know that Thistlewood was an "extensive" rather than an "intensive" reader, in the sense that he read a large number of books instead of repeatedly reading a small number of important books. Intensive reading in the early modern period was mostly associated with close reading of the Bible and a few selected religious works. Thistlewood never read in this way. He also does not appear to have read books out loud—he never mentions it if he did, at any rate. He seems to have read books alone—he noted in one diary entry that he had overheard slaves plotting to murder him "when I was in the back piazza reading"—with a notebook beside him in which he copied arresting passages.[34]

What did he read? In general, his reading was eclectic and mirrored the type of reading that members of the more serious subscription libraries in Britain tended to read. Thistlewood owned six of the ten books most borrowed by members of Bristol's subscription library between 1773 and 1784, including John Hawksworth's accounts of Cook's voyages, David Hume's *History of England*,

Abbé Raynal's polemic on West Indian colonization, William Robertson's *History of the Americas*, and Lord Chesterfield's *Letters to his Son*.[35] Like Bristol merchants and traders, he found history, law, travel, and geography especially congenial. His interests turned toward nonfiction rather than fiction, though he did own a number of works of poetry, both ancient and modern. He also owned works in Latin and French, including favorites by Horace and Ovid. Conspicuously absent, however, were popular novels, such as Henry Fielding's *Amelia* or *Tom Jones* or Lawrence Sterne's *Tristram Shandy*. He owned few religious works. Apart from a Latin and an English Bible, the only religious works he owned were George Whitfield's sermons and *The Whole Duty of Man*. More to Thistlewood's taste were philosophical works, especially some of the great texts of the Enlightenment, such as *Philosophical Transactions*, Voltaire's *Works*, and Montesquieu's *De l'espirit des lois* (in translation), as well as less elevated tomes, such as *Travels of a Philosopher* and the *Ignorant Philosopher*. He kept up with English affairs through subscriptions to Dodsley's *Annual Registers*, *Town and Country Magazine*, the *London Review*, the *Critical Review*, and *Covent Garden Magazine*. He maintained an interest in his adopted land, owning Long's *History of Jamaica*, Browne's natural history of Jamaica, histories of the Americas by Raynal and Robertson, James Grainger's poem on sugarcane, a volume on the laws of Jamaica, and a history of Barbados (presumably by Henry Frere).

Thistlewood the Intellectual

Thistlewood's greatest predilection was for books on science and mathematics, especially botany and horticulture. He was a keen amateur scientist and an accomplished botanist and gardener, and his library reflected these interests. Approximately one-third of the books he owned were scientific. They included books on chemistry, mathematics, mechanics, astronomy, and medicine, as well as numerous books on husbandry, gardening, and botany. He had twenty-six books alone that dealt with plants. Thistlewood's scientific books were both varied and up to date. He owned, for example, Joseph Priestley's *Experiments and Observations on Different Kinds of Air* (1774) and Benjamin Franklin's work on electricity. His commonplace books attest to his interest in science. His annotations on Franklin's experiments with electricity, for example, took up nine pages of close text.[36]

He was a prolific reader, eclectic but sophisticated, and a serious reader, reading demanding major works. The "swarms of insipid Novels, destitute of sentiment, language, or morals," that British critics claimed were cheapening literature and deluding and seducing frivolous readers, especially women with "voracious appetites" who were "not capable of distinguishing between good or bad," were not to his liking.[37] An analysis of the books he borrowed and lent to others in 1777 and 1778 shows that Thistlewood and his friends read both widely and well. They read books destined to become lasting works of importance. Moreover, they kept up with the latest fashions, reading books that had created a stir in London not long after they were published there. Between December 1776 and January 1779, Thistlewood borrowed twenty books from friends and lent out ten books. He also received his regular consignment of titles from Henry Hewitt on 1 May 1778 and spent a memorable afternoon at the house of wealthy planter and future historian of Jamaica, William Beckford, perusing his fine library and "look[ing] over many Folio Volumes of excellent plates of the Ruin of Rome etc."[38] The books he read were a mixture of classics, contemporary treatises, and practical guides to science and planting. He borrowed from Samuel Hayward the works of Machiavelli, as well as the works of the Restoration thinker and critic, Sir William Temple, and the Augustan art critic, Jonathan Richardson. In addition, he borrowed from Hayward in May 1778 a 1777 catalog of English books, enabling him to keep up with the latest publishing trends, such as the works of the Scottish Enlightenment, which were of particular interest. He borrowed Adam Smith's recently published *Wealth of Nations* from King on 12 May 1777 and returned it on 4 August, replacing it with another classic of political economy, Adam Ferguson's *Essay on the History of Civil Society* (1767). At the same time, he borrowed that other great work started in 1776, Gibbon's *History of the Decline and Fall of the Roman Empire*. Having already read Hume's essays, he completed his inquiry into the works of leading Scottish thinkers by borrowing from Mr. Burt on 20 July 1778 thirty numbers of the influential *Edinburgh Review*. He also perused an earlier Enlightenment writer, Jonathan Swift, whose fifth volume of collected works he borrowed from Hugh Wilson on 19 July 1778.

He also dipped into the developing discipline of anthropology, borrowing on 12 May 1777 the four volumes of the *Sketches of the History of Man* from King. He continued to be interested in travel literature, receiving from Thomas Mead the 1733 work, *The Travels and Adventures of James Massey*. In addition, he kept up with current affairs by maintaining subscriptions to local newspapers and London journals. In the late 1770s, the major topical issue was the war in the thirteen colonies. Thistlewood, as we have seen, did not reveal much interest in the American Revolution in his diaries, but he was certainly well informed about it. He borrowed three books concerning the war in America. On 3 March

1777, he received from William Hylton *Sentiments of a Foreigner, on the disputes of Great Britain with America*, translated from the French. He got from Hayward a pamphlet by the radical dissenter, Richard Price, *Liberty and America*, and he borrowed a pamphlet written by the West Indian merchant, Beeston Long, about how the military in North America was supplied. He also gave to his neighbor Hannah Blake a book that he had purchased about the war, *The Present State of Great Britain and America*. He rounded out his reading with a treatise on the philosophical principles of medicine that he borrowed from Christopher Kirkland, a book of practical relevance from William Bodington—Michael Soleirol's *Essay on the Management off the Rum, distilling etc*—and Sir William Hamilton's *Observations on Mount Vesuvius* and *Essays on the Manners and Character of Women*.

What can we discern about Thistlewood's character and opinions from his lifetime habit of reading? The society he grew up in—provincial northern England—was a quiet backwater, similar to Westmoreland, where he spent most of his life. Yet it was not untouched by the intellectual currents transforming society and thought in the eighteenth century. It seems clear in his terse diary entries and his lengthy transcriptions from what he read in his commonplace books that he absorbed much of the common thinking of his day and agreed with the insights that thinking inspired. The sentiments we can discern from his diaries and commonplace books show that he was an Enlightenment man. That statement, however, warrants a caveat. The values of the Enlightenment are hard to distinguish because the Enlightenment itself was so diverse and diffuse. As Mark Goldie argues, "The Enlightenment was not a crusade but a tone of voice, a sensibility." It was not a monolithic project but a pluralistic debate by "a cluster of overlapping and interactive elites who shared a mission to modernize."[39] Moreover, that mission to modernize came from below as well as above: the vulgar shared in the pragmatic and worldly quest to transform the world and emancipate its citizens. In a sense, it is a mistake to try to determine whether Thistlewood shared the values of the Enlightenment because Enlightenment values were so all-encompassing. To be a Briton in the middle of the eighteenth century was to be an Enlightenment person. Roy Porter summarizes the British Enlightenment as "primarily the expression of new mental and moral values, new canons of taste, styles of sociability and views of human nature." It was the creed of pragmatic worldly modernizers, devoted to progress and the increase of both civility and civilization. A belief in the pursuit of happiness displaced the seventeenth-century creed of Calvinism—be it through sensual gratification, the acquisition of wealth, or the increase in knowledge. Thistlewood shared, in his enthusiasm for science, his inattention to religion, and his methodical and rational approach to making money, modernizers' faith that a benevolent and secular Newtonian universe allied with the development of commerce would lead to improved societies and greater individual happiness.[40]

"Learning . . . at the Lowest Ebb"

How did Thistlewood's intellectual ambitions suit life in Jamaica? Was Jamaica a haven of the Enlightenment, or was it one of those outposts of empire that Bernard Bailyn has described as "a ragged outer margin of a central world, a regressive, backward-looking diminishment of metropolitan accomplishment?"[41] Jamaica in the mid-eighteenth century both resembled and differed from the bustling, dynamic, intellectually curious world of England. In some respects, Jamaica was similar to the great metropolis of London. Like London, Jamaica was oriented toward commerce and getting ahead. London, Joseph Addison said, was "a kind of Emporium for the whole Earth," a shrine to consumption, luxury, ceaseless bustle, and naked ambition.[42] Much the same was true for Jamaica. White Jamaicans were devoted, above all, to the main chance and displayed the kind of restless energy and active devotion to the making of a fortune that distinguished the citizens of London from other Britons. Jamaicans were notoriously avaricious and consumed by an aggrandizing self-interest. Their attachment to personal advantage made them behave "almost like a parcel of *Men-eaters* devouring one another, the *greater* eating up the *lesser*."[43] Like Londoners, white Jamaicans were compulsively sociable, expansively extroverted in their behavior, and great attendees of balls, banquets, and concerts. They engaged in a dizzying round of visits to each other in the countryside and prided themselves above all on their hospitality, receiving "in the most friendly manner those with whose character and circumstances they are often utterly unacquainted."[44] It was a place, in short, where that exemplar of the practical Enlightenment, James Boswell, would have felt at home. He would have enjoyed the liberality and religious indifference of Jamaican planters, delighted in the abundance of drink and food that graced their tables, and been unable to contain his excitement at the ample opportunities for sexual encounters that were provided in an exploitative slave society. He may even have been tempted to agree with Long's view that white Jamaicans had so successfully imitated "the manners of Europeans at every point" that they now "differ[ed] not much from their brethren at home, except in a greater profusion of dishes, a larger retinue of domestics, and in wearing more expensive cloaths."[45]

Nevertheless, Jamaica was not London. It was not even provincial Britain. While Boswell might have gained in Jamaica in terms of sexual opportunity, conviviality, and the pursuit of pleasure allied with wealth, he would have lost the access to culture that residence in London afforded. Further, he would have been appalled at the indifference to education, learning, and the polite arts that the majority of white Jamaicans evinced. Even the patriotic Long admitted that there was little reason to "expect that this little island will ever become the seat of philosophy." There were exceptions: Long lauded the intelligence and cultural sophistication of John Fearon, a native-born Jamaican who had never left the island but was as cultivated as any English gentleman and possessed "a library furnished with a collection of the best authors."[46] But, in general, Jamaicans showed little love of learning, were naturally indolent, and devoted themselves more to the pursuit of sensuous pleasure, be it sexual or culinary, than to the disciplined acquisition of knowledge. Leslie was appalled when he visited in the 1730s at how little Jamaicans valued learning. "Learning," he declaimed, was "at the lowest Ebb." He believed that "there are indeed several Gentlemen that are well acquainted with Learning," but "these are few." Most Jamaicans, he believed, "have a greater Affection for the modish Vice of Gaming than the *Belles Lettres*, and love a Pack of Cards better than the Bible." It was "quite unpolite," he found, "to talk of a *Homer*, or a *Virgil*, of a *Tully*, or a *Demosthenes*."[47]

Thus, Thistlewood can be distinguished from most white Jamaicans because he aspired to intellectual pursuits. Jamaica was not a propitious environment for cultivating the life of the mind, as all commentators agreed. Yet culture did exist in Jamaica. Its citizens included members of the Royal Society, the Dilettante Society, and the Royal College of Physicians. Spanish Town had an active theater, a circulating library, a literary society, and an agricultural society. The first oratorio in the Americas was composed and performed in Jamaica in 1775. Thistlewood was unusual but not singular in his devotion to reading and his interest in science and horticulture. Science was popular in Europe's American colonies. James McClellan has highlighted the close links that existed between colonialism and science in St. Domingue in the third quarter of the eighteenth century and has stressed the popularity of science among French colonists and the significance of colonial scientific discoveries for Enlightenment France. The Ministère de la Marine et Colonies dispatched botanists to develop new tropical crops in botanical gardens. Richard Drayton notes that the philosophical and economic foundations of these governmental scientific initiatives were significant, associating natural history, economic inventory, strategic intelligence, and anthropological interests with a new ideal of "Enlightened Administration."[48]

Jamaica was not as advanced as St. Domingue in its pursuit of science, having few of the learned societies and little of the governmental support that distinguished the French colony, but it followed the same trends. In particular, a few white Jamaicans became interested in botany in the 1760s and 1770s and started to press for publicly funded botanical gardens. Jamaicans had shown little interest in improving nature before then. Leslie complained in 1740 that despite having "the finest trees in the world," planters "have no Avenues of them, nor so much of a shady Walk about their Pens or Seats." Lord Adam Gordon complained a quarter of a century later that Jamaica had "scarce any thing deserving the name of [a] Garden in the Island." Despite the benefits of "the inexpressible Bounty of Nature," Jamaicans seldom tried to improve their many "beautiful Prospects . . . beyond what Nature gives them."[49]

But in the decade before the American Revolution, the situation changed. Great planters, such as speaker of the Jamaican House of Assembly, Sir Charles Price, made enormous efforts to develop carefully landscaped estates based on the British model. Price's retreat in St. Mary's Parish—the Decoy—was the closest property in Jamaica to an English country estate. It contained a deer park, a man-made lake stocked with wild duck and teal, and "a very elegant garden disposed in walks, which are shaded with the cocoanut, cabbage, and sand-box trees." Long thought Decoy extremely attractive. More important, it was an outpost of burgeoning civilization. Not only were the "flower and kitchen-garden filled with the most beautiful and useful variety which Europe, or this climate, produces," but "clumps of graceful cabbage-trees are dispersed in different parts, to enliven the scene; and thousands of plantane and other fruit-trees occupy a vast tract, that environs this agreeable retreat, not many years ago a gloomy wilderness."[50] Price had combined European fashion with Jamaican materials to transform a wild site into a place of cultivation—just as Long hoped would occur with Jamaican culture as a whole.

At the same time, the British government and the Jamaican Assembly produced measures designed to develop public gardens that might contribute to economic growth and aid in the transformation of Jamaica into an improved society. The Seven Years' War impelled quasi-public British scientific institutions, such as the Society of Arts, to create colonial botanical gardens as a means of discovering which Asian and African plants capable of agricultural production could be introduced into the West Indies. Beginning in 1762, the Society of Arts announced prizes for anyone who could form a garden "in which plants, useful in medicine, and profitable as articles of commerce, might be propagated." Three years later, a botanical garden was founded at St. Vincent, and in 1775, Hinton East and Matthew Wallen, both of whom had established private botanical gardens in the eastern Blue Mountains in the early 1770s, persuaded the Jamaican Assembly to create two botanical gardens and fund the salary of a full-time botanist. The assembly set up a public garden at Bath in the Parish of St. Thomas in the East. In 1794, it acquired East's magnificent garden, full of exotic plants and tended by thirty-nine slaves, at Spring Garden in the mountains of Liguanea at Gordon Town, in upper St. Andrew Parish. Bryan Edwards took these botanical initiatives as a symbol of Jamaican patriotism—East had emphasized in a 1784 report that he had introduced useful as well as ornamental plants into the garden and had reiterated that acquiring the breadfruit tree from the South Pacific would be useful for feeding slaves and would serve as a sign that an "improving" plantocracy was devoted to Enlightenment ideals. He concluded the first volume of his history with a lengthy appendix based on Arthur Broughton's *Hortus Eastensis*, which was a catalog of 521 exotic plants in East's garden. Its placement there was not accidental. Edwards's major concern in his work was to validate West Indians as enlightened, morally sensitive, and valuable citizens of the British Empire against Adam Smith's fierce economic denunciation of the importance and efficiency of the sugar colonies and against the strictures of abolitionists about West Indians' moral character.[51] Such claims were not unusual in an age when people were convinced that scientific advancement, agricultural improvement, and economic progress went together. If colonial gentlemen were interested in agriculture, especially horticulture, and science, then it might be possible to overlook their moral deficiencies. Even Gibbon, a leading skeptic of imperial ambitions, believed that Britain's "pure and generous love of science" and its diffusion of agricultural techniques to distant parts of the world were exceptions to the rule that empire was the handmaiden of avarice and cruelty. The advance of science in the colonies was evidence of the increase of "the real wealth, the happiness and perhaps the virtue of the human race."[52]

An Amateur Scientist

Thistlewood was intensely interested in science, especially the sciences he could practice himself: botany, horticulture, and meteorology. He was well informed about these fields and about attempts made to advance scientific concerns. On

10 January 1775, for example, Thistlewood "Going home met Mr. Cope who told me of a physic Garden or Botanical Garden being established in Jamaica. That Matthew Wallen is one of the Commissioners; that the King of Spain has given leave to collect seeds, trees, plants &c throughout his Dominions." Six years previously, he had reported that he "hear[d] dr. drummond of Bluecastle have purchased plants at negril, that mr. john pulley Edwards has basney spray and that Montague James Esq. Is introducing the mango into this country."[53] His friendship with Anthony Robinson has already been noted. After Robinson's death, he continued to find congenial friends with whom he could discuss scientific matters. In 1777, he showed off his garden to Thomas Robbins. While the two "walked about the pasture, & examined the Trees, plants etc," Robbins declared that he considered "dr. George Spence in Hanover, to be the greatest Botanist in the Island."[54]

Thistlewood's scientific interests are clear from his inventory, which lists an impressive array of scientific instruments. He owned two telescopes and a convex eyeglass, including a "large 4 feet refractory telescope" worth £15. He possessed a microscope, a hydrometer, a hydrostatic balance, a magic lantern, "Priestly's machine for impregnating water with fixed air," and a full array of math instruments, including instruments required for surveying.[55] Some of these instruments he had made himself. On 26 January 1753, he "Made an hydrometer: the scale an Inch divided into a hundred parts: the card about 31 ½ inches long." He bought others and was given at least one—an optical apparatus "made by B. Martin"—by a friend (Thistlewood noted that it was "a very fine apparatus but is rather hurt being in unskilful hands").[56] His instruments facilitated an active curiosity about astronomy, botany, and physics and encouraged him to become friends with others similarly interested in practical science, such as Samuel Hayward. Thistlewood visited Hayward to view his "new optical apparatus and Electrical Machine" and was impressed by his "6 feet Acromatic Telescope," which he enviously described as "Better than Mine, tho' not in proportion, as six guineas and a half is to Four Guineas." Hayward's telescope allowed him a good look at Jupiter, the moon, and Saturn and its moons. Five years later, however, he proudly boasted that his telescope "beats" that owned by Captain Arthur Forrest. On 11 April 1777, William Woolery, a local grandee, showed Thistlewood and some friends "Cole's forcing pump, a Very Ingenious Machine & easily worked, Cost £30 sterling." A year later, Mr. More visited and "shewed me a perspective glass: the glasses of his own grinding, which he does very neatly," and in 1779, More again "shewed me a small binocular prospect glass of his own construction" that Thistlewood declared "ingenious" and that "gave a very good view." Thistlewood and More examined the night sky with it, seeing "Saturn's Ring and his 4th Satellite."[57] Thistlewood delighted in seeing stars and especially comets. In 1759 and 1769, he observed comets passing above Jamaica and described them minutely in his diary. On 30 April 1759, he stated, "The comet resplendent tonight," and noted that it was "about 50 degrees high in the south, before 8 p.m." Two weeks later, it was 60 degrees high in the southwest. It was probably Halley's comet, which had arrived in England on Christmas Eve, 1758. The comet that blazed across the sky in 1769 was described with even more enthusiasm. Between 31 August and 16 September 1769, Thistlewood made numerous notations about the comet's shape, color, and trajectory. A year later, he sent a "scheme of the comet orbit of 1769" to his brother in Lincolnshire. In 1777, he described in his diary an equally rare event, an eclipse of the moon.[58]

Astronomy was a popular pastime for educated Englishmen in the eighteenth century. An erudite gentleman of means might be expected to own a telescope in Georgian Britain.[59] Even more popular were aspects of science that could be most easily seen as utilitarian, engines of natural progress, and means whereby pragmatic improvement could be made, especially anything involving agriculture and improvements science could make in agricultural production. Moreover, it was only outside the physical sciences that amateurs such as Thistlewood could make a name for themselves.[60] Thistlewood attempted to achieve renown in two areas in which professional skill was not required and empirical observation and the application of extensive industry were most important. He was a collector and list maker by inclination, so it was natural that he would attempt to collect information about the world around him. Plants and the weather were obvious choices for investigation. As early as 1752, he began a weather journal, noting each day the strength and direction of the winds and the conditions of the atmosphere, including thunderstorms, rain, and extraordinary meteorological events. He kept these records in the same systematic way he kept his diaries until his death in 1786. As an employee at Egypt Plantation, he indulged his interest in trees and plants by importing seeds from Henry Hewitt in Britain and expanded his interest in gardening when he moved to Breadnut Island Pen in 1767. By the 1770s, his garden had become a showpiece. The garden had an economic purpose, providing Thistlewood with a small proportion of his income every year. More important, it was an arena in which he could demonstrate to the world at large his talents as an amateur botanist and show that he was one of the leading horticulturalists in eighteenth-century Jamaica.[61]

That his gardening was undertaken for more than economic reasons is clear from Thistlewood's correspondence with Edward Long, preserved in Long's papers at the British Library.[62] Having "seen inserted in the History of Jamaica the quantity of rain that I had observed fall in 1761 at Egypt, which imagine was communicated by my worthy friend dr. Anthony Robinson," in 1776 he summoned up the courage to write to Long, his social and intellectual superior. In a very long letter, he explained that he had allowed Richard Panton, a Savanna-la-Mar physician "engaged in a work on the diseases of the country," to make a copy of Thistlewood's weather journal. Panton had died just before setting sail to Britain and consequently "these Copy's became useless." Thistlewood resolved to send them to Long, after adding to them "the general account of Rain fallen since the beginning of 1761, and some other small matters," assuring Long that "the Observations were made with all care and exactness." On 12 June 1776, he noted in his diary that he "delivered to Capt. Richardson's care, a parcel to Edward Long Esqr. London—Containing a Journal off the Weather from the beginning of 1770 to the 7th Instant inclusive and Quantity of Rainfall, heights of the rain and also a general Acct of Rain fallen since the beginning of 1761." The material sent was copious—amounting to 127 pages, of which 112 were meteorological observations and a summary of annual rainfall. Along with a few recollections about Robinson, Thistlewood added some reflections on his garden and the plants he had in it. He listed the plants that grew at Breadnut Island and noted that "at different times and considerable expense" he had sent for a variety of plants and seeds that had not been successfully transplanted. Added to this list was an explanation for why these European plants and fruits had not prospered at Breadnut.

Thistlewood addressed Long with all the respect one might expect from someone far beneath Long socially and "an intire Stranger." He was delighted when Long replied, thanking Thistlewood for his gift. On 17 June 1777, Thistlewood wrote again to Long, declaring himself "glad" that Long had found his papers acceptable and exclaiming that "as a Correspondence is now begun which you so obligingly approve of, [I] shall not offer any excuse for continuing what is so Agreeable to me." Thistlewood then launched into a lengthy discussion of the techniques he had used to measure the weather and gave his opinion on a variety of scientific matters such as whether Jamaican plants had been described better by Patrick Browne in his *Natural History of Jamaica* or by Nicolaus Jacquin in his *Selectarum* (he preferred the latter). He clearly saw this cor-

Thistlewood was an enthusiastic amateur scientist, eager to participate as much as he could in transatlantic scientific discourse. This letter shows the peak of his ambition—an attempt to initiate correspondence with Edward Long, the leading British intellectual connected to Jamaica. Thomas Thistlewood to Edward Long, 17 June 1777, Long Papers, Add. MSS 18275A, f. 126, British Library.

respondence as a means whereby he could gain an entrée as an expert on the weather and flora of a far-distant periphery of empire into a wider and more distinguished scientific circle. He hoped "to have the pleasure to hear from you again when convenient." Long did not, however, carry on the conversation. Thistlewood's intellectual horizons remained limited to his parish.

Within his intellectual circle, however, Thistlewood achieved considerable acclaim. Douglas Hall has highlighted the significance of Thistlewood and his garden in the development of botanical and horticultural pursuits in Jamaica, even if Thistlewood's efforts were relatively unheralded. Broughton's *Hortus Eastensis* cataloged 521 exotic plants and listed 124 by time of first planting. Thistlewood is not listed as an importer of plants to Jamaica, but of the plants dated by first importation in the *Hortus Eastensis*, Thistlewood recorded in his diaries an earlier planting in 78 cases.[63] In 1762, for example, he noted, "I have now a white narcissus in full flower in the garden. . . . This is probably the first that ever flowered in the garden." In 1770, he wrote with satisfaction that he had "flowered an English pink [rose] (of a beautiful red) in my garden which is the first I have seen, or heard of, to have flowered in the island. The plant is flourishing and will have many flowers."[64] Perhaps his most notable innovation was to plant asparagus, with the help of Francis Scott, a gardener from Hexham in Northumberland. After an initial planting in April 1771, Scott supervised Thistlewood and his slaves in planting 12 asparagus beds in August 1771, each 40 feet long and 4 feet broad and heavily dunged.[65]

By the early 1770s, Thistlewood was recognized in his district as a skilled and knowledgeable horticulturalist. Gardening made him money, but more important, it allowed him to flatter people by giving gifts of his produce. On 7 May 1775, for example, he "Sent to Mrs. Vassall some asparagus and flowers" while he "Sent Mr. [Richard] Vassall an account of plants growing in my garden, May 1st 1775." The beauty and extent of his garden encouraged people to visit him, especially in the years immediately preceding the American Revolution, when Thistlewood's prosperity was at its height. He entertained regally at such functions, treating his guests to the best food he could obtain from his livestock and his garden. On 15 March 1775, for example, he entertained John Cope, Richard Vassall, and William Blake and fed them homegrown "mutton & broccoli, carrots & asparagus," as well as fruit from his orchard. The fame of his garden spread far enough that Governor William Trelawney wanted to see it when he visited Westmoreland Parish. Thistlewood had provided most of the food when the governor dined with the Copes—"a teal, a whistling duck & 2

Spanish snipes, 10 large broccoli, about 3 quarts of English peas in the pods, and a large calabash full of asparagus; also 4 ripe figs, 3 sweet limes, and flowers" —and the governor was so impressed that, according to Thistlewood, he wanted to come see his garden.[66]

The garden represented an enormous effort by Thistlewood and his slaves. It contained a mixture of local and imported plants. Thistlewood was as assiduous in cultivating new trees, plants, and flowers as he was in acquiring up-do-date literature. Between his acquisition of the ruinate (or unoccupied and uncultivated) Breadnut Island in July 1765 and his planting a garden on the property in February 1768, he imported and planted 139 varieties of flora from England. He had to be indefatigable in his gardening because the property was ill suited to the purpose he put it to. As Thistlewood explained to Long, "I am unfortunately fixed on one of the most unfavorable places for the Culture of Plants, off perhaps any in the Island, having hot air, poor soil, and bad seasons. . . . We have not the fine, moderate growing showers that some parts of the Island have, but commonly cross from one Extreme to the other, a great drought, then a glut of rain, a drought again and so on." It was with "great difficulty" that he managed to get native plants of the island to grow at Breadnut, and he made "but little progress" in introducing many European plants and fruits.[67] Many plants, notably English fruits such as pears, peaches, and nectarines, might thrive in the better-situated botanical gardens in the St. Andrew Mountains but could not prosper in a tropical Westmoreland garden close to sea level. On 11 March 1774, he noted sadly that there was "No sign of the artichokes, myrtles, or liquorice plants" he had planted. Despite importing well over 200 varieties by 1770, an initial listing of the plants growing in his garden in September 1770 amounted to just 136 plants. But he persevered. By 1775, he listed over 300 items growing in his garden and in the slaves' provision grounds. Hall estimates that about 60 of the plants had been imported from England, about 25 came from various sources in North America, and the rest were from local gardens, fields, and waysides. His unpromising hilly and rocky piece of land had been transformed into one of the best gardens in western Jamaica. Other gardeners praised what he had done. William Pommells, for example, declared that Thistlewood's indigo was "the best he has ever seen made in the Island, and is equal to Guatemala indigo."[68]

His skills facilitated entry into a small circle of educated men interested in horticulture and botany, such as Samuel Hayward, a merchant and foundry owner; George Spence, a wealthy St. James planter reckoned to be the best botanist in the country; John and William Henry Ricketts and Richard Vassall, wealthy Westmoreland sugar planters; and Richard Panton, Robert Pinkney, and Thomas King, comfortably well-off doctors. As with reading, gardening provided a means of social contact as well as a venue for displaying skill and participation in a wider transatlantic scientific discourse. Thistlewood's involvement with Pinkney was typical. In October 1773, Pinkney sent Thistlewood a list of trees and plants he wanted to order through Henry Hewitt. He also sent him "Milne's translation of Linnaeus." Thistlewood returned the book a fortnight later and gave Pinkney "some ripe seed of the adhatoda or prickly justicia, a pretty shrub bearing purple flowers which smell like violets."[69] Thistlewood was always sending his friends gifts of plants and seeds. He received many in return. When he went to the Hertford estate on 11 June 1778, he not only looked over William Beckford's library and played billiards and cricket but also exchanged plants. Thistlewood gave Beckford rose-apples, and in return, Beckford gave Thistlewood "some geranium slips, flower seeds, jonquil roots etc." He also sent plants to Britain. He sent a box of plants to Britain in May 1775 with Captain Charles Sattie, including "The Clusea, or Balsam Tree; Hippommane; Manganeel [Manchioneel] or Eve Apple Tree; Croton; wild rosemary; Caesalphina [probably Barbados pride]; Braziletto; Ironweed; Whitewood or Tulip Tree [mountain mahoe]; Dogwood; Paulinia, Supple Jack; Crabwood; Adhatoda or prickly justicia; Spathe or Maiden Plum Tree; a young rose-apple," and several seeds. Two months later, he sent apples and spices plus three volumes of the *Western Universal Botanist* for Hewitt to return to a Mr. Nichol.[70]

Indeed, Thistlewood's interest in horticulture linked him to the transatlantic exchange of goods and ideas that marked the beginnings of globalization in the mid-eighteenth century. He sent for plants from Peru, the Mosquito Coast, Georgia, and India, as well as Britain. By the late 1770s, his garden was an oasis of cosmopolitanism in provincial Jamaica—presided over by a man who had rooted himself firmly in western Jamaican soil. The garden was one of the primary sites of Enlightenment culture, on the one hand a source of vegetables, fruits, flowers, perfumes, and drugs and on the other a space for rest and sensuous pleasure. It combined a functional purpose with a spiritual function while being a repository of Enlightenment intellectual energy. Thistlewood's garden certainly gave him great pleasure in life as well as satisfying his considerable intellectual ambitions.[71]

Sensibility

The cosmopolitan side of Thistlewood's nature—his yearning for education and his desire to participate in learned and up-to-date discourse on scientific and botanical matters—helps to explain his hero worship of Anthony Robinson and his sorrow at Robinson's premature death. Mastery of science and gardening accompanied Thistlewood's burning ambition for mastery in other areas. Robinson was knowledgeable in areas in which Thistlewood desired to be recognized. It was for this reason that Thistlewood made copious notes of what Robinson said. On 22 May 1765, Robinson dined with Thistlewood at Egypt and "gave me a Figure & definition off the Tithy malus: a most rare plant." Thistlewood devoted four pages to a detailed description of the plant. Because he identified so strongly with Robinson, it is not surprising that he was upset when Robinson died. The lengthy encomium he wrote about Robinson in his diary contained comments he would have wanted someone to make about him. Robinson, who was "not much older than me," Thistlewood said, was "sober and effective and the most agreeable companion I was acquainted with." He was "a good natural philosopher and the greatest botanist that ever was in Jamaica." In short, Thistlewood lamented, "I was never happier than in his company."[72] Years later, Thistlewood still mourned his loss. He included in his package to Long a copy of an elegy published in the *St. Jago Intelligencer* commemorating his "beloved friend." Thistlewood commended the author as one "possessed off a great Share [of] the benevolent and amiable qualities he has so well described" in Robinson and praised the elegy as "a most exact and true portrait of this worthy man." Indeed, the poem, he felt, was "deserving of being included among our best Collections of poems."[73]

In his reaction to Robinson's death, Thistlewood exhibited the feelings one associates with the culture of sensibility that was a conspicuous feature of eighteenth-century life. His response was far from stoic; it demonstrated that he had "a sensibility of heart" that "fit a man for being easily moved and for readily catching, as if by infection, any passion."[74] Thistlewood shed abundant tears for his friend, showing himself to be a man of sensibility and a man capable of sympathetic identification with another. Nothing could be more representative of his times than sensibility—rooted in the scientific understanding of the nervous system as the trigger of both thought and feeling—which encouraged the expression of emotions and instinctual passion.[75] Sensibility led to sympathy, or an emotional engagement with others. Sympathy was a key Enlightenment concept. David Hume, following from Lockean notions of associational psychology and the theories of philosophers such as Berkeley, Butler, and Hutcheson who believed that being human was based on man's innate capacity for sympathy, even argued that nature's "great resemblance among all human creatures" led to people imbued with sympathetic feelings toward others who could feel unhappy about injustice or misfortune even "when the injustice is so distant from us, as no way to affect our interest." What Hume realized was expressed better by Adam Smith, who saw that imaginative projection was the vehicle through which sympathy, or compassion with the situation of others, was released: "How selfish soever man may be supposed, there are evidently some principles in his nature, which interest him in the fortune of others. . . . Of this kind is pity or compassion, the emotion which we feel for the misery of others, when we see it, or are made to conceive it in a very lively matter."[76]

Nevertheless, Thistlewood had no sympathetic identification with the majority of people with whom he passed his life. We have already seen his indifference to the deaths of slaves convicted of capital crimes. He was also capable of mind-boggling savagery toward slaves who committed what he deemed offenses. He seldom expressed strong emotions when his slaves died, even if he had spent considerable time in their company. He noted dispassionately the deaths of many slaves, seldom adding to the recognition of their deaths any appreciation of their particular human qualities. Typical was his reaction to the death of Cambridge, a slave on the Egypt estate who had been found dead in a morass by two other slaves. Thistlewood commented: "The cattle boys say they heard him holler last night, but thought it had been canoe-men in the river. Imagine he was murdered by runaways who, it seems, threatened to murder him the last time he was runaway if he did not leave them. . . . Wrote an account to Mr. Cope, per Prince." No expression of regret for Cambridge's death or expostulation against the enormity of the crime committed against the slave accompanied Thistlewood's diary entry. The next day, Cambridge was buried without ceremony. Thistlewood was no more emotional when his own slaves died. Syphox was the first slave he owned who died. Bought on 29 April 1765, he died a year later. Thistlewood made no comment save that Syphox "had been long ailing." Will was the next to die. Bought at the end of 1761, he died on 7 August 1767. All Thistlewood had to say was that "Will died about breakfast time this morning. Sent Cudjoe and Solon to bury him." Thistlewood was no more communicative when Johnnie died in 1770, although Johnnie had been the second slave Thistlewood had purchased and had lived with him for twelve years. Johnnie's fellow slaves were upset and buried him with ceremony, putting on a "play" for him in the evening, but Thistlewood only noted that "Johnnie died of a flux." The only slave that Thistlewood owned whose death elicited any sympathy was Chub, who died in 1775. The day after relating that Chub had died "at 8 o'clock" after having been "very ill indeed," Thistlewood noted that "At night the Negroes buried poor Chub. I gave them a bottle of rum."[77]

In part, Thistlewood's indifference to his slaves' deaths reflected white Jamaicans' fatalism or even levity toward death, which arose from living in a society with a high mortality rate. Because the deaths of family and friends, let alone slaves, were so frequent, white Jamaicans did not often allow death to distract them from their everyday business. Thistlewood's indifference to slaves' deaths was also a result of his exposure to the harsh realities of Jamaican slavery. Whites' lack of concern for slaves, even in death, initially shocked Thistlewood. On 12 May 1751, he confided to his diary: "In the afternoon Mimber, a Fine Negro Woman, [was] buried today . . . like a Dog! She died yesterday." Burying slaves without ceremony was part of a white man's acculturation process. Yet it is noticeable that no slave's death occasioned in Thistlewood even a measure of the grief that overwhelmed him when his nephew died in 1765, when his son died in 1780, or after the deaths of his closest friends—James Crawford in 1750, Anthony Robinson in 1768, and Samuel Hayward in 1781.[78] He not only never expressed doubts about the rightness of slavery but also barely acknowledged that most Afro-Jamaicans suffered under that condition. His only recognition that slaves might not have enjoyed enslavement came in 1757 when he was separated from his partner, Phibbah, after taking a position as overseer of the Kendal estate. He related that Quashie, a slave from Egypt who visited him bearing gifts of a turtle and eighteen crabs from Phibbah, told him that Phibbah "is sick, for which I am really very sorry." He added, in the sole occasion in his lengthy diaries when he showed a degree of sympathetic identification with a slave, "Poor girl, I pity her, she is in miserable slavery."[79]

Thistlewood and Slavery

Thistlewood's detachment from the predicament of Jamaican slaves indicates that he perceived that there was an unbridgeable gap between him and them. He lived with slaves, socialized with slaves, especially when he went hunting or fishing, and saw individual slaves as human beings with recognizably different personalities and behaviors. Yet he never identified with them or contemplated treating them in the same way he treated whites. He was careful not to use violence against whites, even if whites were his subordinates and had behaved very badly toward him, as had Thomas Fewkes in 1757. With slaves it was a different matter. Thistlewood accepted that violence against blacks—both physical and sexual—was part of the natural order and that terror was a sensible strategy for keeping them overawed and docile. Even though the race and status of slaves were not "a reason for not treating them as Rational Beings," their condition as slaves was unalterable: they were not like whites, who should be treated as "parts of his Family," but alien creatures, excluded from polite discourse.[80]

It is difficult to explain Thistlewood's views about blacks because he so clearly felt that slavery was natural and inevitable that he seldom concerned himself with reflecting on its morality or on what slaves felt about slavery or about being African. As far as can be discerned, Thistlewood believed slavery to be normative and Africans to be natural slaves. They were slaves because they fell outside the social contract that secured individual rights, a blessing reserved for European insiders. Thistlewood never questioned the right of white dominance. Although he read extensively from Enlightenment texts, he never internalized the Enlightenment insight that recognition of slaves' humanity might lead to recognition of their equality—a dangerous concept in a society where people of African descent were a substantial proportion of the population. Instead, he worked from ancient assumptions that humanity included a hierarchy of degrees between the "base" (African slaves) and the "noble" (elite European men). Within that framework, he recognized, though only to a limited extent, slaves' humanity. But he never considered the possibility that slaves might be in any way equal to white men—or that they might show any sign of sensibility or emotional pain. Africans were outsiders; he did not need to consider their rights, especially in a society in which white control was always tenuous.[81]

Thistlewood's opinions about slaves and blacks are instructive because we have few records that rival Thistlewood's diaries in regard to the extent of contact between a white man and black slaves. Thistlewood lists thousands of slaves by name. Most are referred to only a few times, but some, such as his mistress Phibbah and his first slave, longtime companion, and occasional irritation Lincoln, are mentioned frequently, enabling us to reconstruct their lives to an extent unparalleled for almost any other eighteenth-century slave. The evidence concerning what Thistlewood thought about these constant companions is contradictory. On the one hand, he was very aware of their individual personalities and seldom referred to slaves as a collective, using derogatory racial epithets. On the other hand, he was conscious that slaves were different, especially in skin color, from Europeans and believed that their skin color suited them for slavery. He seldom referred to his slaves as slaves. Instead, he denoted them by color. He used a universal social language based on racial identification to describe slaves. He almost always referred to them as "negroes." Between 1751 and 1782, he used the word "slave" in his diaries just 55 times, compared to 3,166 references to "negro."[82]

Thistlewood was no stranger to Africans or to slavery when he arrived in Jamaica. His position as a supercargo on a worldwide trip had exposed him to Indians, African slaves in Bahia, and Africa itself at the Cape of Good Hope. He undoubtedly had also come across portrayals of Africa and Africans in books and plays. Thistlewood gives little clue as to what he thought of Africans when he first came to Jamaica, but if he was a typical Englishman of his age, he would have grown up with a highly unfavorable image of them. Drawing on earlier Iberian notions of Africans as culturally inferior and marked by their race as savages and idolaters with subhuman, bestial characteristics, the English stigmatized blacks as wild men, beasts, and savages. Although the explicit biologically based racism of the late eighteenth and early nineteenth centuries was absent, the sheer accumulation of derogatory references to Africans in the seventeenth and eighteenth centuries indicates that the belief that sub-Saharan Africans were uniquely deficient in color, character, and culture was widespread.[83] Enslavement entrenched such attitudes further and encouraged observers to confirm Africans' bestiality. Both Richard Ligon and Hans Sloane—influential seventeenth-century commentators on Barbados and Jamaica, respectively—compared Africans to beasts. These writers noted that African women's breasts "hang down below their Navels" and were "lank . . . like those of goats," while Ligon compared slaves who were wrestling to "two Cocks, with heads as low as their hips."[84]

Nevertheless, attitudes toward Africans were not as negative as they would become in the late eighteenth century. Long was entirely dismissive of Africans' capacities. Africans were "void of genius," without "a system of morality." "Their barbarity to their children debases their nature even below that of brutes," he opined, and they were "idle . . . proud, lazy, deceitful, thievish, addicted to all kinds of lust, incestuous, savage, cruel, and vindictive, devourers of human flesh, and quaffers of human blood, inconstant, base and cowardly."[85] Earlier observers were prepared to credit Africans with having some positive qualities, even within a discourse that was generally negative about African capacities. Unlike Long, Ligon and other seventeenth- and early-to-mid-eighteenth-century commentators granted that African women could be physically attractive. When Ligon saw a black woman for the first time, he thought she had "the greatest beauty and majesty together: that I ever saw in one woman."[86] Of course, such imagery was self-serving, allowing white men full license for sexual opportunity, but it still betokened a discourse around race, or rather around culture, in which there was some scope for black individuality.

James Knight and Charles Leslie, both of whom wrote histories (one unpublished, one published) of Jamaica in the 1740s, had a more nuanced and balanced appreciation of African character than did Long, whose view of Africans was so hostile that he speculated that they belonged to a different genus than did Europeans. Neither were particularly positive about Africans' character—Knight believed that many were "sullen, deceitful, [and had a] Refractory Temper" while "some are Careless, others Treacherous or Idle"; Leslie thought that Africans on arrival "start off simple and innocent but they soon turn out to be roguish enough"—but both accepted that Africans varied in personality and behavior and saw slaves as fellow human beings with ordinary virtues and vices. Knight carefully delineated the characteristics of different ethnicities with a commendable, if inaccurate, focus on establishing collective personality types. Both were less concerned than Long with justifying African slavery by dint of innate African inferiority. Instead they wanted to allay white fears that Africans would rise up against them by arguing that Africans from separate tribes had a "mutual antipathy" to each other and were in awe of white might and authority. They also wanted to counter metropolitan accusations that Jamaican slaveholders were excessively cruel. Leslie accepted the brutality of slave management but thought it understandable "given how impossible it were to live amongst such Numbers of Slaves, without observing their Conduct with the greatest Niceness and punishing their Faults with the utmost Severity." Knight adopted an et tu quoque argument, claiming that Africans left behind brutal tyrannies in Africa and lived, under slavery, better than poor people elsewhere, including England, lived.[87]

Thistlewood's attitudes were closer to those of Knight and Leslie than they were to those of Long. He considered slaves to be human like himself with distinct personalities that arose less from innate African character than from individual makeup. He only rarely treated slaves as a collective instead of individuals. After his first week supervising slaves at Vineyard Pen, he declared that the slaves there were "a Nest of Thieves and Villains," but this assertion reflected his inexperience with slavery as much as any belief in racial denigration.[88] The assertion, moreover, was exceptional: thereafter he hardly ever lumped slaves together in such a fashion. One of the remarkable features of his diaries is the extent to which slaves emerge as fully rounded individuals. He was not slow to assign pejorative epithets to slaves when they did things that annoyed him (as they did frequently), but these epithets were generally exasperated responses to individual behavior rather than expressions betraying racial stereotyping. Thistlewood often lambasted, for example, the behavior of his longest-serving slave, Lincoln. He described Lincoln as "headstrong," "roguish," "incorrigible," "lazy and impudent," and untrustworthy. Yet Thistlewood's actions belied his harsh words. He deployed Lincoln as a fisherman and hunter (with access to firearms) and invited him to accompany him on hunting expeditions. He installed him in positions of responsibility, such as that of a driver. He trusted him to take messages to other plantations. He gave Lincoln larger rations and presents when he was pleased with what he had done. Lincoln is portrayed in the diaries as a complex, if flawed, human being. Slaves' faults arose from human frailty rather than imbecility. Thistlewood did not see blacks as biologically different or inferior in capacity to whites—they were human, as he was, even if their color and condition disqualified them from membership in civil society. Nevertheless, although Thistlewood was able to recognize and act on slave individuality, he did not consider blacks to be equal to whites. Africans may not have belonged to a different genus than did Europeans, but they were distinctly inferior humans whose claims to justice did not have to be given the same respect as those of whites. Consciously or subconsciously, he placed blacks in a separate category from whites—treating them as outsiders to whom little consideration needed to be expended.

Thistlewood showed little interest in either Africa or Africans—remarkable given his general intellectual curiosity and his close proximity over thirty-seven years to large numbers of Africans. Even when he first arrived in Jamaica, he seldom commented on African practices, unusual though most of them would have seemed to a man raised in Lincolnshire. He did, out of curiosity, go to see slaves dancing and playing African music in his first months in Jamaica and learned from Africans both local lore and African tales.[89] But most of Thistlewood's references to cultural borrowings from Africa came in the first years in Jamaica when he was still struck by the novelty of his surroundings. They also came when he was a novice at interpreting slave behavior. From the perspective of scholars interested in the transmission of African culture to the Americas, Thistlewood's diaries are disappointingly thin on African habits and customs.[90] As he became more established in Jamaica and more knowledgeable about his slaves, he commented less and less about what they had retained from Africa.

When he did comment on Africans, however, his remarks were invariably negative. He was impressed with some of their physical skills, noting approvingly that "Negroes are expert at throwing a Rope to catch Cattle" and that "some of Mr. Dorrills Negroes can write in their way."[91] But as the tone of the latter observation suggests, Thistlewood was surprised at any indication of African intelligence. Africans were the least distinguished of humankind and the opposite of the chosen people. Thistlewood speculated: "[I]f the Negroes are the seed of Cain, how were they Preserved in the Universal Deluge?"[92] He related William Dorrill's observation that "as a Mule has not the feeling of a Horse, So . . . a negroe has not the Perfection of feeling equal to White People, himself has Seen them have their Limbs Cut off, and never Shrink."[93] Typically, what could be seen as a positive quality—extraordinary physical courage—was turned into a denigration of Africans' ability to feel. They were, according to this view, related to other humans only in the same way that mules were inferior versions of horses. The easy juxtaposition of animals and humans emphasized a recurrent theme in early modern commentary on Africans—that they resembled animals. Whites continually singled out Africans' supposedly animal-like traits. Africans were sexually promiscuous, ate improper foods (including human flesh), had a strong odor, went naked, and were indifferent or cruel to their offspring.[94] Thistlewood shared such assumptions. He appears to have believed a story told to him by Wannica that she had seen "Man Eaters . . . cook man's flesh to eat," which they reckoned "more sweet than hogs flesh." Significantly, African cannibals were supposed to prefer "the flesh of yellow and red peoples . . . for they say the flesh of Black people is bitter."[95] Wannica was probably telling Thistlewood what he wanted to hear—that Africans were close to beasts. The beast they most resembled was the ape. Thistlewood noted that, like monkeys, "Negroes have an ugly Custom . . . off picking lice off their heads with their fingers, putting them in their mouths and eating them."[96] But Africans differed from apes in being domesticated and able to be tamed. Thistlewood learned to inventory animals and slaves together as "stock" and occasionally gave slaves and livestock common names.[97] He also learned to judge, buy, and sell human stock in ways similar to the ways in which cattle were purchased. On 17 March 1762, he wrote a lengthy commentary on the sorts of slaves that were best to buy. They should have a "good Calf to their Leg and a small or moderate Sized Foot," but a buyer had to be careful since sellers "shave the men so close & gloss over them so much that a person cannot be certain he does not buy old Negroes."

In his daily contacts with Africans, Thistlewood tended to ignore slaves' innate animalism and deal with them as humans. But although he could ignore their bestiality, he could not avoid thinking about them in highly color-coded ways. Jamaica had a well-developed and all-embracing system of categorizing people by color, using language as the principal determinant of racial identification. Ordering people by color was so natural that whites found it reflexive. An analysis of Thistlewood's language reveals that he virtually always identified people by race, even when it would have been linguistically easier not to do so. Thus, he received a note from John Cope about Myrtilla and "her 2 Mulatto and one Negroe child." It would have been simpler to say "Myrtilla and her three children," but he could not do so because each child had to have a separate racial moniker. Racial identification was so essential that only .1 percent of the people Thistlewood introduced in his diaries were not assigned a racial classification. Even his son was generally denoted as "Mulatto John." Color was more important than genealogy. Hardly anyone in Thistlewood's ambit is just a man or a woman: they are invariably a "negro" (sometimes qualified by ethnic origin, such as "Coromantee or Gold Coast Negroe"), a mulatto, a "sambo," or a white person. Thistlewood's consciousness of color is all-pervasive and consistent.[98]

Thistlewood's color-consciousness is the key to understanding why an Englishman attached to the modernizing project of the Enlightenment and capable of sympathetic identification with Robinson showed little feeling toward Jamaican blacks and subjected those blacks to a brutal and tyrannical regime of power. Thistlewood's indifference and brutality toward his slaves betokened more than just the recognition that a white man on the Jamaican frontier needed to be tough and ruthless in order to survive. It demonstrated that there were observable limits to sympathetic identification. Color was the principal barrier to being able to feel "pity or compassion, the emotion which we feel for the misery of others."[99] The development of a humanitarian sensibility relied on people coming to believe that it was necessary and comparatively easy to right wrongs. It also relied on people having sufficient empathetic identification with others to feel some causal responsibility for the suffering that others endured.[100] Empathy comes when people realize they have something in common with suffering people. As David Hume argued, people engage sympathy only when they realize that external objects have a particular relation to them and are associated with them.[101] Thistlewood had no empathy with slaves whom he conceived as different from himself primarily by virtue of their color. Slaves may have been rational creatures, but they were not equal to Europeans. Identification depended on a fantasy of like social standing, which Thistlewood did not have toward slaves but which he did have toward Robinson. He was in certain respects a "man of feeling" and a typical Enlightenment man, but he limited the range of his feelings, placing blacks outside the boundaries of his concern. If he had lived longer, he might have been forced to modify his views. The rise of abolitionism and the advent of sympathetic responses to slave suffering would force slaveholders to confront, in ways Thistlewood did not have to do, the question of how civilized people could be indifferent to the pain they inflicted on slaves.

chapter five

Weapons of the Strong and Responses of the Weak

Thistlewood's War with His Slaves

There is not one planter who has not seen with concern the daring walk of my negroes. . . . What safety will three or four whites have among one or two hundred men, whose courage will be strengthened by the support you give them? My cause in this matter becomes the cause of every *colon*. . . . The un-happy condition of the Negro leads him naturally to detest us. It is only force and violence that restrains him; he is bound to harbor an implacable hatred in his heart, and if he does not visit upon us all the hurt of which he is capable it is only because his readiness to do so is chained down by terror; so, if we do not make his chains as proportionate to the dangers that we run with him, if we let loose his hatred from the present state in which it is stifled, what can prevent him from attempting to break the chains? The bird locked in his cage profits from the slightest negligence to escape. I dare to say that our negroes lack only sufficient courage or resolution to buy their freedom with the blood of their masters. Just one step can enlighten them about what they have the power to undertake. . . . It is not the fear and equity of the law that forbids the slave from stabbing his master, it is the consciousness of absolute power that he has over his person. Remove this bit, he will dare everything.—Speech of Nicolas Lejeune, a coffee planter in Plaisance, St. Domingue, to the Superior Council of Le Cap, 1788, defending himself on a charge that he had tortured to death four slave women by burning them

"However They May Disguise It, [Slaves] Hate
Their Masters and Wish Them Destroyed"[1]

One Saturday in late March 1765, Thistlewood's nephew John, a young white
servant, decided to spend an afternoon shooting and fishing. He never returned. A search party was formed, which found a hat and an overturned canoe. The next day, his body was discovered floating in the river. Flanders, a
slave, made a coffin, and John's distraught kinsman read prayers over him and
buried him. Another white man and two male slaves were in attendance. The
next day, Thistlewood wrote in his diary that he divided his kinsman's "old
cloaths" between a fellow white servant, two slaves who had retrieved his body
from the river, and Flanders. He noted, "I feel Strangely, pain all over me and
can eat nothing etc." Yet not everyone on the estate mourned John Thistlewood's death. Four days after the funeral, Thistlewood wrote in his journal that
"Last Night between 8 and 9 O'Clock heard a Shell Blow on the River, and afterwards in the Night 2 guns fired with a loud huzza after each, on the River
against our Negroe houses for joy that my Kinsman is dead, I imagine. Strange
Impudence."[2] Here was one of those rare occasions when the hidden transcript
of a subordinate group suddenly became public.[3] Here the artifice that prevented slaves from speaking their own minds was dropped. Thistlewood was
made aware once more of a fact he had known very well for most of his fifteen-
year residence in Jamaica: the relationship between him and his slaves and between all whites and all blacks was an undeclared war, always likely to erupt, as
it had done in May and June 1760, into sudden violence.

Whites were in an extremely precarious situation in mid-eighteenth-century
Jamaica. On the one hand, they had established an awesomely productive economy in which they made enormous profits.[4] On the other hand, they made
those profits within a highly distorted social structure that included a mass of
exploited, brutalized, and resentful African slaves. The result was a society in
which fear was, as the historian Bryan Edwards argued, "the leading principle
upon which the government is supported."[5] Although, as Edwards noted, a
"sense of that absolute coercive necessity which . . . supersedes all questions of
right" was evident in "all countries where slavery is allowed," fear was much
more firmly established in Jamaica than elsewhere. Africans outnumbered Europeans by a ratio of nearly 9 to 1, and slave revolts and Maroon attacks were
common.

A growing literature on slave resistance in the Caribbean points to the ever-
present desire of slaves to overturn their masters' rule, the considerable solidar-

ity and secret complicity that determined slaves were able to achieve, and the numerous methods of covert and open resistance that slaves were able to employ against their enemies.[6] The outpouring of work on the weapons the weak used to oppose their masters leads one to wonder how whites were ever able to withstand slave assaults on their property, authority, and person. Yet except in late-eighteenth-century St. Domingue, slaves never managed to overcome white rule. Although slaves contributed to their own liberation, the principal destroyer of the flourishing plantation system in the British West Indies was metropolitan authority. It is appropriate, therefore, to consider the weapons that the few but powerful whites used to prevent continual war between themselves and their slaves. Thistlewood's diaries are a useful medium through which to view the strengths and weaknesses of white power and the methods by which whites kept slaves, usually successfully, in check.

We need to do this in part because explaining the success of masters in maintaining their rule in frontier areas of Jamaica is more difficult than explaining the power of masters in places where whites were more numerically dominant, such as the American South. Peter Kolchin succinctly summarizes what slaves were up against in the antebellum American South, concluding that conditions were such "as to make organized rebellion virtually suicidal." Whites' numerical dominance and control of firepower in the South prevented violent resistance. Most slaves were Creoles with no experience of Africa or life outside slavery. They enjoyed relatively good living conditions in comparison to slaves in the West Indies. More important, they lived in small units among generally resident planters and a large, stable white population unburdened by major military conflicts between 1783 and 1861. Slaves were physically outnumbered, isolated, and economically impotent. Moreover, a resilient and enormously confident planter class, which employed a wide variety of psychological techniques to cow its bondspeople, confronted them at every turn. Increased settlement reduced slaves' ability to escape and prevented them from forming outlaw bands. Not surprisingly, revolts were few and easily suppressed. Slave rebellion was so clearly suicidal that most rational slaves knew it was pointless. By 1830, only a half-crazed visionary such as Nat Turner would embark on open rebellion and only desperate slaves careless of the future would join such a doomed attempt to overthrow white power.[7] As Eugene Genovese concludes: "The slaves of the Old South should not have to answer for their failure to mount more frequent and effective revolts; they should be honored for having tried at all under the most discouraging circumstances."[8]

Eighteenth-century Jamaica was different. The relatively large black population posed a great threat to continued white dominance and provided a prime opportunity for oppressed slaves. As the anonymous author of *An Essay concerning Slavery and the Danger Jamaica is expos'd to from too great Number of Slaves* . . . put it, "if some Stop not be put to it [the buying of Negroes], or if better Discipline not be observed, the Island must be overrun, and ruined by its own Slaves."[9] Jamaican whites' fear of a slave revolt is palpable in the complaints they made to imperial authorities about the danger they were in, the draconian laws they passed to keep their servile population in check, and the grandiose, expensive, and ultimately unsuccessful schemes they hatched to increase white settlement in the island.[10]

"They Being Very Ripe for It"

Whites were right to be afraid. Jamaican history was punctuated by numerous slave revolts and rumors of revolt. Even though his thirty-seven years in Jamaica were a period of relative quiet,[11] Thistlewood experienced a number of revolts and near revolts in Jamaica. No revolts occurred in his first decade in the island, despite considerable worry in 1751 that there would be "an insurrection of the Negroes; they being very ripe for it, almost all over the Island."[12] But in 1760, Thistlewood found himself in the middle of one of the largest revolts ever staged in Jamaican history—Tackey's revolt. Whites in Westmoreland had to contend with a well-organized revolt that nearly replaced European rule in the island with an African kingdom. Thistlewood never came so close to disaster again, but he noted at least three other rebellions in his diaries: one in 1765 in St. Mary's; one in northeastern Westmoreland, not far from his estate, in October 1766, during which he participated in a "slave rebel hunt"; and an islandwide revolt, concentrated in the northern parish of Hanover, in July 1776. To these actual revolts should be added potential rebellions, such as the foiled attempt of urban slaves to burn down Kingston in 1769, and the fear of revolt, such as the panic following the hurricane of 1780, when local leaders asked the Jamaican House of Assembly for a sloop to provide protection against "exceeding turbulent and daring" slaves.[13] In addition, the day-to-day business of running a plantation was fraught with danger. Individual slaves occasionally murdered their masters and mistresses, or at least were rumored to have done so. In 1760 and again in 1764, Thistlewood reported rumors of slaves killing their masters.[14]

Severe penalties were meted out to slaves who dared to strike whites, as we have seen. Not many slaves were willing to risk such punishment, and consequently, most slaves put up with whatever provocation whites gave them. Yet the fact that a number of slaves were prepared to resort to violence was sufficient to give white Jamaicans pause. Thistlewood found it necessary to carry a stick, and sometimes a gun, for protection. As early as 3 August 1750, he was confronted by a slave who "pull'd out his knife" when apprehended gathering fruit. On several occasions in his early years on the island, he was forced to defend himself from slave attacks by knocking down recalcitrant and hostile slaves.[15] Thistlewood often found slaves on his property who were carrying guns and endeavored to take the guns away.[16] In January 1752, he noted that Ambo very nearly had an accident with a gun that "our Negroes brought with them from Salt River, with intent to Shoot the Monkey yt troubles their grounds."[17] Thistlewood helped train the first slave he purchased, Lincoln, to become an excellent shot. He often sent Lincoln out shooting, as in October 1758, when he "Sent Lincoln into the Morass with a gun, [and] he Shott a whistling duck."[18] Thistlewood did this despite laws that prevented blacks from carrying arms. Allowing armed slaves to wander the countryside posed a constant danger to whites. In March 1761, for example, two runaway slaves with guns who were pretending to be Maroons came to a Mr. Torrents, who "suspecting them to be Rebells, order'd one off them to be Seized, upon which he resisted, killed one off Mr. Torrents dogs with his Cutlass, snap't his piece at Mr. Torrent, and made his escape from 4 Armed Negroes."[19]

Thistlewood realized as soon as he arrived that whites faced physical danger every day from their slaves. Any doubts he had about the perilousness of his situation were erased in late December 1752 when he encountered a runaway, Congo Sam, on a narrow causeway near a morass. Attempting to capture Sam, Thistlewood met with spirited resistance. Sam tried to "chop" him with a machete and drove Thistlewood into the morass, declaring, "I will kill you, I will kill you now." Thistlewood called for assistance, but no one responded, although many slaves were watching. He was only just able to hold the blade while Sam retained his grip on the stock or handle. After a fight lasting perhaps twenty-five minutes, Thistlewood overcame the runaway slave and persuaded a watching slave to help him. It was a very close call, as Thistlewood realized at once. What was most disturbing was that the attack was probably premeditated. Thistlewood recalled a conversation a few days earlier with Quashie, a slave who had told him "(before all the Negroes) that I should not eat much more meat here!" In all probability, Thistlewood speculated, many of the slaves "knew that Sam had an intent to murder me when we should meet, by what I heard them speak one day in the cookroom when I was in the back piazza reading." The premeditated nature of the event was confirmed by the slaves' unwillingness to assist him. London, the slave who eventually did help him, was particularly suspect. Thistlewood believed that London loosened Sam's bonds after his capture in order to join with the runaway against the overseer and had only desisted when he heard two white gentlemen riding by. Thistlewood believed that his slaves wanted to kill him.[20]

Weaknesses Inherent in White Rule

The uncertainty of whites' position in the island was heightened by their profound lack of knowledge about Africans and African society. One of the conceits that many whites had was that slaves were hopelessly divided by language, ethnicity, and status in the plantation system. Charles Leslie noted that slaves were brought to the island from a number of different countries and that, consequently, they "cannot converse freely; or, if they could, they hate another so mortally, that some of them would rather die by the Hands of the English, than join with other Africans in an Attempt to shake off their Yoke." In addition to such divisions between African-born slaves, Leslie argued, Creoles—slaves born in Jamaica—had little to do with slaves brought to the island.[21] The latter claim had some small truth to it. Until the early nineteenth century, few Creoles participated in largely African-led revolts.[22] But Leslie was deluded in thinking that slaves lived together as mutually uncomprehending and hostile individuals—perhaps it was for this reason that Thistlewood and his friends felt that Leslie was such an unreliable witness.[23] West African societies had sufficient commonalities, especially linguistic commonalities, to enable slaves to communicate intelligibly with one another and share a common cosmological understanding.[24] Moreover, the nature of the slave trade and the structure of the slave community on large plantations ensured that West Indian slaves lived among sufficiently large concentrations of their fellow countrymen to allow many African traditions to be transplanted to the New World, including language. Bilingualism and multilingualism were common in Africa. Jamaica was probably multilingual from its colonization, and linguists argue that a Gold Coast language, Twi-Asante, very quickly became a lingua franca among slaves, in addition to Creole English.[25]

Olaudah Equiano in his autobiography confirms the relative ease by which slaves from different regions of West Africa were able to communicate with one another. Equiano was kidnapped in 1756 and sent to the coast from his native

Ibo homeland; during this journey, he recalled, he passed through "many strange lands" where he met new people who "resembled our own in manner, customs, and languages." Although initially he was not able to understand the language of these strangers, spending a short time together led to mutual comprehension. Arriving in Barbados in a cargo of slaves with "Africans of all languages," including slaves who he thought were "from a distant part of Africa," he had little difficulty "convers[ing] with different Africans."[26] Although some hereditary tribal animosities remained after transplantation to the New World, the common experience of slavery and slaves' subjugation to European masters bound slaves together more effectively than most whites realized.[27] The degree of unity among slaves and the danger that unity posed to whites who knew little and understood less of African customs and language can be seen in Thistlewood's encounter with Congo Sam.[28] At a crucial moment in his fight with Sam, Sam called out to two slaves, neither of whom was from the Congo, "in his language," which everyone except Thistlewood understood. Unsurprisingly, Thistlewood "was much afraid of them" and their collusion.[29]

Whites' difficulties were compounded by their need to allow slaves considerable freedom: to move around the countryside unsupervised, carry guns, and gather at slave markets on Sunday where they traded, drank, and plotted. In short, whites allowed slaves to violate most of the laws that were meant to guarantee whites' safety on a daily basis. Thistlewood's diaries are full of slave derelictions of slave laws.[30] He supplied alcohol to slaves, allowed favored slaves to travel when they pleased to neighboring plantations and Sunday markets, and trained slaves to be highly proficient shots. He did so in order to provide food for his plantation and acquire additional income. Nevertheless, whites' latitude toward slaves caused problems. He dealt daily with slaves found wandering on his estate, slaves catching crabs and fishing, slaves stealing property, and slaves quarreling with slaves under his control. On 3 August 1750, for example, Thistlewood "Catch'd a Negroe fellow gathering fruits in ye Penn, he pull'd out his knife and refus'd to give account of himself for some time—he belongs to Salt Spring, his name is Duke, I sent him home and wrote to Mr. Clarke to punish him." Still new in Jamaica, he was unsure whether he had acted properly, but this type of episode happened so frequently that he soon perfected his response. Believing himself absolutely in control on his own estate, Thistlewood seldom left punishment to others, as he did with Duke, but whipped first, then asked questions later. When one of his slaves brought a slave of Nathaniel Herring's to Thistlewood, Thistlewood gave the slave a sound thrashing, commenting that the man was "Notorious for taking Money, Crabbs etc from our Negroes."[31] Such determined exercise of independent authority by Thistlewood did not endear him to fellow members of the master class, as we have seen.

Slaves were quick to exploit such tensions. They were formidable enemies, able to organize and carry out revolts. Whites knew they had to be prepared to meet slave violence with superior violence of their own. A well-regulated militia was thus essential, but the effectiveness of local militias was uncertain.[32] Governors who had been military men dismissed Jamaica's militia as woefully deficient. Governor Robert Hunter, a "brave old soldier," lamented in 1730 that "our indifferent Militia" was comprised mostly of white servants "of whom much the greater part is not to be trusted with arms."[33] The Jamaican militia was unlikely to strike fear in invading regular troops or fierce Maroon guerrillas. It may have been sufficiently awe-inspiring, however, to cow recently arrived Africans. That, at least, was what Leslie argued, stating that when Africans "see the muster and exercise, there can be no Terror in the World greater than what they lay under at that time." This terror only applied to African-born slaves: "'Tis true that the Creolian Negroes are not of this Number: They all Speak English and are so far from fearing a Muster, that they are very familiar with it and can exercise extremely well."[34]

Thistlewood took his militia duties seriously. Between December 1752, when he was first called to exercise with the local militia, and August 1758, the parish held forty-three musters. He went to all but five, being sick once, being excused two times, and sending a substitute on another occasion. Absences were taken seriously. When Thistlewood did not attend a 19 October 1753 exercise and gave no excuse for his absence, he was fined, much to his annoyance. Exercise was more than just an occasion for men in an isolated rural area to socialize. Arms were checked regularly, and officers and men were expected to do duty when, as happened in 1756, 1757, 1760, 1776, 1780, and 1781, the island was placed under martial law. In November and December 1756, for example, Thistlewood was called to exercise eight times. On three of these occasions, he had to stay all day and stand guard for hours at the courthouse door. On Sunday, 12 December 1756, the Westmoreland militia put on a more elaborate display than usual. After being on guard at Savanna-la-Mar, Thistlewood marched with the rest of the troops to church, where he "heard Mr. Ramsay preach a very good sermon" and then was feted at Colonel James Barclay's house before "marching to the Bay, with Beat of drum and Colours flying." Thistlewood's morale was boosted by the day's events. Slaves watching this show of force and display of white unity also may have been impressed or awed. Yet a moment's reflection would have assured a thoughtful slave that the white militia was not that impressive. No matter how well disciplined and well trained white militiamen were (and Thistlewood was not alone in being an accomplished marksman: he and his friends often had shooting competitions in which they sharpened their skills), resident whites were too few in number to be able to overcome a body of blacks bent on overthrowing white rule. Whites needed allies. In Westmoreland Parish, these allies came in two forms—Maroons and British soldiers. Neither Maroons nor soldiers, however, were entirely reliable.

Maroons formed a semi-autonomous African community in the interior of western Jamaica. Resolute adversaries of white rule for the first third of the eighteenth century, Maroons and whites agreed in 1739 to an often uneasy truce in which both sides recognized the other's authority in their respective regions of power. Determined to preserve their rule in their own area, Maroons were relentlessly fierce, especially against runaway slaves. In 1763, Thistlewood related that "the wild Negroes (Cudjoe's I mean) lately Come up with eleven Runaways in a hut in the Mountains, kill'd three and took the rest."[35] Yet he was wary of these "wild Negroes," as he significantly called them. Maroon ferocity was extreme, even in an island that was no stranger to savagery. In 1757, whites called on the Maroons to capture a runaway slave who had murdered his own child, a white overseer, and several Maroons. The Maroons obliged, but in a chilling way. Taking "that villain Bowman" prisoner, they were carrying him to Montego Bay when, sick of Bowman's abuse, one Maroon said that Bowman "had a damned foul Mouth" and shot part of his mouth off. Another said "he had a damn'd ugly Belly" and bayoneted him. The group then cut out the man's heart, roasted it, and ate it. Whether the Maroons in fact did this—and there is no reason to suspect that they did not—is less important than the fact that Thistlewood believed them capable of such things.[36] The Maroons received a large reward, but their actions were disturbing. Was it wise to trust such savage allies? Maroons had their own agenda that sometimes coincided but sometimes clashed with what whites desired. By the last quarter of the eighteenth century, as white settlement began to intrude into Maroon territory, Maroons began to reconsider their willingness to act as a police force for whites. In 1776, Thistlewood reported that Maroons might have been at the bottom of a recent uprising in Hanover.[37] By the 1790s, consensus had changed to conflict and white Jamaicans once again had to battle their most resolute internal foes.[38]

It could be expected that "wild Negroes" would have no loyalty to Europeans who held blacks in bondage. But British soldiers were only marginally more reliable. Soldiers were necessary to supplement local militias, but they caused a great deal of trouble. In 1756, Thistlewood encountered three deserters who were refused lodgings for the night by his employer, John Cope. The soldiers, "for malice," pulled down stakes used in sugar cultivation. In 1760, in the aftermath of the great slave rebellion, Thistlewood was forced to put up a body of rangers (mostly mulattoes and blacks) for the night. After he gave them a gallon of rum, the rangers got drunk and tried to procure slave women. Thistlewood was "obliged to get out off Bed, take my pistolls and go quiet them, which Soon affected but they fought after, one against another till almost Midnight." Early in 1762, Thistlewood came under real danger from four soldiers, armed and "much in liquor," who had wounded the slave London "barbarously" and threatened to run Thistlewood through when he intervened. Thistlewood was forced to call other plantation whites to help him keep order. Thistlewood was reminded of the danger he faced from soldiers later in the year when five soldiers called on him and demanded refreshment. Thistlewood refused, believing them to be "impudent in an Extraordinary manner." He endeavored to throw the soldiers out, but one "Struck me with a Naked Masheat over my left hand and Wounded me." Such an attack was not a freak occurrence: Thistlewood recalled that an overseer named Ned Stephens had been murdered in similar circumstances.[39]

The Sources of White Dominance

The weaknesses inherent in white rule in Jamaica were only partially alleviated by the support whites received from purported allies. How, then, did whites survive? In part, of course, experienced overseers such as Thistlewood relied on well-documented day-to-day methods of social control.[40] But as important as these methods were in ensuring slaves' submission to masters' authority, they do not explain why white control over blacks was so infrequently challenged. The numerical imbalance between whites and slaves was clearly in slaves' favor, blacks hated whites, and the conditions of slavery were so obviously appalling that almost any other condition was preferable. The reasons for Europeans' safety amid great insecurity must be sought elsewhere.

One theory advanced as an explanation for continuing white dominance in the antebellum South is that whites fashioned an ideological strategy after 1750 in which paternalism and white supremacy combined to implant in blacks an assuredness of their inferiority and a willingness to accept racial subservience to whites.[41] Drew Faust has described the effectiveness of such a strategy in her

We have no likeness of either Thistlewood or his mistress Phibbah. William Blake's famous engraving of a Surinam planter and his maid or mistress gives some idea of how Thistlewood and Phibbah might have dressed. William Blake, *A Surinam Planter in His Morning Dress*, in John Gabriel Stedman, *Narrative of a Five years' Expedition, against the revolted Negroes of Surinam* (London, 1793), 2:56.

exploration of how antebellum South Carolina planter James Henry Hammond sought to exert mastery over his slaves. Hammond "developed a carefully designed plan of physical and psychological control intended to eliminate the foundations of black solidarity" while attempting, with only a limited measure of success, to present himself to his slaves as "a beneficent master whose guidance and control represented the best of all possible worlds for the uncivilized and backward people entrusted to him by God."[42] Hammond was firmly convinced that Africans were an inferior race ideally suited to slavery and committed to the powerful antebellum notion of stewardship as a rule governing the behavior of superiors toward inferiors, and his theories of slave management were designed to inculcate in his slaves a sense of their master's overwhelming moral and physical authority.[43]

This explanation does not work for eighteenth-century Jamaica. Some white Jamaicans, of course, caricatured Africans as racial inferiors. The virulent racism of antebellum proslavery advocates in the American South echoed the themes developed by Jamaican Negrophobes such as Edward Long in the late eighteenth century. Long's diatribes against Africans are couched in a racial philosophy that assumed a biological basis for white supremacy.[44] Yet there were several varieties of thinking about Africans in eighteenth-century Jamaica, and it does not seem that Thistlewood shared Long's scientifically based theories about black inferiority. He uttered virtually no racial diatribe against blacks in his diaries. As discussed in chapter 4, Thistlewood was able to see Africans as humans, if distinctly inferior humans. He believed they could be excluded from polite discourse mainly because they were outside the social contract that secured individual—and exclusively white and European—rights. But he was no paternalist. He did not see himself as a "beneficent master," nor did he attempt to mask the exercise of his authority through psychological inculcations of his racial and moral superiority. He did not appeal to his slaves; he threatened them. Thistlewood's attitude toward slavery was that it was a natural condition that arose out of the power of Europeans and the powerlessness of Africans. He was, in a sense, a patriarch, but one unconstrained by any sense that his patriarchal power needed to be tempered by a recognition of reciprocal duties. He did not need to reciprocate with slaves because, as Africans, they were not part of a patriarchal familial model in which unequal social relations could be naturalized.

The clearest guide to how the racial thinking of Thistlewood and other white Jamaicans influenced their slave-management strategies is found in the commands of Richard Beckford to his Jamaican attorneys in 1754, instructions that

Thistlewood dutifully copied in full. Beckford was an enormously wealthy planter who became a British MP before dying at a young age. The proprietor of nearly 1,000 slaves, he began his instructions on the care of his charges with a lament for the state in which he forced his slaves to live. "The Unhappy Situation of a Slave," he started, "is a Circumstance that will touch every Generous Breast with a Sentiment of Compassion." After recommending that slaves be treated with "Justice and Benevolence," Beckford gave detailed instructions about the feeding and care of slaves before concluding with a reminder that "ye Success of my Plantations will chiefly depend upon your Prudent direction in governing ye Mind of my Slaves as well as exercising their bodies in a Reasonable manner." But by "governing ye Mind," Beckford did not mean the comprehensive reordering of the social and cultural world of slaves that Hammond envisioned. He did not mention altering slaves' devotion to African culture and an African cosmological worldview. Slaves were free to fashion their own culture as they saw fit or were able to do, given the strictures they were under. This indifference to the cultural practices of slaves was found not only in Beckford's schema but also in Thistlewood's daily slave-management techniques. He made no attempt, for example, to regulate how slaves worshiped and, unlike Hammond, never considered "destroying the autonomy of the slave community" as a means of forcing slaves to accede, seemingly willingly, to a master's dictates.[45] By "governing ye Mind," Beckford meant that whites were to exercise "a Steady and Temperate Government" with "a firm reliance on your Justice and Humanity." Slaves, it was assumed, were as intolerant of injustice as were whites (they were human, after all), and although their "Colour of Condition" and "want of education" suited them to be slaves, this condition was not "a reason for not treating them as Rational Beings" or for supposing that they did not have a "Sense of Injury which will dispose them to Revenge that may produce more fatal Consequences than desertion." Whites, in short, should do unto slaves as they, if slaves, would have masters do unto them.[46] White despotism, at least in the mid-eighteenth century, did not extend to psychological domination that rooted out all cultural traces of Africa.

The principal method of controlling slaves in Jamaica was through terror, as the St. Domingue planter Nicolas Lejeune argued. Terror, or naked power, was at the core of the institution of slavery. Jamaican slavery was especially brutal even by the elevated standards of New World brutality. Whites were encouraged to keep firm discipline and to punish slaves frequently and harshly. Thistlewood whipped slaves; rubbed salt, lemon juice, and urine into their wounds; made a slave defecate into the mouth of another slave and then gagged the unfortunate recipient of this gift; and chained slaves overnight in "bilboes" or stocks. Indeed, whites frowned on overseers and planters who were deemed to be lenient toward their slaves. In 1763, Thistlewood noted that his neighbor had dismissed an overseer because he did not discipline slaves sufficiently.[47] A more common complaint by experienced white Jamaicans, however, was that newcomers were overly rigorous in punishing slaves. In the middle of Tackey's revolt, when the danger to whites was most acute, Thistlewood commented that the new white man on the plantation, John Groves, was "in a frenzy," shooting randomly both rebel and faithful slaves. Groves may have been unhinged by the revolt because henceforth he was overly violent toward his charges, at least in the view of Thistlewood, who was himself no lax disciplinarian. In January 1761, Thistlewood was forced to reprimand his underling for being "like a Madman amongst the Negroes flogging dago, primus etc without much occasion." The reproach caused Groves to depart in protest because "he might not flogg the Negroes as he pleased: very Stubborn and resolute."[48] In short, Thistlewood was a brutal and cruel master—but he was not alone and, at least according to his own testimony, was far from being the most sadistic or tyrannical master in his area. Tyranny was the natural by-product of the transition from Europe to the savagery of a slave society. An English doctor commented on this transition in his description of the ubiquity of flogging of male slaves by Dutch women in Dutch Guiana in the 1790s: "The corporal punishment of slaves is so common that instead of exciting the repugnant sensations, felt by Europeans on first witnessing it, scarcely does it produce, in the breasts of those accustomed to the West Indies, even the slightest glow of compassion."[49]

Public punishment of slaves was equally barbaric. Persistent runaways faced bodily mutilation or execution. In March 1765, Thistlewood appeared as a witness against his slave Plato, who had been sent out with a machete to look for runaways "with a Tickett" and had then run away himself for nearly three months. Plato was found guilty and "Sentenced to have 100 lashes at 4 difft places on the Bay . . . and to have his right Ear cut off." In 1753, several of William Dorrill's slaves were tried for running away. One was hung, and two had "both ears Cropp'd, both nostrills Slitt and mark'd in both Cheeks." Whites constantly reminded slaves of the punishment they faced for committing a serious crime. After Robin was hung for running away in 1751, Thistlewood mounted his head on a pole, where it stayed as a grim reminder of white power for four months.[50] Nervous whites also punished slaves when they suspected them of plotting rebellion. Thistlewood commented in 1771 that he had heard that "Frazier's Beck, on Thursday last, tried for having a Supper and a great number of Negroes at her house last Saturday night." Her punishment was to have "her ear Slit, 39 lashes under the gallows, and 39 again against the Long Stores."[51]

Not surprisingly, the most gruesome punishments were reserved for those slaves who had nearly brought the colony to its knees in 1760. Tackey's lieutenants suffered slow torments and lingering deaths after their revolt was quashed (Tackey fell in the rebellion itself). Over 100 slaves were executed and 500 transported, mostly to Honduras, as revenge for the murder of 60 whites and free coloreds and blacks in the revolt.[52] Executions of slaves in Westmoreland began shortly after the revolt was quelled. On 31 May, Salt River Quaw was burned to death over a slow fire, while Paradise Dover was hung. These were the two preferred methods of killing rebels, but an even more sadistic punishment — gibbeting alive — faced the principals in the revolt. The leader of the revolt in Westmoreland was Apongo, or Wager, a supposed "Prince in Guinea," who was condemned to "hang in Chains three days then be took down and burnt." Wager died before his three days on the gibbet were up, but some slaves lingered there for a considerable length of time, all of which Thistlewood carefully recorded. One slave, Cuffee, was "Jibbetted 43 hours, then took down & Burnt."[53]

In the aftermath of Tackey's revolt, Jamaican whites demonstrated remarkable unity. That unity was not always so apparent in peacetime, when whites quarreled with one another over women, work, politics, and property. Yet, on the whole, white society was remarkable for its solidarity. In many respects, whites formed the strongest and certainly the most unified tribe in the country, with remarkably few divisions between classes and ethnicities. They were unified around a number of firm rules. The first rule was a presumption of white egalitarianism, as has been outlined above, manifested principally in ostentatious hospitality. The presumption of hospitality was so strong that it served a crucial role in uniting all ranks of white society. Whites were obliged to acknowledge the special character of having a white skin in a society predicated upon white dominance. In order to protect themselves from a hostile black majority, whites needed to know that they were all members of a privileged community that also had shared communal duties.

Whites stuck together against blacks even when they had private misgivings about the behavior of individual whites. Beckford emphasized that servants should be treated with consideration and according to the laws of the land. Indeed, servants were to be considered part of an overseer's family. More concretely, Beckford insisted that "it must be laid down as an inviolable Rule never to proffer a stranger to be a Storekeeper distiller or Overseer whilst there is a

Servant in my Employ of Sufficient Abilities to fill any Vacancy yt: may happen."[54] Thistlewood followed such policies of special treatment toward white servants as much as he could. One afternoon, when out making holes to plant sugarcane, Thistlewood ordered "Lewie to flog the Negroes that were holing because they did not work." Thistlewood's subordinate, Robert Lawrence, however, countermanded the order and told Lewie "not to regard" Thistlewood. Thistlewood was irate but vented his anger at the unfortunate Lewie, whom he had flogged and demoted from his position as driver. He said nothing to Lawrence in front of the slaves, but he later informed him of the etiquette by which whites did not publicly contradict each other. Thistlewood noted: "Robert afterwards was Submissive."[55] He had absorbed a valuable lesson, one that slaves also would have observed. Slaves learned that although they might sometimes be able to play off one white against another, in the end whites would stick together, whatever provocation there might be between individuals.

Slave Acceptance of Enslavement

Nevertheless, white solidarity and the implementation of terror were not enough to keep slaves in check. If we are to understand the sources of white safety in a hostile environment, we need to examine the extent to which slaves were willing to accept their condition. Slaves may have been in a birdcage, as Lejeune opined. But if they wished to, they could always force open that birdcage and escape, as Lejeune's slaves did in the Haitian revolution. The numerical dominance of Africans in Jamaica and the limitations of whites' coercive powers meant that slaves always had it in their power to overthrow slavery, difficult though that may have been. What preserved slavery in Jamaica was that slaves accepted, albeit reluctantly and conditionally, that they were slaves and that masters had the right, or at least the capacity, to force them to do what they wanted them to do. Without some measure of consent, masters such as Thistlewood would have been unable to survive.

That slaves accepted the inevitability of their condition does not mean that they welcomed it; that slaves did not resist slavery to the full extent of their ability does not mean that they were contented. Slaves did not like being slaves. They actively resisted both slavery as a system and those aspects of enslavement they particularly disliked. An extensive body of work has made us aware of slave resistance. But slaves had much to lose if resistance was unsuccessful, as slave resistance almost always has been throughout history. One key to understanding how whites could be relatively safe in a society in which they were in great danger was the position of slaves within the plantation economy. Slaves, as Sidney Mintz and Douglas Hall argue in a seminal essay, were petty producers, wedded to an ideology of protopeasant capitalist accumulation. Slaves cultivated a large proportion of the food needs of plantations and were allotted individual provision grounds in order to achieve the planters' goal of slave-based slave maintenance. Slaves provisioned themselves and much of the white population as well. In this respect, Jamaican slaves operated within economic and social parameters that were fundamentally different from those within which slaves in Barbados and the American mainland operated. There, slaves (even those involved in local provision markets) were outside the realm of ordinary market relations: they had the "privilege" of producing garden fruits and vegetables, as Virginia tobacco planter William Tatham observed, but their efforts were not essential to the maintenance of the plantation system and the feeding of the white population. In Jamaica, the internal economy operated by slaves was crucial to maintaining the plantation system.[56]

Turning over the provisioning of slaves to slaves had two contradictory consequences. Because blacks fed themselves, theoretically they were not dependent on whites for their physical survival (although in practice the amount of food slaves eked out from provision grounds put them only at subsistence level and they still needed white help in times of famine or personal difficulty). Their provision grounds gave slaves a measure of economic independence, allowing slaves to act as if planters owned only their labor, not their lives or personalities.[57] Jamaican slaves were thus able to maintain more autonomy than slaves in the colonial American South and Barbados, where masters preferred to feed slaves from rations produced on their plantations rather than through a provision-ground system.[58] But although provision grounds liberated slaves from the economic and cultural control of their masters, they tied slaves firmly to the physical ground of the plantation and induced in them a wary conservatism typical of peasants and petty commodity producers. Planters may not have grasped all of the implications of turning over slave maintenance to slaves themselves, but they were conscious of the value this process had in reconciling slaves to their condition. They eagerly advocated the laying out of provision grounds for slaves. Beckford, for example, placed special emphasis in his instructions on the importance of provision grounds. Significantly, he discussed the need to give provision grounds to "New Negroes" not because slave production would supplement planter-provided food allowances but because it would help reconcile newly arrived Africans to their position. He insisted that new slaves be given "a little property of their own and for yt: Purpose every New Negroe must receive a gratuity in Stocks, a house built, and at least a quarter off an Acre of ground Planted in Some Species off Provisions." Slaves, in effect, were to be pro-topeasants, able to accumulate property while being property themselves.[59]

Nevertheless, it was not to their masters that slaves became reconciled when given provision grounds. Slaves became committed to their particular patch of ground and their particular plantation. The slaves under Thistlewood's care had little fondness for their overseer, as was evident in their rejoicing over the death of Thistlewood's nephew and their refusal to offer assistance in his fight with Congo Sam. But they were attached to the piece of land on which they lived and planted. Like most preindustrial peoples, Africans invested land, and residence on land, with a host of meanings, cultural and social as well as economic. In particular, genealogy and locality were linked. Barry Higman notes that a source of the isolation that newly arrived Africans in the New World felt was their removal from ancestral land, a process that "dislocated their linking of genealogy and locality, and the veneration of specific pieces of land."[60] Cultivating their provision grounds, which slaves considered heritable estates distributed to relatives upon their death, reconciled Africans to their dispossession and removal from Africa.[61] Slaves bitterly resented any disruption of their attachment to their land and property. In 1754, when it appeared that slaves might be moved from the Egypt estate, Thistlewood noted that there was a "Visible grief in all our Negroes, upon acct off Moving."[62] When slaves were forced to move, they usually protested vigorously. In 1784, Thistlewood arranged for the sale of fifty-three slaves of Samuel Hayward to Julines Herring. He reported that the slaves protested vociferously, declaring that "they will not go" and being "quite refractory."[63]

Slaves as Propertied Persons

The difficulty that slaves faced, however, was that their ability to control their economic production and maintain their own patch of ground was very tenuous. Slaves lived in a world of radical uncertainty, always vulnerable to attack from both inside and outside the plantation. Slave attachment to property was merely custom, not law, and was dependent on masters' sufferance. In short, slaves were capitalists without the benefit of laws protecting property and person. Whites could use their access to the mechanisms of law to take advantage of slaves' attempts to enter into market relationships. Whites could change any relationship entered into with a slave from one between buyer and seller to one between master and slave.[64] Slaves' lack of legal protection meant they could never fully enter into a market economy. Masters' control of the laws that governed market exchange severely limited slaves' freedom to act within the market by rendering them dependent on whites' continued tolerance of their market activity. Slaves' vulnerability as propertied persons made them conservative and encouraged, on most occasions, a temporary truce between slaves and whites because whites were not only the principal predators on plantations but also sometimes the only protectors slaves had. Slaves needed white protection because they lived in a classic Hobbesian world. The long-term battle was between blacks and whites, and when the opportunity was ripe, slaves acted against whites. But in the short term, whites benefited from the temporary accommodations slaves were forced to make with whites in a white-controlled market in order to protect their property and person.

The life of a slave on a Jamaican plantation in the mid-eighteenth century was an extraordinarily difficult one. Thistlewood's diaries merely reaffirm and add a fresh gloss on the universal opinion of modern scholars that Caribbean slavery was one of the most dehumanizing systems ever devised. The work regime was debilitating. Overwork, malnutrition, accidents, harsh punishment, and disease all contributed to low fertility, high mortality, and fragile and uncertain family relationships. Masters generally did not interfere in slaves' cultural, social, and family lives, but slaves found it difficult to establish viable social and cultural practices given the hard work they were forced to endure and the remarkable flux that characterized life in eighteenth-century slave communities. Slaves came and went so frequently that it is misleading to even describe groups of of slaves as communities. Slaves were always dying or, given high white mortality rates and rapid estate turnover, being sold. Unacclimatized slaves from Africa were continually being imported to the island and placed into ever-fluctuating slave communities where they had few kin or friends to help them adapt to their frightening new world.

These traumatized and bewildered plantation slaves found that they were constantly under attack. These attacks came from three directions: from resident whites; from slaves on the same plantation; and from slaves and whites on other plantations. Thistlewood was one of the principal predators on the properties he controlled. Few days went by without Thistlewood recording that he punished a slave for some infraction or other. His subordinates and superiors did the same. What was most worrisome, from the perspective of his slaves, was the unpredictability of Thistlewood's punishments. What passed without comment one day was viciously punished the next, depending on Thistlewood's mood. Undoubtedly, Thistlewood's slaves watched their master's moods very carefully and avoided him when they saw he was irritable.

Thistlewood's Sex Life

Slave women probably observed Thistlewood's moods very carefully. He satisfied his sexual urges by having sex with slave women, particularly those under his care. He recorded all of his sexual conquests in schoolboy Latin in his diary, and it is clear that few slave women were safe from him. He had sex with slave women from early in the morning to late in the evening and in places that ranged from his dwelling place to cane fields to curing houses to slave houses. He did not have sex in Jamaica for four months after his arrival, although he learned on arrival that white men had free access to black women. He does not explain, of course, why he waited so long to avail himself of sexual gratification. But following his first sexual experience in Jamaica, on 10 August 1750, he embarked on an active sex life. Thistlewood engaged in 3,852 acts of sexual intercourse with 138 women in his thirty-seven years in Jamaica. To reduce these intimate acts to the banality of statistics, in an average year (excluding 1750 and 1786, the year he arrived and the year he died, as exceptional), Thistlewood coupled 108 times with 14 different partners. The intensity of his sexual activity varied over time, peaking in 1754, shortly after he took up with Phibbah, when he had sex 265 times, then gradually declining from an average of nearly 200 sex acts per annum in his thirties, to over 100 sex acts a year in his forties and early fifties, to around 80 sex acts per annum in the last decade of his life. The number of separate partners he had each year also declined, from a high of 26 in 1755 to under 10 in the 1780s. His sexual activity suggests that he was a highly but not inordinately sexed man. Modern surveys indicate that the average Briton who has sex (23 percent of adults do not) has sex around 96 times per annum and has 10 sexual partners in a lifetime. Thistlewood thus had sex slightly more often than the average person who has sex nowadays. His situation, however, gave him virtually free access to slave women, meaning that he had more opportunity to have sex with larger numbers of partners than is common today.[65]

The pattern of his sexual activity shows both continuity and change. Although he had many sexual partners, the majority of his sexual congresses were with a principal partner who served as his "wife." From August 1750 until September 1751, he lived with a slave called Marina. That relationship ended when he left Vineyard Pen. After moving to the Egypt estate in 1751, he took up with

Jenny, a Nago slave woman. His relationship with her proved stormy. Phibbah replaced Jenny in his bed and in his affections in late 1753. He and Phibbah lived as master and concubine, except for when he left for the Kendal estate in 1757, until his death in 1786. Phibbah was far and away his most frequent sexual partner. He records having sex with her 2,142 times, accounting for 55 percent of his total sex acts. The degree of his attachment to Phibbah varied—it was strongest in the earliest years of their relationship between 1754 and 1759, when sex with her accounted for 63 to 88 percent of his sexual activity each year—but at no time did any slave displace Phibbah as his most frequent sexual partner. The only times Phibbah did not monopolize his attentions came in the early 1760s, when Phibbah had a young child to care for, and between 1771 and 1774, when Abba was his partner on 128 occasions, which constituted 29 percent of his sex acts in those years.

Nevertheless, Thistlewood never confined his attentions to Phibbah alone. Even in the year of his death, he had sex with 6 other women besides Phibbah. Thistlewood had sex with 2 women—Egypt Susannah and Abba—172 and 169 times, respectively, and had sex with 10 other women more than 30 times each. In total, he had sex with these 12 slaves 871 times, accounting for 23 percent of his sexual activity. All of these women were slaves he controlled—5 slaves belonged to the Egypt estate and 7 slaves were among those he owned. The only slave he did not own or control with whom he had a significant number of sexual encounters was Mulatto Bessie, a slave owned by his friend Samuel Hayward. He had sex with her 25 times between 1776 and 1779. He had sex more than once with another 33 women. Of these, 22 were women he either owned or controlled. Thistlewood did not confine his attentions solely to his own slaves—63 of his partners, with whom he had 374 sex acts, were slaves who lived on other plantations. Few of these women were white. On 30 October 1752, Thistlewood had sex "cum mulier, in Sam's hutt in Paradise." On 4 February and 6 April 1758, he had sex "cum mulier sup terr. Hill sea side." Given that Thistlewood was very precise about racial nomenclature, the lack of a racial signifier here probably indicates that the women were white. He never showed any interest in white women besides these prostitutes. Predictably, he never explains why, but an obvious reason must have been that it was easier to have sex with black women, especially when they could not escape him, than it was to seek out white women, whom he would have to woo. He mostly preyed on slaves who were answerable to him. Besides the sex acts he had with Phibbah, 1,336 of his sex acts were with slaves who resided on the four properties he managed. He was especially likely to have sex with his own slaves. None of them escaped his attentions, and all, except Abba's daughter Blind Mary and Fanny, who had sex with him once and twice, respectively, had sex with him on numerous occasions. Abba, Bess, Sukey, Franke, and Phoebe had sex with him more than 50 times each. At Egypt, he also had sex with most female slaves. He had sex with 42 women and did not have sex with 10 women, at least 4 of whom were designated as old and superannuated. From his perspective, he was a sexual opportunist or sexual enthusiast; from the viewpoint of his female slaves, Thistlewood was the quintessential sexual predator and exploiter. Only the very young and the very old could be hopeful that Thistlewood would not have sex with them, and even they probably had their doubts. He had sex with his slaves when they were either in puberty or not long after—he had sex with Bess, Sally, Maria, Sukey, Coobah, and Phoebe for the first time when each was only fourteen or fifteen and had sex with Abba perhaps before puberty—and made them have sex even when they were very heavily pregnant. Thistlewood had sex with Abba twice when she was over eight months pregnant, once a month before she gave birth in 1776, and most notably on 23 August 1772, two days before she was "brought to bed of a girl." Similarly, Thistlewood had sex with a heavily pregnant Franke on 16 March 1776. Eight days later, she miscarried.

The essential features of his sex life—sex with a regular partner interspersed with sex with secondary favorites and opportunistic sex with his own slaves and strangers—changed little over time. Nevertheless, we can discern several phases. The first phase was before Phibbah became his principal partner. He had sex relatively infrequently—227 times in three years—but with a comparatively large number of partners, few of whom predominated as his sexual partner. Between 1753 and 1767, his Egypt years, he was very sexually active. Most of his sex was with Phibbah, except when she had a young child in the early 1760s, but he also had sex with lots of other women, averaging over 20 partners a year. An analysis of his sex acts in 1758 gives us some indication of his patterns in this phase of his life. He had sex 179 times that year with 23 partners. Phibbah was his partner in 131 of his sex acts, all of which were in his bed at night. Of his other 22 partners, only Mazerine, with whom he had 9 sexual encounters, had sex with him more than 5 times. The only slave to share his bed apart from Phibbah was Abba, whom he had recently purchased and who was still a girl. He had sex with her "sup lect" on 19 April, but it was "non bene," which is not surprising given that Abba was probably very young, possibly a virgin, and certainly still recovering from the traumas of the Middle Passage. He had sex with 4 other women in his house: once with Cynthia in his parlor and once each, "sup chest lid mea room," with Chrishea, Little Doll, and Egypt Susannah. The remainder of his sex acts took place on Egypt's grounds, except for an encounter with Esther, a Congo slave belonging to Mrs. Appleby, with whom he had sex near a loading place by the sea. He had sex twice with Cynthia (alias Worsoe) in the curing house and once with Nancy in the washhouse. Otherwise, he had sex on the ground—"sup terr"—in various clearings near cane pieces and coffee grounds, near the guava walk, and near the morass. Two favorite locations were on a hill looking out to sea and in the "Negro grounds," where he had sex 6 times. In total, he had sex in 18 different places. He provides few other details besides place, time (more often P.M. rather than A.M.), and participant, except to note that on four occasions he had sex "Stans! Backwd." He also noted when he paid the woman involved. In 1758, payment was relatively uncommon. He gave his partner either 1 or 2 "bitts" only 18 times and did not do so 30 times (excluding the times he had sex with Phibbah, whom he did not pay).[66]

The number of his partners declined by half after he moved to Breadnut Island and reduced even further, to less than 10 per annum, as he aged in the 1780s. He also became less enamored of Phibbah, especially between 1771 and 1776, when he showed partiality to Abba, and after 1781, when Bess (then in her late twenties or early thirties) became a favorite. Nevertheless, Phibbah was always his most frequent partner, accounting for over two-thirds of his sex acts in the late 1770s and around 60 percent of his sex acts in the years immediately before he died. His sexual activity also became more predictable. In 1776, for example, he had sex 101 times with 11 women, including 62 times with Phibbah, always at night in his bed. He had sex 3 times in his library, with Abba and Damsel, and had sex with 10 women in 7 separate outdoor locations. Two of these locations—"sup bench, under shed, in New Garden" and "sup Terr, over morass, near duck pond"—accounted for 19 of his sex acts. He had sex away from Breadnut Island only once, when he had sex at 7:00 P.M. with Robert Chambers's Mirtilla "sup terr in kirkpatrick's pen pasture, to the East of the Coromantee pond and North off the road." Many more of these acts involved financial transactions than his sex acts in 1758. He gave between 2 and 4 bits to every partner except on 5 occasions—3 times with Hayward's Little Mulatto Bessie (each time resulting in the comment "sed non bene" being recorded) and twice with Abba. Only Little Mulatto Bessie and Phibbah never received payment for having sex with Thistlewood. By 1776, Thistlewood's sex life was more routine than it had been in 1758. He tended to have sex with the same slave in the same place at the same time and was much more likely to view sex as a form of prostitution rather than opportunistic exploitation, which had been a feature of his sexual activity earlier, especially in the mid-1750s.

Sex and Social Control

White men molested slave women in part because they could do so without fear of social consequence and in part because they constantly needed to show slaves the extent of their dominance. The institutional dominance of white men had to be translated into personal dominance. Slave owners needed to show that they were strong, violent, virile men who ruled the little kingdoms of white autocracy that were Jamaican plantations as they pleased. What better way for white men to show who was in control than for them to have the pick of black women whenever they chose? What black men and women thought of these transgressions can only be surmised, but they could not have accepted such violations of their sexual autonomy with equanimity. On occasion, they took revenge. Thistlewood reported, as we have seen, that slaves murdered his former subordinate, Harry McCormick, "for meddling with their women."[67] The already strife-torn fabric of slave community life was further weakened by white men's continual sexual exploitation of slave women. Sexual relations between black women and white men made dramatically clear not only the powerlessness of blacks against white dominance and white exploitation but also the differences between the experiences of men and women in enslavement. Men faced physical punishment; women faced the same punishment as well as the additional burden of having to provide sexual services to white men.

Thistlewood was probably a rapist in deed. He was certainly a rapist in thought. He harbored attitudes concerning the sexual exploitation of black women that were deplorable, even for men of his time and place. He related, for example, a story from a Mr. Banton about "ye Barb[ados] woman that was rap'd by three of them (at Kingston) in a short space, he ye Middle one yet she laid ye Bastard Child to him and how he made her explain herself."[68] A gang-rape of a black woman was only cause for comment when there was a story attached to it. Thistlewood made it clear to female slaves who were caught transgressing that they could avoid punishment by having sex with him. On 1 February 1753, Clara was "wanting" all afternoon. On her arrival home, Thistlewood promptly had sex with her "by the Coffee Tree." On 16 September 1753, he had sex with "Waadah in the Still House sup floor," having found her there, "runaway I suppose." Refusing to have sex with Thistlewood was not a realistic option. Clara and Waadah knew they had to submit to his sexual demands or else receive physical punishment—punishment that may have been more severe as the result of their refusals.

Black women's capacity to resist the sexual advances of white men was extremely limited, as the following accounts show. On 12 March 1755, Thistlewood noted that his employer, John Cope, brought a party of six men to the Egypt estate, where they caroused. Late in the evening, "all except Cope and one other, after being heartily drunk, haw'led Eve separately into the Water Room and were Concern'd with her[.] Weech 2ce [twice]. First and last." Thistlewood's tone suggests he disapproved; his subsequent failure to punish Eve when she ran away after her ordeal confirms his distaste. But he did nothing to stop the rape—it was hardly possible for him to do so when his employer was involved—and continued to associate with the men who committed the rape. Two years previously, however, he had intervened in an attempted rape: "At Night Mr. Paul Stevens and Thomas Adams going to tear old Sarah to pieces in her hutt, had a quarrel with both of them. They burnt her and would fire the hutt Note they both drunk." Thistlewood was not so much alarmed at the attack on Sarah as concerned at the white men's presumption in interfering with one of his charges. He was disturbed that Stevens and Adams had attempted to damage estate property. The episode demonstrates how perilous it was for slaves to resist white advances: Sarah was burned for trying.[69]

Certainly the cost of resistance could be high. Following a drinking session with a Mr. McDonald ("who had Eve to whom he gave 6 bitts"), Cope made "Tom fetch Beck from the Negroe's house for himself with whom he was with till morning." Beck, however, was not his first choice, as events the next Monday proved, when Cope ordered "Egypt Susannah and Mazerine whipped for refusal." Cope's actions so outraged his slaves that they exacted revenge. Thistlewood tells that "Little Phibbah told Mrs. Cope last Saturday night's affair. Mrs. Cope also examined the sheets and found them amiss."[70] The slaves' sense of moral economy had been sufficiently upset by what they considered an unfair whipping that they chose to inform on their master to their master's wife. Nevertheless, the effect of such disclosures was minimal. Cope continued his escapades in the slave quarters and became an assemblyman and custos of the parish. The whipped slaves received no recompense, and Cope's young wife, Molly, was forced to turn a blind eye to her husband's infidelities.

A minority of slave women tried to make the best of their uneasy situation as the sexual playthings of white men. Having sex with Thistlewood could be turned to a woman's advantage. Thistlewood often gave money to his sexual partners, as we have seen. The sums earned from what was essentially forced prostitution could be considerable. Two of Thistlewood's sexual partners—Egypt Susannah and Mazerine—each earned sufficient money from their sexual encounters to either buy enough food to last half a year or purchase half a pig. Slave women were active participants in a dynamic internal commerce based on exploitation of their sexuality. Earnings from prostitution were one means whereby they could pursue entrepreneurial activities and enhance the likelihood that they would someday own property.[71] Slave mistresses of white men were especially adept at turning their liaisons into commercial gain, as we will discover in chapter 7 when we examine the life of Thistlewood's mistress, Phibbah. Nevertheless, although a few slave women may have achieved measurable benefits from their association with white men, the overall effect on slave communities of white men's sexual pursuit of black women was mostly detrimental. Thistlewood's sexual opportunism reinforced slaves' already-strong sense of helplessness and contributed to the psychological damage suffered by slaves living under traumatizing conditions in a radically unstable society. We can see this in Thistlewood's admonishments to underlings to desist from pursuing the wives of slave men. He was especially firm in his condemnation of his nephew's attempted conquest of Little Mimber, the wife of Johnnie, the driver on the Egypt estate and thus a man of some importance in the slave community. Johnnie strongly resented John Thistlewood's "taking" Little Mimber and attempting to keep her as his wife and complained vociferously to his master. Thistlewood took his slave's side, remonstrating with his nephew that he needed to confine his attentions to women who were not attached and refrain from angering slaves whose support was crucial for the smooth management of the estate.[72] Nevertheless, the damage had been done. Little Mimber had been with John Thistlewood. Johnnie's only recourse was to complain—a complaint he knew might be taken seriously or might be ignored.

Thistlewood's Management of Slaves

White men's sexual avidity was not the only issue that fractured harmony in slave communities. Slaves had to fear others besides resident whites. Slave men and women quarreled and fought with each other frequently. Sexual relations on the plantation were like a complicated game of musical chairs, and the many permutations of partners often created problems and disputes. In 1773, for example, Thistlewood "Flogged Maria for cuckolding Solon at the Retrieve, and stirring up Quarrels etc." In 1774, Maria was again flogged "for leaving Solon and running to her sweetheart at the Retrieve." After that affair foundered, she lived with two men from neighboring estates in quick succession before setting up housekeeping with a slave named Monday. That relationship soon ran into trouble. On 13 November 1778, Lincoln visited the couple, at 3:00 A.M., ostensibly to give Maria some sugarcane. But when he "began to inquire for his countryman [Maria]," Monday refused to let him speak to her. Lincoln persisted. He went "into her room to stay with her." Monday, however, "laid hold of him first" and beat him. Monday incurred no further punishment from Thistlewood. By 1787, Maria was living alone. Maria was not unusual in her variegated sex life. In 1774, Thistlewood noted, "Understand Jimmy wants to throw away Abba, he having long kept Phoebe slyly, Phoebe has also thrown away Neptune (or wants much to do it) upon Jimmy's account."[73]

Thistlewood's slaves experienced marked domestic discord. Monogamy was as unfashionable among slaves as it was among whites, and slaves sometimes changed partners with dizzying rapidity. In part, slaves tolerated promiscuity because West African practices such as polygamy allowed it.[74] But whereas in Africa polygamy operated within a secure social context and served to reduce domestic friction, in Jamaica African rules governing polygamous relationships no longer applied. African women in Jamaica had more control over domestic arrangements than women in Africa had. In West African cultures, women were expected to live in families and have children who would perpetuate the families. They were "valued for child-producing properties, for their economic contribution to the household, and for the affinal relationship they represent to husband and his kin." These traditional African assumptions about the role of women did not hold in Jamaica. As Michael Mullin has argued, women in slavery in Jamaica may have had more say, power, and independence compared to men than women in Africa had. A skewed sex ratio, combined with the propensity of some slave women to reserve themselves for white men, meant that many black men were left without partners. Competition for women was thus keen, and disputes often arose when men found their "rights" to sexual access frustrated or challenged. Some women recognized their value and the inability of slave men to become controlling patriarchs and insisted, like Maria, on playing the field. The sexually independent slave woman was not uncommon. For example, Thistlewood's principal partner on the Kendal estate, Aurelia, did not confine her attentions to her master alone: Thistlewood was told that "six different men lay with Aurelia" one night, by her own volition. Her deviation from traditional models of African female behavior, moreover, did not lessen her status as the leading woman on the plantation. Slave men were dominant within slave communities, but their authority was precarious and was shaken by the insistence of some slave women on sexual independence. The peculiar conditions of slavery rendered black men's attempts to control the sexuality of black women problematic, especially when white men could always undermine black men's sexual authority and power. Changed gender expectations may have increased slave men's demoralization.[75]

Thistlewood used this sexual climate to advance his slave management. Slaves often needed to refer disputes about sexual infidelities to him. Sometimes he interfered; sometimes he punished transgressors; sometimes he let slaves mete out justice themselves. When Sancho complained to Thistlewood about the infidelity of his wife in 1752, he "advised them to part, which they accordingly did." When London molested Hannah in 1755, Thistlewood, "upon Hannah's complaint Whipp'd London." London "went to complain to his Master and Mistress but they w[ou]ld not hear him then he Absconded." In the case of Cobbena, however, who "catchd London and Rosanna [Cobbena's wife] at work upon London's bed," he let Cobbena act the part of the master and refrained from punishing him for giving London "a good thumping."[76]

To a limited extent, Thistlewood recognized slaves' relationships and honored slaves' rights in these relationships. He also, as we have seen, tried to prevent white servants from interfering too blatantly with what he considered to be the sexual rights of male slaves. He chastised his nephew for trying to sleep with the partner of the driver on the Egypt estate. But it is clear that slaves' relationships were at the mercy of the master. That the most important slave in the slave community had to appeal to Thistlewood's authority to secure his sexual rights showed how Thistlewood exploited the chaotic conditions that characterized slave life—chaos that he, through his sexual opportunism and ready resort to violence, in large measure created—to solidify his hold over a harassed, tormented, and brutalized slave population.

Thistlewood also exploited general conditions of lawlessness in a lawless society. Slaves stole from him and from each other constantly. Thistlewood frequently flogged slaves at Egypt for stealing cane or corn. On 1 January 1763, for example, he flogged Will for stealing corn and a month later caught "Col. Barclay's boy stealing cane." On 18 December 1764, he "Flogg'd my Johnie for stealing corn and Agnes and Solon for breaking cane." A week earlier, he had caught three slaves eating cane and had flogged Quamina a month before that for "destroying the Cane in the old Neg. gd. pce."[77] On 27 June 1763, he flogged Dago for stealing oranges and, on 29 August 1763, punished Primus, whom he caught "filling a large pint Bottle with Rum." Slaves also stole from each other.

On 28 October 1763, for example, Cudjoe robbed Neptune of a pair of shovel-billed ducks that Thistlewood was sending to Richard Hungerford. Thefts were most frequent between slaves living on different plantations. In 1763 and 1764, Thistlewood noted nine examples of his slaves being robbed of property by slaves from other estates. He noted on 22 March 1763 that "a shirt of Mason Quashie, got up and ironed, was stolen out of the washhouse & pawned" by a slave of Elizabeth Bennett. On 12 November 1764, he wrote to George Lesley complaining that Quashie and Sukey had had "6 bitts worth of Corn, took from them by Long Pond Negroes." On 27 October 1763, a runaway female "whom Cubbena & Rosanna, Quamina & Quasheba, had long harboured in their houses" stole chickens belonging to Egypt Lucy and Dago. Thistlewood ordered Cubbena and Quamina to "make Them Satisfaction." Again, on 13 April 1764, Thistlewood's "Negroes were fishing in the Salt Savanna at dinner Time" when "[William Henry] Ricketts Negroes Come and Robb'd them off the fish." Thistlewood sent his nephew and "some Negroes" to bring in the six slaves concerned, all of whom he flogged, much to the displeasure of their wealthy owner, who confronted Thistlewood the next day. Slaves had little protection from thieves besides the intervention of their masters. Their vulnerability can be seen in the successful thievery of "a Negroe man Named Julius" who was marked as a "Notorious runaway" because his left ear was cut off. When Thistlewood apprehended him a week after he had stolen new hoes belonging to newly purchased slaves, he was also carrying "2 dead pigs a dead fowl & a living one 2 womens pockets [and] a Black Jack."[78] If Thistlewood had not apprehended him and given him 100 lashes, Julius could have continued to steal with virtual impunity. When a thief was from within a slave community, slaves could humiliate or ostracize the violator of group norms. But when a thief came from outside the closed society of the plantation, slaves had little option other than to turn to their masters, who alone had recourse to the law and the authority to apprehend and punish slaves, wherever they came from. When a white person attempted to take slave property, slaves were entirely defenseless and relied absolutely on their masters' protection. Thistlewood realized this early in his time in Westmoreland. On 27 September 1752, he quarreled with "Messrs. Jemmison and Mason," who "pretend to bring an order from John Filton for the fishing dory, [and] old canoe, he gave the Negro driver (Quashe), [and the] old seine he gave Phibbah." Thistlewood was not prepared to let them abscond with his slaves' property and "desired them get out of the plantation."

Slave criminality and misbehavior were enhanced by the policy of providing slaves with provision grounds. Slaves moved easily from rationalizing a theft of food or supplies from the master to rationalizing purloining food from fellow slaves. When slaves were given ready access to markets, the temptation to steal increased.[79] It was just as easy, if not easier, to become a property-owning individual through thieving as it was to become a property-owning individual through the careful cultivation of provision grounds. Pervasive slave criminality in an essentially unregulated society must have caused slaves to become wary and conservative.[80] Eugene Genovese points out the negative implications of slaves' thievery, even if we accept that slaves did distinguish between stealing from other slaves and taking the goods of the master and thus transferring his property from one form to another. Of course, stealing or taking did have positive connotations if viewed as part of an alternative morality in which the oppressed saw themselves as having the right to use whatever weapons they could, including thieving, to counter the hegemonic rule of masters. But as Genovese insists, making a distinction between stealing and taking was easier in theory than in practice. For many slaves in many slave systems, from eighteenth-century Jamaica to newly independent Haiti to the antebellum U.S. South, stealing became a way of life and was not just confined to stealing from the master. More important, constant thievery passed the moral advantage to the planter. Stealing conflicted with the moral values most slaves held—notably those who were Christian or Muslim but also other slaves who sought to live morally respectable lives. Even if stealing can be seen as resistance (and it was only so in some cases), Genovese is surely correct in arguing that it encouraged slaves to slip into degradation, division, and self-contempt and weakened their self-respect.[81]

Yet although frequent disputes between slaves weakened communal solidarity and reduced the likelihood of collaboration between slaves across estates, an embryonic social consciousness and awareness of the necessity for slaves to join together for mutual safety also slowly developed. Attacks from outside slaves, either runaways or slaves from other plantations, were far more frequent and dangerous for slaves attempting to increase their wealth and prosperity through acquisitive individualism than were day-to-day conflicts with slaves from the same estate. In resisting incursions from hostile outsiders intent on extending their own economic interests, Thistlewood's slaves were forced to join together as a collective unit. In the process of creating slave communities that exhibited considerable cultural and political autonomy, they needed on occasion to enlist the help of Thistlewood to protect their interests, particularly their interests in property. The short-term need for white support helped to preserve white dominance and prevented the undeclared battle between whites and blacks from erupting into an all-out war. Even when it seemed as if whites might be wiped off the island, as in 1760, the conflict between long-term objective and short-term necessity kept whites in their precarious position of power in the island.

The world outside the plantation could be very dangerous for slaves. Thistlewood details many instances of his slaves being attacked when traveling for business or pleasure outside the estate. The roads were full of brigands and runaways who attacked slaves. In 1758, for example, "Mr. Cope's Simon's head broke by Negroe men in the Road, who took a Crabb from him."[82] A year later, he found Cambridge dead in the morass and speculated that "he was Murdered by Runaways, Who it seems threatened to murder him the last time he was runaway if he did not leave them, least they should be found upon his account, by our looking for him."[83] Whites also attacked slaves. In 1756, for example, Thistlewood wrote that a white man was brought "before Mr. Cope by Peter the Constable upon Complaint made by William Crookshanks off his Robbing and abusing House Franke yesterday Evening, near Paradise." Sometimes slaves could be attacked for no reason save a man's fancy. In 1764, Thistlewood wrote a long account of the shooting and death of Humphrey—"a Stout hopefull young Fellow, and begun to Understand his Business"—by white, mulatto, and quadroon servants in a canoe. The men called Humphrey over to the canoe, demanded that he give up his fish, and then shot him when he refused. Thistlewood expostulated that Humphrey was shot "Wilfully and purposely (out of Mere Wantonness) without giving them any Manner off Provocation."[84]

In such cases, slaves found whites of material assistance. Thistlewood's subordinate, William Crookshanks, helped House Franke in her complaint against her white attacker. Crookshanks brought the white man before the justice of the peace, who imposed a fine. Thistlewood presumably stopped Sarah from being raped or burned to death when attacked by two white men. He also tried to avenge Humphrey's death (and recoup his losses from the early death of a promising worker) by having his killer brought before a court. Yet white assistance to blacks attacked by whites was not always successful, given Jamaica's legal presumptions in favor of whites. Although Thistlewood's nephew cornered three of the men in the canoe in Savanna-la-Mar and extracted a confession in front of a judge that they had shot Humphrey, Humphrey's murderer was acquitted when one of the two white men in the canoe swore that it was the mulatto (presumably long since vanished) rather than the quadroon who had mortally wounded Thistlewood's slave. The testimony of white men was always preferred in any case involving blacks.[85]

One way slaves could avoid being harassed was to join together for mutual protection. Planters designated slaves according to who owned them. Thus, the slaves of Colonel Barclay became Barclay's Ned and so on. Slaves also identified themselves by reference to the plantations they came from, but for different reasons. Slaves had a clear sense of belonging to a particular patch of ground and being part of a group with shared interests. Consequently, when Thistlewood stumbled upon a group of Barclay's slaves fishing at a bridge demarcating Thistlewood's and Barclay's estates, Barclay's slaves repelled Thistlewood from an area in which they believed they had customary economic privileges. Thistlewood noted that the slaves were "very insolent with menaces and Threatenings etc refused to go at my Bidding etc." After Thistlewood and his companion escaped, he reported, they were "glad to find our Selves Safe away." When he took matters into his own hands a week later and whipped "some of their Negroe women," he noted that "the Negroe Men followed us home, with menaces and Impudence." Clearly Thistlewood had interfered with what Barclay's slaves saw as their exercise of customary economic rights. They were prepared to challenge Thistlewood's violation of their privileges. They complained to Barclay, the leading magistrate in the parish, who immediately confronted Thistlewood on their behalf and threatened to whip Thistlewood if he caught him punishing his slaves again.[86]

Thistlewood's slaves used him in a similar fashion to protect their economic interests when other slaves threatened them. Thistlewood often intervened to protect his slaves' property and person. He was continually writing letters to other whites asking that slaves who had intruded onto the provision grounds of his slaves be punished. On 6 September 1763, for example, Thistlewood wrote to Aaron Moffat "acquainting him off more than Twenty Negroes being seen [to] go thro' this Estate to Windward last Saturday." Occasionally, slaves dealt with intruders themselves. On 10 September 1756, for example, a watchman "Shot and Cut" Mr. Mould's Scotland "with a Machete till he died in Colonel Barclay's Negroe Ground." The slave escaped punishment because Thistlewood considered his actions reasonable since he was defending slave property from a slave who was "stealing corn, plantanes etc." More often, however, Thistlewood's slaves called on him to take action against offending slaves. On 3 July 1759, he rode to a neighboring estate to talk with a fellow overseer about "Yaw robbing Quasheba off 7 Bitts worth of fish." His intervention worked: "[T]hey agreed to make satisfaction."

In many respects, the interests of Thistlewood and his slaves coincided, especially when outside slaves made incursions onto estate property that was valuable to his slaves. An episode in 1764 reveals the degree to which masters' and slaves' interests overlapped. On the afternoon of 18 February 1764, a slave woman, Chrishea, brought word to Thistlewood that "many Negroes were fishing in the greenwood ponds." Thistlewood armed himself with a cutlass and went with ten slaves in search of the offending slaves. He was told the band of thirty belonging to George Williams's estate had gone "Thro' the Estate to the Leeward, Vapouring their Sticks in an Impudent Manner, and Singing Country etc." Heavily "in liquor," Williams's slaves had already "robb'd Melia off her fish" and beat her and cut her face. Giving chase, Thistlewood and his slaves caught up with the slaves, who "behaved very impudently." Thistlewood fired buckshot at one and took two others who had beaten and robbed Melia into custody, flogging them on the spot. Proceeding to the Greenwood Pond, he apprehended "many Negroes, belonging Col: Barclay and the Retrieve" and confiscated their fishing gear and the fish they had caught. Both Thistlewood and his slaves returned home satisfied with a job well done. Thistlewood had preserved the safety of his estate and defended one of his slaves; his slaves had protected their right to fish in the Greenwood Pond undisturbed.

The property rights of slaves within the slave economy weakened slave resistance to white power. On the one hand, the tendency of slaves to engage in capitalist market-oriented activity worked, in the long run, against the logic of plantation slavery because it reduced slaves' dependence on the bounty of the master and thus reduced his control over them. On the other hand, private property and market exchange fractured slave communities. Disputes over property and property-related crimes opened fissures within slave ranks. Confronting attacks on slave property rights from outside often healed these fissures, but it also often weakened the black community as a whole. The idea that slaves approved of all types of resistance, even when it made them suffer, is a myth. Slaves, for example, were reluctant to succor runaways when they could survive only by raiding slave provision grounds. When London and Quaw came upon two runaways on 10 March 1755, they immediately tried to apprehend them, taking away a gamecock and a "Bag of Plantanes." They were not going to allow foreign slaves to acquire their hard-earned property or property they believed they had a right to by virtue of being slaves at Egypt. In trying to secure the miscreants, however, London cut his hand very badly with a knife, allowing the two men to escape. The traffic, however, between runaways and resident slaves was not all one way. Slaves exploited runaways just as they believed runaways exploited them. When one of Thistlewood's slaves escaped, others sometimes used the incident as an excuse to raid the master's property and then blame the loss on the unfortunate runaway. This seems to have occurred on 17 July 1750 when Robin escaped. The storehouse was broken into, goods taken, and Robin blamed. Although the slaves reported the thief to be Robin, Thistlewood thought it "pretty certain to ye contrary as they found everything so readily."

Establishing a moral economy in which slaves had customary rights and could engage in primitive capitalist accumulation was one thing, but translating theoretical property rights into an actual economy was quite a different matter. Slaves had neither laws nor customs to protect them in their pursuit and defense of economic gain. Slaves sought and gained considerable economic autonomy within the plantation economy but in so doing trampled on the economic autonomy of other slaves who were equally determined to seek power by owning property. Slaves did develop some sense of community and probably some political consciousness as members of plantation communities with interests, especially property interests, to protect against hostile forces who wished to take slave-produced resources for themselves. But this communal solidarity was limited and territorially defined. Thistlewood's slaves knew who the real enemy was: their actions when John Thistlewood drowned and when Thomas Thistlewood was attacked by Congo Sam showed that they were aware that whites were their ultimate enemy. Both whites and blacks knew this fundamental truth of Caribbean existence. The ever-present fear of black servile revolt transfixed white minds. It was the ultimate weapon slaves knew they could always employ against whites. They knew that whites feared them and that it was this fear, as Lejeune bluntly suggested, that led them to treat slaves with unremitting ferocity. Yet, especially before the advent of such ideological unifiers as Christianity, which transformed Afro-Caribbean culture in the early nineteenth century, it was difficult for slaves to overcome the inherent tensions and suspicions based on conflict over property that existed between differing groups of plantation slaves. Those inherent tensions and suspicions probably saved whites in the very dangerous near-disaster of Tackey's revolt in 1760.

Tackey's Revolt

The revolt that first swept through St. Mary's Parish in north-central Jamaica and then spread to Thistlewood's Westmoreland Parish in May 1760 was the most significant Caribbean slave revolt before the Haitian Revolution of 1791–1804. In its shock to the imperial system, it would not be equaled until the Jamaican rebellions of 1831 and 1865 and the Indian Mutiny of 1857.[87] Thistlewood's diary is an excellent eyewitness account of the revolt by a coolheaded but frightened participant at one of the centers of the storm. What emerges is the atmosphere of rumor, panic, and confusion that swept over Westmoreland in late May 1760. The degree to which this revolt shook the colony to the core is evident in the many diary entries referring to the revolt's aftermath as Thistlewood and other whites tried to make sense of the revolt and did their best to exact fierce vengeance on those slaves who had been bold enough to try to overcome white rule. The revolt was a highly organized conspiracy planned in remarkable secrecy by Akan slaves from the Gold Coast in several places in the island. The impressive organization of the rebellion was matched by the ambitiousness of its intentions. According to Edward Long, Tackey and his followers aimed at "the entire expiration of the white inhabitants; the enslaving of all such Negroes as might refuse to join them; and the partition of the island into small principalities in the African mode; to be distributed among their leaders and head men."[88] It very nearly succeeded in its objective to create a West African state in the Caribbean. Bands of rebels rose against whites in St. Mary's, Clarendon, St. Elizabeth, St. James, and Westmoreland. Considerable success was achieved in both St. Mary's and Westmoreland. Militias were routed, estates were torched, and slave rebel numbers exceeded 1,000 in each parish. Only the death of Tackey, whose leadership had been crucial in the conflict in St. Mary's; resolute action by the competent Jamaican-born governor, Henry Moore; and the assistance given to hard-pressed settlers by British regular troops and the British navy, as well as, more problematically, by Maroons, allowed whites to survive the rebels' determined onslaught.[89]

The revolt was also foiled at the local level by the resoluteness and courage of whites such as Thistlewood and the ambivalent reaction of many slaves to a revolt in which they were more likely to lose their painstakingly acquired property than they were to achieve freedom. On 26 May 1760, four of Thistlewood's neighbors rode bareback, wearing very few clothes, to inform him that an overseer had been murdered, another had been "sadly chopped," and Thistlewood "should probably be murdered in a short time." Thistlewood fled in panic to Savanna-la-Mar, where he did his "duty" until daylight. Bravely, he then returned home to secure his property and defend his estate. Thistlewood knew he was in great danger. The day of greatest crisis was 29 May. On the nearby Jacobsfield estate, rebels tore down the great house. Meanwhile, news of the militia's rout had reached the ears of Thistlewood's slaves. Thistlewood noted, "[O]ur Negroes have good intelligence [of the rout], being most elevated, and ready to rise, now we are in the most imminent danger." The evening was spent in confusion, with Thistlewood seeing a house burning in the distance while parties of soldiers tramped through the estate "on the way to Leeward." It was not until 2 June that the tide turned in favor of the whites when a force comprised of regular troops, the Westmoreland militia, and Cudjoe's Maroons, the latter performing "with great bravery," overcame a large body of rebels. By early July, with the capture of "William Grove's Apongo . . . King of the Rebels," the danger had effectively passed. Nevertheless, Jamaican whites remained very fearful. The revolt had shaken their confidence in the assertion that white dominance would last in Jamaica. Many people were so discouraged that they left the island. Thistlewood commented in August, "It is said a Thousand people are already gone off upon account of the Negroe Rebellion." The fear remained even after the principal rebels were tortured, executed, or transported. In October, Thistlewood supped with John Stewart, who told him of an old proverb "which frights many people: 'One thousand seven hundred and sixty three, Jamaica no more an Island shall be,'" with Thistlewood adding, "(Not for the whites)."[90]

What remains particularly curious about the revolt, as seen in Thistlewood's tense diary entries, is the degree of ambivalence of his slaves toward rebel objectives. Thistlewood had good reason to believe that several of his slaves knew about the plot and were sympathetic to it. On 28 May, he noted, "When the report was of the Old Hope Negroes being rose, perceived a strange alteration in ours. They are certainly very ready if they durst, and am pretty certain they were in the plot, by what John [Groves] told me on Sunday evening . . . that he, what signified him, he would be dead in a Egypt etc etc, and from many other circumstances, Lewie being over at Forest's that night etc. Cuffee and Job also being very outrageous." Lewie may have been a conduit between slaves planning to rebel on Forest's estate and slaves at Egypt. When Apongo was condemned, Thistlewood asked him if he knew "any of our Negroes." Apongo replied that "he knew Lewie & wished him good bye." Thistlewood thought only three of his slaves—Quacoo, Abraham, and Achilles—were active in the rebellion, but he suspected that many others at Egypt knew what was going on. In October, still reflecting on the events of late May, he noted, "[A]t the beginning of the rebellion, a shaved head amongst the Negroes was the signal of war. The very day, our Jackie, Job, Achilles, Quasheba, Rosanna etc had their heads remarkably shaved. Quasheba's brother fell in the rebellion."[91] Yet even though he suspected his slaves of complicity in the rebellion, Thistlewood was forced to rely on their assistance. As far as possible, he maintained his normal working routine in the worrying days of late May, giving slaves tickets, for example, to go to Roaring River and Savanna-la-Mar to buy provisions. He tried, nevertheless, to ensure that all of his slaves were close at hand and under strict surveillance. At night, four slave men were given arms and told to guard the estate buildings while Thistlewood and Groves took turns sleeping. On 29 May, when things were most desperate, Thistlewood armed most of his slaves and "kept a strict guard and a sharp lookout."

It is difficult to be sure why Thistlewood's slaves did not rebel. Wisely, they kept their thoughts to themselves, leaving Thistlewood unaware of which slaves were loyal to him and which were not. But they clearly knew of the plot and had access to firearms. Why did they not rise against their beleaguered overseer? Possibly, slaves hesitated before committing themselves to a revolt that, if unsuccessful, promised torture and death. Thistlewood's clearheaded and determined actions probably compounded their hesitation. Thistlewood knew what was going on, even if imperfectly; had a plan of action that defended his property effectively; and was prepared to send "suspicious" slaves to jail. Matters may have been different if Egypt had been under the control of Thistlewood's sole white companion, Groves, who panicked dreadfully, shooting at strange slaves on sight, wounding a harmless domestic, and bolting to Savanna-la-Mar when the situation was most desperate. Slaves may have been willing to take their chances against Groves but not against Thistlewood.

Another reason why Thistlewood's slaves did not rebel was their desire to retain control over their own property. The problem with a slave rebellion, from a wavering slave's point of view, was the immense destruction of property involved. Long estimated that the damage caused in the 1760 rebellion amounted to over £100,000. In the great Baptist War of 1831, the damage to white property was estimated at over £1,000,000.[92] These figures related only to white property, but much slave property was also destroyed in the conflagration. The major weapon that rebel slaves employed against whites was fire. In 1831, the "whole surrounding country was illuminated" by "distant houses in flames."[93] But fire destroyed slave provision grounds as well as cane pieces and great houses. Rebels also took supplies from estates they had overrun and slaves who did not join their rebellion. Thistlewood, for example, was told by Thomas Reid, who had fled to him, that a slave had informed him that "one of their Coromantees was expected to come in the night, with a party of the rebellious Negroes to take all they could with them." Reid had escaped, along with "Many of the well-affected Negroes," who had left "lest they should be forced to join the rebels."[94] These slaves may have been "well-affected" because they feared losing all they had worked for in order to support a rebellion that was uncertain of success. Slaves' commitment to their individual patches of land blunted some of the harshness of slavery by allowing them a measure of economic autonomy: it also blunted the edge of resistance by making slaves hesitate before committing to rebellions with revolutionary implications. Slaves feared what would happen if the consequences of revolution were the destruction of existing property rights. That hesitation to commit fully to the implementation of slaves' long-term objective to extirpate whites from the island may have preserved white rule in a society where, by rights, that rule should have been vanquished. Slaves were "certainly very ready if they durst" to overcome white rule. It was becoming "durst" that proved the stumbling block.[95]

chapter six

Cooperation and Contestation, Intimacy and Distance

Thistlewood and His Male Slaves

Their master's character and repute casts, they think, a kind of secondary light upon themselves, as the moon derives her lustre from the sun; and the importance he acquires, in his station of life, adds, they imagine, to their own estimation among their neighbour Negroes on the adjacent estates. Their attachment to the descendants of old families, the ancestors of which were the masters and friends of their own progenitors, is remarkably strong and affectionate. This veneration appears hereditary, like clanships in the Scottish Highlands; it is imbibed in their infancy, or founded perhaps in the idea of the relation which subsisted between, and connected them in, the bond of fatherly love and authority on the one side, and a filial reverence and obedience on the other.—Edward Long, *History of Jamaica*

Whoever considers the Negroes Superiority in Number, the sullen, deceitfull, Refractory Temper of most of them, that some are Careless, others Treacherous or Idle, and apt to Run away; and how much their Masters Interest depends on the Care, and Diligence of His Slaves must needs be Convinced, that there is an Absolute necessity of keeping a Vigilant Eye, and Strict hand over them.—James Knight, "The Natural, Moral and Political History of Jamaica and the Territories thereon depending"

The Death of a Slave

Thistlewood recorded a curious event early in 1756. On the morning of 3 February, John Cope Sr. died at age fifty-six. "A Negroe Man about 24 years of age," Thistlewood related three days later, "so soon as he heard his old Master was dead went to the Negroe house privately and shot himself, to Accompany him into the Otherworld and there wait upon him (his name was Roger and was Learned to be a Mason)." It is hard to know what to make of this episode. It violates what we think of slavery in a number of ways. As discussed in chapter 5, slaves hated their masters. Few masters were as deeply implicated in slavery and the Atlantic slave trade as John Cope Sr. An Englishman, he had served as the governor of Cape Coast Castle in West Africa, at the center of British slave-trading efforts in Africa.[1] From there, he had turned to slaving himself, owning and operating slave ships out of London, before moving to Jamaica and setting himself up as a sugar planter. Conceivably, Cope had been instrumental either directly or indirectly in the process through which Roger had been taken from Africa to Jamaica. Occasionally, the transactions that resulted in slaves being forcibly moved across the Atlantic were echoed on New World plantations. Only six days before Cope's death, Thistlewood remarked on a tense encounter between two slaves who had last seen each other under different circumstances in Africa. "It is remarkable," Thistlewood noted, "that one of the New Negroes named Achilles, is he who took Doll and sold her." Achilles was "robbed going home" of "some Clothes, some Tobacco, and a gun." The African now called Doll whom Achilles had sold into slavery may have had something to do with Achilles' misfortunes. It is not totally impossible, though unlikely, that Achilles, Doll, Roger, and Cope were all involved in the African side of the slave trade at the same time—Achilles and Cope as beneficiaries, Doll and Roger as victims.[2]

To act as Roger was reputed to have acted was decidedly odd. It is strange that a slave would have such affection for his white master that he would sacrifice himself at his master's passing. But what is equally odd, at least to modern minds, is the manner of Roger's self-destruction. Roger killed himself with a gun. One of the essential rules in any slave society was that blacks should not be entrusted with weapons. Such a rule was common sense in societies where whites were heavily outnumbered. Yet Thistlewood notes several cases in which slaves used guns. He does not find it unusual that his slaves celebrated the death of his kinsman by firing guns into the air or that Achilles had a gun stolen from him, even though he was "one of the New Negroes." Thistlewood often armed his slaves. He even bought firearms from and sold firearms to slaves. On 13 March

1760, just two months before Tackey's revolt shook white rule to its very foundations, Thistlewood noted that he had "Sold Old Sharper the gun I bought from driver Quashe, Many years ago, he gives me only 10 shillings for her but paid ready Money."[3]

That one slave had such a misguided sense of loyalty to his master that he was willing to commit suicide in order to serve him in the afterlife and that slaves often had access to weapons, contrary to law and common sense, are small matters in the overall system of slavery. They do not substantially alter our understanding of slavery in mid-eighteenth-century Jamaica. Yet these seemingly isolated events should give us pause. At the very least, they indicate that master-slave relationships were very complex and highly personal. Masters' power over slaves was never absolute. It was always contingent on slaves' recognition that masters had to be obeyed. Slaves did not always give that recognition, although the consequences of not obeying masters were extraordinarily severe. Slavery was a continual battle of contestation and cooperation between two parties with different objectives that sometimes coincided and sometimes clashed. In order for slavery to work, both master and slave had to concede a degree of legitimacy to the other, even if the legitimacy thus recognized was grudging, conditional, and a second-best alternative to what masters and slaves truly desired. Masters would have preferred that slaves do their will because slaves freely accepted masters' right to command slaves as they pleased. Slaves would have preferred to have no masters at all and to be free. Both needed to accept some compromise that involved recognizing the power the other party held, even if, of course, the degree of compromise masters needed to make with slaves was much less than that slaves needed to make with masters. The master-slave relationship was subject to continual negotiation, even though it was profoundly asymmetrical, with slave owners holding enormous power and slaves holding very little power. But if slave owners, as Ira Berlin notes, "held most of the cards in this meanest of contests, slaves held cards of their own." Moreover, "even when their cards were reduced to near worthlessness, slaves still held that last card [refusal to obey], which, as their owners well understood, they might play at any time." In the final analysis, "the web of interconnections between master and slave necessitated a coexistence that fostered cooperation as well as contestation."[4]

Mastery and Force

At bottom, of course, Europeans upheld their mastery over Africans through their near monopoly of force. Mastery in a land where hostile, brutalized, barely assimilated Africans vastly outnumbered Europeans was necessarily achieved through physical violence, unvarnished brutality, and terror. But, as chapter 5 has detailed, whites devised management strategies to control slaves that exploited the uncertainty that slaves necessarily felt in a system predicated on absolute, arbitrary power. Everyone was brutalized by slavery, both the whites who meted out punishment and the slaves who suffered that punishment. But it was slaves who suffered most. Thistlewood's diaries reveal a slave population severely bruised—psychologically even more than physically—by the torments they faced every day. Jamaican plantation slavery was especially dreadful and particularly brutal and dehumanizing. It is hard to disagree with Richard Dunn's claim that "Caribbean slavery was one of the most brutally dehumanizing systems ever devised."[5] We can measure its dreadfulness by any number of means, but perhaps the most revealing is the number of suicides or attempted suicides of slaves that Thistlewood recorded over thirty-seven years. Jamaican slavery was so appalling that many slaves felt the only response was self-destruction. Roger was not unique. In 1756, for example, Moll drowned herself "wilfully," fearing that she had killed "Mr. Mould's Lydde," whom she had beaten in a fit of rage because she thought Lydde had taken up with her partner Cobbena.[6] Two years earlier, Thistlewood reported that a recently purchased African called Nero "Would not Work, but threaten'd to Cutt his own throat. Had him Whipp'd, gagg'd, & his hands tied behind him so that the Mosskitoes and Sand flies might torment him to some Purpose."[7] On 23 July 1776, Thistlewood flogged Phoebe "for wishing she was dead already." Five years earlier, Jimmy put into words what many slaves may have thought about their lives. Caught "throwing the fire about the cookroom, and being otherways very impudent," he retorted to Thistlewood that "if this be living he did not care whether he lived or died." Thistlewood responded by putting him in the bilboes overnight and flogging him the next day.[8]

Commentators on Jamaican slavery are divided about the dehumanizing effects of slavery. Some insist on the vitality of slave culture in Jamaica, emphasizing that slaves were able to construct institutions that to a large extent they made themselves. Scholars have shown, for example, that Jamaican slaves were able to reconstitute family life based on African models. They have stressed the importance of the slave-oriented internal economy in which slaves pursued economic activity partly free from white control. Through familial relationships, community interactions, and the pursuit of acquisitive individualism, slaves were able to dilute white pretensions that slaves could be depersonalized and regimented through constant application of force. Other historians, however, stress disorganization, instability, and chaos as the principal characteristics of Jamaican slavery. They highlight the savageries of slavery and point out how these savageries led to significant slave dehumanization as masters sought, with considerable success, to obliterate slaves' personal histories.[9] I favor the latter interpretation. Slave owners not only tormented their slaves physically but also subjected them to intolerable psychological stress. Jamaican slaves lived in a world of radical uncertainty. They were always vulnerable to the depredations of whites and fellow slaves. This uncertainty was heightened when slaves were unseasoned migrants from Africa, when slave populations were continually in flux, and when the only shared experiences that slaves had were those gained through suffering. All of these conditions existed when Thistlewood lived in Jamaica.

Yet, as Roger's suicide attests, behind the collective experience of slaves in Jamaica lay the experiences of many individuals who fashioned highly personal responses to enslavement. One of the great virtues of Thistlewood's diaries is that they allow us to recapture the individual experiences of slaves in Jamaica more fully than is possible through other sources. His diaries tell us most about Thistlewood and his interactions with his slaves. We will not lose that perspective in this chapter: the information we get from his diaries on slave character and slave activities is refracted through the lens of his particular concerns. But the diaries are also valuable in introducing us to thousands of individual slaves, some of whom are discussed in enough detail that they emerge as nearly fully rounded human beings. In this chapter and the next, we will, for example, gain some appreciation of the personalities of Lincoln, Thistlewood's longest-serving and perhaps longest-suffering slave, and Phibbah, Thistlewood's mistress. Even if our understanding of these slaves' lives is mediated by the fact that we see them through Thistlewood's eyes and thus view them only as Thistlewood saw them, Thistlewood's diaries are a rare and valuable resource for understanding slave experience.

Generally, slaves in Britain's American empire left few traces of their existence, although, as Jerome Handler and Vincent Carretta have revealed in painstaking reconstructions of existing documentary and pictorial evidence, we have more information about the experiences of enslaved Africans from the standpoint of Africans themselves than we might once have realized.[10] Nevertheless, few sources are as rich as Thistlewood's diaries in capturing the quotidian existence of slaves' lives in the Caribbean. Thistlewood's diaries allow us to view slaves, many African rather than Creole, as humans. Examining slaves as individuals is important for two reasons. First, looking at slavery through the eyes of individual slaves adds flesh and bone to the dry statistics on slavery that are usually the only information we have on slave societies. The reconstruction of some slaves' lives offers much insight into how slaves coped with slavery. Second, if we are to understand the contours of white lives in early Jamaica, it is important to know what whites were up against. Slavery was not an abstraction but a real, immediate, personal, and immensely varied institution. In order to be "masters," whites had to exert their mastery over fellow humans who displayed a full range of human behaviors and human weaknesses.[11]

Thistlewood's Slave Forces: Egypt

Hundreds of slaves populate the pages of Thistlewood's diaries. Some slaves, notably slaves at Egypt and the slaves he owned, are mentioned enough times for us to get some appreciation of what their lives were like. This chapter and the next focus on seven slaves. Thistlewood owned six of them; the remaining slave, Phibbah, was owned by Thistlewood's employer, John Cope, and became Thistlewood's principal sexual and emotional partner. Three—Johnnie, Chub, and Lincoln—were men; four—Coobah, Sally, Abba, and Phibbah—were women. Johnnie and Chub died in Thistlewood's service; Coobah and Sally were transported off the island; and Abba, Lincoln, and Phibbah survived Thistlewood. Together, they lived 181 years with Thistlewood. All except Phibbah were African. I have concentrated on slaves owned by Thistlewood because it is these slaves about whom we can gather the fullest information. I have included Phibbah as well because her life was so intimately tied to Thistlewood's and because she is easily the most fully drawn character in Thistlewood's diaries, apart from Thistlewood himself.

The individual experiences of these slaves make sense only if we understand the slave communities in which they lived. Slaves' experiences varied dramatically depending on the plantation they were on; the ethnic and sexual makeup of the slave force they were part of; and, most important, the nature of the work they were expected to do. Their experiences were also greatly affected by the character of their owner or supervisor. Thistlewood was the master of four slave forces during his time in Jamaica. Between 1750 and 1751, he supervised between 37 and 42 slaves on a livestock pen in southwestern St. Elizabeth Parish. In 1757 and 1758, he was overseer of 61 slaves at the Kendal sugar estate, on the border of Hanover Parish and Westmoreland Parish. The short time he spent at each of these places makes them unsuitable for deeper analysis.[12] The two estates where Thistlewood spent most of his life and where he had the fullest interactions with slaves were Egypt Plantation, where he was overseer between 18 September 1751 and 1 September 1767 (except for a year at Kendal), and Bread-nut Island Pen, Thistlewood's own property, where he lived from 1 September 1767 to his death with between 24 and 34 slaves whom he owned, plus his mistress Phibbah. These two estates were in southern Westmoreland, separated by no more than three or four miles. Nevertheless, they were very different in their economic orientation and in the size, composition, and duties of their respective slave forces. The Egypt estate was a 1,500-acre property located near the coast and along the Cabaritta River among a maze of swamps and man-made canals. Most of the property was water or swamp. It contained around 300 acres of habitable land, including 150 acres of cane land divided into 33 separate cane pieces, 65 acres of pasture, and land given over to slaves' provision grounds.[13] It had many weaknesses as a property. It depended heavily on hired slave labor, it had an unreliable mill that broke down nearly every year, and it did not have very good cane land or the capacity to access more land, given the parlous financial situation in which John Cope always found himself.[14]

When Thistlewood took over Egypt, it contained 89 slaves, of whom 31 were adult men, 29 were adult women, 6 were boys of working age, 9 were girls of working age, and 14 were children. By the standards of the 1740s and 1750s, the size of this slave force was probably a little below average for a sugar estate. Richard Sheridan's analysis of slave forces in inventories suggests that in the early 1740s the average number of slaves on a sugar estate was 99. By 1768, the average number of slaves on a sugar estate had jumped to 150, and by 1788, it had risen again to 181.[15] These slaves faced a life of constant toil, frequent hunger, continual violence, and ever-present uncertainty. Working on a sugar estate was the hardest work a slave could do, and the harshness of the labor was reflected in atrocious mortality rates. Barry Higman has shown that slaves working on sugar estates had appreciably worse demographic prospects than slaves working in other enterprises, even after ameliorative policies were introduced in the late eighteenth century.[16] Nearly every estate had more deaths than births. Dunn's extensive analysis of slave patterns on the nearby Mesopotamia estate shows that between 1762 and 1831, 504 females had just 410 recorded live births. During the same period, the estate recorded 749 deaths, resulting in a ratio of deaths to births of 1.83 to 1.[17] Mortality was exacerbated by excessive morbidity. Estate records suggest that at any one time large proportions of slaves in sugar labor forces were sick. On Simon Taylor's Golden Grove estate in St. Thomas in the East Parish, the percentage of slaves who were ill in the 1760s and 1770s never fell below 10 percent and was usually much higher.

The Fort William estate was part of the vast sugar holdings of the Beckford family in Westmoreland. This engraving was owned by the planter-historian William Beckford of Hertford Pen. Beckford was so impressed by Thistlewood's company that in July 1778 he sent him six engravings depicting views of rivers, which included this illustration and the following two illustrations. These illustrations provide one of the rare links outside his diaries to Thistlewood and his Jamaican life. *View of Fort William Estate, Westmoreland, 1778*, engraved by Thomas Vivares from a painting by George Robertson. Courtesy of the National Library of Jamaica.

On the estate of John McLeod, a St. Dorothy sugar planter who left a well-documented inventory in 1775, the percentage of all slaves who were unhealthy was 28 percent and the percentage of slaves of working age (between fifteen and forty-four) who were sick was 22 percent. On the York estate in Hanover in 1778, the percentage of slaves of working age who were "able" or "healthy" was 62 percent.[18] Slaves were similarly unhealthy at Egypt. An unusually detailed listing of slaves' occupations made by Thistlewood on 11 March 1752 showed that 20 of 60 adult slaves (33 percent) were ill or disabled. The result of high morbidity rates was low fertility and high infant mortality, heightened by slave owners' practice of making young adult slaves, especially slave women, do back-breaking field labor. Over two-thirds of men and over three-quarters of women between ten and thirty-five years old worked in the fields. Over two-thirds of all women compared to under one-third of all men were field workers.[19]

Slaves sickened and died disproportionately more often on sugar estates than on other types of estates because the work was so hard. Slaves had to "hole" or

View of Roaring River Estate, Westmoreland, 1778, engraved by Thomas Vivares from a painting by George Robertson. Courtesy of the National Library of Jamaica.

"trench" the land in order to plant cane. The strongest and youngest slaves were assigned this arduous, boring, mechanical work. In a ten-hour day, each slave was expected to dig 60–80 holes. Later they would plant canes in them. In following years, the cane could be "ratooned" or cut to the root so that new sprouts would bloom, but every few years, holing would have to be done again. Then the cane had to be harvested. The cane was cut, ferried to the sugar mill, and then fed into a series of three vertical rollers that crushed it for boiling. Slaves had to be very careful during this process to avoid having their limbs crushed in the rollers or being burned by the pans that boiled the sugarcane into sugar or rum. The whole process involved extreme danger, considerable haste, and maximum effort, both on the part of the slaves and on the part of the white operatives who had to force slaves, usually through abundant use of the whip, to stick to their unpleasant task.[20] It is not surprising that the daily sick list often included more than ten slaves.[21]

Managing a sugar estate was hard work and required a hard man. It was no accident that the most egregious examples of sadistic behavior from Thistlewood came when he was in charge at Egypt. It was during this period that he invented Derby's dose and engaged in other practices, such as on 22 November 1764, when he "Picketted Douglas' Coobah on a quart bottle neck, till she begged hard." It was also no accident that it was at Egypt that Thistlewood faced the most opposition from slaves. The episode with Congo Sam, for example, oc-

View of Bridge over Cabaritta River, engraved by Thomas Vivares from a painting by George Robertson. Courtesy of the National Library of Jamaica.

curred in his first year as an overseer at Egypt. The period between 1754 and 1756, when the crops failed and slaves could not support themselves through their provision grounds, saw Thistlewood at his fiercest. Slaves continuously raided the sugarcane for food, and Thistlewood constantly whipped them. He whipped them so much that by 24 March 1759 he wrote, "My pocket Whip is broke and Wore out." Slave management required positive as well as negative incentives, such as the granting of special allowances, especially at Christmas, occasional monetary payments, and short-term freedoms.[22] But physical coercion was crucial, and fear of the lash was what dragged most of the work out of slaves producing sugar. Thistlewood may have copied Beckford's recommendation that it was in "the Interest of every Master to treat his Slaves with Justice and Benevolence that their lives may be render'd as cosy as their Condition will permit" and he may have shown considerable concern for slaves, ministering to them, for example, when they were sick. Nevertheless, he followed his copying of Beckford's instructions with a chilling poem on slaves turning on whites in a "Bacchanalian Frenzy" when "Full Acts of Blood and Vengeance they pursue," indicating that he thought slave management on sugar estates was so violent that it was likely to inculcate "a Sense of Injury" in slaves that would "inspire a general Rancour and hatred of ye Person who inflicts it."[23]

Life at Breadnut Island, on the other hand, was a good deal easier for slaves since work on a pen was less demanding than work on a sugar estate.[24] It was also easier for Thistlewood. Although he continued to punish slaves regularly and arbitrarily, the acts of savagery that had distinguished his rule at Egypt diminished. The relative ease of management at Breadnut may have been the result of his long experience in managing slaves, but it was more likely to have arisen from the more relaxed work regime that existed outside the sugar economy. Breadnut Island Pen was not an especially auspicious purchase. It was hilly and rocky with poor soil. Nevertheless, its position on a bend of the Cabaritta River provided swamps full of wild fowl and fish, the higher ground allowed livestock to graze, and the hollows gave protection to Thistlewood's plants. A diary entry on 2 July 1770 gives us an idea of what his working slaves did on the property: "Sally tending the corn. Sukey and Mirtilla weeding the garden. Pompey has the day [off] and Caesar is minding the goats. Maria and Dick lame, Coobah run away and Lincoln given a ticket and sent in search. Chub fishing. . . . Cudjoe, Solon, Johnie, Jimmy, Franke, Phoebe, Nanny and Peggy cleaning pasture." In addition, three slaves—Abba, Bess, and Damsel—assisted Phibbah around the house, and five children were not yet ready for work. Slaves involved in gardening, tending livestock, working as domestics, or fishing had less onerous duties than slaves working on sugar estates.[25] Nevertheless, many of the slaves who worked at Breadnut Island were still involved in sugar production. Thistlewood regularly hired out slaves to work on nearby plantations. They earned Thistlewood good money but at the expense of their health: jobbing slaves were given the hardest work on estates, with planters preferring to work them harder than their own slaves.[26]

Thistlewood's Slave Forces: Breadnut

When Thistlewood arrived at Breadnut Island Pen, he brought with him 27 slaves of his own and Phibbah, a slave belonging to John and Molly Cope, whom he rented for £18 per annum. Of these, 20 were Africans he had bought in five separate purchases between 1756 and 1765. In addition, he had acquired 6 children and a slave girl called Bess, a present from Sarah Bennett to his slave mistress Phibbah. He purchased 3 more slaves between 1773 and 1776, lost 4 adult slaves and 5 children through death, and transported 2 off of the island. By the time of his death in 1786, he owned 34 slaves, of whom 17 were Africans he had purchased, 1 was a Creole he had purchased, and 16 were Creole children of African slaves. The origins of the slaves he bought between 1756 and 1775 were diverse. Of the 27 he bought, the origins of 16 are known: 3 were Ibo from the Bight of Biafra, 4 were from the Gold Coast, 3 hailed from the Congo, 1 was from Sierra Leone, 3 were from the Bight of Benin, and 2 were Creoles.

The result of his purchasing policies was that in 1767 he had a slave force with a disproportionately large number of men and women in their teens and twenties. Apart from 6 children who were between 1 and 9 years old, all of his slaves were between 13 and 29, with 16 between 19 and 27.[27] At his death, he had 1 slave in her twenties (and that slave was blind), 3 slaves who were 14 years old, and 5 slaves between 32 and 34. A further 12 slaves were between 38 and 46 years old, and another 12 were 11 or under. His slave force was thus considerably less productive at his death than it had been when he first moved to Breadnut Island. Nevertheless, the majority of his slaves—21 of 34—were able, health permitting (4 of Thistlewood's slaves were handicapped, 2 to the extent that they were incapable of heavy work), to undertake the full range of work that Thistlewood needed done. The increasing age of his slaves and growing proportion of children would have posed a problem for Thistlewood only if he had lived another decade.

By Jamaican standards, Thistlewood was extremely fortunate in having a slave force that remained highly productive over an extended period. Part of the reason for the good health and high productivity of his slaves was that they did not work completely within the sugar economy, even though most of his slaves were hired out at some time to work on sugar estates. The hardiness of his slaves also reflects well on Thistlewood's skill and care in keeping them healthy. Beckford instructed his underlings, "A particular tenderness must be Exercised towards those that are Sick and proper Physick administered, and the Overseers are admonished not to force any Sick or Infirm Negroes to Labour." Thistlewood took these words to heart. His diaries are replete with accounts of treating slaves' illnesses. In 1770, he compiled sixty-one medical recipes he had used during his twenty years of looking after slaves, demonstrating how much interest he took in slave medicine. His attention to slaves resulted in a relatively healthy and productive slave force.[28] Of course, slaves' good health also derived from the ministrations of slaves themselves, but Thistlewood's diaries say little about slaves' role in their own treatment.

Household Structure

Unlike most appraisers of Jamaican inventories, the appraisers of Thistlewood's estate grouped his slaves according to the type of household in which they lived.[29] On three occasions, Thistlewood also noted in his diaries the type of household in which slaves lived. Thus we have a rare opportunity to survey household arrangements in a colonial West Indian labor force four times over a twenty-year period.[30] In September 1767, he owned 27 slaves who lived in 12 households, ranging in size from 1 slave to 5 slaves. Slaves lived in seven types of household. Three households contained a man and woman living as husband and wife. Two contained a woman, either 1 or 3 children, and an unrelated woman. Two households were comprised of 2 unrelated men living together, and 2 contained 2 unrelated women living together. Only 1 household contained a nuclear family of husband, wife, and child. Altogether, 25 slaves lived with other slaves and 2—Damsel and Johnnie—lived alone. Sixteen slaves did not live with either a partner or children. Eleven slaves lived with people they were connected to by birth or by virtue of being in a relationship. We do not know who all of the partners of male slaves were, but only 3 women lived with partners who were also Thistlewood's slaves. Four women were attached to men from the Egypt estate, which is hardly surprising given that Thistlewood had just left that estate, and Abba was attached to "Emotson's Neptune," which makes sense since she had worked for Thomas Emotson and his wife. Three women were unattached.

By 1770, Thistlewood's slave force had shrunk by 1 slave to 26 slaves, who lived in 11 households, 2 of which contained 4 slaves apiece. Abba and her 3 children now lived by themselves. Sally had been placed in a household of 4 young adults that also included Bess, Jimmy, and Damsel. The number of slaves living with kin[31] or with people they were in a relationship with had increased to 14, and the number of slaves living with people they had no attachment to had declined to 12. Overall, Thistlewood's slaves in 1770 lived in eight different types of household. By 1776, the number of different household types had decreased to six, although the number of slaves Thistlewood owned had increased to 28. The young adults' household of 1770 had broken up. Damsel had taken up with Solon, who had previously been with Maria and Maria's daughter Lucy. Damsel and Solon had 2 children, Nelly and Quashie, born in 1772 and 1775, respectively. Jimmy and Phoebe were now living together and had 1 child. Bess was attached to "Mr. Wilson's Jimmy." She also had a child, Bristol, whose paternity is unclear. Sally was living by herself after an attempt to match her with Chub failed dismally. Three women were involved with slaves from neighboring estates, and 6 of Thistlewood's women were attached to Thistlewood's men. Altogether, 15 slaves lived with a partner. The most significant change was in the number of slaves who lived with consanguines (23) compared to the number who did not (5). Each of these 5 slaves lived alone; Thistlewood's slaves no longer dwelled in households in which unrelated or uninvolved adult slaves lived together. Thistlewood's slaves lived in only four types of households—husband and wife; husband, wife, and children; woman and children; and adult solitaires.[32]

By 1786, Thistlewood's slaves' household structures had changed again. Thistlewood's slaves now lived in 12 households of five types. The majority—22 of 34—lived in just 4 households, containing husbands, wives, and children. The largest was a polygamous household, headed by Lincoln and his long-term partner, Sukey, which included Lincoln's additional wife, Abba, Abba's 5 children (1 adult, 2 teenagers, and 2 infants), and Abba's infant granddaughter. For the first time, therefore, Thistlewood's establishment contained a multigenerational, polygamous household. Three households contained husband, wife, and children. Bess continued to live without a partner on the estate and resided with her fourteen-year-old son and six-year-old son. Nevertheless, given that her long-term partner, Jimmy, lived very close, Bess and her 2 children to all intents and purpose lived in a standard nuclear household. Dick and Mirtilla continued in the most stable of all of Thistlewood's slaves' households. They became attached in the late 1760s and were still together, childless, in 1786. Only Lincoln and Sukey and Thistlewood and Phibbah had been together longer. Franke and Strap were still together, and the other 5 adults all lived alone. The slaves living alone were the only slaves who did not live with slaves they were attached to by blood or by relationship. The other 29 slaves all lived with consanguines. Thus, 9 slaves lived in a polygamous, male-headed household; 21 lived in nuclear households of husband, wife, and children (assuming that Jimmy and Bess lived as husband and wife); and 5 lived as solitaires. All slaves except for Nanny, Maria, and Peggy, who lived as solitaires, would probably have lived in male-headed households.

The trends within these shifting household arrangements are clear. As Thistlewood's slaves aged, they gravitated toward forming a smaller number of household types, each of which increasingly contained only people connected by blood or by relationship. Overall, Thistlewood's slaves lived in ten different types of household during the twenty years of residence at Breadnut Island, but the eight types of household that existed in 1770 shrank to five in 1776 and 1786. None of the households in 1776 or 1786 contained adult slaves unconnected to other slaves in the household. They also moved toward living in male-headed rather than female-headed households. The number of female-headed households, excluding solitaire households, declined from 4 in 1767 to at most 1 and probably none in 1786. Even in 1767, however, 4 of the 7 women seemingly living in female-headed households were attached to men from nearby estates. Only Coobah, Peggy, and Coobah's infant daughter Silvia lived in a truly female-headed household. The woman and children household form was generally not important at Breadnut Island, whatever the significance of the mother-child link. Only 9 of the 49 households described between 1767 and 1786 contained only women and children. Households also increased in size over time. By 1786, 3 households contained 5 or more slaves compared to just 1 in 1767, 1770, and 1776. The existence of a polygamous household containing 1 man and 2 wives suggests that slaves replicated West African familial practices when possible. The slave system heightened familial instability. No single household remained the same over twenty years, and only Sukey—who remained throughout with Lincoln—and Peggy, Johnnie, and Caesar—who do not seem to have had any permanent attachments—did not change or acquire new partners. Nevertheless, Thistlewood's slaves worked hard to establish strong family bonds based on a mixture of African-derived and European-influenced forms.

One cannot draw too many implications from an analysis of one small slave grouping, but in the absence of other listings of slave households over time in eighteenth-century Jamaica, the conclusions we can draw from Thistlewood's slaves' family arrangements provide an interesting gloss on a long-standing and controversial historical argument. Historians have vigorously debated the nature and purpose of family and household units established during slavery in the Americas, though usually at a high level of ideological abstraction. Thistlewood's diaries and inventory do at least allow for a study of household structures rooted in actual practice and permit an analysis over time. They suggest that the extent of matrifocality within Jamaican slave family structures has been exaggerated and, more important, that slaves tried to reduce the matrifocality that did exist. Changes over time also suggest that Orlando Patterson was correct to argue that the mating system of Jamaican slaves passed through a series of stages, culminating in an ordinary monogamous union of man and woman in middle or late middle age. Slave households followed a developmental cycle of young adult solitaires forming households that became more complicated as the members of the household aged. It was the nuclear family that eventually predominated. Nuclear families were especially important for Africans since they were separated from adult kin. Nevertheless, as the household arrangements of Thistlewood's longest-serving slaves, Abba and Lincoln, indicate, the long-term trend was that slaves established extended multigenerational households by the time they entered their forties, within which they had a measure of polygamy. In this way, African-born slaves tried to reestablish in Jamaica patriarchal polygamous West African practices. It seems that the early-nineteenth-century pattern whereby Creoles lived in often complicated extended family structures while Africans were largely isolated from family life did not hold true during the African-dominated period of Jamaican slavery. In this period, Africans were as likely as Creoles to establish viable family groups and to live within increasingly larger nuclear family households. Later differentiations between African and Creole familial practices probably relate to the declining percentage of Africans within slave populations and their increasing isolation from ever more firmly established Creole slave populations, especially large Creole populations on sugar estates. Isolating Africans from Creoles was difficult on smaller slaveholdings such as Thistlewood's where relatively few slaves were Creoles.[33]

The Invisible Field Hands

Analyzing household structure tells us little about how slaves lived their lives and slaves' varying responses to enslavement. Biographies of individual slaves help us flesh out more about what slave lives were really like. They demonstrate that slaves had to make a clear trade-off. The closer a slave was to a master, the greater the benefits and privileges the slave might achieve, but being closely attached to a master entailed great risks. Distance brought safety. Intimacy provided privileges but led to danger. Individual slaves had to choose (to the extent that they were free to make such a choice) how closely to ally their lives with that of the master. Slaves could achieve a measure of autonomy if they were willing or required to labor in the obscurity of field work, away from the master's gaze. But that autonomy provided few tangible benefits save being unlikely to suffer their master's wrath. The following explorations of the lives of three male slaves demonstrate the consequences slaves faced in choosing different trade-offs. They reveal, too, that we cannot view slaves' lives in isolation from the lives of their masters. Thistlewood did not control all aspects of his slaves' lives and did not wish to do so. He had little interest, for example, in exploring slaves' cultural aspirations or regulating their behavior outside of work hours. But he nevertheless had an enormous impact on how slaves lived their lives, and slaves constantly had to deal with him.

Johnnie, who was purchased by Thistlewood on 20 February 1758, is the most shadowy figure of the seven slaves studied in these two chapters. He came close to becoming invisible within Thistlewood's establishment. In the thirteen years

Thistlewood owned him before he died, probably in his early to mid-thirties, on 22 July 1770, Johnnie was hardly mentioned by Thistlewood, except in relation to his work duties. Johnnie was a field worker who was first employed making sugar on the Egypt estate and then worked in the garden and as a fisherman at Breadnut. Thistlewood also hired out Johnnie in 1768 and 1769 to work on nearby sugar estates. He does not appear to have had a partner and lived alone. His life, at least so far as Thistlewood was aware of it, was one of hard work and few rewards. Thistlewood did not go hunting or fishing with him, never sent him on errands, and displayed no interest in his character or behavior. There is no touch of individuality in Thistlewood's descriptions of him. Perhaps because of the backbreaking work he was required to do, Johnnie was often sick. He contracted yaws, a highly contagious disease characterized by skin eruptions followed by fever and sores that developed into foul and fungous tubercles and ulcers,[34] in November 1758 and suffered stomach pains from June 1769 onward that eventually killed him. He attempted to supplement his meager food allotment by selling food but was not always successful. On 27 September 1758 and 28 April 1765, Johnnie was robbed of his fish by other slaves and was forced to ask for Thistlewood's help. Thistlewood interceded with the owners of the guilty slaves to seek compensation for him. Most of the time, he stayed out of trouble, but on three occasions, he earned Thistlewood's displeasure, twice for breaking and eating cane and once, along with another slave, "for neglect of their Business." Johnnie was indelibly marked (literally) by indiscretions that may have been motivated by hunger as much as by disobedience. On 18 October 1769, Johnnie was discovered to be absent from the place he had been hired at, and three days later, he was "put . . . in the bilboes." Thistlewood exercised his incipient sadism by "mark[ing] Johnie in the right cheek, [and] put[ting] a collar and chain about his neck" after releasing him.[35] Even a faceless slave who kept to his own business could fall victim to his master's caprices or rage.

Chub was only slightly more visible than Johnnie. A young boy of thirteen or fourteen with "3 perpendicular scars down each cheek" when purchased by Thistlewood on 19 July 1765, he took some time to adapt to Jamaican ways. On 31 July 1765, Thistlewood recorded that Chub had become very ill from "eating bitter Cassada." He only recovered when Thistlewood "work'd him well" and "gave him a double vomit." Chub was often sick and died young. At fifteen, he had his first bout of venereal disease; by the age of seventeen, he suffered from yaws; and at eighteen, he was partly lame. In 1771, at the age of nineteen, he had measles, and on 15 October 1772, he fell seriously ill with a fever. He remained sickly until his death on 20 October 1775, after "a violent cold, fever,

headache etc." Thistlewood noted on 21 October 1775 that "At Night the Negroes buried poor Chub. I gave them a bottle of rum." Chub was twenty-four.[36]
Most of his short life in Jamaica had been spent in the fields. Chub's work experience, however, was more varied than that of Johnnie, partly because he was
a boy rather than a man when purchased and partly because Thistlewood moved
from the Egypt sugar estate to his own pen eighteen months after he purchased
him. Chub was delegated to help build "Negroe houses" and cared for Thistlewood's horses. When Chub was sixteen, Thistlewood attempted to transform
him from a field worker into a fisherman, with limited success. He occasionally
sent him on errands, and on 29 June 1768, he sent Chub (along with six other
slaves) to the market at Savanna-la-Mar to sell "16 bundles of Scotch grass."[37]

Slaves appreciated being relieved of the heavy burden of field labor. That
slaves disliked field labor more than any other task is clear because slave owners
used assignment to the fields as a punishment. Yet the great advantage of working in the fields was that it allowed distance from the slave owner. As Fernando
Ortiz has described in his classic comparison of slave life on sugar and tobacco
plantations in Cuba, the nature of master–slave relations owed much to the type
of work a slave did. Sugar was an impersonal industry and did not necessitate
close contact with masters. In tobacco growing (and other kinds of work besides sugar production), "the personal element always predominated . . . and
there was a patriarchal, intimate quality about its work."[38] Such increased contact between masters and slaves was fraught with difficulties. Slaves wanted to
work in jobs outside field labor because the work was easier, the tasks were more
varied, and opportunities for financial gain and a measure of personal independence were more abundant. Yet slaves favored in this way were also more liable than field slaves to incur their master's wrath. With privilege came responsibility, and with responsibility came risk. In short, the greater the intimacy
with the master, the greater the possibility for individual advancement but the
greater the risk of physical and occasionally psychological punishment. The
primary risk was that privileged slaves would do things that displeased their
masters. A secondary risk, of more momentous consequence, was that privileged slaves would lose their autonomy. Slaves with specialized responsibilities,
Philip Morgan notes, mediated "either directly or indirectly between the worlds
of master and slave, meeting whites on an intermittent but more regular basis
than ordinary field hands."[39] Greater contact meant more circumscribed autonomy. It allowed for greater manipulation of masters, but it inevitably made privileged slaves more dependent on the system and those who controlled the system than field hands.

Thistlewood demanded more from slaves in positions of responsibility than he did from other slaves. When he perceived that these slaves failed, he was not slow to punish them, usually brutally. Chub never had a position of responsibility such as being a driver, but he experienced the perils of privilege to some extent when he moved out of field labor. Thistlewood was annoyed that Chub, while tending horses, "by neglect let the grey and white horses" escape. They subsequently "almost killed mackey before a negroe could get to his assistance." Chub received a sound flogging. On 21 November 1769, a similar incident occurred. As part of his job tending livestock, Chub had been told to mind Thistlewood's geese. He "won't mind" them, Thistlewood complained, and Thistlewood sent him back to the fields.[40]

Thistlewood decided intermittently to use Chub as a fisherman. He used the fish that slaves caught to feed himself and to supplement the food supplies of needy slaves. He also sold the surplus at market in Savanna-la-Mar. Becoming a fisherman was one of the better jobs a slave could do. The task itself was neither onerous nor unpleasant, especially compared to the drudgery of field labor, and it allowed slaves a degree of latitude and autonomy. In order to catch fish, slave fishermen needed to wander widely through the estate and nearby countryside. As Philip Morgan notes for low-country South Carolina, "watermen and fishermen enjoyed unusual mobility, and their daily routines had none of the monotony of field labor."[41] Moreover, catching fish provided slave fishermen with a convenient source of income. Although Thistlewood expected to receive all of the proceeds of his slaves' fish sales, slave fishermen found it easy to keep some of the proceeds for themselves.

Conflict over fishing was very much evident in the complicated relationship between Thistlewood and Lincoln, but it also marked relations between Thistlewood and Chub. Late in 1767, Thistlewood sent Chub to Egypt, where he was to be taught by an Egypt slave, Kinsale, "to learn how to strike and set fish pots etc."[42] Chub soon got into trouble. On 4 January 1768, Thistlewood "flogged him for neglect," and on 21 November, he relieved him of his duties and sent him back to the fields. He was back fishing by mid-February 1770, placed under the supervision of Egypt fisherman, Cyrus, but he was soon in Thistlewood's bad graces again. On 26 February 1770, Thistlewood "Trimmed Chub well for not coming till past one o'clock, and bringing very little even then." In March, May, and twice in June, he flogged Chub for bringing in no fish. Exasperated, Chub and his fellow fisherman, Cyrus, ran away for a week. The result was predictable: Chub was flogged, put in stocks, and sent back to the fields. There he stayed, increasingly prone to sickness, until he died in 1775.[43]

We do not know much more about Chub than we know about Johnnie. His personal life and his relations with other slaves are almost completely unknown. We do know that he was sexually active in his mid-teens, but with whom is unclear. Certainly he never established a long-term relationship with any woman and did not have any children. Thistlewood "made a match between Chub and Sally" on 7 July 1768, when Chub was sixteen or seventeen and Sally was fifteen or sixteen, but the matchmaking was unsuccessful.[44] As we shall see, Sally was a slave with many problems. Chub and Sally lived in a house with Abba and her three young children but moved out within a year. In 1769, Chub was housed with the twenty-four-year-old Pompey, with whom he alternated fishing duties, and from 1770, he lived with Cudjoe, a twenty-five-year-old Coromantee who had come to Jamaica in 1765. Pompey and Cudjoe both survived Thistlewood. Pompey, a Coromantee, was purchased in 1761, worked mostly as a goat herder, did not have a partner, and never had children. Thistlewood's will described Pompey, who was about forty-two at the time, as old, distempered, and suffering from elephantiasis. He was valued at just £5, suggesting that he was unlikely to live long. He was also a prodigious farter: "Pompey frequently lets such loud farts that we hear him plain & loud to my house & cookroom, between 130 and 140 yards from his hut."[45] Cudjoe worked in the fields until falling ill in June 1776. In 1787, he was described in Thistlewood's inventory as "ruptured" and was valued at £10. Sometime in 1773 or 1774, he joined up with Fanny, a Creole slave purchased from Thistlewood's neighbor, Samuel Say, with whom he had at least three children before Fanny's death in childbirth on 6 December 1782.[46]

Lincoln the Survivor

We know much more about our final male slave, Lincoln. He was a constant presence in Thistlewood's texts and in his life. Lincoln was the first slave Thistlewood bought, and he outlived his master. We even have a record of him after Thistlewood's death. He was described in a runaway notice in 1795 as an Ibo who had come "to the Island quite young." He was now stout and elderly (he would have been fifty-four or fifty-five) and was a fisherman in Savanna-la-Mar who claimed the right to "hire his own time."[47] Between 1756 and 1786, Lincoln was mentioned several times a week in Thistlewood's diaries. Indeed, the last entry in Thistlewood's diaries concerns Lincoln. On 14 November 1786, Thistlewood recorded that "Lincoln shot 9 teal. Sent Mr. Wilson a pr."[48] It was appropriate that Lincoln was the last slave mentioned since for over thirty years he and his master had been intimate, if unequal, companions. Their lives were inextricably linked. Thistlewood intruded constantly in Lincoln's life, and, as is evidenced by the numerous references he made to Lincoln in his diaries, Lincoln was no less frequent a presence in Thistlewood's life. Only Phibbah, Thistlewood's mistress, was more important to Thistlewood. Phibbah's relationship with Thistlewood, however, was complicated by their physical attraction to each other and was as much a meeting of minds and bodies between two partners as a relationship between a slave and a master. The relationship between Lincoln and Thistlewood, however, was mediated primarily by their respective status as slave and master. Their contestations confirm the statement made by Eugene Genovese in the opening of his magnus opum, *Roll, Jordan, Roll*, a quarter of a century ago: "Cruel, unjust, exploitative, oppressive, slavery bound two peoples together in bitter antagonism while creating an organic relationship so complex and ambivalent that neither could express the simplest human feelings without reference to one another."[49]

Stating that Lincoln was a very important person in Thistlewood's life implies that the slave and his master had an intense emotional attachment to each other. Some scholars insist that in the asymmetrical power relationship between a slave and a master, personal ties could not be anything but shallow and false. Orlando Patterson argues, "No authentic human relationship was possible where violence was the ultimate sanction. There could have been no trust, no genuine sympathy, and while a kind of love may sometimes have triumphed over the most perverse form of interaction, intimacy was usually calculating and sadomasochistic."[50] Patterson emphasizes more strongly than most contemporary scholars the destructive nature of slavery in Jamaica. He insists that slavery completely stripped slaves of their cultural heritage, brutalized them, and rendered ordinary life and normal relationships extremely difficult.[51] In the main, I agree with Patterson. Nevertheless, personal ties linking master and slave did exist. Rhys Isaac, for example, has examined the intense relationship between Landon Carter of Virginia and his manservant, Nassau. Nassau was Carter's constant attendant, almost an extension of his master's eyes, ears, and arms. He was also a drunkard, much to his master's despair. Carter tried to convince himself that he could cope without Nassau—in 1775 he confided to his diary, "I have been learning to do without [Nassau] though it has been but very badly yet I can bear it and will"—but the bonds between the two were too strong to be broken by anything but death.[52] Lincoln and his master were similarly tied to each other. As Douglas Hall notes about the two men, "one senses a mutual understanding which might even have touched upon affection."[53]

In one respect, we know more about Lincoln than we do about Thistlewood —we know a little about his appearance. Lincoln enters Thistlewood's diaries on 3 January 1756 when Thistlewood purchased him from Robert Mason at Hertford for £43. Lincoln was "an Ebo, about 16 years of age, measures 4ft 9 ⁷⁄₁₀ inches." Lincoln remained short into adulthood, being several inches shorter than fellow male slaves Dick, Syphox, and Cudjoe. On 22 July 1770, Thistlewood wrote that he was "about 5ft 2 ⁷⁄₁₀ inches high." He went on to describe him more fully: "[H]is teeth not filed, crabyaws on hands and feet, so tender footed; on each cheek, and each shoulder; some weals on his back."[54]

The relationship between master and slave was often tense. Thistlewood was frequently exasperated with Lincoln and called him a "rogue." On 5 December 1768, Thistlewood had an argument with Lincoln and demoted him from driver to field laborer, exclaiming that "he is Notoriously head-strong and Roguish." In 1770, Thistlewood knocked Lincoln down with a stick when Lincoln refused to trim some trees and lamented, "he is very deceitful, lazy and impudent." On 6 October 1786, less than two months before Thistlewood's death, Thistlewood remonstrated that Lincoln "is a great villain" after he "shot 3 times this morning, at large flocks and brought a pair of teal only."[55] Of course, such statements should be viewed with skepticism. Thistlewood's behavior toward Lincoln indicates that he did not generally view Lincoln as negatively as these outbursts suggest. He favored Lincoln over other slaves, always giving him a full bottle of rum at Christmas when most slaves were expected to share a bottle between several people.[56] He was the first slave Thistlewood thought of when distributing his old clothes and petty possessions.[57] More important, Thistlewood entrusted Lincoln with comparatively important tasks. He was usually the first person chosen to look for runaways. In 1770 and 1771, for example, Lincoln was sent out several times to search for Coobah, a persistent runaway. This task afforded him several days of leisure to wander the countryside. No doubt it was a task that was a welcome relief from his usual duties. Lincoln was also frequently chosen to take letters or goods from Thistlewood to other people. In 1757, when Thistlewood was pining for Phibbah after leaving Egypt to become an overseer at the Kendal estate, Lincoln was sent almost every week to Thistlewood's old estate to convey messages and gifts to his lover. On 26 August, for example, Thistlewood "Sent Lincoln with my horse to Egypt for Phibbah tomorrow, if she can come. He carried her some plantains, and Mrs. Cope some roses."[58]

Thistlewood's preferential treatment of Lincoln was partly due to the fact that he was his first slave. Even though Thistlewood was very experienced in dealing with slaves before he purchased Lincoln, it was in his dealings with Lincoln that he discovered what it meant to be a slave owner. In the first two months that he owned Lincoln, Thistlewood learned about the normal relationships between slave and master. Two days after his purchase, he "gave Lincoln a mat to sleep on and cut up ten yards of Brown Oznabrig to make him Cloaths." Within a month, he had taught Lincoln how to fish and hunt. By the end of January, Thistlewood was contemplating how to better communicate with his slave. He noted that his friend Thomas Emotson claimed, "If you can learn a New Negro to Count Twenty, he will learn to pronounce most English words very well." On the same day, Thistlewood proudly displayed Lincoln as his manservant when he went "to the Bay to exercise" in a muster of local militia. Owning a slave was a marker of status in Jamaica, placing Thistlewood above the common ranks of white servants. It is not unreasonable to assume that being able to show off his status as a slave owner made him feel kindly toward the slave who was the source of his good feelings about himself. Some of the reflected glory of slave ownership probably passed on to Lincoln, making him special to Thistlewood in ways that were impossible for slaves purchased later.[59]

Another reason why Thistlewood treated Lincoln differently from his other slaves was that Lincoln demonstrated an abundance of talents that Thistlewood considered useful. Lincoln was no fool. He quickly became an accomplished fisherman and hunter, and even though Thistlewood often became exasperated with Lincoln's perceived deficiencies as a hunter and fisherman, he never doubted his expertise in the field. Such expertise endeared Lincoln to his owner, who was himself an accomplished outdoorsman who enjoyed tramping about the morasses and swamps of southwestern Jamaica in search of wildlife. Lincoln frequently accompanied Thistlewood on such trips, during which the line separating master and slave became blurred. At these times, Lincoln was more companion than bondsman. Lincoln's skills with gun and rod were vital to both Thistlewood and his slaves. In 1780 and 1781, in the aftermath of devastating hurricanes, Lincoln's ability as a fisherman and hunter probably prevented some of Thistlewood's slaves from perishing from famine.[60]

Thistlewood also thought highly enough of Lincoln's talents to allow him, along with Phibbah, to choose where slaves' provision grounds would be located at Breadnut Island. Moreover, he used him at Breadnut as a driver. The driver was, in effect, the head slave. Nevertheless, Lincoln's behavior as driver occasionally exasperated Thistlewood and led him to send him back to the fields. On 5 December 1768, for example, Thistlewood "Broke Lincoln from his driverships and made him weed with the rest! he is Notoriously headstrong and Roguish."[61] The most significant indication that Thistlewood, despite his several exclamations to the contrary, was prepared to repose confidence in Lincoln came during Tackey's rebellion of 1760, when Thistlewood armed Lincoln and ordered him to keep very strict watch.[62] Thistlewood trusted Lincoln enough to believe that he would protect his master even in a slave rebellion. It is difficult to know whether Thistlewood's trust was misplaced. Lincoln's loyalty to Thistlewood was certainly conditional and was determined by his subordinate slave status. He had good reason to be wary of Thistlewood because he often suffered from Thistlewood's wrath. Lincoln was flogged much more frequently than either Johnnie or Chub, showing that intimacy with whites greatly increased the likelihood of punishment. Lincoln received his first flogging within two months of purchase and was branded on each cheek within two and a half years.[63] Floggings continued regularly thereafter.

The Problem with Fish

Most disagreements between slave and master concerned the amount of fish and game that Lincoln provided. Thistlewood wanted the majority of fish and game that Lincoln caught; Lincoln used his talents as a fisherman and hunter to make money for himself. The ambitions of both led to conflict. On occasion, Lincoln brought the desired amount of fish to his master.[64] But often Thistlewood complained that Lincoln brought "scarce . . . any fish" or only "enough for a cat."[65] On 7 May 1776, Thistlewood elaborated on his dissatisfaction with Lincoln's fishing practices: "About half past noon Lincoln came, but did not bring . . . of a bitt's worth of fish; which has been his practice a good while past, and when he perceived I would punish him, he threatened to make away with himself if I troubled him. However, gave him a good flogging and put him in the bilboes. He sells all the fish that he ought to bring me, cannot be kept fishing in my own morasses, or the rivers, but will go out to sea etc and does not come at all until past dinnertime; is extreme impudent."[66] Thistlewood considered Lincoln's fishing a way to help him lower the costs of feeding his slaves. Lincoln thought of his fishing as a means of advancing his economic self-interest.

As in South Carolina and other parts of the Caribbean, blacks monopolized the provision of fish to Jamaican fish markets.[67] It is possible that Africans with experience as fishermen in West Africa dominated this trade. Ibos from coastal Nigeria were especially skilled watermen.[68] Since Lincoln was an Ibo, he may have had some familiarity with watercraft. Certainly he was a skilled canoeist.

In any event, it is clear that he was actively engaged in selling fish at Savanna-la-Mar. He was thus a participant in the busy internal marketing system that was a vital part of the Jamaican economy. In 1760, Thistlewood gave him a ticket of leave "to go sell crabs." He regularly went to market to sell fish. In addition, he sold land turtles and "Indian grass," mostly on his own account. We can gain some idea of the process from an entry in 1781 when Thistlewood complained that a white man had bought "Many fine land Turtle from my Jimmy; Jimmy Confesses it, he was Lincoln's factor Neither does Lincoln deny it."[69]

Lincoln made money in two ways. First, he sold fish and game that he had caught, either directly or in partnership with others. Second, he diverted some of the proceeds for goods that Thistlewood had given him to sell into his own pocket. Thus, on 2 July 1768, Thistlewood made an account of the money he had received for selling "Indian grass" but noted, "Lincoln does not give a clean account of 7 bitts worth, which was sent more, and he pretends he could not sell, etc, etc, cannot trust him. However, told him he might have what he could get for it."[70] Thistlewood was rarely so forgiving. Usually he felt Lincoln was cheating him. Convinced, undoubtedly correctly, that Lincoln was working for himself rather than working for him, he "flogged Lincoln, for disobedience in not fishing for me as I ordered him." He suspected that Lincoln was working for himself again in 1779 when Egypt's new overseer, the Barbadian Mr. Whitehead, found "Lincoln . . . shooting pigeons, 3 days last week in Egypt morass." Lincoln had told the overseer after shooting six pigeons that Thistlewood "was going to have company" and that he had been sent out "to shoot me some." Interestingly, and disturbingly for any white person worried about whites' safety, he had shot the pigeons with "a soldier's musket, which he told them was John's gun [Thistlewood's son, Mulatto John]; but Waterford [an Egypt slave] says, is Mr. Wesley's Cuffies."[71]

Disputes over property caused conflict between the two men. In 1778, Thistlewood "Flogged Lincoln well, new marked him on the right shoulder low, and put him in the bilboes, as he scarce brought any fish, and threatened if I insisted on fish that he would run away and a great deal more impudence."[72] The vehemence of Lincoln's response suggests that he believed Thistlewood had overstepped his mark in refusing to acknowledge Lincoln's customary rights to the fruits of his own labor. Slaves grudgingly accepted slave owners' rights to resolve grievances and adjudicate disputes in the slave community and to punish slaves for running away, shirking work, or being impudent. But slave owners had to tread warily before interfering with what slaves considered their property rights. What slaves saw as rights slave owners tended to see as privileges.[73] My guess is that Lincoln saw access to fish as his right and did not accept Thistlewood's claims to all of the fish he caught.

"He Is a Great Villain"

A wise master recognized slaves' claims to property as long as these claims did not compromise his control or interfere with economic production. Recognition of slaves' right to own property and right to trade and barter contradicted many of the basic tenets of slavery, but it served the short-term goals of both master and slave, as was stressed in chapter 5. Slaves gained a degree of economic independence but became wary of outright rebellion.[74] Masters played a significant role in resolving slave grievances. Jamaican slaves were traders and entrepreneurs but had virtually no recourse when other slaves stole their property, except for slave owners' intervention.[75] Slaves stole constantly from one another, Lincoln offending as much as anyone. In the summer of 1770, "Vine and Nancy come with a complaint of Lincoln's stealing their fowls." Thistlewood investigated and was told by Hannibal of the Old Hope estate that "Lincoln had brought a hen to his house . . . dressed it and eat it, then went and fetched a pullet which he wanted to sell him; told him of Nancy's hog, which he wanted Bacchus to assist him to catch. He also spoke several threatening words etc." Thistlewood had Lincoln flogged. But punishing Lincoln was less an assertion of Thistlewood's power than an intervention into a dispute between property-owning slaves. Thistlewood was careful to hear the accusations against Lincoln in front of the slaves he had stolen from—Vine, Nanny, and Mr. Say's Nancy. Lincoln was not only flogged but also ordered to pay restitution to his victims.[76] On at least one occasion, Lincoln put his "threatening words" into action. In 1778, two months after Thistlewood had predicted a famine during a period of severe food shortages, Lincoln was caught stealing canes on a nearby property by a slave called Simon. Lincoln did not take kindly to being discovered "in this villainy" and "attempted to drown or choke Simon." He was quickly apprehended and given "a good flogging at once."[77]

Lincoln also stole in order to ingratiate himself with fellow slaves. Lincoln's first flogging, less than two months after his purchase by Thistlewood, came when Thistlewood discovered that he had gone "privately to my Case" to steal a bottle of rum, which he then "Mashed . . . in pieces." Upon inquiry, Lincoln revealed that a fellow slave, Dover, had set him up for the theft. It appears that Lincoln had agreed to steal Thistlewood's property in order to become friends with Dover. In the following two years, Lincoln suffered three more floggings for stealing in combination with other slaves. He gave Neptune plantains stolen from Thistlewood's battery, conspired with Oronogue "to shoot my ducks," and robbed a neighbor's corn field with Hector.[78] In 1773, Lincoln was flogged again for what Thistlewood perceived to be criminality. Lincoln caught a hog with Thistlewood's dogs and brought it home. After he discovered that the hog belonged to "old Hannibal," bearing a grudge against Hannibal for causing him to be flogged three years previously, he told the elderly slave that his hog had been confiscated and killed it.[79]

Thistlewood's diaries provide some hints about how Lincoln was viewed by his fellow slaves. He attained a measure of authority over other slaves, in part due to Thistlewood's preferential treatment of him and in part due to his long residence in Jamaica. By the time of Thistlewood's death, Lincoln, now forty-seven, had been a slave longer than any slave in Thistlewood's establishment, save Phibbah. He had approached Thistlewood several times on behalf of other slaves when they needed help. In 1771, Cudjoe fell into the fire after suffering a fit. Lincoln fetched Thistlewood to assist Cudjoe. Thistlewood had Cudjoe "brought into the cookroom, senseless, the Negroes thick about him." Thistlewood's discussion of the event gives a good indication of the ways in which slaves used their masters' authority and their solidarity against informing on fellow slaves. Although Thistlewood tended to Cudjoe by applying "spirits of hart shorn," he suspected that Cudjoe was suffering from a more everyday and easily diagnosable problem common in both the white and black populations—he was drunk. But every slave Thistlewood asked "denied" that Cudjoe had been drinking, except for Egypt Harry, who "told me the truth." Harry's betrayal of a fellow slave made him unpopular—for telling the truth, Thistlewood said, "they hate him." Cudjoe had gone on a bender after selling grass at Savanna-la-Mar and buying rum from the proceeds. He "drank a good deal by itself, then more in hot punch etc, till it overcame him." Only then did Thistlewood's slaves take action, "call[ing] me, and join[ing] to impose upon me."[80]

Lincoln protected Cudjoe on this occasion. He may have hoped to have been similarly protected when he did wrong. Lincoln seems to have relied on this expectation of mutual protection when another slave accused him of taking justice into his own hands. In 1770, Coobah ran away yet again, and Lincoln was sent after her. He found out that she was being held in the stocks at a nearby estate. One of that estate's slaves was ordered to bring her home. The slave, however, was deceived by Coobah, who pretended to faint and thus was able to make her getaway. Thistlewood placed some of the blame on Lincoln, who "neglected to inquire for her there, or I might have had her immediately." Presumably he conveyed as much to Lincoln, who therefore had reason to be displeased with Coobah. Lincoln found Coobah two days later and brought her home. The next day, Coobah was flogged and sent into the fields, where she once again pretended to faint. She accused Lincoln of "beat[ing] her on her breast in the field." Whether Lincoln (a man who was violent on other occasions) did or did not beat Coobah is impossible to tell. What is important is that his fellow slaves were unwilling to snitch on him and that Thistlewood preferred to believe Lincoln rather than the difficult Coobah. When Thistlewood asked his slaves whether Lincoln beat Coobah, "all the rest of the Negroes say not."[81] This betokens a measure of respect for Lincoln by his fellow slaves.

"An Amorous Man of Many Attachments"

Thistlewood also provides us with abundant information about Lincoln's love life and how he formed a family. Lincoln was a man with many attachments. He was sexually active within two and a half years of his purchase and soon suffered the usual consequences of sexual activity in eighteenth-century Jamaica. On 14 April 1757 and 12 June 1759, Thistlewood noted, "My Lincoln has got the clap." By April 1757, he was the partner of Egypt Susannah, who was also a favorite of Thistlewood's. Lincoln then opportunistically began a relationship with Gordon's Polly at Kendal. He had a tendency to attach himself to other men's women. In January 1760, Thistlewood "Flogged Lincoln and Violet for Crim[inal] Con[versation] [i.e., adultery] to recompense Job," who, presumably, was Violet's former partner. But Lincoln stayed with Violet and, by 23 January 1760, had "made a match" with her. The relationship was not a happy one. Lincoln physically attacked Violet several times and took up with other women. At the end of 1760, Lincoln contracted his third dose of venereal disease, which he blamed on a liaison with Little Doll. By this time, Lincoln and Violet had parted company.[82]

Lincoln was not alone for long. He quickly took up with the fourteen-year-old Sukey (Lincoln was twenty-two) in December 1761. Sukey became Lincoln's principal wife. She still lived with Lincoln when Thistlewood's estate was appraised in 1787. The couple never had children. Their "marriage" appears to have been relatively happy. When Lincoln was ill in late June and early July 1785, Thistlewood reported that Sukey "attended" him constantly, indicating a degree of affection between the couple.[83] On 2 March 1782, Thistlewood noted that Sukey "fell in one of her fits" after being punished along with Lincoln for stealing a box and harboring a runaway. Lincoln was so upset that "When she was in the fit, [he] told Jimmy Stewart, that if she did not recover he would cut his own throat." Thistlewood noted only two major conflicts between the couple. The first dispute, however, puts Lincoln in a particularly bad light. At eight o'clock on the morning of 5 February 1767, "Franke ran from the Pen, and gave an account that Sukey was very bad, Lincoln having beat her terribly." Thistlewood, still at Egypt, rode to see what had happened and found Sukey "speechless." Lincoln had run away. Thistlewood attended to Sukey's injuries, which were severe. Meanwhile, Lincoln had persuaded a friend of Thistlewood's to write a note on his behalf. Thistlewood was unimpressed: he "seized [Lincoln], had him to Egypt, flogged and pickled him well, then put him in the bilboes."[84] If Thistlewood was unimpressed with Lincoln, Lincoln might have been equally angry with his master. Thistlewood had usurped Lincoln's patriarchal rights by interfering with his punishment of his wife. A slave's domestic affairs were never immune from a master's watchful eye.[85]

Thistlewood seldom interfered in the domestic affairs of his slaves. He was not concerned about "a great outcry at the Negro house" in 1782 when Lincoln "catched the Retrieve Shamboy in bed with his wife Sukey."[86] Nor did he involve himself in a disagreement between Lincoln and Monday over Monday's wife, Maria, as related in chapter 5. Lincoln suffered a severe beating from the slave he had attempted to cuckold. But Thistlewood's power to intervene in interslave disputes was important and undermined male slaves' patriarchal authority. When Lincoln and Abba (who were sexual partners since the early 1770s and living in the same household since 1777) "got to fighting in the cookroom and hurt Phib[bah]'s arm in endeavoring to part them," Thistlewood quickly dealt with the matter. He blamed Lincoln for the affray and put him "in the bilboes for a while."[87]

Slave owners assumed that slave men should be dominant over slave women. They placed men rather than women in positions of responsibility and taught them useful skills. On the rare occasions when they acknowledged family relationships, they placed men at the head of households. Lincoln was the head of a household that included his first wife, Sukey; his additional partner, Abba; and Abba's five surviving children, three of whom were Lincoln's. Lincoln was able to transfer African notions of family and kinship, especially polygyny, into Thistlewood's slave community.[88] Early in the 1770s, Lincoln took up with Abba. Abba and her five children and grandchild were living with Sukey and Lincoln at the time of Thistlewood's death. He also kept a third woman, Clarissa, who lived on the neighboring Prospect estate. He had a son, Davie, with

Clarissa in September 1777. Clarissa died on 9 January 1778, and Davie died on 19 December 1778. By 1783, Lincoln had another third wife, this one living on the neighboring Three Mile River estate. Thistlewood recorded that he "flogged Lincoln about his 3 Mile River wife" on 13 September 1783. Lincoln had thus established himself as a patriarchal head of household within an African pattern of polygynous marriages.

Yet Lincoln was not an unconstrained African patriarch. African male patriarchal authority was diluted in New World slavery. As Michael Mullin has argued, slave women in Jamaica had more independence and power in domestic arrangements than women in Africa.[89] It was not so much that slave women were powerful as that slave men were powerless. The peculiar conditions of slavery rendered black men's attempts to control the sexuality of black women problematic. Women often insisted on their ability to play the field, believed they had a right to stop men from philandering, and were willing to break out of traditional African gender arrangements.[90] Male slaves attempted to place limits on these newfound female freedoms. Masters were convinced that supporting male authority was the way to prevent social discord in the slave quarters. They made men heads of households and accepted that slave men had rights over their wives and children. Yet slave patriarchy was a tender fruit, always likely to be stamped out by masters' assertions of authority. In any battle between the authority of slave men and the authority of masters, masters invariably won. Lincoln's authority over his wives and children was thus always precarious, mainly because Thistlewood undermined Lincoln's control over his womenfolk by insisting on having sexual relations with Sukey and Abba. Between 1770 and 1776, Thistlewood had sex with Sukey 26 times, paying her 2 bits on each occasion, and had sex with Abba 155 times, also usually paying her 2 bits for each encounter.

An Intimate Relationship

Lincoln emerges from Thistlewood's diaries as someone with a full range of human characteristics. At times, he was trustworthy, at other times, not. He was a talented hunter and fisherman who did not always do as he was told. He was a lover with a wandering eye and a tendency for domestic abuse. He was also a respected long-term resident of the slave community who on occasion violated other slaves' respect and trust through unwise actions and small betrayals. He was a trusted confidant of his master who often roused his owner's violent rage.

Much remains unknown, of course. We do not know enough about him to assess the psychological effects on his personality of capture and enslavement in Africa, the Middle Passage, or the brutal treatment often extended to him. But he did not let the everyday humiliations of slave life diminish him or reduce him to abject dependence. Mutuality, rather than dependence, is ever-present in his relations with his master. Thistlewood's diaries, moreover, do not suggest that Lincoln was especially deferential to his owner. Lincoln was no Quashie or Sambo, even if he was no rebel either.[91]

Lincoln was a survivor, if not a very heroic one, who scraped together the lineaments of a fulfilling life from the unpromising conditions of plantation life in eighteenth-century Jamaica. He continually negotiated with Thistlewood about the conditions of slavery. In May 1771, for example, he returned late from an excursion with "a note from mr. Hughes begging I would forgive him, he having been at the Prospect Estate to see his wife, and overslept himself." Thistlewood and Lincoln agreed that a suitable recompense would be for Lincoln to bring Thistlewood "24 crabs to pay for the loss of yesterday forenoon, which he promised to do but never troubled himself to perform." Thistlewood retaliated by confiscating Lincoln's greatcoat. He "sold it (before his face), to Egypt Daniel, for 26 lbs, to mortify him." Lincoln was so enraged that he ran off to Savanna-la-Mar, from whence he was brought back by Jimmy and Solon, secured in the bilboes, and flogged.[92] The relationship here was not between benevolent paternalist and a slave outside of civil society but between two men within the same patriarchal social order, albeit in different positions within that order. In this case, as in most cases, Lincoln lost. But he never stopped trying to assert himself. Thistlewood rationalized his indifference to slaves' rights by conceptualizing them as people without rights by virtue of their African heritage, but he never saw them as essentially different in personality and ability from himself. Lincoln was disobedient and "rogueish," but he was still distinctively a man, "a luckless unfortunate barbarian" rather than a child "expected never to grow up," as Willie Lee Rose put it in summarizing changes in how slaves were treated over time.[93] The reality of Lincoln's existence tempered Thistlewood's theoretical appreciation of African abilities. Lincoln's continual contests with Thistlewood forced Thistlewood to grant him a degree of legitimacy that compromised Thistlewood's sense of absolute sovereignty, even though he was usually able to assert his will over his slave. The point is, however, that Lincoln never accepted that he was solely the instrument of his master but acted as if he had a mind of his own and a destiny that he could influence.

Lincoln's humanity marks him out. He was African and retained African habits. In 1771, "Lincoln was at a play, at the burial of a Negro at the Retrieve all Sunday night." Similarly, two years later, Thistlewood notes that he found "Mrs. North's George playing upon the Banjo to Lincoln." This time, Thistlewood was less tolerant than when Lincoln was "at a play," perhaps because he associated banjo playing with drumming and obeah. Thistlewood noted, "I chopped all up in pieces with my cutlass, and reprimanded them."[94] Yet although he retained African customs, he also adapted to European mores. He learned to use European technology, such as guns; participated in the market economy; and adopted English as a language. Culturally, he moved between two worlds. The same was true of his life as a slave—he had to assimilate himself to Thistlewood's opinions and moods, but he maintained his own autonomy as much as he could. His life was one of continual negotiation, in which he battled to acquire advantages through his intimacy with his master. He also sought to minimize the dangers that intimacy brought to slaves trying to establish themselves within negotiated relationships that were profoundly asymmetrical in favor of masters.

Lincoln was marked not only by his humanity but also by his position as the slave closest to his master. That closeness, or intimacy, brought advantages and disadvantages that Johnnie and Chub did not have to contemplate, given their distance from the person and thoughts of their master. Closeness cohabitated with conflict. As Genovese argues in relation to privileged slaves in antebellum America, "If closeness bred affection and warmth it also bred hatred and violence; often it bred all at once, according to circumstances, moods and passions."[95] For slaves, closeness to masters was both a matter of ambivalence and a symptom of the contradictions rooted in slavery. It was only through intimate contact with their masters that slaves were able to carve out a measure of independence that allowed for economic and cultural advancement. Lincoln used his close contact with Thistlewood to establish himself as an African patriarch and an economically autonomous individual. Lincoln was successful enough in gaining his independence that by the time of Thistlewood's death, he was master of his own household and controlled to some extent the conditions under which he worked. Within a decade of Thistlewood's death, he had formalized those arrangements and, while remaining a slave, was quasi-autonomous in the sense that he could hire himself out for pecuniary gain.

Nevertheless, Lincoln's intimacy with his master came at a personal cost. He did not adopt the Quashie persona whereby his personality was usurped by the cultural power of the master. But he was not unaffected by his constant interactions with Thistlewood. His closeness to Thistlewood meant that he bore the brunt of Thistlewood's displeasure. His frequent floggings are evidence of how often he annoyed his master. The continual negotiations he embarked upon with his master in order to achieve some space for his own ambitions were often tense, resulting in Thistlewood ruminating on the deficiencies of Lincoln's personality, as he saw them. Their thirty-one-year enforced intimacy tied them together in a web of mutual dependence that was unsatisfactory for both but vital in shaping their respective identities. In Lincoln and Thistlewood's constantly renegotiated battle over how much a slave had to submit to a master's will and how much a master had to recognize his dependency on his supposed inferior, we see a real-life model of Hegel's dialectic of dependence and independence, of losing and finding one's identity in the consciousness of another person. Thistlewood as master saw himself as an omnipotent lord—consciousness in action, in Hegelian parlance—but that omnipotence was limited by his need to have his omnipotence recognized by the slavish Lincoln, who was not the Aristotelian slave who was the extension of his master's will. By his actions, Lincoln showed that he did not recognize that the master alone had autonomous consciousness. The slave had it as well, if only to ensure self-preservation. In discovering, as Hegel argues, that he had a "mind" of his own, Lincoln denied that his master could indeed use him solely as his tool or instrument. In their continual battles and negotiations, Lincoln and Thistlewood demonstrated the futility and absurdity of masters' assertions of total power and showed that the endless process of cooperation and contestation that slaves and masters engaged in compromised masters' ideology of enslavement.[9]

chapter seven

Adaptation, Accommodation, and Resistance

Thistlewood's Slave Women and Their Responses to Enslavement

I have frequently seen our female domestic[s] . . . , when sent to the stocks, make a very low curtsey, and with the most ironical smile of insolence say, "Thank you massa, much obliged to you for let me sit down softly." The stocks are a wooden bed; at the foot of it is a board with circular holes, which open to admit the feet. The feet are fastened and padlocked. . . . I regret to say it, that female negroes are far more unmanageable than males. The little girls are far more wicked than the boys and I am convinced that were every proprietor to produce the list of his good negroes, there would be, in every instance, an amazing majority in favour of males.—Mrs. A. C. Carmichael, *Domestic Manners and Social Conditions of the White, Coloured, and Negro Populations of the West Indies*

Saturday 1 October 1768: Phibbah's Coobah marked on Silvia's smock bosom, D T S J H, for Dago, her husband; Mr. Meyler's Tom, her sweetheart; and John Hart[nole], who she is supposed to love best; and other ornaments [a sketch follows]:

D T S J H

(all that heart loves best)

[a flourish]

Here's meat for money

If you're fit I'm ready

But take care you don't flash in the pan.

—Thistlewood's diary, 1 October 1768

Women and Resistance

All of Thistlewood's slaves were, to some extent, psychologically damaged by their experiences as slaves. Their community, to the extent that it existed, was one marked by personal devastation and social trauma. Thistlewood's slaves were trapped in a dehumanizing life of exhausting labor, debilitating disease, and demeaning social relationships; they were constantly tired, frequently frightened, and subject to continual flux in their living and work arrangements. Thistlewood deliberately fostered these conditions. His carefully controlled but deliberate savagery toward his slaves destabilized slave communities and allowed him to act as a vengeful facilitator who intervened powerfully, violently, and usually successfully in slaves' domestic and personal lives, bolstering his authority in a world where custom was attenuated, the law was of no avail, and a master's power was close to absolute.[1]

Thistlewood's female slaves faced especially difficult problems, partly because of the nature of female slaves' experiences but mostly because Thistlewood paid them special attention and made their lives particularly difficult. Slave women were workers, mothers, and sexual partners. Thistlewood interfered in all three areas and accentuated their trauma. Male slaves could avoid Thistlewood by working in the fields and keeping well away from their master. Women did not have that option. The big difference between slave women and slave men was that women were both producers and reproducers. Thistlewood wanted them to work and make him money. He also wanted them to increase his wealth through the production of children. In addition, he was drawn to slave women for sexual gratification. As we have seen, Thistlewood's relentless sexual opportunism meant that only very young and very old women were safe from him. Slave women consequently did not have the option of distance—they were intimate with Thistlewood whether they wanted to be or not.

How, then, did Thistlewood's women cope with their master's continual involvement in their work, family, and reproductive lives? How did they balance the demands of their master with their own desires? How did they resist becoming mere extensions of their master? How did they escape the most debilitating aspects of slavery in a society where black women were discriminated against on account of both race and gender? It is unlikely that we will ever be able to get beyond the tyranny of the sources—produced invariably by white males—to explore what slave women actually thought and to understand what the experience of slavery meant to them. Thistlewood's diaries tell us most about Thistlewood, and it is pointless to try to use them to examine too deeply the lives of his slaves. Nevertheless, as in our examination of the experiences of his male slaves, Thistlewood's diaries are sufficiently rich and detailed to enable us to explore the individual circumstances of a few of his female slaves. I focus in this chapter on the lives of four slave women whose experiences show us to some extent the problems slave women faced and how they overcame them, bearing in mind that not all slaves were able to surmount the obstacles they faced. Their interactions with Thistlewood, as he has related them to us, suggest two conclusions about female slaves' experience. First, there was little middle ground in female slaves' lives. Slave women were either especially oppressed or comparatively privileged. For most slave women, their daily work was debilitating and unsatisfying; their family life was fraught and unstable; and their contact with whites was miserable and confined mostly to punishment or sexual exploitation. As one white doctor condescendingly put it, the slave woman's life was "upheld by no consolation, animated by no hope." Her children were "doomed like herself to the rigors of eternal servitude."[2] For the mass of black women, therefore, slavery was an intensely depressing and frightening existence. A few slave women, however, were able to transcend the horrors of slavery through their skillful manipulation of privileges gained as a result of close involvement with whites. These women enjoyed the best work conditions within slavery and were the most likely to secure freedom for themselves. Second, each of the four women studied resisted slavery to some extent or at least resisted the dehumanization implicit in enslavement. Their resistance took several different forms. Direct, outright resistance was singularly unsuccessful, as can be seen in the unfortunate lives of Coobah, the closest of Thistlewood's slaves to a rebel, and Sally, a slave whose unhappy experiences led her to give up hope and passively accept whatever her master did to her. Abba was also at times a pathetic creature traumatized by slavery. Yet she responded to her mistreatment differently from Sally, coping to some extent with what she was forced to endure. She had to cope. She was the mother of seven children and had to ensure that those children were fed and nurtured. She was forced to accommodate herself to enslavement and to her master's demands. Accommodation, however, could easily turn into collaboration, as can be seen in the life of Phibbah, Thistlewood's long-term mistress and the most remarkable person mentioned in Thistlewood's diaries. She not only survived slavery but also transcended it. In part, she did so through associating with Thistlewood—literally by sleeping with the enemy. But she also transcended slavery through her determined efforts to carve out a place for herself and her family that resembled freedom rather than the nominal enslavement that was her formal status.

Viewing a collaborator through the prism of slave resistance raises some important historiographical questions. The current historiography of slavery persists in viewing slaves either as victims of oppression or as determined rebels whose "every willed response . . . could be interpreted as resistance." But as the author of this statement adds, "such responses can also be interpreted as adaptation."[3] Moreover, we may know that slaves performed acts that intentionally and systematically hampered the plantation system on a day-to-day basis, but it is difficult to distinguish between acts that were active examples of nonacceptance of the slave system and acts that signified individual failings or criminality. If everything that did not directly aid planter oppression of slaves can be seen as resistance, then, as Michel-Ralph Trouillot laments, it is hard to know whether resistance "stands for an empirical generalization, an analytical category, or a vague yet fashionable label for unrelated situations."[4]

One way in which we can transcend the conceptual difficulties inherent in examining resistance is to distinguish between strategies of resistance and tactics of opposition. Michel de Certeau has theorized the differences between the two. He argues that resistance is only possible when the dominated group or dominated individuals act outside of the system of domination that encloses them. Resistance requires an "elsewhere" from which the system may be perceived. But slaves' struggle against domination occurred in everyday life, including the domain of permissible activities. These everyday practices of resistance interrupted and defined the constraints of life under slavery and exploited openings in the system for the benefit of slaves. They took place, however, by necessity *within* the system, on ground defined by the controllers of slavery, and were undertaken without any hope of ultimate success. The tactics of slaves in everyday practice involved exploiting "the gaps which the particular combination of circumstances open in the control of the proprietary power," but the small victories that resulted from these internal manipulations of the established order were ephemeral since slaves had no space in which they could maintain what they believed they had won. Theorizing everyday practices that disrupted slavery as "opposition" rather than resistance allows us to acknowledge the strength of masters' domination and recognize that it was nearly impossible for slaves hoping to survive under slavery to break down that dominance. Forms of power determine the practices that are possible within a given field of action.[5] In mid-eighteenth-century Jamaica, the vast asymmetry of power, especially physical power, that existed between slaves and masters and the regular exercise of violent power on slaves who transgressed made slave agency very difficult. As Michel Foucault contends, "There cannot be relations of power [as opposed to domination] unless subjects are free. If one were completely at the disposition of the other and became his thing, an object on which he can exercise an infinite and unlimited violence, there would not be relations of power. In order to exercise a relation of power, there must be on both sides at least a certain form of liberty."[6] Of course, the power of the master was not complete and the liberty of the slave was not totally circumscribed. But the dominance of the powerful was sufficiently strong, except at moments of extreme rupture, such as Tackey's rebellion, that the weapons slaves used against their masters were the tools and tactics of people excluded from the locus of the "political proper."[7]

Gender also complicates our understanding of slave resistance because the features of women's lives as slaves were appreciably different from those of men. As Arlene Gautier insists, the appropriation of slave women's sexuality "redoubled women's exploitation as workers," whereas male slaves could at least take some comfort in "the fantasies of their sexual powers."[8] Men more often than women undertook violent resistance to masters. Female slaves, however, tended to focus on resistance that ate away at the efficiency of the slave system. Possibly, women were even in the vanguard of cultural resistance. Barbara Bush has interpreted women's behavior, especially in family and sexual relations, "as part of a wider pattern of resistance informed by African cultural practices." Black women were intransigent workers, were persistent runaways, and practiced methods of family limitation that frustrated planters' attempts to naturally increase the slave population.[9] Robert Dirks argues that women were the "organs of discontent" on slave plantations because they were less likely to be flogged than men, soon becoming the "more unmanageable element of the work force."[10] Women were in the vanguard of cultural resistance because they were more closely connected than men to whites. The female-centered nature of the slave system, concerned with maternity, fertility, and sexuality, made slave women more intimate than slave men with owners.[11]

The House and the Fields

Contemporaries were well aware that slave women's experiences were very different from those of slave men. Thistlewood's wealthy planter neighbor, William Beckford, explained it carefully in 1788: "A negro man is purchased for a trade, or the cultivation and different processes of the cane—the occupations of the women are only two, the house, with its several departments and supposed indulgences, or the fields with their exaggerated labors. The first situation is the most honourable, the last the most independent."[12] Women, on the surface, had a more limited range of work possibilities than men. This narrow range, moreover, was highly polarized. Female slaves were either house slaves —the most privileged of all slaves (although, as we shall see, these privileges came with considerable costs) who had the most intimate relationships with white men and white women—or field slaves. The few slaves who attained positions of responsibility within the household were the most likely of all slaves to have lives of relative ease, acquire substantial amounts of property, and gain freedom, either for themselves or for their children. The mass of female slaves in Jamaica, however, enjoyed none of these advantages. Most female slaves worked as field laborers on sugar plantations.[13] Black women were valued mainly for their labor and were more likely than men to be engaged in the tedious and backbreaking work of planting sugar. The majority of slave women, therefore, were victims of an especially brutal and exploitive labor system.[14] Perhaps the only compensation available to women suffering such strenuous and hazardous labor was that they may have been able to retain more cultural autonomy than was possible among slaves more intimately connected to slave owners. Elsa Goveia has intriguingly suggested in her masterful survey of slavery in the British Leeward Islands at the end of the eighteenth century that masters thought so little of field slaves that they made no attempt to divert them from what they considered to be inferior African habits and practices.[15]

Yet Beckford's description of the differences between men and women in slavery is incomplete. Beckford concentrates only on the productive roles of slaves. What really differentiated female slaves from their male counterparts was their dual role as producers and reproducers. A female slave could contribute in two ways to a slave owner's prosperity: she could produce profits from her bodily labor, and she could add to her owner's wealth by producing additional laborers in the form of children, although children took a long time to recoup their rearing costs. By rights, female slaves should have been valued more highly by slave owners than male slaves given the two ways women contributed to their quest for economic advancement. In West Africa, as Philip Curtin has detailed for Senegambia, women were indeed sold at higher prices than men, primarily because women were more easily absorbed into West African patriarchal systems but also because women provided their owners with additional sexual and reproductive benefits.[16] In Jamaica, however, planters did not value women as highly as men, except possibly in urban areas and there only occasionally. A sample of 13,008 adult male slaves and 8,511 female slaves in 1,954 inventories made in the second and third quarters of the eighteenth

Thistlewood would have lived in a house similar to this at Breadnut Island. Unlike this scene, slaves would have been conspicuous by their presence. Detail from map by Thomas Craskell and James Simpson, *Map of the County of Cornwall, in the Island of Jamaica* (London, 1763).

century indicates that the average man was valued 18.2 percent higher than the average woman.[17] One possible reason for the disparity in slave prices is that the reproductive value of women slaves was more problematic in Jamaica than in West Africa. Planters preferred to buy rather than breed, as polemicists fearing cultural and physical disaster from the continual infusion of fresh Africans into the country lamented.[18] Slave infant mortality remained extremely high through-out the eighteenth century.[19] Thus, slave owners were unlikely to gain signifi-cant increments of labor by encouraging women to give birth. Moreover, child-birth accentuated problems of morbidity. Data is sketchy, but it seems clear that women's sicknesses were very often gynecological in origin.[20] Even if a preg-nancy proceeded normally and resulted in a healthy child, planters were still loath to lose women as productive workers in order to gain advantages from their reproductive potentialities. Jamaican planters were notoriously indifferent to the needs of pregnant women, flogging them even when they were in advanced stages of pregnancy and making them work at strenuous field labor both imme-diately before and soon after childbirth.[21] Thistlewood compounded pregnant women's difficulties by having sex with them when they were in later stages of pregnancy.[22]

It would be a mistake, however, to assume that the conditions of reproduction were determined only by slave owners' wishes. Reproduction caused women problems, but it also offered possibilities. Slave women tried to control their reproduction either through abortion and infanticide or through long lactation.[23] Women actively resisted slave owners' attempts to interfere in childbirth and deliberately limited their fertility in a variety of ways. They objected to working when heavily pregnant and even more to attempts to separate them from their children before they were willing to wean them.[24] Women attempted to control their reproduction while gaining as many advantages as possible from their reproductive capacities when they did reproduce.

As in their work lives, the family lives of women had a more divided character than those of men. Motherhood allowed them niches and gaps within slavery that they could exploit to their own advantage. Planters conceived of slave family relationships entirely in terms of women and children. They virtually never noted the fathers of slave children in inventories, for example, but frequently connected slave women to slave children, as in "Benneba and her child Silvia," and sometimes described slave children as "belonging" to slave women, as in "Hagar's Cuba." Women played on this conception of family to assume a dominant role in child rearing and adopted positions of influence and autonomy in the family. Nevertheless, slave mothers suffered continual frustration at being forced to combine parenthood with field labor. It was difficult for them to celebrate motherhood when they had to endure what must have seemed like an almost inevitable series of heartaches over dying infants and children sold away from them. Bush argues that the insuperable difficulties of pregnancy, childbirth, and motherhood may have caused considerable numbers of slave women to develop amenorrhoea—an incapacity to bear children caused by severe psychological trauma.[25]

Another difficulty slave women faced was the constant threat of sexual exploitation. Some male slaves were sexually assaulted by male owners—Thistlewood notes two instances of this ("Report of Mr. Watt Committing Sodomy with his Negroe waiting Boy" and "strange reports about the parson and John his man")—and others were tormented by amorous female owners—Thistlewood reported one rumor of a white woman who was reputed to be "making free" with male slaves—but the incidence of such sexual exploitation was undoubtedly low compared to the almost continual sexual molestation of slave women.[26] Even a cursory reading of Thistlewood's diaries alerts one to the enormous frequency of sexual exploitation of women on the estates that Thistlewood controlled. Women's continual vulnerability to sexual assault may have exacerbated the psychological trauma inherent in slavery. Some women slaves, such as Sally, whom we shall come to shortly, became so traumatized and demoralized by the manifold injuries they suffered under slavery that they essentially gave up or refused to continue surviving. Not all slaves were like Lincoln, determined to survive whatever slave owners threw at them. But some women used their sexual exploitation to gain advantages for themselves. Interracial relations gave some black women an entrée into the white world and some space for themselves within the all-encompassing structures of white male dominance.[27]

The Slave Rebel

Some slaves found it impossible to accept white male dominance in any form. Thistlewood faced dissent and insubordination from one slave in particular— Coobah. Coobah was a rebel who refused to accept the strictures of slavery. She was what white Jamaicans in the eighteenth century called "an incorrigible runaway." Thistlewood bought her on 7 December 1761, at which time he described her as "4 ft 6⁶⁄₁₀ ins. Tall, about 15 yrs. Old, Country name Molia, an Ebo." He assigned her quarters with Egypt Princess and, the following week, sent her, with five other new slaves, to work in the fields. He initiated her in another way nine months later when he had sex with her, noting in his diary, "Stans! Backwd: gave her a bitt."[28] By 17 August 1765, she had suffered her first bout of venereal disease. She had already had yaws in 1762 and had spent much of the first few months of 1764 ill in the hothouse. On 12 November 1766, at about twenty years of age, she had a child with her husband, a free black man, but the child did not survive long, dying at fifteen months old on 16 March 1767. Whether the death of her child triggered something in Coobah is impossible to tell, but she increasingly became unmanageable. She first ran away in August 1765, a five-day absence that resulted in her being flogged and having a collar and chain put around her neck. She did not run away again until 20 March 1769, but from 1769 onward, she ran away at every opportunity when she was not sick (as she was throughout most of 1772). In 1770, she ran away eight times, and in 1771 she escaped five times. Coobah's persistent running away resulted in increasingly harsh punishments. By 1770, she was receiving severe floggings and was being kept in the stocks overnight. She was branded on the forehead and forced to wear a collar and chain for months at a time.

In addition to running away, Coobah indulged in what both Thistlewood and his slaves considered antisocial behavior, such as stealing food from white neighbors of Thistlewood and fellow slaves. She also had arguments with other slaves when working in the fields about the amount of work she was expected to do.

By this time, she had become openly rebellious to Thistlewood, refusing to accept his authority in any matter. The nadir was reached on 4 October 1770, when Thistlewood reported: "[A] punch strainer hanging up against the buttery, Coobah sleeping in the cookroom, last night took the strainer and shit in it, wrapping it up and covering it with a piece of board, this breakfast time had it rubbed all over her face and mouth, but she minds not." Her rebelliousness made her a liability. Thistlewood had to divert slaves from the fields to go look for her on the frequent occasions she was away, and it often took these slaves three or four days to find her. He also could not employ Coobah as he wished. He was not able to send her, for example, to work on neighboring estates because "she is so troublesome in running away, &c," thus depriving him of one of his most profitable sources of income.[29]

What provoked Coobah's intransigence is, of course, unknown, but it did result in Coobah being parted from her master. Thistlewood resolved to get rid of Coobah, which he eventually did on 18 May 1774, when he sold her for £40 and had her transported to Georgia. Coobah succeeded in ridding herself of her owner and managed to escape the harsh sugar regime of Jamaica for the relatively more benign one of Georgia, but at considerable cost. She left for Georgia with the marks of her insubordination on her body: pocked by smallpox, debilitated by repeated bouts of venereal disease, lacerated by numerous floggings, and branded on her forehead as a troublemaker. Thistlewood was not sorry to see her go. She had produced no money for him as a field hand, had borne no children who could augment his fortune, and had caused him grief. Coobah achieved her aims insofar as she made it impossible for Thistlewood to control her. Nevertheless, her rebellion was opposition rather than resistance. It operated only within the system of slavery and never really threatened the continuation of the system itself. It thus must be accorded a failure since slave resistance, especially individual slave resistance, was never successful.

The Demoralized Slave

Sally was also a troublemaker, but her case is different from Coobah's. Sally did not so much resist enslavement as become completely overwhelmed by the life she found herself in. Sally was so traumatized by slavery that she gave up. In the 1780s, when she was in her early thirties and had spent over twenty years as a slave, she reverted to infantile behavior as a response to her condition. Originally from the Congo, she was purchased by Thistlewood on 1 April 1762 from the Savanna-la-Mar attorney Jeremiah Meyler when she was nine or ten years old and four feet one inch tall. Thistlewood "named her Sally and intend[ed] her for a seamstress." On 2 May, Thistlewood sent her to Hannah Blake "to learn to be a seamstress, I am to feed her, She is to work for doll whilst learning, and I am to give Doll a doubloon when learnt." The experiment was not a success, although Thistlewood persevered for three years before recognizing that "she will by no means learn to be a Seamstress."[30] Her initiation as a field hand was no more successful. Within a month of returning from Thomas Emotson's, where she had been working as a poor seamstress for four months between May and August 1766, she got a bad case of yaws. Within six months, she had run away to Savanna-la-Mar. Thistlewood had her "flogged . . . [and] marked . . . on the shoulder and sent . . . to work at the Penn," but such harsh treatment did not deter her. She ran away again the next month and the month after that.[31] A pattern had been established that was not to change for the rest of the time Thistlewood owned her. Every year, she ran away two or three times for a couple of days at a time and then was either returned by another slave or came back of her own accord. She does not appear to have intended to run away permanently since she was usually easily recovered (in this respect, the differences between her and the more clearly rebellious Coobah are obvious). She often ran away in response to a perceived injustice. She ran away three times, for example, soon after having sex with Thistlewood.[32]

Sally suffered a great deal from forced sex with Thistlewood and other men. On 22 August 1768, Sally was reported missing. When she was returned "by a negroe woman of Mrs. Blakes," Thistlewood "Put a collar and chain" around her neck and "branded her with TT on her right cheek." He also discovered "her private parts is tore in a terrible manner which was discovered this morning by her having bled a great deal, while she lay in the bilboes last night." "When threatened a good deal," Sally admitted that she had had sex with a "sailor [who] had laid with her while [she was] away." Thistlewood had sex with her thirty-seven times but often recorded that the sex was unsatisfactory, suggesting that his sex with Sally involved rape. In addition, he tried to choose her sexual partners, matching her with Chub on 4 July 1768, when Sally would have been fifteen or sixteen. The partnership was not a success. Sally was not permanently attached to any man, living for the most part after breaking up with Chub either alone or with the house slaves. This did not mean, however, that she was sexually inactive or that she did not fall victim to venereal disease. On 20 November 1774, for example, Thistlewood recorded that "Sally has the clap very badly." She was particularly badly affected by venereal disease in 1782, when she was sick for nearly two months.[33] These bouts of venereal disease accentuated her general unhealthiness. She was often ill, suffering especially acutely from yaws. In 1772, she had one of her toes amputated, and for nearly six months, she was too lame to work. She did not go back to work in the fields until 10 May 1773.

Possibly, Sally's frequent illnesses made her infertile. Thistlewood noted only one time when she was reputed to be "breeding" and that resulted in a miscarriage, which led to her being laid up for two weeks.[34] Low fertility and high infant mortality were significant problems for Jamaican slaves and their owners. Thistlewood records 121 live births from 153 pregnancies in his diaries.[35] Of these live births, we can ascertain the fate of 66 children. At least 51 children died before the age of seven, and just 15 survived past seven years of age. Slave women may have been reluctant mothers, consciously avoiding having children in response to the adverse conditions in which they lived. Certainly some contemporaries thought the low breeding rates of slave women were a deliberate strategy to frustrate their masters' purposes.[36] The Gothic novelist and Jamaican slave owner Matthew "Monk" Lewis colorfully remarked in the early nineteenth century: "I really believe that the negresses can produce children at pleasure; and where they are barren, it is just as hens will frequently not lay eggs on shipboard, because they do not like their situation."[37]

Why Sally had no children is impossible to discern. What we can say, however, is that if she had had children she would have found it very difficult to provide for them since she could barely support herself. Sally did not get along with her fellow slaves and was forced to cultivate her provision grounds entirely by herself. Her efforts were not successful, and she could not produce enough food to prevent being constantly hungry. When times were hard, as they were in the latter half of 1778 and between April and June 1781, Sally was forced to ask Thistlewood for money to buy provisions.[38] Sometimes she took matters into her own hands. On 23 March 1781, Mary, a slave belonging to Jeremiah Meyler, complained to Thistlewood that Sally, who had been a shipmate of hers, had "inticed her to Sleep in her husband's house at Mr. Haywards and in the morning stole her of her pocket, with 2 knives etc in it & her Victuals." Thistlewood "could find nothing of the victuals" but nevertheless gave Sally "a good flogging." Three years later, she stole a basket of peas from House Franke.[39] She had stolen food from her fellow slaves before. Eleven years previously, she had stolen, boiled, and eaten a young fowl from the cookroom belonging to Jimmy. She had tried to blame the theft on someone else, waking Jimmy to tell him that "somebody had come and stood a long time looking upon her then took out the chicken & went away." But Thistlewood found "some of the feathers . . . in the pot in which she boiled it, this morning, and she soon confessed," earning a flogging for her misbehavior.[40]

The most telling example of how Sally was treated and how she was degraded occurred on 7 August 1770. Thistlewood wrote, "As Sally steals everything left in the cookroom, and eats it if eatable, Phibbah had her tied with her hands behind her naked for the mosquitoes to bite her tonight." Not surprisingly, Sally ran away even though "Her hands were tied up so tight that the string hurt her very much." Thistlewood "Brought her home and secured her for this night in the bilboes." Her degradation was complete when Thistlewood raped her as punishment when she was caught—"Cum Sally (mea) Sup. Terr. In Rockhole Provision Ground." The event seems to have been pivotal for Sally since henceforth she made no attempt to fit into the slave community and accepted any punishment she was given. On 22 June 1776, for example, Thistlewood put her in a collar "as she will not help herself, but attempts to run away." She hardly looked after her provision grounds, relied on handouts from Thistlewood, ran away frequently but to little effect, stole from other slaves, and became so disagreeable to other slaves that they refused to have anything to do with her. Phibbah, for example, was incensed that Sally refused to work in the kitchen and sat dejected and dispirited rather than proceeding with her work. By the early 1780s, Sally had lost the will to survive. She had given up. It was no surprise that on 30 November 1784 Thistlewood sold Sally for £40, along with another persistent runaway, Barton's Mary, and had her shipped off the island. It was a sad end to a sad story.

The Slave Mother

Abba's story also has elements of tragedy about it, although in her case this had less to do with her reactions to slavery than with the difficulties she faced as the mother of a large family. Purchased in February 1758, Abba remained with Thistlewood until his death in 1786 (although she was sent by her master to live with Thomas Emotson and his wife on 17 July 1758 to learn to be a seamstress and did not return permanently to Thistlewood until the mid-1760s). In that time, she became pregnant thirteen times, had ten live births and one stillbirth, and had six children who survived the first year of life, four of whom were still living at Thistlewood's death (between the ages of five and twenty-five), and one grandchild. Such fecundity was highly unusual. Most slave women in Jamaica in the period of the Atlantic slave trade were either childless or had no more than one or two children. Richard Dunn's studies of slave fertility on the

Mesopotamia estate in Westmoreland between 1762 and 1831 show that the birth rate in late-eighteenth-century Jamaican slave communities was feeble. In an average year, seventy-five women of childbearing age produced on average only six recorded live births. Deaths exceeded births by 749 to 410.[41] By the mid-eighteenth century, slave women in the Chesapeake, especially Creole women, were each bearing between six and eight children, of whom about four survived into adulthood. Few Jamaican slave women were so prolific. Inventories made in Jamaica in 1753 connecting women with children list 106 women who had 180 children. Nearly 60 percent of women with children had just one child, fewer than 6 percent had four or more children, and just 1 percent had seven surviving children. Fewer than 17 percent of children listed with their mothers lived in families with four or more children. These statistics understate the number of children women had since adolescent and adult children would have been listed separately from their mothers. Nevertheless, few women had large numbers of surviving children.[42] The inventory of Robert Needham, taken in 1739, lists 74 women among his 205 slaves. These women had 50 children. There were nearly as many women without children (36) as with children (38). Over 70 percent of Needham's female slaves who had children had only one child, and only one woman had more than two children.[43] Among Thistlewood's slaves alive at his death, no slave had been pregnant or had given birth as many times as Abba, although Damsel (Solon's wife) had four living children and Phoebe had three. Maria, Mary, and Bess each had one living child, while Sukey, Peggy, Mirtilla, Nanny, and Franke were all adult slave women with no surviving children. Abba accounted for a full quarter of all pregnancies of Thistlewood's slave women.[44]

Abba's high fertility affected her experience as a slave. She never entered into a permanent monogamous relationship with any man. She was the matriarch of a family of four children and a grandchild by 1785. Nevertheless, even though she cared for her family mostly by herself, she seldom had independent control over how her family was treated. In the first place, her precarious financial position and the many mouths she had to feed made her dependent on her master for support. She was never able to engage in the outright rebellion that childless women such as Coobah and Sally evinced toward Thistlewood because she needed his protection and financial aid to help her large family. She also relied on other slaves, especially slave men, for help in providing for her family. Abba had many partners, several of whom were not slaves under Thistlewood's care. As a young woman, she was briefly attached to Hazat, a slave belonging to William Mould, before entering into a long-term relationship with Neptune, a slave belonging to Thomas Emotson. She lived with Neptune for at least four years and had four children with him, three of whom survived past infancy, including Mary, who lived into adulthood despite being blinded after a bout of smallpox when eighteen months old. In 1767, Thistlewood moved her to his pen and had an Egypt slave, Cumberland, build her a thatched house. Abba and her three children lived in this house along with Sally until the hurricane of 1780, when she moved in with Lincoln and Sukey. She remained attached to Neptune until sometime after 1769. In 1770, she took up with another slave who lived off of the estate. Thistlewood recorded on 13 December 1770, "Last night a negro [was] here from John Ricketts estate ([named] Cudjoe) who it seems has made, or is about making, a match with Abba slyly." Two weeks later, "Abba's new sweetheart Cudjoe at the pen today asked me leave to have her [Abba], which I consented to."[45] Within five months, Jimmy, a slave owned by Thistlewood, had replaced Cudjoe. Thistlewood was not impressed by this new match, flogging both Abba and Jimmy when he caught them sleeping together, the main reason being that "One of the children was upon the bed with them, full of the yaws, although Jimmy has never had them; and the cookroom left to itself, although all the utensils in it, and all the clothes in this week's wash."[46] By 11 December 1774, the affair was over, as "Jimmy wants to throw away Abba, he having long kept Phoebe slyly." Abba moved on as well. She became pregnant by Lincoln in late 1775, having already had a child that was probably his on 25 August 1772, and on 26 January 1776, she was attached to yet another slave from another estate, Jeremy, who was owned by a Mr. Johnson. She continued to sleep with Lincoln and by 1780 had entered into a polygynous union with him. Lincoln took Abba and her children into his house to live with him and his principal wife, Sukey, creating an extended polygynous and, after Mary gave birth to Prue in 1785, multigenerational household. It was only at the end of Thistlewood's life that Thistlewood once again contemplated providing Abba with her own house. He began to put up a house for her on 30 October 1786, a month before he died.

Abba's life was defined more by motherhood than by her serial relationships. What sort of mother was she? Contemporaries thought slave women were generally feckless parents who neglected their children and were cruel to them.[47] Thistlewood sometimes shared this view. He castigated his slave Bess for mothering in "her usual careless manner" after her young son got a fish bone stuck in his throat and blamed her and the midwife, Egypt Quasheba, for being "bad nurses indeed" when another son of Bess's died soon after birth in February 1776. On another occasion, he claimed that a slave mother had stood by and let a mule kick and severely injure her infant child. He also blamed fathers for mistreating children, flogging slave men on three occasions when he felt they were deliberately or carelessly starving infant children. He locked up Jimmy after the death of one of Abba's children on 17 October 1771 because he "Attribute[d] the death of Abba's child to his disturbing them in the night."[48]

Thistlewood never made such criticisms of Abba. Abba cared for her children as much as she was able to, was solicitous about them when they were ill, and was distraught when they died.[49] Abba lost four children soon after birth and two sons who were about six years old. When her son Johnnie fainted on 5 January and died on 8 January 1771 from "a spasm, or locking of the jaws" and her young boy Neptune died on 2 August 1773 of "a most violent cold, got I suppose by the water running thro' her house & making the floor wet," Abba was beside herself with grief. Thistlewood described her as "almost out of her senses" and "quite frantic & will hear no reason." Johnnie's death, in particular, affected her deeply. She buried him near her house with singing and dancing, as was the custom in West African funerals, and mourned his loss six months later in a postinterment ceremony by "Throw[ing] Water (as they call it)" and by "beating the Coombie loud, singing high &c. Many Negroes there from all over the country."[50] Abba found it difficult to accept these deaths. On 28 December 1780, she invited an obeah man, Mr. Wilson's Will, to her house because she believed that Solon's wife, Damsel, was "the occasion of her children being sick & her miscarriage etc." She needed, it seems, some explanation for why her children had died. The result was "a sad uproar." Thistlewood disapproved of obeah, and when he caught the obeah man, he gave him a good flogging. But he did nothing to Abba, the instigator of the "uproar," suggesting that he sympathized with her grief over the fate of her children.

The apparent cause of Neptune's death, however, suggests that Abba found it difficult, despite her best intentions, to look after her children and ensure that they had enough food to survive and safe conditions in which to live. Thistlewood's brief description of her house—so open to the elements that water could flow easily through it—indicates that she lived in abject poverty. Her inability to provide for herself and her large family meant that she was more reliant on Thistlewood's largesse than most slaves. The inadequate house that she had was given to her by her master, as was the more substantial dwelling he finally provided in the last month of his life. Abba lived so close to the edge that she was forced to rely heavily on Thistlewood's assistance. She could not afford to rebel or offer resistance to her enslavement when she had so many mouths to feed. Resistance made little sense when a slave had many dependents and could provide for those dependents only by remaining in the good graces of a vengeful master. Her acquiescence to enslavement can be seen in how few times she was punished. She was flogged only three times in her twenty-eight years with Thistlewood, twice in 1770 with Damsel for neglecting to clean the great house and once in 1784 with Sukey "for making such a noise last night."[51] Significantly, Abba never ran away. To do so would have meant abandoning her family.

Slaves lived close to subsistence and near to disaster even at the best of times. The provision-ground system, which was the main source of slave subsistence, often fell short of satisfying slaves' basic needs. When a slave had a large family to look after, the chances of destitution and starvation were greatly increased. As Gilbert Mathison argued in 1808, "If it should happen that, through idleness, or sickness, or old age, or in consequence of too numerous a family of children, the provision-ground should be neglected, or become unproductive or insufficient, the Negro is not allowed to expect, nor in fact, does he obtain, assistance from the stores of the plantation."[52] When hurricanes struck, as they did five times between 1780 and 1786, or when there were periods of scarcity, even the hardest-working slave endured a subsistence crisis. The results were poverty, malnutrition, disease, and death. An anonymous critic of Jamaican slavery painted a bleak picture of one such subsistence crisis in 1746: "[S]ome of the poor Creatures pine away and are starved, others that have somewhat more spirits, go a stealing and are shot as they are caught in Provision Grounds; others are whipt or even hang'd for going into the Woods, into which Hunger and Necessity itself drives them to try and get Food to keep Life and Soul together."[53]

Abba could supplement her income from her provision grounds in a variety of ways. Unlike most African-born slaves, she had been trained to do more than just field work. Thistlewood had sent her to his friend, Mrs. Emotson, soon after he bought her to learn to be a washerwoman and seamstress. Thistlewood fostered such efforts by providing her with large quantities of cloth to make into clothes that she could sell at market. He treated her not as a field slave but as a domestic slave, whose main duties were washing clothes and cleaning house. Domestic duties were relatively light and gave her more opportunities to make money than field slaves had. On 8 March 1765, for example, Thistlewood noted, "My Abba Called, Selling Goods, bought off her a Silver Thimble for 5 bitts, which gave Phibbah." But Abba was not a natural saleswoman. On

3 June 1770, Thistlewood gave Abba a ticket to sell produce that Thistlewood estimated was worth five cobbs. But Abba "made scarce three. She is very wrong-headed and obstinate." Later in the same year, Thistlewood commented on the poor sums Abba had received for her corn and plantains: "Abba is a very negligent market woman."[54] Even if she had been an excellent saleswoman, the amounts she could have earned from selling produce would have been limited. As Richard Sheridan argues, few slaves were able to produce a surplus. He notes that whatever surplus slaves produced was generally used to purchase imported food. Supplementing food allowances was essential if slaves were to receive anything close to the nutrition they needed to do the work masters required them to do. In general, food supplies for slaves were very sparse, even in times of abundant harvest. Adverse circumstances, such as the closing of North American trade with Jamaica during the American Revolution or the series of hurricanes that devastated the island in the early 1780s, led to famine.[55] Moreover, slaves had little margin for coping with disaster—natural or man-made. Abba suffered when a fellow slave, Solon, stole her corn. She suffered even more when Thistlewood accidentally killed her prize possession, a sow. Thistlewood gave her 32 bits "to lessen her loss," knowing that "this sow was the support of herself and children," but the loss would have been hard to bear. In addition, much of her energy was taken up with providing food and clothing for her large family, leaving her little time to produce a surplus. Thistlewood gave Abba "3½ yards of Irish linen and thread & cut off near 2 yards to make me 6 night caps." But Abba needed almost all of the 5½ yards of linen for herself and her children and could not provide more than three caps for Thistlewood.[56]

Abba supplemented her income in three ways besides selling clothes and produce, all of which relied on white assistance and were dependent on Thistlewood. Given her experience in childbirth, it was natural that Thistlewood would think her suitable to act as a midwife. She started midwifery rather late, the first instance recorded by Thistlewood on 10 June 1784, when she assisted her daughter Mary in the birth of a baby girl (who died a week later). She received a dollar from Thistlewood for help in "laying up" on this and five other occasions.[57] She also received money for providing sex to white men, notably Thistlewood. Abba was one of Thistlewood's favorite partners, especially in the mid-1770s. Between 1771 and 1776, Thistlewood had sex with Abba 156 times, often in his house, sometimes in the fields, and occasionally on a garden bench. Usually, Thistlewood gave Abba 2 bits each time he had sex with her. In the 1770s, when times were generally good, such additional income was probably sufficient to allow Abba to provide for herself and her family. In the more desperate years of the 1780s, a period when Thistlewood had sex with her only three times, Abba did not have sufficient money to supplement her inadequate provisions and was forced to beg for extra money from her owner. In 1777, Thistlewood gave her 16 bitts "to assist her."[58] He gave her a further 10 bitts in 1781 and began to give her a dollar every Christmas. In 1785, Abba received another 10 bitts "to buy provisions," 6 bitts "to buy meat, rice etc," and a "dollar to assist her, she being ill and [having] a large family to maintain." By the middle of 1786, times had become very hard—Thistlewood commenting that he "never saw Such a Scarce time before, that is Certain"—and Abba's children complained of hunger. Thistlewood gave Abba more money "to assist her" and began to construct a new house for her and her family. When he died, however, Abba was in desperate straits, unable to support herself or her family.[59]

Abba was neither a reluctant mother nor an uncaring and negligent one. But whatever personal pleasures she derived from motherhood, it is clear that the number of children she had severely reduced her capacity to cope with the conditions of slavery. She was not a resourceful survivor like Thistlewood's mistress, Phibbah. Instead, the size of her family greatly reduced her independence and sacrificed her health. The system worked against her. Slaves could survive only if they remained healthy, could protect their provision grounds from theft by other slaves, worked hard, and were working either for themselves alone or for a small family. Slaves who became ill, could not protect their provision grounds from other slaves or whites, or were burdened by a large family were forced, like Abba, to rely on the help of their owners to survive. Slave owners encouraged such dependency. Keeping slaves dependent protected them from what might happen if slaves gained some independence. But such slave-management strategies also worked against slave owners' interests. It showed slaves that they could maintain a degree of independence and subsist with a degree of comfort only if they had no dependents. The conditions of slave life encouraged slaves not to have large families. As Barry Higman concludes, "There is no doubt that the slave system disorganised patterns of family and kinship organisation." Because every aspect of the Caribbean slave regime worked against the stability of slave family life and because, despite whites' continual assaults on slave life, slaves still had a strong attachment to and love for their children, it would not be surprising if individual slave women chose to limit their fertility so they would not end up like Abba—the parent of a large family she could not support or protect.[60]

The Slave Mistress

Not all women refused to adapt to their unfortunate situation, like Sally and Coobah, or were forced to rely on the support of their master in order to survive, like Abba. A minority of women managed to not only survive enslavement but also transcend its limitations. Easily the most remarkable slave encountered in Thistlewood's diaries was his long-term mistress, Phibbah. What is most remarkable about her is how skillfully she was able to exploit her relationship with Thistlewood to gain personal advantage and social benefits for the entire slave community. Phibbah was able to transcend slaves' powerlessness through her privileged position as the mistress of a white man—a position that enabled her to purchase property, advance the social status of herself and her family, and engage with Thistlewood on a more equal basis than was possible for any other slave. In doing so, she undermined the principle of black subordination and weakened assumptions of white dominance.

The story of how Phibbah secured individual and familial advantages demonstrates how the personal agency of one actor could disrupt seemingly rigid networks of social rules that were intended to secure the dominance of one group over another. She was a slave who acquiesced to her master's demands but also used the privileges she wrested from her master to benefit her enslaved compatriots. Phibbah's lengthy sexual and emotional relationship with Thistlewood was more than just the exploitation of a black woman by a powerful white man. By the end of her thirty-three-year relationship with Thistlewood, Phibbah was attached to her lover and longtime partner by bonds of affection and possibly love. Thistlewood and Phibbah were, to all intents and purposes, husband and wife. As his wife, Phibbah established for herself an enviable position as a privileged slave, enabling her to have a richer and fuller life than was possible for most slave women.

The rich detail of Thistlewood's diaries provides a wealth of material about Phibbah, making her life extraordinarily accessible in comparison to the lives of other eighteenth-century black women. Nevertheless, as with Thistlewood himself, we lack much vital information about her. We do not know what she looked like, what her ancestry was, or what her life was like before she met Thistlewood. What we do know is that she was a Creole who had a sister, Nancy, who was a slave on a nearby estate. She remained close to Nancy all her life. When we first meet her on the Egypt estate in 1751, she was owned by William Dorrill, who bequeathed her to his colored mistress, Elizabeth Anderson, who in turn left Phibbah to her and Dorrill's daughter, Molly Dorrill, later the wife of

John Cope. By then, Phibbah was already a mother, with a young child called Coobah (not the Coobah discussed above). If we assume that Coobah was at least fifteen when she first gave birth in 1762 and that Phibbah was at least a similar age when she gave birth to Coobah, then Phibbah's birth can be estimated at no later than the early 1730s. She was thus at least in her early twenties and possibly older—perhaps close to Thistlewood's age (he was thirty-two)—when she became Thistlewood's partner in 1753. The last mention of Phibbah comes in 1792, when she was finally given the manumission promised her in Thistlewood's will of 1787.[61] She was probably well into her sixties at the time, perhaps even in her seventies. She was already adjudged old by the time of Thistlewood's death: his appraisers described her as "Pheba (the old woman that lives with Mr. Thistlewood)" in his inventory.[62] Besides Coobah, who was also alive in 1792, Phibbah gave birth to two children, a stillbirth in 1755 whose paternity Thistlewood attributed to John Cope and a son, John, in 1760, who died at age twenty in 1780.[63]

Thistlewood did not take up with Phibbah immediately upon meeting her. Indeed, some of his first references to her were unflattering. On 27 February 1752, he gave Phibbah a flogging of seventy lashes for "harboring" John Filton, Thistlewood's predecessor as overseer at Egypt, in her house. After beating off Congo Sam's attack on 27 December 1752, Thistlewood noted in his diary that evening that he had had "reason to believe" that three slaves, including Phibbah, "knew that Sam had an intent to murder me when we should meet, by what I heard them speak one day in the cookroom." It was not until 11 October 1753 that he first had sex with her. She became his regular mistress in February 1754. Before that date, Thistlewood's principal partner had been an African field hand called Jenny, who shared his bed as his "wife" between January 1752 and December 1753. It was not a happy partnership. Jenny's fellow slaves resented her rise in status after she became his mistress. Quashie, a slave driver and thus one of the most important slaves on the estate, was so bold as to make "impudent" remarks about Thistlewood's lover directly to the overseer's face. Moreover, Jenny was not indifferent to the attractions of "negroe fellows" and was reprimanded by Thistlewood for being "Concerned" with them and for "importuning" Thistlewood "for Sugar, Rum &c." for her fellow slaves. Such importuning showed that Jenny's loyalties lay with her fellow slaves rather than with Thistlewood. Thistlewood was not impressed. Nor was he pleased by "her damn'd obstinate humour" and incessant quarreling. The final straw came when he discovered that she had brought a knife with her to his bed. Not surprisingly, Thistlewood was "afraid" of her "intent." Equally unsurprisingly, Thistlewood decided that Jenny was not a suitable principal partner and returned her to the fields. Jenny had overplayed her hand. She was, unlike Phibbah, unable to steer a careful course between the Charybdis of overidentification with her master and the Scylla of too close commitment to slave interests.[64]

Phibbah was a much more sensible choice for Thistlewood as his principal partner. The success of long-term interracial pairings depended very much on the character and status of the black mistress. Just as a wise planter made sure when choosing a driver that he chose someone who could retain the respect of the slaves he needed to control, so too did he endeavor to choose as his mistress a woman with authority in the slave community. Becoming the mistress of a white man accentuated a slave woman's status, but the exercise of that status fomented resentment within the slave community if the master's mistress did not command respect. A mistress was not so much chosen by the master as co-opted with the tacit consent of other slaves. She occupied a distinct position of leadership within slaves' internal hierarchy. A mistress gained power through her special access to the master. She fulfilled a vital role within the slave community as an intermediary able to intercede on behalf of slaves. She also provided the slave community with crucial information about the master's thoughts and actions. With power, however, came responsibility. If the master's mistress abused her privileged status by lording it over other slaves, as Jenny appears to have done, or if she played favorites or alienated the master by pleading too vigorously on behalf of other slaves, thus usurping the master's power to discipline slaves, she would lose the respect of the master or the slaves or possibly both. From a master's perspective, a mistress who caused trouble with slaves weakened his ability to control his slaves—Quashie's "impudent" remarks about Jenny were an indirect challenge to Thistlewood, as Thistlewood himself recognized. From a slave's perspective, the master's mistress needed to be someone who could serve as a reliable conduit of slaves' concerns. The mistress, therefore, was a crucial linchpin in the negotiated relationships that constituted slave-master interactions.[65]

Phibbah was no Jenny, as Thistlewood soon discovered. She had two distinct advantages over her unfortunate predecessor. First, she was a recognized leader within the slave community with a privileged position as the chief housekeeper. Second, she knew how to act the part of the master's mistress, exhibiting throughout her thirty-three years as Thistlewood's chief concubine a remarkable capacity to maintain her lover's affection while remaining well regarded within the slave community. As far as can be discerned from Thistlewood's diaries, she got on well with her fellow slaves, participating, for example, in slave activities and festivals. When she fell dangerously ill in 1768, "many Negroes came to see her," and her closest friends—House Franke, Vine, and her daughter, previously named Coobah but now called Jenny Young, were extremely solicitous of her health and well-being. Similarly, when her son John died in 1780, many slaves from several plantations attended the funeral and comforted Phibbah in her grief.[66]

A Privileged Slave

House slaves frequently became the concubines of white men. Indeed, having sex with the master was almost an expected part of the job, part of the price they paid for the privilege of being removed from plantation labor. As Barry Higman has demonstrated, female domestics in the early nineteenth century had the greatest chance of any slaves (except for slave drivers, who were usually comparatively old when they were appointed to their positions) of reaching sixty years of age.[67] The brutality of field labor may have been one reason why Phibbah and other privileged house slaves sought white men as partners. Hilary Beckles has traced the family history of one group of household domestics— Old Doll and her three daughters on the Newton estate in Barbados—who used their positions as household slaves and their relationships with white men to obtain substantial social authority within their slave community, acquire property of their own, and avoid being relegated to the fields. These four women thought of themselves as a slave elite. They evaded hard manual labor and socialized with whites and free blacks rather than slaves. Their high status can be seen in the fact that they "owned" slave assistants. They adopted strategies designed to protect their interests as a family, making sure, for example, that if any of them was sent into the fields, other family members would entreat estate managers to return that slave to house duty. They also eschewed any sexual or emotional involvement with slave men. Instead, they consorted entirely with whites, which meant that over the generations they transformed themselves from dark-skinned Africans into a mostly free and lightly colored Creole family. Fittingly, Old Doll's family buried her in a manner normally reserved for whites. She and her family had left their slave roots behind. But it is misplaced to view them as turncoats. Rather, they should be seen as "women—mothers and grandmothers—struggling to improve the intellectual and material lot of their families against reactionary plantation policies and the constraints imposed by the wider slave system."[68] Phibbah and Old Doll were sisters under the skin—privileged house slaves with slaves of their own (Phibbah was given a slave girl called

Bess in 1765 by a free colored woman, Sarah Bennett, to keep as her own, although legally, as a slave herself, Phibbah could not own slaves) who associated sexually only with white men. Both women achieved freedom through accommodation with white men rather than through resistance, as resistance is commonly understood.[69]

House slaves had little choice but to accept white men's sexual advances. They were more likely than field slaves to be on hand when white men sought black women, as Eve, a young house slave, found out on 12 March 1755, when a drinking party of six men gang-raped her. Depersonalized, quasi-commercial sex between white men and slave women was pervasive in slave societies at all levels but was especially common between European migrants and female domestics. House slaves were expected to provide sexual services for masters as part of their domestic duties. John Stedman in his narrative on life in Surinam in the 1770s candidly outlined how customary such practices were. "The batchelors in this Climate," he opined, "all without Exception have a female slave (mostly a Creole) in their keeping who preserves their linnens clean and decent, dresses them Victuals with skill, carefully attends them . . . during the frequent illnesses to which Europeans are exposed [and] prevents them from keeping late Hours, knits for them, sows for them etc." Such attachments, Stedman claimed, were matters of great pride to "these Girls," so much so that "they hesitate not to pronounce as Harlots, who do not follow them (if they can) in this laudable Example in which they are encouraged by their nearest Relations and Friends."[70]

The semi-institutionalized commercial arrangements whereby "Relations and Friends" bargained away young women's individual sexual rights in return for positions for them as domestic servants had major cultural consequences. Although working in the house with its "supposed indulgences" was "the more honourable" situation for slave women, "the most independent" slave women were those who worked in the fields "with its exaggerated labours." Women who worked in the fields had some choice over their living arrangements and retained considerable cultural autonomy. Female house slaves, however, may have found it hard to follow African traditions. Long's dismissive comments about white women "insensibly adopt[ing]" the "fawning, dissonant gibberish" of their "sable handmaids" also operated in reverse. Female domestics were the most Europeanized and Creolized of black slaves, and they risked becoming culturally isolated. Thistlewood disapproved of "African superstitions" and punished those discovered practicing obeah. Phibbah distanced herself from such activities, informing Thistlewood, for example, that her daughter Coobah had held two myall dances in her house. Female domestics found it hard to escape white men's gaze and suffered for such close proximity.[71]

Nevertheless, Phibbah recognized in ways that Jenny did not that in order to maintain her power she needed not only to continue to receive Thistlewood's favors but also to perform a useful role as intermediary between slaves and master. Phibbah knew more about slave life than Thistlewood. When Thistlewood had sex with Eve rather than Mountain Lucy, the slave Phibbah had provided him "to keep as Sweetheart the Time she lies in" during late pregnancy in 1755, Phibbah found out almost immediately. Thistlewood mused that he did not "know who could have told her," but Phibbah evidently had her sources.[72] Even after she became Thistlewood's mistress, slaves continued to tell her things Thistlewood did not know. Thistlewood noted that Phibbah intervened with him on behalf of other slaves, three times expressing his displeasure when she pushed slaves' claims too far. On 11 January 1760, for example, he reprimanded Phibbah "for intermeddling with Field Negroes business with me."[73] Phibbah's sphere of influence was the cookroom and did not extend, in his opinion, to the fields. In the cookroom, however, Phibbah was able to punish slaves or forgive them as she saw fit.[74]

Friends and Family

As her willingness to punish slaves suggests, Phibbah had divided loyalties. She probably provided Thistlewood with information. It was natural that two people in a long-term relationship would talk about people they both knew. Thus, Phibbah told Thistlewood when he was at Kendal that Old Sambo had taken to "walking around Cabritto upper bridge with white men who promised to carry him to his country." Phibbah was also privy to many white people's secrets. She told Thistlewood, for example, that Molly Cope had asked Phibbah "slyly" whether Thistlewood "had made a will" after Thistlewood had been very ill.[75] Phibbah's contacts with whites were extensive but not close. They were usually limited to assisting Molly Cope in childbirth, at christenings and weddings, and during children's illnesses. Nevertheless, by the 1770s, Phibbah had become sufficiently respectable to be able to entertain white women. In 1779, she hosted two local grandees and their wives to "tea and porter under ye guinep tree in ye garden." Such intermingling with white dignitaries never happened again, but that it happened even once suggests that John Stewart was right when he claimed that there was social intercourse between white women and colored mistresses.[76] Nevertheless, Phibbah's preferred milieu was among her own kind: privileged house slaves and the mistresses of white men. As in North America, "adult female cooperation and interdependence was a fact of female slave life."[77] Privileged house slaves formed networks of friendship and mutual assistance. Phibbah had very intense relationships with two fellow house servants at Egypt, House Franke and Egypt Lucy, in the 1750s and 1760s and, after moving to Breadnut Pen, became close to Thistlewood's neighbor's mistress, a slave called Vine. The relationships were mutually supportive. When Phibbah gave birth to Mulatto John in 1760, House Franke came from the Salt River estate to assist her, and Egypt Lucy gave "Phibbahs Child Suck." The three women engaged in business together, selling produce at market, and used the money they earned to free Phibbah's sister, Nancy, and Phibbah's mulatto granddaughter (the daughter of Coobah). After Egypt Lucy died on 27 June 1772, Phibbah organized her funeral.[78]

Phibbah's family was small but close-knit. It comprised Phibbah, her sister Nancy, and her two children, Coobah, or Jenny Young, and John. It also included Phibbah's close friends, business partners, and housemates, House Franke and Egypt Lucy. The five women shared especially strong links, visiting each other frequently and joining in trading. Phibbah did her best to advance the interests of her friends and family, importuning on their behalf with Thistlewood, attempting to purchase their freedom, giving them gifts, and assisting them in their work. She was especially solicitous of the interests of her children. Coobah followed in her mother's footsteps and became a house slave and the mistress of white men. But Coobah's experiences were more varied than her mother's. The first mention of her was inauspicious and suggests the danger black women faced from the attentions of white men, even when they were children. Thistlewood notes that on 19 February 1758 he prevented Coobah from being raped by a white bookkeeper who had lured her "into the Boiler Room by [a] Stratagem" and "Attempted to Ravish her, Stopp'd a handkerchief into her mouth etc." Coobah was probably still a child at the time. Three and a half years later, she had become Molly Cope's waiting maid and was due to have a child, which Thistlewood thought was fathered by either her partner, Mulatto Davie, or John Cope.[79] Six years later, she enjoyed an opportunity granted to very few slaves—a yearlong trip to England as the servant of the Copes' son, William Dorrill Cope. Such an experience would surely have given Coobah a better understanding of Europeans and European society and perhaps explains why, despite her fondness for myall and obeah in her youth, she became more Europeanized than her mother. Unlike Phibbah, Coobah became a Christian, converting along with her husband, Jimmy Stewart, on 13 November 1771, and taking the name Jenny Young after baptism.[80]

Jenny visited her mother frequently and was particularly helpful to her in times of distress. When her half-brother died in 1780, she stayed with her mother for two weeks. Increasingly, Thistlewood came to see her as his own daughter, giving her presents when she was ill, selling her livestock, and employing her to make clothes. Thistlewood's developing affection for Jenny was an important step in his own maturation. As Douglas Hall suggests, Thistlewood's open and affectionate association with Phibbah and her family encouraged him to temper his behavior toward his slaves and provided him with a greater appreciation of their world. In this respect, creolization was a two-way process: Jenny "Africanized" Thistlewood as he and other whites "Europeanized" her.[81]

Phibbah's other child, John, was the only surviving child she had with Thistlewood, born on 29 April 1760. One reason why black women attached themselves to white men was that the children produced in those relationships were likely to be more privileged than ordinary slaves. The privileges given John—he was freed on 25 May 1762, educated from the age of five at a local school, trained in a profession (he was apprenticed to a carpenter in his teens), and allowed to join the colored militia—were powerful reasons why Phibbah would want to stay with Thistlewood, besides ties of affection and the personal advantages that being a mistress of a white man afforded. If John had not died of fever at age twenty and had grown out of his teenage delinquencies,[82] he might have become a member of Jamaica's brown elite, enjoying a status and standard of living higher than that which Phibbah had acquired for herself.[83] He would have been Thistlewood's principal heir and would have inherited Phibbah's not inconsiderable estate as well. In effect, by "whitening" her children, Phibbah had accentuated their advantages in life.[84]

Phibbah's strong commitment to her family and close friends pervades Thistlewood's revelations of her life. Phibbah was a warm and affectionate mother, who cared deeply for her children. When John was ill, she looked after him; when he needed clothing, she made it herself; when she went to see friends, he went with her; and when John angered his father (as he often did), she sought to help him. When he came down with fever, Phibbah walked a long distance to attend him, and when he died, she was inconsolable.[85] Indeed, Thistlewood felt she was indulgent to a fault with her often-wayward son: "His mother promotes his Ruin, by excessive indulgences and humoring him beyond all bounds."[86] That she was able to maintain a vibrant emotional life is remarkable given the chaos that characterized Jamaican slavery. The circumstances of slavery usually militated against slaves forming stable families. The brutality, flux, and trauma of slave life made slave family life and community life highly dysfunctional. Phibbah was insulated from the dehumanizing tendencies inherent in Jamaican slavery because she was both a household slave and a Creole.

A Wealthy and Independent Slave

Being the mistress of a white man also had economic advantages, which recommended it to ambitious slave women. One of Phibbah's major priorities was to become economically independent. Attaching herself to Thistlewood allowed her to achieve this aim. Phibbah was a wealthy woman for a slave by the time Thistlewood died. She owned both land and livestock as a result of her successful "huckstering"—small-scale vending of surplus agricultural products, clothing, and trade goods. Phibbah drew on Thistlewood's resources in developing her huckster activities, which gave her a competitive advantage over other slaves. She traded the gifts he gave her for livestock and consumer goods. In addition, she was an accomplished seamstress and sold clothing to both whites and blacks. For example, when Thistlewood first arrived at Egypt and before he attached himself to Phibbah, he gave her 8 bitts for making him a waistcoat. Later on, he and Phibbah teamed up: Thistlewood provided her with cloth, and Phibbah turned this cloth into finished products. They shared the profits. In 1757, Thistlewood gave Phibbah "goods worth £5 that she was to sell and give me the money." By the 1770s, these arrangements had become regularized.[87]

These activities resulted in Phibbah making a lot of money. On 31 August 1761, Thistlewood reported that he held nearly £67 on Phibbah's behalf—over two years' salary for a white bookkeeper or enough money to buy seven or eight head of cattle or two slave children. Most of her money was made from sewing, baking, and selling surplus agricultural goods. She also profited from buying and selling livestock. On 27 May 1758, she bought a mare and arranged for a slave driver to look after it in return for every third foal the mare produced. On 5 April 1760, she sold a foal for £7. She sold others on 22 March 1765, 27 September 1767, and 17 May 1772. Along with livestock, she also owned slaves, as noted above. Thistlewood recognized her right to control the slave girl Bess, given to her by Sarah Bennett, and legalized the arrangement in his will by formally bequeathing to her Bess and Bess's child Sam, thirty-three and seven years old, respectively. He also confirmed her right to the land she had long cultivated, ordering his executors to "lay out the sum of One Hundred Pounds current money . . . in the purchase of a Lot or piece of land for the said Phibba wherever she shall chose and that they do build thereon a dwelling-house for the said Phibbah suitable to her station so that land and house do not exceed the said sum of One Hundred pounds." In 1784, he had agreed to fence in Phibbah's land.[88]

In gaining property of her own, Phibbah achieved a limited but measurable independence for herself and even more independence for her children. Economic and familial independence went hand in hand. Phibbah's involvement with Thistlewood was at least partly an attempt to ensure that her family could replace the dependence and uncertainty that marked the slave condition with the independence and security that characterized free society. Phibbah had obtained by the time of Thistlewood's death a family estate whereby she and her family could support themselves through subsistence production. Phibbah and her family were "protopeasants"—subsistence farmers engaged in independent production on their own land. The family unit was central to this transformation since food production was organized around the labor of family members. Family estates were more than economic units; they were also "the basis for the creation of family lines and the maximization of kinship ties, in contrast to the kinlessness of the enslaved." Phibbah's determination as the matriarch of her family to forge an independent protopeasant estate demonstrated her concern that her family prosper.[89]

The Lover

Achieving economic and familial independence was not easy. It involved a long association with a white man over whose actions Phibbah had little control. As we have seen with Jenny, a mistress could fall out of favor with her master very easily, with dramatic and negative consequences—Jenny was returned to the fields, where the slaves over whom she had lorded her former position no doubt exacted their revenge. Slave mistresses had to put up with male philandering and brutality. Hugh Wilson, Thistlewood's neighbor, for example, frequently beat his mistress, Miss Sally, a free mulatto woman who was Phibbah's friend. Thistlewood recalls Sally receiving three beatings between 1775 and 1781. Sally was nevertheless better off than Sappho, the mulatto mistress of Thistlewood's friend, Francis Ruecastle, who "beat etc his Wife sadly" so that Sappho died.[90] White men could act with mind-numbing savagery and get away with it. Thistlewood recorded a conversation with Harry Weech, an overseer who had worked for him, who had "cut off the lips, upper lip almost close to her Nose, off his

Mulatto sweetheart, in Jealousy, because he said no Negroe should ever kiss those lips he had."[91] In this respect, Phibbah was relatively fortunate. Thistlewood recorded only one act of violence toward Phibbah in the thirty-three years of their relationship. On 6 December 1755, he wrote that he gave Phibbah "some correction." Both Thistlewood and Phibbah were philanderers. Thistlewood suspected her of having affairs with his employer, John Cope, and his predecessor, John Filton.[92]

Nevertheless, they had a warm and loving relationship, if such a thing was possible between a slave and her master. Their vigorous sex life was an obvious manifestation of the bond between them. Phibbah was far and away Thistlewood's principal partner, participating in 65 percent of his sex acts between 1754 and 1764. In the first year of their relationship, they had sex 234 times. Thirteen years later, they had 87 sex acts a year, and ten years after that, in 1777, when Thistlewood was fifty-six and Phibbah was at least in her late forties, they still had sex four times a month. They had an active sex life right up to the end: Thistlewood last had sex with Phibbah two months before his final illness, at age sixty-five. More important, their active sex life appears to have been consensual. Alone of female slaves under Thistlewood's control, Phibbah could refuse to have sex with him, as she did ten times between 1754 and 1759.[93] By the 1760s, the two seldom quarreled and demonstrated an unforced affection for each other. When John Thistlewood drowned, Phibbah was disconsolate—"ill with grief," as the equally distraught Thistlewood put it. When Phibbah became so ill that she was feared near death, he "got up and tended her . . . getting no rest in the evening" and cared for her after a doctor had bled her.[94]

Nevertheless, Phibbah and Thistlewood reached this happy state only after overcoming a major crisis in 1757—Thistlewood's move to Kendal. It was only following this crisis that the relations between the two could accurately be described as those between husband and wife. The crisis, moreover, was not just a crisis in their relationship; it betokened a challenge to Phibbah's position as a privileged slave. If she lost Thistlewood, which was possible if not probable, her status would be reduced to that of an ordinary housekeeper without all of the advantages that followed from being the mistress of a white man. She would have lost much of her status as a leading slave on the Egypt estate. Phibbah was extremely unhappy about Thistlewood's move for two reasons. First, she was emotionally attached to him—he noted at his departure that "Phibbah grieves very much." She gave him a gold ring when they parted on 23 June 1757 "to keep for her sake." Phibbah did not follow him to Kendal because her owner, Molly Cope, refused to let her go. Thistlewood "begged hard of Mrs. Cope to sell or hire Phibbah to me, but she would not; he [i.e., John Cope] was willing."[95] Second, whatever Phibbah did was likely to lead to a diminishment of status. If she followed him to Kendal, she would have had to establish herself among a community of slaves with whom she had had no previous contact and would have needed to usurp—with unknown consequences—the position of Kendal's leading female slave. If she did not go with him, her position as leading female slave at Egypt would be jeopardized, especially if Thistlewood replaced her in his affections and his bed. Could she rely on Thistlewood's successor finding her suitable to be his mistress? Even Thistlewood recognized her dilemma: "Poor girl, I pity her, she is in miserable slavery."[96]

Phibbah played a very difficult game and played it with consummate skill. She realized that Thistlewood missed her terribly. After Phibbah visited him on 4 July 1757, he commented, "Tonight very lonely and melancholy again. No person sleep in the house but myself and Phibbah's being gone this morning still fresh in my mind." She kept those melancholy feelings fresh by reminding Thistlewood of what he was missing in frequent visits during which she showered him with gifts, such as turtles, eggs, pineapples, biscuits, cashews, roses, and foodstuffs. He was immensely grateful, commenting, "So good a girl she is."[97] But Phibbah needed to do more than provoke fond feelings in her lover. She knew that if Thistlewood stayed at Kendal, he would eventually replace her. He started to do so in 1758, taking up with Aurelia, a slave he had previously denigrated as a "Madam." Phibbah could not move to Kendal since her mistress would not let her, therefore, she would have to reconcile Thistlewood with his previous employer, John Cope. It was a difficult task since Thistlewood believed Cope feckless and was irritated not only at Cope's many reckless and unfulfilled promises but also at his treatment of Phibbah and his unwillingness to force his wife to allow Phibbah to be rented out to Thistlewood. But Phibbah was determined to get Thistlewood back to Egypt and ferried offer after counteroffer between the two men. Eventually, Thistlewood relented. On 27 June 1758, he agreed to return to Egypt with a considerable salary increase and improved conditions. In part, he returned because his terms of employment had improved, but he had had equally generous offers elsewhere. What clinched the deal were his deep feelings for Phibbah. She had won a major victory. John and Molly Cope never again tried to dictate what Phibbah could do. When Thistlewood left Egypt for Breadnut Pen, the Copes immediately agreed that Phibbah could go with him as long as Thistlewood paid a rental fee for her services. From 1758, she was in effect a free woman. Moreover, she retained her position as the leading female slave at Egypt and later Breadnut.[98]

A Heroic Accommodator?

How, then, do we make sense of Phibbah? She was neither a victim nor a rebel. To see Phibbah as a resister of slavery stretches the concept of resistance almost to the breaking point. If anything, Phibbah collaborated; she did not resist. She became a slave owner herself, was not averse to punishing slaves under her care, and informed on slave delinquencies to her master.[99] She sought out the company of whites, free colored people, and privileged slaves and encouraged her daughter to do the same. Most important, she was the principal comfort and emotional support of Thomas Thistlewood, the mortal enemy of the slaves under his control. Her love and counsel may have tempered Thistlewood's behavior, but it mostly contributed to his well-being and, in this respect, hindered rather than aided slaves' attempts at resistance.

Nevertheless, Phibbah did not become the slaves' enemy. It is best to see her not as a victim, a hero, or a resister or collaborator but as an accommodator. She recognized the realities of life in Jamaica and realized that it was fruitless to try to fight against being enslaved. She did not try to validate the negative view that whites had of slaves' capacities. Indeed, she accommodated herself so well to slavery that in the end she transcended it. Phibbah acquired through her hard work and assiduous cultivation of Thistlewood a measure of prosperity and independence and a sense of self-worth usually denied to slaves in a regime where slaves were systematically stripped of honor. She is revealed in Thistlewood's diaries as a real, flesh-and-blood woman, capable of both love and disdain, strong if sometimes foolish, a loyal friend, a devoted if occasionally exasperated partner, a loving if sentimental mother, and a resourceful entrepreneur. She transcended slavery by demonstrating through her behavior that slaveholders' claim that slaves were dependent and without honor was a lie. In this respect, Phibbah dealt the Jamaican slave system a more severe blow than did Tackey. Phibbah's activities blurred the distinctions whites believed separated them from Africans. Her involvement with Thistlewood made her less African but it made him less European; her acquisition of a family estate belied notions of slaves being propertyless; her eventual freedom complicated the easy equation of whites with freedom and blacks with slavery. Messy reality thus softened and disturbed rigid theories about what slaves could and could not do. Phibbah's actions cast doubt on the complete supremacy of whites and the complete inferiority of blacks. By doing so, she achieved more than was possible by the most active resistance.

chapter eight

The Life and Times of Thomas Thistlewood, Esquire—Gardener and Slave Owner

It is only by leaving to the masters a power that is nearly absolute, that it will be possible to keep so large a number of men in that state of submission which is made necessary by their numerical superiority over the whites. If some masters abuse their power, they must be reproved in secret, so that the slaves may always be kept in the belief that the master can do no wrong in his dealings with them.—Cited in Pierre de Vassière, *Saint-Domingue (1729–1789): La Société et la vie créole sous l'ancien régime*

We are alienated from nature and we are not free; we are reduced to maintaining an inhuman politics, by a course of cruel actions . . . and dragged along by a host of passions that we want to satisfy: not being able to break so many chains, we want to polish them and make them shine, and in this work, we use thousands of arms that nature has made for liberty.—Michel-René Hilliard d'Auberteuil, *Considérations sur l'état présent de la colonie française de Saint-Domingue*

The Death of Thomas Thistlewood

On Monday, 28 August 1786, Thistlewood received an invitation to attend the funeral of Major General John Myrie at George Goodin's pen. Thistlewood does not say so, but he may have felt his age. Myrie was buried "a little before Noon with Military honours" on 29 August 1786, with "An abundance of people there." Born in July 1732, Myrie died at age fifty-four, having achieved very high status. He was nearly twelve years younger than Thistlewood. Some of Thistlewood's newest acquaintances in 1786 were younger still. In the last weeks of his life, he struck up a friendship with a young doctor, Samuel Bell, who spent a "very agreeable afternoon" with him on 9 September 1786. He dined with him the next day and stayed until the evening and did so again the following week. On 17 September 1786, Thistlewood noted, "Dr. Saml Bell born January 1st 1750 old Style. Somewhat about 35 & ¾." Bell was thus a newborn child when Thistlewood arrived in Jamaica in 1750. A new generation was taking over. It was a generation that would be forced to deal with the advent of abolition, the pressure of amelioration, the gradual weakening of Jamaica's privileged place within the empire, and the increasing denigration of West Indian planters as a social type by missionaries, abolitionists, and humanitarians. Thistlewood's time was passing. He would not live to see the emergence of the abolition movement. He lived in Jamaica when the viability of the institution on which Jamaica's prosperity depended was not questioned.

Thistlewood was clearly weakening by the autumn of 1786. The day after Bell came for his second dinner, Thistlewood related that he was "Still greatly out of order, pains all over." By 23 September, he reported that he was "having violent Rheumatic pains." In October, his condition worsened. On 4 October, he was "Exceeding Weak." On 11 October, he was "very ill yet & rest exceeding bad O'Nights." By 22 October, two days after a hurricane blew down his piazza roof and took some shingles off his house, he noted, "Last Night intolerable, restless & in great pain." Laudanum eased the pain but not for long. On 25 October, he described his previous night as "Never had a Worse Night, Within my Memory." Bell was with him nearly every day, prescribing laudanum and other medicines. Still, Thistlewood was "quite confused, don't know how things are going on." His neighbors and friends feared the worst. They came to comfort him and bid him farewell. By 15 November, Thistlewood's condition had deteriorated to such an extent that he had abandoned the habit of a lifetime—he stopped keeping his diaries. His illness must have been acute for him to discontinue a practice that had sustained him through nearly thirty-seven years of residence in Jamaica. On 25 November, he wrote his last will and testament, and on 30 November 1786, he died. He was buried the next day in the church-yard at Savanna-la-Mar. The last record we have of him is the inventory of his estate taken by Hugh Wilson and Samuel Delap a week before what would have been his sixty-sixth birthday, on 12 March 1787.[1]

His death was as unexceptional as his life. No doubt many of his white friends and neighbors attended his funeral—not many people had lived in Westmore-land as long as he had and he had built up many friendships in the parish. His slaves would not have attended and may not have mourned Thistlewood's de-parture. One can assume, however, that his first slave, Lincoln, was affected by the passing of the man who had owned him for nearly thirty-one years, and Phibbah, now an old woman, probably grieved at his passing. But the mourn-ing would have been muted—he had reached a good age by Jamaican standards and, though well respected, did not have many close friends. Within a few months, he would have been forgotten. Once his inventory had been taken; his slaves, house, and other property had been sold; and his mistress freed, all of which had been done by 1792, the memory that Thistlewood had once lived in the parish would have quickly faded. Nothing he had done in his lifetime marked him out as someone whose life would be remembered. It is difficult to imagine that his activities, behavior, and thoughts could become a primary reference point for understanding Jamaican life in the mid- to late eighteenth century, as I have argued in this book. When one visits the land that once was the Egypt es-tate and Breadnut Island, along the Cabaritta River a few miles west of the small town of Savanna-la-Mar in southern Westmoreland, nothing survives that reminds us of him. The church where he was buried no longer exists, and the new church built on the property has obliterated the grave site where his re-mains rest. Similarly, nothing now stands at Tupholme, where he was born, in Lincolnshire, England, once a small hamlet but now empty fields.

But Thistlewood's diaries allow him to live on, albeit in a form he would not have liked or perhaps even recognized—as a brutal, sexually voracious master of traumatized slaves rather than a cultivated Enlightenment man, accomplished gardener, and amateur scientist. His diaries—fortuitously preserved, alone among diaries written by whites in the island in the eighteenth century—give Thistle-wood a voice. They encourage us to re-create his experience and, more impor-tant, allow us an entrée into the extraordinary society of which he was an unex-ceptional member. The material drawn from the diaries is fascinating in itself. More important, it helps to evoke a world that is past but was important in its time and whose memory still lingers in the West Indies and beyond.

Whites in a Slave Society

This study of Thistlewood's diaries casts light on three important topics. It explores the nature of power in a mature and brutal slave society, especially the relationship between hegemonic rule and negotiated consent. It illustrates the character of white society in eighteenth-century Jamaica. Finally, it elucidates how traumatized African slaves coped with the new and violent forms of discipline introduced by planters in the plantation revolution that changed societies with slaves in the American South and the British West Indies into slave societies. Each of these topics demonstrates the significance of the transformation of Jamaica into a slave society in shaping the lives of white and black Jamaicans.

Drawing from studies of ancient slavery, historians have made a distinction between societies with slaves, in which slavery was marginal to the central productive processes, and slave societies, in which slavery was central to economic production and the model for all social relations.[2] Jamaica became a slave society within a generation of first British settlement, before the plantation system had been fully developed and during the transitional period of Jamaican history when piracy competed with plantation agriculture for economic and cultural supremacy. By 1750, Jamaica had been a slave society for at least three-quarters of a century. It was one of the most complete slave societies in history, with over 90 percent of the population racially distinctive chattel slaves and with a system of laws predicated on the nearly total obedience of slaves to white authority. The impact of slavery was thus absolute, as Frank Tannenbaum recognized over fifty-five years ago in his pioneering study of slavery in the Americas. Slavery was at the center of both economic and social relationships: "Slavery changed the form of the state, the nature of property, the system of law, the organization of labor, the role of the church as well as its character, the notions of justice, ethics, ideas of right and wrong. Slavery influenced the architecture, the clothing, the cooking, the politics, the literature, the morals of the entire group—white and black, men and women, old and young. . . . Nothing escaped; nothing and no one."[3] Contemporaries knew of slavery's powerful hold even when they were determined to resist its horrors. The early-nineteenth-century missionary William Knibb knew what he was up against as an advocate of abolition in an island devoted to slavery's preservation. On his arrival, he declared: "I have now reached the land of sin, disease, and death, where Satan reigns with awful power and carries multitudes captive at his will." But exposure to slavery made him fearful that he would come to accept the peculiarities of a slave society as normal. Four years into his stay in Jamaica, he worried, "I am fearful of becoming habituated to its horror; sincerely do I hope I never may."[4] Even a determined opponent of slavery feared he could not escape the power of slavery to compel people to adopt the assumptions that undergirded it.

Thistlewood's diaries bear constant evidence of the all-pervasive effect of slavery on white society. He spent most of his nearly thirty-seven years in Jamaica supervising slaves, punishing slaves, having sex with slaves, quarreling with slaves, socializing with slaves, and intervening in disputes between slaves. He was both contemptuous of slaves as racial inferiors and afraid of what they might do to him if he relaxed his guard. His most intense relationships were with slaves, notably with Lincoln and Phibbah. He was immersed in a society that was dependent on the labor of black slaves for its wealth and prosperity. He lived among people who were fearful that the dreadful torments it inflicted on people it categorized as racial inferiors might one day be inflicted on them.

But we should also look, as we have done in this book, at white society outside of the overwhelming prism of slavery. We cannot understand Jamaica without assessing slavery, but slavery was not all there was in eighteenth-century Jamaica. The culture that blacks established was not the only cultural form that existed. Whites may have been small in number, but they developed a rich, vibrant, and distinctive culture that left a legacy in Jamaica well after the people who developed it vanished.[5] It was not necessarily an attractive culture. White Jamaicans were widely reckoned to be engaging but indolent, hospitable but avaricious and vain, lively but with a fiery temper, and egalitarian but capable of mind-numbing savagery. They were devoted above all to the main chance, which stimulated their avarice, supported their extravagance, and underlay their indolence and desultory inability to persevere at any task. The evidence from Thistlewood's diaries does nothing to dispel these eighteenth-century commonplaces about white Jamaican character. Yet a study of Thistlewood and his white compatriots reveals that whites were more than a flighty and ill-disciplined mob of extreme hedonists. They were also a tough people. A succinct summary of Thistlewood's life is that he was a tough man in a tough place who was prepared to do whatever it took to secure power and enforce his dominance over blacks. They were also more unified, less debauched, less selfish, and less self-serving than some think. They were the strongest and most determined "tribe" in the island and were formidable enemies of Africans. Understanding why slaves did not rebel more often or more successfully requires appreciating the strength and determination of this white "tribe."

We still know relatively little about these people and what they did and thought—the literature on whites in eighteenth-century Jamaica is sparse compared to the outpouring of work on the planter elite and common folk of the colonial Chesapeake and the lower South.[6] Thistlewood's diaries help us understand the contours of white society in this period and give us insight into the rules that governed white relations. They mostly confirm and deepen what we already know about white society from the writings of historians such as Edward Long and Bryan Edwards.[7] Nevertheless, they contradict at several points the established view of white Jamaican society. In many respects, Thistlewood was a typical white Jamaican. His diaries give us an excellent picture of the opportunities Jamaica offered and help explain why whites flocked to the island, despite the very real likelihood of early death from disease and their constant and justified fear that slaves would attack them. Edwards' telling aphorism about the underlying truth of white existence in slave societies bears restating: "Fear —that absolute coercion that supersedes all questions of right—is the leading principle upon which all governments in slave societies are supported."[8]

Thistlewood's diaries help us understand what it meant to be an ambitious white migrant in a mature slave society. He was interested in getting ahead economically in a society predicated on individual aggrandizement. Jamaica proved to be a land of opportunity for impecunious English migrants of ability and determination. From humble beginnings, he rose to a position of considerable comfort, becoming a landowner, sizable slave owner, and local worthy. By the time of his death, he had attained an estate that, though moderate by Jamaican standards, was appreciably greater than any estate he could have obtained if he had remained in England and large by the standards of British America. Thus, his move to Jamaica turned out to be a success. His success, however, was rooted in aspects of his character and behavior that were not usually renowned as features of a typical white Jamaican's personality. Jamaica was famed as a land populated by chancers, people who were reckless and intemperate, flitting from one project to another without finishing what they started. Thistlewood, instead, was careful, calculating, and sober. He worked hard. He was not self-indulgent, indolent, and full of overbearing pride, like most Jamaicans. He was persistent, steadfast, and mentally and physically resilient. Making money in Jamaica was hard work and required impressive industry and constant perseverance. Circumstances in the third quarter of the eighteenth century were propitious for the making of fortunes, but wealth did not just drop into white men's hands. The misfortunes, mostly self-inflicted, of Thistlewood's feckless and incompetent employer of fifteen years, John Cope, show that even men who had huge initial advantages, such as owning a large sugar estate, as Cope did, did not automatically become rich, especially if they did not plan carefully, manage their money skillfully, and attend with due diligence to the multifarious demands of running a plantation. Thistlewood was successful, unlike Cope, because the skills he acquired as a manager of slaves at Vineyard Pen and then the Egypt estate between 1750 and 1767 stood him in good stead when he purchased his own property.

The paucity of experienced and talented slave overseers on the mid-eighteenth-century Jamaican frontier meant that Thistlewood—tough, accomplished, resourceful—could name his own price when seeking employment. White planters relied on Thistlewood to run their plantations just as they relied on slaves to produce the crops that provided them with their wealth. Further, as Thistlewood's detailed accounting of his assets and debits show, poorer whites had a signal advantage over rich planters in that their handsome wages had to be paid in cash. Thistlewood was careful to never get into debt, possibly because he had firsthand evidence in his dealings with Cope of how easily indebtedness could compromise personal independence. As a result of his skill, careful husbanding of his assets, and determined exploitation of his value in a labor market that favored him, he was able to achieve by the 1770s his dream of landed independence and financial security. Contrary to a wide literature that assumes that the rise of large plantations in the British West Indies reduced opportunity for poor whites, the ordinary man, at least in Jamaica, was able to prosper. It is quite possible that Jamaica was the "best poor man's country" in the eighteenth century. If one survived its fierce disease environment and did not succumb to drink, gambling, or excessive wenching, few better places existed for a person seeking a competency or even a fortune. The sugar economy provided an ideal foundation for wealth, especially for servants willing to work under capricious owners. Thistlewood prospered as a functionary on a sugar estate and used the money he gained from this lucrative activity to take up pen keeping—an ideal profession for men of moderate wealth who had to buy their own slaves and land.[9]

But obtaining wealth was possible only through the agency of slavery. It was the acquisition and employment of slaves that led to making money. We have known for a long time that it was slavery that secured colonial prosperity in the eighteenth-century British Atlantic world.[10] Thistlewood's diaries confirm that proposition. Not only did slaves produce the goods and provide the services that gave whites most of their ongoing income, but they were also whites' principal assets. The value of slaves was especially pronounced in the third quarter of the eighteenth century as slave prices soared and slaves became valuable appreciating assets. But in order to gain value from slaves, their owners needed to know how to employ them and how to manage and control them. Thistlewood was in high demand as an overseer because he knew how to manage slaves. His ability to control slaves was his passport to prosperity. He acquired his landed estate from savings he accumulated from his employment as a manager of slaves and the substantial income he gained from the employment of his own slaves. He maintained his landed estate and was able to cultivate his garden and pursue his interest in amateur science through the labor of his thirty or more slaves. Slaves secured his financial independence, but at a cost. At bottom, Thistlewood never achieved what he most desired—physical and financial independence from others—because that independence always rested on the broad but scarred shoulders of his hardworking slaves.

Thistlewood was also a typical white Jamaican in being a fierce egalitarian. Jamaica was notorious for its intransigence to imperial authority, insisting that Britain treat it as an equal. That intransigence was rooted in white Jamaicans' touchiness about white equality within their sociopolitical structures. White Jamaicans, as an early-nineteenth-century governor lamented when turning down an offer to populate the island with lower-class females from England's jails, were committed egalitarians: "[T]he Description of Females which you mention would not be well received here. Every white Person is upon the same Footing in Jamaica."[11]

White equality arose primarily out of white demographic failure and Jamaica's immense economic productivity based on the backbreaking labor of more and more African chattel slaves. Because whites were few in number and the danger of black rebellion meant that all whites had to stick together, ordinary white men were in an extremely advantageous situation—politically as well as economically. In a country where whiteness was everything, wealthy men were forced to recognize that white men had a special claim on their attention. The rich were dependent on the poor, not only for their economic prosperity but also for their physical survival. Thistlewood was a vital cog in the successful continuation of white society in the island, and he knew it and acted upon it. He took liberties with wealthy white men that would have been considered outrageous in England and got away with it because rich whites knew it was important to keep skilled white operatives on their side.

Unlike the majority of white men, Thistlewood was not relentlessly sociable and hospitable, even though he did socialize with other whites and entertained them in his house. He was not an especially outgoing man but a loner, most comfortable with his own company. Nevertheless, he was public-spirited and participated in a full range of community activities, especially the political duties incumbent upon white residents in a rural parish. His contemporaries may not have been particularly fond of Thistlewood, although it is difficult to elucidate community opinion of him from Thistlewood's own words. We can only make assumptions based on odd hints from his diaries that suggest that he was a prickly character, determined to stand up for his rights even against the leaders of local society. But whatever they privately thought of him, well-off whites recognized that he was a significant person in the community and accorded him a degree of respect that would not have been possible in England. He was appointed to a range of local offices, culminating in his becoming a member of the local judicial bench, which honored him as a person of importance in Westmoreland. He achieved the much-vaunted personal independence that was a central animating impulse of men moving to eighteenth-century British America. He did so mainly through exploiting his advantages as a skilled and trustworthy white man of long residence in the island in a society desperately short of such crucial mediating figures. In Jamaica, the economic dependence of rich whites on poor whites had a powerful leveling effect, raising men of lowly status such as Thistlewood to positions of relatively high status and prestige.

Jamaica was a curious combination of eighteenth-century hierarchical assumptions and nineteenth-century democratic pretensions. Few societies have ever been so unequal, with over 90 percent of the population owning very little of the total wealth and being subject to the will of a very small minority. Even within white society, wealth was very unevenly distributed, with the wealthiest whites owning the great majority of Jamaican wealth. But within the structural inequality that characterized Jamaica was a remarkable ideological egalitarianism whereby all whites were recognized as being in important respects the equals of all other whites. White egalitarianism, however, was predicated upon nearly absolute racial supremacy. White Jamaicans were able to retain their belief in the naturalness of subordination by translating subordination and hierarchical domination from a British context into that of a racially polarized slave society in which white power and white egalitarianism were based on separating privileged free whites from brutalized black slaves. Upholding white supremacy replaced the protection of property and propertied persons as the basis of political legitimacy in a significant departure from the political culture of eighteenth-century Britain. Because white Jamaicans were afraid of what slaves might do to them if they were not kept brutally in check, they needed to ensure that all whites were united in their commitment to the maintenance of white rule. White unity was fostered through a compulsive cult of hospitality toward fellow whites, whereby even humble whites were included in the political process. Most important, whites prioritized the interests of whites at all times over the interests of blacks. By the last third of the eighteenth century, Jamaica had developed into a caste society, in which the social and political distances between white men and slaves and between white men and free coloreds were immense and insurmountable. This development was well under way by the time Thistlewood arrived on the island but was by no means complete. Women such as Elizabeth Anderson, a free mulatto or quadroon woman, mistress of William Dorrill, and probably the mother of Molly Cope,[12] were able to pass as whites before mid-century. After mid-century, however, the process whereby whites were distinguished from free coloreds was intensified. The shock of Tackey's revolt, in particular, convinced white Jamaicans that their safety resided in fostering white unity and making whiteness the badge of political and social inclusion.

The concessions that wealthy whites made for poorer whites were rooted in the leverage that ordinary whites had over wealthier whites as employees able to command their own price and essential allies against slaves. Yet the concessions were easy to make because so many whites were similar insofar as they were all masters over slaves and thus were implicitly concerned with supporting and continuing subordination. Even before Thistlewood became a slave owner in 1756, he had become accustomed to exercising mastery over slaves. Whites could luxuriate in a society known for its remarkable egalitarianism because so many whites—perhaps three in four adult men—shared a similar status as people complicit in the command of dependents. The habits of command went far down the social chain and gave white men a common identity. Thistlewood could insist on being treated as an equal to rich whites because he was a master of slaves. Any master of slaves had a special claim on the public weal. White egalitarianism in a society in which people believed in the naturalness of subordination created tensions when the interests of independent men clashed with the interests of other independent men, as was shown in Thistlewood's many disputes with other white men determined to stress their own independence. But in the main, white egalitarianism allowed whites to become a remarkably unified and formidable force in Jamaica. Thistlewood's diaries help us to see that whites did manage to create a viable society in the Caribbean that was characterized by more than just untrammeled individualism, self-centeredness, and lack of concern for the commonweal.[13] Thistlewood did not live in an anarchic society, although elements of anarchy, lawlessness, and disorder emerged from time to time among highly individualistic whites. Instead, he was part of a society with rules and reason, founded on the recognition of whiteness as the defining condition for social privileges.

But equality went only so far. It extended only to whites, not to free coloreds and most certainly not to slaves. Thistlewood's views on blacks and slavery were entirely conventional and were founded on his belief—unstated but explicit in his actions toward slaves unfortunate enough to be under his care—that blacks were a lower form of humanity whose sole purpose was to work for and be obedient to whites. In perhaps no other aspect of his life in Jamaica was Thistlewood more typical than in how quickly and avidly he turned to purchasing slaves. He knew that owning slaves was both a way to make money and a way to attain a degree of respectability. But respectability was not accompanied by restraint in how slaves were used or abused. Thistlewood was also typical in his treatment of slaves after he bought them. He bought slaves as soon as he had enough money for their purchase and gradually increased his slaveholding. His slave force reached thirty-four slaves by the time of his death. He looked after his slaves as well as he could, especially in regard to their health, but he did so less because he was concerned for them as people than because they were valuable investments. Thus, their health and welfare were of paramount importance. Thistlewood saw slaves as people rather than racial categories. He was no Edward Long with a well-developed theory of scientific racism that justified treating Africans as subhumans. Nevertheless, his treatment of slaves indicates that he saw Africans as distinctly inferior to whites and as people whose concerns need not be of much moment to him.

His diaries catalog a story of unremitting brutality against slaves. Indeed, his depredations against the slaves under his control are the most striking features of his diaries and make it hard to see him as anything other than a tyrannical and sadistic monster. He punished his slaves relentlessly and viciously, molested his slave women continually, and demonstrated a remarkable lack of concern about the effects of his actions on his slaves. Ironically, though one doubts that his slaves would have appreciated the irony, the chaos that Thistlewood cultivated largely through his own precipitate and vicious actions facilitated his control over his slaves. Richard Dunn has called the slave system in mid-eighteenth-century Jamaica one of the most dreadful systems of human exploitation ever developed. Thistlewood's diaries provide ample proof of this claim.[14] But the picture of slavery as revealed in Thistlewood's diaries is also a surprising one. It shows that his power may have been theoretically absolute but in practice was always modified by the realities of being a slave owner in an under-institutionalized society. Thistlewood governed his slaves partly through coercion and fear, partly through skillful manipulation of slaves' desires, partly through keeping slaves traumatized and dependent on him, and, most important, partly through negotiation. The extent of his power over slaves was far from total, as his diaries reveal on almost every reading. He could not control slaves' movements on and off the plantation. He was uninterested in directing most aspects of their social and cultural lives (and could not have done so even if he had wanted to). In particular, he depended on slaves' agreeing to do the work for him that he insisted they do.

At bottom, Thistlewood could not force his slaves to remain his slaves or accept his authority, but he could make life very unpleasant for slaves like Coobah and Sally who defied his control. In the last resort, he relied on his slaves' resigning themselves to their condition. Slaves accepted enslavement, albeit reluctantly and with reservations about the extent to which they would agree to masters' demands in any particular instance. They did so because it was difficult for them to see any viable alternative to the situation they found themselves in short of rebellion, resistance, and running away. All of these possible actions entailed enormous risks. Slaves who took these risks were more likely to suffer physical punishment, even death, than to gain any advantage over their masters. The odds were stacked so firmly in favor of masters that slave actions did not constitute resistance in any real sense. They may have opposed masters' policies and battled, sometimes successfully, to counter actions and customs they considered unfair or undesirable, but they had no chance of overturning the system, save through violent revolution. Slave "resistance" was opposition—internal manipulation of the established order that disrupted but did not threaten or transform the system within which slaves were trapped. Whites were too powerful in mid-eighteenth-century Jamaica for slaves to be able to challenge their authority except in a piecemeal and limited manner.

What we need to recognize as well, however, is that slavery was not maintained by force alone (though, of course, force was what sustained it). It was a negotiated relationship subject to continual renegotiation and redefinition. That negotiation, moreover, was done at the level of individual relations because, although the state mandated and supported masters' control over slaves, masters' control was bolstered only through a complex web of continuing interactions between two unequal parties.[15] Thistlewood's diaries provide a rich account of how that endless process of negotiation and renegotiation worked. The process was asymmetrical—Thistlewood had most of the power, and slaves had little to none; Thistlewood had the protection of the state and the law on his side, and slaves did not—but although the playing field was uneven, slaves did not always lose and masters did not always win.

It worked for Thistlewood mainly because he was able to exploit slaves' desire to possess goods and property of their own in a society that did not recognize slaves' rights over property. He was useful as the only person who could protect slaves' economic interests. The imposition of the provision-ground system, which made slaves protocapitalists as well as protopeasants, accentuated how much slaves needed his support to protect their property from attack by other blacks or whites. They had no choice other than to rely on their oppressor if they wanted their property to be safe from depredation. Unlike Thistlewood, slaves lived in a Hobbesian world, liable at any time to have their person or property attacked, without having any recourse to law or custom.

Thistlewood exploited very well the predicament slaves found themselves in, which may explain why he faced relatively little dissent or rebellion from his slaves after he took up residence on his pen. Even in Tackey's revolt, when Thistlewood's estate was directly threatened by advancing rebels, his slaves remained loyal to him. They were loyal less because they felt any sympathy for Thistlewood or any solidarity with him—it is clear that they resented, possibly hated, him and had good cause to do so—than because they had much to lose if the rebellion was not successful. In particular, slaves feared that rebels would destroy the property they had painstakingly acquired. Slaves hesitated before committing fully (though it is clear that several slaves at Egypt were at least sympathetic to the rebellion and had foreknowledge of what happened) to what was most likely to be an unsuccessful rebellion, the consequences of which would be the destruction of existing property rights. Rebellion served slaves' long-term interests, especially their desire to end enslavement and rid Jamaica of the whites who tormented them. Nevertheless, their principal opponent best protected their short-term interests. Only Thistlewood was able to mobilize the forces of the law to protect slave property. Only Thistlewood had the power to punish slaves who took advantage of the lawless conditions that pertained in the Jamaican countryside and threatened slave property. The result was an unholy alliance between oppressor and oppressed, with each dependent on the other. Slavery was not only a negotiated relationship. It was also a mutually dependent relationship. Thistlewood needed slaves in order to produce income and give him status. Slaves needed Thistlewood, much as they wished they did not, to secure their interests in a world where their interests were constantly under attack. Accommodation was as essential a part of slaves' existence as opposition.

Thistlewood's diaries provide a wealth of detail about slave life in eighteenth-century Jamaica, especially concerning the backbreaking work slaves were required to do. Cutting cane was one of the hardest tasks slaves had to do. Although this print is from a later period, showing slaves with more clothing than would have been customary in the eighteenth century, it illustrates the type of work slaves were expected to perform. *Jamaican Negroes Cutting Cane in Their Working Dresses*, in H. T. De La Beche, *Notes on the Present Condition of the Negroes in Jamaica* (London, 1825). Courtesy of the John Carter Brown Library at Brown University.

A study of Thistlewood's diaries shows the daily accommodations slaves and masters had to make with one another. It reveals, in particular, the accommodations Thistlewood had to make with his charges. Recognizing them as people was the most important concession, but there were others as well. More important, it shows how he took advantage of the accommodations slaves were forced to make with him in order to achieve harmonious slave management.

We sometimes look at what slaves did and examine how they resisted slavery without taking proper account of the fact that they were not alone on plantations and pens. Slaves in Jamaica enjoyed more autonomy, especially in cultural matters, than did slaves in British America, especially once paternalism began to replace patriarchalism as the dominant creed of American slave owners in the last third of the eighteenth century. But they were never members of autonomous communities. Masters interfered constantly in the workings of slave communities, either positively when they resolved disputes between slaves or, more often, negatively when they punished slaves for various infractions or sought women for sexual gratification. The point is that masters were always there, a presence that every slave had to deal with. Thistlewood was a skilled and successful manager of slaves. His ability to manage slaves improved over time as he moved away from the harshness of the sugar regime to the relatively benign environment of a garden and livestock pen. But he recognized the importance of imposing his will on slaves from the start and was good at doing so. In retrospect, few of the actions detailed in Thistlewood's diaries are as significant—or as chilling in their assertion of Thistlewood's ability to manifest his power over his slaves—as his first actions at his initial post, Vineyard. Having watched his employer, Florentius Vassall, demonstrate his dominance by giving the leading slave on the estate, the mulatto driver Dick, "300 lashes for his many crimes and negligences," Thistlewood proceeded to make an example of Titus, one of the oldest slaves on the pen. Thistlewood made him the first object of his punishment regime, giving him 150 lashes for harboring a runaway.[16] That Thistlewood's arrival triggered the savage punishment of two leading adult male slaves in a small community of forty slaves was not coincidental. It showed that Thistlewood was indeed, as his slaves at Egypt privately called him, "ABBAUMI APPEA," that is, "No for Play."

A Violent and Enlightened World

Thistlewood's diaries are extraordinary documents detailing years of involvement and thousands of interactions between blacks and whites. They provide a close view of the workings of the institution of slavery, an institution more complex, more variegated, more brutal, and yet more open than we had realized. Reading Thistlewood's diaries is like watching a soap opera in which the plot seems familiar but the working out of familiar scenarios takes unfamiliar turns. Yet for all of the information we are given about slaves and especially about how a no-nonsense manager dealt with the slaves under his control, we learn disappointingly little about what Thistlewood really thought about his charges. He tells us little about his views on Africans, slavery, and the morality or immorality of what he did to his slaves. Even more frustrating, the more Thistlewood knew about slavery and Africans, the less he confided to his diaries. By the time he became a landowner and pen keeper, Thistlewood would have acquired, through watching and socializing with a large number of slaves over the course of a decade and a half, a large body of information about how Africans acted, what they believed, and how he thought they should be controlled. He would have formed strong opinions about African capacities and the intimate workings of the slave system. But despite his close connections to slaves and his growing experience of slavery, Jamaica, and Africans in Jamaica, he became less and less revealing over time in his written records about Africans and slavery. He felt no need to share with potential readers what he would have considered obvious insights not worth telling himself in his daily record of his life.

But although detailing what he knew about Africans and slaves was not important to Thistlewood, it is important to us. For a modern reader, there is a massive contradiction about Thistlewood. On the one hand, he was a brutal and even sadistic tyrant, subjecting his charges to all manner of physical, psychological, and sexual ordeals over a sustained period. On the other hand, he was a cultivated man of the Enlightenment, an avid reader, and an amateur scientist. He was notably up to date with modern ideas and trends, even though he lived at the farthest reaches of the British Empire. One of the most surprising features of Thistlewood's life as revealed in his diaries is how far the ideas and values of the English Enlightenment reached. Even at the far edges of the Jamaican frontier, not all people reverted to "barbarism," which metropolitan observers condescendingly thought was a universal tendency of Europeans in the Tropics. Some, like Thistlewood and a small group of friends, were active participants in types of intellectual exchange that would not have disgraced ordinary men and women in metropolitan and provincial Britain. The question we cannot help but ask is how Thistlewood could be both cultivated and savage at the same time. Of course, this question is not one that was a contradiction in Thistlewood's lifetime, a period when savagery and civilization mixed happily together for most people most of the time. The leading intellectuals of Thistlewood's time, such as David Hume and Edward Gibbon, were generally in favor of slavery rather than opposed to it. The revolutionaries who took power in France after 1789, despite their supposed hatred of slavery, supported the rights of slave owners on every critical issue before events in St. Domingue forced their hand.[17] Moreover, the ability of seemingly cultivated men and women to demonstrate atavistic qualities that can only be described as barbaric is a startling feature of most modern history, notably the dreadful history of the twentieth century. Nevertheless, the demonization of West Indian planters in metropolitan opinion in the late eighteenth and early nineteenth centuries as unredeemable reprobates, uninterested in learning, and at odds with new humanitarian assumptions about the right way to treat other people makes this seeming contradiction in Thistlewood's character worthy of investigation.

Thistlewood was well read and au fait in the latest scientific fashions. His diaries show that metropolitan charges that Jamaica was a barbaric wasteland, devoid of intellectual activity, were overstated. Thistlewood was part of an active circle of friends interested in a wide variety of issues central to the "practical" Enlightenment. He and his friends read widely and well. They practiced astronomy, physics, chemistry, and biology. That such pursuits were not general does little to diminish their importance in showing how far the ideas of the Enlightenment spread in the eighteenth century. The customary image of the West Indian planter class is that it "constituted the most crudely philistine of all dominant classes in the history of Western slavery," according to Gordon Lewis, author of the leading intellectual history of the Caribbean. Lewis continues: "[O]ne whole minor theme of Caribbean literature . . . is almost unanimous in its general portrait of a planter way of life that is at once crassly materialist and spiritually empty."[18] In general terms, such condemnation is true. But it is not the whole story, as Thistlewood's diaries reveal and as the historians of eighteenth-century Jamaica and St. Domingue discussed in chapter 4 confirm. Thistlewood was not quite the tropical intellectual. But he contributed to the developing intellectual life of the island through his studies on meteorology (which found a place, much to Thistlewood's delight, in the work of a genuine tropical intellect, Edward Long) and his hard work in creating a showpiece garden. He was also part of an intellectual group of small planters and professionals who kept themselves informed about the principal philosophical, political, and scientific ideas circulating in Europe's metropolitan centers.

Yet some ideas that gained currency among Enlightenment philosophes — that Africans were worthy of being treated as human beings, that freedom was the appropriate status for Africans rather than slavery, and that all colonial rulers should respect the inherited cultural forms of colonial subjects — were never countenanced by Thistlewood and his friends. Indeed, what is remarkable about Thistlewood's intellectual assumptions is how little attention he paid to either slavery or Africans. His commonplace books are concerned more with natural phenomena, such as electricity, than with social phenomena, such as slavery. The principal obsession of most eighteenth-century scholars of British plantation settlements was to dissect the institution of slavery and show that it was a legitimate social order for a developing society. The legitimacy of black chattel slavery in a society otherwise devoted to liberty is the leitmotif of Long's long and Whiggish overview of Jamaican society immediately prior to the American Revolution. Jamaica's other major eighteenth-century historian, Bryan Edwards, was also primarily concerned with defending slavery from hostile attacks from the metropolis while reaffirming his humanitarian credentials. In South Carolina, as Jack Greene has shown, political discourse concentrated in-

cessantly on the relationship between slavery and liberty, an obsession powerfully informed by the ubiquity of slavery in the colony and local perceptions of
the nature of chattel slavery, as daily observed.[19]

Thistlewood, by contrast, betrays little interest in slavery. To the extent that
he considers it at all, slavery seems a natural condition, especially for Africans,
who he never doubts are suited to enslavement. He only once makes an empathetic identification with a slave, when he laments that Phibbah is "in miserable
slavery." It is significant, of course, that the slave he identifies with is his mistress and that he does so at a moment of great domestic crisis. Otherwise, slaves
are merely "negroes" or "mulattoes." He may not have demonstrated the scientific racism that characterized the writings of Long about Africans, but he
was similar to Long in seeing slaves as outside the social contract that entitled
people to rights and privileges. In this respect, we can see that in Jamaica, as in
other plantation societies with large slave populations, the existing order was
rationalized and naturalized through use of racial ideologies and a comprehensive racial coding. Thistlewood was a cultural racist who believed Africans were
culturally inferior. He was a white supremacist, almost in an unthinking way.
He demoted people of African descent to the base of civilization as savages,
even while he was prepared to have sex with them and mingle with them extensively.[20] Thistlewood's broad reading suggests that he was forward looking, in
touch with the latest intellectual developments in Britain and France. His attitude toward Africans, however, at least so far as it can be discerned, was backward looking. He continued to uphold old ideas that conceived of society as a
hierarchy of degrees, with Africans at the base and Europeans at the top. He
never internalized the Enlightenment insight, derived from a growing scientific
and philosophical emphasis on the importance of sympathy, that if slaves were
human, they were in important respects equal to whites. A cultural racist was in
effect little better than a biological racist, even if his ideas about black inferiority were less well developed and allowed for more fluidity in social interactions.
For both, color was crucial in determining who did and who did not belong to
the body politic. The taint of blackness was enough for Thistlewood to have no
sympathetic identification with a person. By conceptualizing Africans and people of African descent as people outside the bounds of sympathetic concern,
Thistlewood was overcome by the contradiction that we see, but he did not see,
between being a man of the Enlightenment and being a brutal and sadistic slave
owner.

The World of the Jamaican Slave

This book is about Thomas Thistlewood. It takes his words as the starting point for larger discussions about slavery and white society in Jamaica. Inevitably, it sees these issues as Thistlewood would have seen them, even if the perspectives we take are not necessarily those Thistlewood would have taken. The main value of this book is to introduce to a modern reader the world of an ordinary white Englishman living in a historically interesting society. Yet Thistlewood is not the only person who comes to life from a reading of his diaries. No other eighteenth-century diary contains the wealth of material that Thistlewood's diaries offer about Africans and people of African descent. From Thistlewood's diaries, we get a glimpse, albeit distorted, into the lives of hundreds of illiterate, if not inarticulate, slaves, mostly born in West Africa. These insights into the lives of people we rarely get the chance to examine make Thistlewood's diaries more interesting and more important.

In this book, we have concentrated on the experiences of seven slaves—though we could have added several more whose experiences would also have been interesting—who were part of Thistlewood's household at Breadnut Island. We have detailed their interactions with their master and assessed the impact on the slaves of those interactions. There are other ways of approaching this topic, such as attempting to re-create the contours of slave existence through the information and the silences contained in Thistlewood's diaries. But the approach taken here does more than reveal the means whereby Thistlewood retained control over a brutalized and hostile work force. It also allows us to glimpse what life was like for slaves. Thistlewood's slaves varied greatly in character and condition. They ranged from anonymous field hands about whom little information can be gathered, like Johnnie and Chub, who died young and without families, to determined rebels, such as Coobah and, in a different way, Sally. Other slaves were mothers, such as Abba, who faced a difficult time trying to provide for a large family. We have focused most attention on the two most intriguing slaves about whom we know the most—Lincoln and Phibbah. Their complex characters are fully realized in the diaries, even if, obviously, they did not reveal some aspects of themselves to Thistlewood or he did not bother to note them in his diaries.

The description of slavery contained in the pages of Thistlewood's journals is a deeply disturbing one. Slaves lived in a frightening world in which they were continually assaulted, constantly terrified, and had few people or institutions they could turn to for help. Law was of no avail, and custom was so attenuated that it was virtually of no use. Brutality and terror were their principal companions. The result was traumatized populations and psychologically disturbed individuals. Flux and uncertainty characterized slave lives. It preceded their lives in Jamaica—most of the slaves mentioned in Thistlewood's diaries were Africans transported to the island and thus experienced the horrors of the Middle Passage—and was a noticeable feature of their time with Thistlewood. In some respects, the longevity of Thistlewood and the relative stability of the slave forces he controlled, first at Vineyard, then at Egypt, and finally at Breadnut Island, underplay the extent of volatility within Jamaican slave communities. Most slave communities were excessively fragile, hardly communities at all, full of recently arrived Africans who were barely acclimatized to the island and subject to frequent disruption as slaves died, were sold to reduce debt, or were dispersed from the estates of dead whites.[21] By the standards of early Jamaica, Thistlewood's slaves experienced relatively little disruption. When he died in 1786, his inventory reveals that eighteen of his thirty-four slaves had moved with him from Egypt to Breadnut in 1767. Lincoln and Abba had been his slaves since before Tackey's revolt in 1760—an event that defined the experiences of whites and blacks in Jamaica of a previous generation. Nevertheless, even within this remarkably stable slave force, four slaves were sold and transported from the island—Simon in 1761, Coobah in 1774, and Sally and Mary in 1784. The threat of being sold was ever present for Jamaican slaves, even if most slaves may have remained on a single estate for most of their lives.

Even more likely than the possibility of being sold was that slaves would have physical pain inflicted on them. Women faced in addition the near certainty that their master would sexually molest them and the possibility that other whites would also see them as fair sexual game. Thistlewood was a fierce disciplinarian. He whipped slaves often and without discrimination. Douglas Hall's summary of the life of slaves at Breadnut Island between 1770 and 1776 indicates that Thistlewood whipped each of the twenty-two adult slaves who lived on the property at least once in that period.[22] Some slaves, such as Coobah, Sally, and Lincoln, were flogged much more regularly. Moreover, Thistlewood had been a considerably more vicious taskmaster when governing ninety slaves producing sugar at Egypt. Not only did he flog with abandon, but he went out of his way to devise especially sadistic punishments. In 1756, for example, he devised an ingenious and especially humiliating form of punishment, which demonstrated utter contempt for his charges, termed Derby's dose after its first recipient. Derby suffered the punishment on 28 January 1756, when Thistlewood "made Egypt shit in his mouth." He suffered it again on 26 May, when Port Royal caught him eating sugarcane and Thistlewood "made Hector shit in his mouth." Hector was involved in this degrading punishment once more on 23 July 1756, when Port Royal—the slave who had caught Derby two months earlier—was returned to the estate after having run away. Thistlewood "gave him a moderate whipping, pickled him well, made Hector shit in his mouth, immediately put in a gag whilst his mouth was full & made him wear it 4 or 5 hours." Phillis was given the same treatment, minus the gag, a day later. Six days later, Hector was himself punished for losing a hoe. Thistlewood inducted a new slave, Joe, into the travails of slavery by having Joe "piss into [Hector's] eyes & mouth etc." The same day, 30 July 1756, Thistlewood whipped two slaves and "washed and rubbed in salt pickle, lime juice & bird pepper." On 1 August, he caught a runaway, Hazat, and "put him in the bilboes both feet; gagged him; rubbed him with molasses & exposed him naked to the flies all day & the mosquitoes all night, without fire." The circle of degradation was completed on 27 August 1756 when Derby, the first recipient of the punishment that Thistlewood named after him, was made to shit in the mouth of Egypt, who had shit in his mouth seven months earlier.

Such sadism was extreme, even for Thistlewood, but it was at the far end of a continuum of violence against his slaves that he persisted in until his death. Thistlewood regularly flogged slaves, placed collars and chains on them, branded them with his mark, locked them in stocks, and subjected them to other punishments, such as "picketting" them on a bottle or smearing excrement over their faces. Some of these punishments, like Derby's dose, seem to have been devised more to humiliate his slaves and demonstrate to his charges the gratuitous assertion of his total power than to correct them for what Thistlewood considered misdemeanors. Slave women suffered other manifestations of his need for dominance and his indifference to their welfare and humanity. Thistlewood was a sexual opportunist, as his diaries graphically reveal. He undoubtedly raped slave women either in lieu of other punishments or merely for sexual gratification. Few slave women were safe from him, although he did draw the line at having sex with prepubescent children—he was contemptuous of his employer John Cope in part because he believed rumors that Cope was taking girls as young as nine or ten into his bed.[23] That white men in Jamaica sexually abused slave women is, of course, hardly a new revelation. Thistlewood's diaries, however, do more than just confirm the practice: they proffer firm evidence of the systematic and widespread practice of sexual molestation of black women by white men from all social backgrounds. We do not know what effects this sexual abuse had on slave women—Thistlewood never cares to tell us how his sexual encounters came about or what meaning either he or his partners attached to the events he describes with such clinical detachment. But we can speculate that the effects were profound and disturbing from what we know of modern research into the long-term consequences of sexual harassment, molestation, and abuse.[24]

The suffering that slaves were forced to endure was so great that even whites recognized it. Possibly, the torments that slaves faced may have damaged the psyches of nonslaves, as Thomas Jefferson argued when he noted that slave ownership "nursed, educated and daily exercised" habits of tyranny so that "the man must be a prodigy who can retain his manners and morals undepraved by such circumstances." Outside observers condemned Jamaicans for their brutality, wondering if residence in "the Torrid Zone" and world leadership in the "barbarous treatment of slaves" had changed the "natural Disposition" of white Englishmen "from Humanity into Barbarity." Even Thistlewood obliquely acknowledged that slaves were so damaged by what had been done to them that they were likely to respond with savage violence. In 1778, he copied into his commonplace book a poem that ended with the chilling couplet:

> Some Afric chief will rise, who, scorning chains,
> Racks, tortures, flames—excruciating pains,
> Will send his injur'd friends to bloody fight,
> And in the flooded carnage take delight;
> Then dear repay us in some vengeful war,
> And give us blood for blood, and scar for scar.[25]

But the major casualties of enslavement were blacks, not whites. They bore the marks of their mistreatment on their bodies—lacerations, brandings, and amputations. The bodily mutilation of slaves was undertaken by the state and by slave owners. On 2 November 1771, for example, a female slave called Frazier's Beck was convicted of having an unauthorized party at her house. She "had her ear slit, 39 lashes under the gallows, and 39 again against the Long Stores," while "Tomlinson's Abbington . . . [had] a bit cut out of his ear, and ditto lashes. Also several others flogged, &c." Slave rebels were burned in slow fires and gibbeted alive and then displayed until their bodies rotted. Persistent runaways were hung and decapitated and their heads were placed on poles as an example for other slaves. We can see the physical effects of punishment on individual slaves by tracing what Thistlewood did over six years to Mary, a slave he purchased in 1778 from Samuel Barton, who had to sell her to satisfy a debt.

Thistlewood described Mary at purchase as from "the Chambah Country, about 20 years of age, pitted with the smallpox & has had the yaws, her ears are bored; tolerably black, with black mark under each eye, thus." Thistlewood marked her with his brand "on each shoulder, but fairest on the left."[26] She was just under five feet tall. She was flogged three times by Thistlewood between 1778 and 1780. She was also whipped (probably under Thistlewood's instruction, but the context of the whipping is unclear) by a fellow slave, Strap, who himself was flogged because "in whipping Mary, it seems, almost cut one of Peggy's eyes out, her right eye." Mary received another flogging as well for Peggy's misfortune. In 1781, she ran away after complaining of a sore belly — Thistlewood thought, "She has got the clap I believe." That same year, she ran away for two weeks and was flogged, forced to wear "a steel collar with a few links of chain to it," and marked on her cheek with Thistlewood's brand. She ran away several more times, the longest absence lasting for nearly a year until she was captured, flogged, and put in the jail at Lucea in Hanover Parish. Thistlewood got her out of jail, paid her fine of £2.91, and "secured her in the bilboes." The next day, he "had Sally's collar with two prongs put on her secure. Marked her on each cheek, gave her a new bill and sent her into the field to work." He never took the collar off Mary until he sold her, eleven months later, on 30 November 1784. When she ran away again a month later, Thistlewood put her in irons as well. From 8 August 1784, Thistlewood locked the traumatized and depressed Sally to Mary's chains during the day. Thus, after being shackled to an intensely depressed and infantilized slave, branded on her cheeks and shoulders, pocked by smallpox, scarred by yaws, and lacerated by numerous floggings, she was shipped off of the island.[27]

The physical scars were easy to see and are easy to recapitulate. The psychic wounds were less obvious but no less real. A recent work on colonial North America aptly describes the process of enslavement as "a systematic assault on [slaves'] sense of self," in which the true brutality was "the psychic condition it imposed upon survivors."[28] The trauma that enslavement induced is everywhere apparent in Thistlewood's terse descriptions of slave behavior. His slaves' psychological distress was manifested in self-destructive behavior and violence and cruelty toward other slaves and animals. A few examples will suffice. On 8 December 1756, "Moll being jealous of Mr. Mould's Lydde with Cobbena, she beat Lydde so that we were forced to have her carried home." Moll threw herself in the river and drowned. Thistlewood was afraid that Cobbena and Quamina would follow suit since "they seem to be much concerned, & by their looks." On 6 June 1780, Thistlewood reported another attempted suicide, this one unsuccessful: "Mr. Wilson's Jimmy (Mocho Jimmy) Bess's husband attempted to hang himself &c, and was very refractory. He is of a very sullen disposition." A week earlier, he had found his prized horse, Mackey, in a distressed state, with his belly slashed. He had been stabbed by Strap, whom Thistlewood flogged for this misdeed on 9 June 1780. Slaves were constantly stealing from and fighting with each other, as on 10 September 1780, when Phibbah was hurt trying to separate Lincoln and Abba in the cookroom, where they were quarreling.

Reading Thistlewood's diaries makes one realize how deeply dysfunctional and conflicted the eighteenth-century Jamaican slave community was. We do not have enough information to psychoanalyze Thistlewood's slaves, and twenty-first-century psychology would not provide the keys to eighteenth-century mentalities even if we could put his slaves on the couch. But the truism that abused persons are more at risk for depression, self-mutilation, suicide, and a host of other personal problems and that people who are abused are likely to become abusers themselves is exemplified in a study of Thistlewood's slaves. Few of his slaves appear to have been able to escape the dehumanization and self-loathing that arose from being part of a brutal slave system. They were all damaged to a greater or lesser extent by their participation in a system in which to survive they had to compromise with their oppressors and accept the values and imperatives of their masters. The "savage paradox" of surviving slavery, as Primo Levi notes memorably of the even more pathological environment of Auschwitz, was that embedded in the triumph of survival was an implicit guilt in being one of those who survived rather than one of those who failed to survive.[29] For some slaves, it was too much to endure. Thistlewood mentions several slaves who killed themselves and several others who threatened to do so. Some slaves, notably Sally, became so demoralized by their mistreatment that they were overwhelmed. Sally's spirit was crushed by what she endured, and, reduced to a listless child, she accepted the contempt that masters believed was the lot of slaves. Slavery was more than just an economic system; it was also a system of social domination and alienation in which the dishonoring of slaves was a crucial element.[30] Sally demonstrated in her behavior that she had internalized the relentless dishonoring and had lost her sense of self.

Nevertheless, most slaves had ways to adapt to the pressures they were under. Thistlewood could not destroy slaves' sense of psychic personhood, although he could severely damage it, because he was not the only person to whom slaves became attached and he was not the only source of value in their lives. Moreover, he demonstrated little interest in becoming an all-powerful father and authority figure. He was brutal and sadistic, but he was no paternalist who believed in the convenient fiction of the contented slave and the benign master and was determined to control all aspects of slaves' personal and working lives.[31] In this way, he was quite different from the familiar stereotype of the slave master drawn from portraits of the antebellum southern planter elite. Thistlewood's slaves did have some space to be themselves. These opportunities were heightened by the Jamaican practice of making slaves provide for themselves by working on slave provision grounds. Although the provision-ground system provided only a bare minimum of support for most slaves and failed signally to help slaves in special circumstances, such as Abba with her large family, it did allow ingenious, entrepreneurial, and lucky slaves to attain some degree of economic independence. Jamaican slaves' tendency to engage in capitalist market-oriented activities enabled them to reduce masters' control over their activities. Slave communities were attenuated and fragile and constantly subject to being harmed by masters' interference. But they did provide slaves with a measure of protection, especially against slaves from other plantations. Moreover, they allowed them to attain meaning in their lives through the fulfillment of roles separate from those assigned to them by their masters.

What emerges from the mass of detail about slaves' lives and masters' strategies is how immensely complicated the system was. It was not a system in which masters could enforce the provisions encapsulated in Jamaica's various slave codes. Slaves violated whites' customary understandings of how slavery ought to work all the time. They wandered through the countryside without leave, participated in a multitude of economic and social exchanges that masters had no involvement in, carried weapons they were not allowed to carry, and had parties and practiced obeah despite strict injunctions against such activities. No doubt, they also plotted and conspired against whites in myriad ways that whites were unaware of and would have been unable to prevent even if they had been aware of them. Moreover, slaves were adept at finding niches and gaps in the slave system to advance themselves, even in those areas that seem at first glance to be notable arenas of slave oppression. Take sex, for example. The sexual molestation of black women by white men was persistent and highly detrimental, one presumes, to most slave women's sense of themselves. It probably had the greatest negative reverberation of all forms of oppression endured by slaves. But to view whites' sexual depravations against slave women solely as exploitation is incomplete. The sexual experiences of some slaves, like Sally, whose sexual encounters with Thistlewood and other whites seem to have been entirely coerced and were central to her gradual self-abasement, can be viewed solely within the prism of sexual exploitation. Other slaves' sexual involvements with whites were more complicated. Slave women were forced to put up with whatever sexual abuse whites gave them, but they could gain power and possibly wealth by taking advantage of the sex they were forced to endure. Thistlewood customarily, for example, paid his slaves, especially his favorite slaves, when he had sex with them. Over time, the payments for such encounters could add up to a large sum. Egypt Susannah, for example, a frequent sexual partner of Thistlewood's during the 1760s, saved enough money from having sex with Thistlewood to purchase pigs and cattle. Slave women who became mistresses could gain significantly greater advantages from their sexual hold on infatuated white men. Thistlewood was convinced, for example, that Myrtilla, whom he believed had his underling William Crookshanks under her thumb between 1754 and 1756, managed to eke out a number of advantages for herself through her involvement with a white man. He also thought she helped to provoke a conflict between Crookshanks and Myrtilla's white owners that violated deeply held principles about an owner's absolute right to control his or her slave. More to the point, however, were the advantages that Thistlewood's own mistress obtained through her involvement with a white man. Phibbah acquired land, property, slaves, and her own and her children's freedom by being associated with Thistlewood. Slaves thus sometimes had the ability to turn even the worst features of enslavement to their own account.

We can see how slaves survived slavery most clearly in the lives of Lincoln and Phibbah. Lincoln was Thistlewood's first slave and the slave with whom he was most intimate. That intimacy created problems but also allowed Lincoln to exploit gaps in the slave system. Lincoln became a skilled hunter, fisherman, and occasional driver. He also became a leader within the slave community of Breadnut Island, eventually establishing himself as the head of a large, African-influenced polygynous household. Like Thistlewood, Lincoln was a patriarch and exercised patriarchal authority, when he could, over his wives and children. He, too, was capable of brutality and insensitivity toward his dependents. I would not want to suggest that Lincoln and Thistlewood were particularly similar—the crimes of one were much greater than the other, and even privileged slaves had little power compared to the least-powerful white. But they were similar insofar as both were determined to exert mastery whenever they could. Lincoln constantly tried to wrest small privileges from his master. He was a survivor who maintained a sense of self and self-worth that was independent of Thistlewood's estimation of him.

Thistlewood's mistress Phibbah was even more of a survivor than Lincoln. Indeed, she was so resourceful that in the end she transcended slavery by becoming to all intents and purposes free. She manifested her freedom through her development of a family estate and her persistent and successful attempts to advance the interests of herself, her family, and her friends. By doing so, she illustrated the falseness of white beliefs that slaves were, in Long's hysterical denunciation of African character, "void of genius," "a brutish, ignorant, idle, crafty, treacherous, bloody, thievish, mistrustful, and superstitious people," concerned with little besides "the common occurrences of life, food, love and dress" —in short, a people "possessing, in abstract, every species of inherent turpitude that is to be found dispersed at large among the rest of the human creation, with scarce a single virtue to extenuate this shade of character."[32] None of these characteristics fits Phibbah's remarkable personality. In her thirty-three-year association with Thistlewood, she demonstrated that slaves were not just the extension of their master's will but that they could exercise some agency over how their lives would turn out. In exercising that agency, she helped shape the world in which she lived and the world in which Thistlewood sought to exercise his dominion.

Jamaica as a British Society

Thistlewood was an ordinary man living at the edges of the British Atlantic world. Does this re-creation of the daily rhythms and routines of his mostly uneventful life tell us much about larger themes? Or does it merely give us an entrée into a particular community and society with assumptions about the rightful order of things that not only are distasteful but also no longer exist? Do these tales of Thistlewood and his slaves, entertaining and disturbing as they are, have any wider application? I think they do. They not only allow us to glimpse what life was like for a white man and his slaves in one of the most complete slave societies that has ever existed but also provide insight into the nature of power in premodern societies populated by Britons. Britons prided themselves as being lovers of liberty and people who would never be slaves. Their constitution and system of government in the eighteenth century were based on their devotion to liberty, their commitment to the protection of property rights, and their determined resistance to real or perceived tyrants. But they did not extend to others, especially Africans, what they insisted on for themselves. Britons sought out Africans whom they could transform into slaves to work the plantations that were the foundation of a portion of their eighteenth-century prosperity. They also lusted after slaves as persons who could satisfy their sexual longings and their fantasies of mastery. The plantation societies they perfected in the British West Indies in the seventeenth and eighteenth centuries were modeled on the political structures of eighteenth-century Britain, especially those of metropolitan England, but the presence of slaves changed the nature of power in those societies. An analysis of Thistlewood and his diaries provides us with an understanding of power in a society dominated, at least numerically, by racially distinctive slaves and illustrates the extent to which the nature of power in Jamaica had diverged from the nature of power in contemporary Britain.

Of course, in many respects the culture of power in eighteenth-century England was not unlike that which operated in Jamaica. Both societies worshiped the rule of law, but the rule of law in both places was as much a weapon of the rich and propertied as it was an impartial means of regulating and reconciling conflicts to the satisfaction of all groups in society. As a generation of historians have illustrated, England was a violent and brutal place with the bloodiest criminal codes in Europe, where people were regularly arrested and convicted under an ever-expanding proliferation of statutes that mandated capital punishment. As in Jamaica, the interests of propertied persons were paramount. Strong evidence exists that Britons' vaunted celebration of their laws and constitution was a superficial cover for a concerted attempt on the part of a self-confident ruling class to aggrandize power for themselves at the expense of poorer people. In this view, England's rule of law was, in Adam Smith's words, "a combination of the rich to oppress the poor" by protecting "the inequality of goods." The slave codes and informal practices of Jamaica whereby slaves faced draconian physical punishment for minor infringements mirrored the law of eighteenth-century England. The Black Act of 1723 allowed men to be hung and left to rot in chains for such minor offenses as poaching rabbits, stealing fish, cutting down trees, and burning a haystack. Soldiers in the British Army were just as likely as slaves to be whipped or hung for insubordination or for absconding without leave, and the ferocity of the punishments inflicted were probably greater than even slave owners, who did not want to destroy valuable property, were prepared to dish out.[33]

Yet the operation of power in Jamaica and other slave societies in British America was different from the operation of power in England in two crucial respects. First, justice was always tempered by mercy in eighteenth-century England. A large proportion of sentences mandating capital punishment were never inflicted but were reduced upon appeal to members of the governing class. In addition, the notion that the law of England was the same for rich as for poor was not just a convenient social fiction. The political and social elite were expected to observe and be bound by the law and were occasionally forced to do so, as in the cases of the executions of Lord Ferrers and the Reverend Dr. Dodd. To depict the law of eighteenth-century England as the exclusive agent of class power is a gross simplification because it also acted to integrate individuals and communities and probably enjoyed the confidence of a broad majority of the English people, most of whom accepted the rightness of a deferential order. The ruling class recognized that the authority they wielded was not absolute and had to be exercised in ways that commanded the respect of the governed. Consent was vital. As the conservative clergyman William Paley argued in 1785, in all forms of civil government, "the physical strength lies in the governed," and therefore wise governors should know "that general opinion ought always to be treated with deference, and managed with delicacy and circumspection."[34] Moreover, the terror of the law should not be overemphasized. Torture was forbidden and was generally not practiced even informally, in great contrast to what happened in slave societies. Trial by jury and the rule of habeas corpus were sacrosanct. Second, the rule of law was founded firmly on the rights of property and was designed to protect the rights of the propertied, including their lives and liberties. Such a statement is generally agreed upon, but what is sometimes missed is that the middling orders and some poorer people also used the law to protect their position and their property. When William Blackstone argued that the law supported "the meanest individual . . . from the insults and oppression of the greatest," he was being neither naive nor disingenuous. The protection of property rights by the law was often extended to the poor, and equality of justice for rich and poor alike was not entirely a myth.[35]

White Jamaicans accepted both of these principles—the equality of all before the law and the sanctity of property rights—in how they governed themselves. Indeed, their treatment of fellow whites was remarkably enlightened and progressive by the standards of contemporary England, let alone Europe. But in their dealings with their slaves, different principles pertained. The culture of power in Jamaica as it related to white control over blacks was a form of absolutism. Jamaica was akin to a police state based on a commitment to terror as an instrument of rule. People like Thistlewood acted as the enforcers of submission to terror. Catherine the Great's aphorism about how she exercised absolute power—"Je travaille sur le peau humaine"—was true for every apparatchik of the Jamaican state. Thistlewood also etched his dominance on the very skin of slaves. Whites justified their actions by repeating the claims made in the most influential of British American slave codes, the Barbadian code of 1688, declaring that slaves were so barbarous that they were unfit to be governed by the laws and customs of England. But as conservative opponents of the slave system such as the ex–West Indian and early abolitionist Reverend James Ramsay recognized, the basis of power in what Ramsay called "the Kingdom of I" was arbitrary authority of a kind that Englishmen believed to be contrary to the laws of nature as prescribed by Locke, Montesquieu, and Rousseau. Even proslavery apologists acknowledged that whites governed through coercion rather than consent. Bryan Edwards attempted to show planters in a humane light. Nevertheless, his determined effort to defend West Indian planters from the slurs of people outraged about how they used their "plenitude of power" was compromised by his admission that planter kindness "affords but a feeble restraint against the corrupt passions and infirmities of our nature, the hardness of avarice, the pride of power, the sallies of anger, and the thirst of revenge." White West Indians thus did not have any defense against the insolent but truthful remarks of the French West Indian torturer and slave owner Nicholas Lejeune in his celebrated trial in St. Domingue for excessive cruelty against slaves in 1788. Lejeune insisted that a slave could only be kept in check by "the consciousness of absolute power that we hold over his person." A slave detested his master, Lejeune argued: "[I]f he does not commit against us every evil that he could, it is only because his will is enchained by terror." Lejeune was right. Despite his long history of barbaric tortures against slaves, which included leaving slaves to rot in irons, he was acquitted and the slaves who denounced him to the court at Le Cap were punished. Whites had a torturer's charter. Lejeune could flourish unchecked in the Caribbean—in Jamaica, such a psychopath would not even have gone to trial.[36]

Just as important, white Jamaicans deviated from the example of metropolitan Britain in abandoning the principle that property was paramount in favor of doctrines that increasingly emphasized the supremacy of race in all matters. Race was the foundation of the social system—white skin meant freedom, dominion, and power; black skin meant slavery, submission, and powerlessness.[37] By the time Thistlewood came to Jamaica, Jamaica was becoming a caste society in which whiteness was the measure of all things. The fact that a few blacks overcame to some extent their presumed powerlessness did not weaken the strength of the racial divide between blacks and whites. Thistlewood benefited greatly from the premium placed on being white. It is hard to imagine that he would have done as well as he did in Jamaica in another country where whiteness did not confer so many advantages. It allowed him space in which he could seek mastery—over himself and over dependents—and satisfy his desires—intellectual, social, and sexual. In the final analysis, however, Thistlewood's lifelong search for mastery, a quest that led him to write his remarkable diaries and seek both a competency and status as an educated and enlightened man, must take second place to the realities of his conduct toward slaves. These showed him to be the opposite of what Englishmen considered themselves to be—a tyrannical and cruel despot. I imagine he would be horrified at this final estimation of his character, but, as the evidence of this book shows, we are right to remember him for his cruelties and brutalities rather than for the other, more attractive features of his personality. Tyranny in the end accompanied whiteness, and it undid Thistlewood as it eventually undid the pretensions of whites wishing to create Albion in the Tropics.

Abbreviations

Add. MSS	Additional Manuscripts
BL	British Library, London
CO	Colonial Office Series, Public Record Office, London
IRO	Island Record Office, Twickenham, Jamaica
JA	Jamaica Archives, Spanishtown, Jamaica
S&A	*Slavery and Abolition*
WMQ	*William and Mary Quarterly*

Chapter One

1. Diary of Thomas Thistlewood, 20 October 1749, Monson 31/1, Lincolnshire County Archives, Lincoln. All subsequent citations to Thomas Thistlewood's diaries—archived in thirty-seven volumes as Monson 31/1–37—will be by date only. I thank Lord Monson for permission to quote from the diaries.

2. 13, 24, 28 April 1750.

3. 27, 29 April, 1 May 1750.

4. 15, 18 May, 16, 20 July, 1 August, 1 October 1750.

5. For Thistlewood at Vineyard, see Douglas Hall, "Thomas Thistlewood in the Vineyard, 1750–51," and "The Vineyard Slaves," *Jamaica Journal* 21, no. 3 (1988): 16–29, and 21, no. 4 (1988–89): 2–16, and Philip D. Morgan, "Slaves and Livestock in Eighteenth-Century Jamaica: Vineyard Pen, 1750–1751," *WMQ*, 3d ser., 52 (1995): 47–76.

6. 12, 19 August, 18 September, 25 December 1750, 4, 5, 26 January, 10 May, 25, 27 June, 6 July 1751.

7. 7 July 1751.

8. 17 July 1750, 28 January, 27 February, 10, 16 May 1751.

9. 3 June 1750, 3, 11 January, 5 February, 11–13 September 1751.

10. 17, 31 July 1751.

11. 1, 30 October 1750, 9 October 1751, 9 February 1752.

12. Trevor Burnard, "'Prodigious Riches': The Wealth of Jamaica before the American Revolution," *Economic History Review* 54 (2001): 506–24.

13. Thistlewood recorded his early life in Monson 31/83.

14. 5–6, 27 March 1749.

15. William Beckford, *Remarks upon the Situation of the Negroes in Jamaica* (London, 1788); William Beckford, *A Descriptive Account of the Island of Jamaica*, 2 vols. (London, 1790); Ricketts and Jervis Papers, Add. MSS 30001, BL.

16. Long Papers, Add. MSS 18275A, BL.

17. David Johnson, *Regency Revolution: The Case of Arthur Thistlewood* (Salisbury, England: Compton Russell, 1974).

18. 21 February 1781.

19. Edward Long, *History of Jamaica . . .* , 3 vols. (1774; reprint, London: Frank Cass, 1970), 2:447–62; Bryan Edwards, *The History, Civil and Commercial, of the British Colonies in the West Indies*, 2d ed., 3 vols. (London, 1793), 2:64–79; Michael Craton, *Testing the Chains: Resistance to Slavery in the British West Indies* (Ithaca, N.Y.: Cornell University Press, 1982), 125–39.

20. 7 August 1781.

21. 4, 8 October, 31 December 1780.

22. 8 October 1780.

23. Andrew O'Shaughnessy, *An Empire Divided: The American Revolution and the British Caribbean* (Philadelphia: University of Pennsylvania Press, 2000), 207, 243–44.

24. P. J. Marshall, ed., *The Oxford History of the British Empire: The Eighteenth Century* (Oxford: Oxford University Press, 1998), 584; O'Shaughnessy, *Empire Divided*, xi–xii.

25. For the early history of Jamaica, see Richard S. Dunn, *Sugar and Slaves: The Rise of the Planter Class in the English West Indies, 1624–1713* (Chapel Hill: University of North Carolina Press, 1972). For the mid-eighteenth century, see Richard B. Sheridan, *Sugar and Slavery: An Economic History of the British West Indies, 1623–1775* (Bridgetown, Barbabos: Caribbean Universities Press, 1974), 222–32, and J. R. Ward, *British West Indian Slavery, 1750–1834: The Process of Amelioration* (Oxford: Clarendon Press, 1988). For Jamaica in the late eighteenth and nineteenth centuries, see Edward Brathwaite, *The Development of Creole Society in Jamaica, 1770–1820* (Oxford: Clarendon Press, 1971), and B. W. Higman, *Slave Population and Economy in Jamaica, 1807–1834* (Cambridge: Cambridge University Press, 1976). For Jamaican shares of West Indian produce imported into Britain, see Sheridan, *Sugar and Slavery*, 470–71, and Phyllis Deane and William A. Cole, *British Economic Growth, 1688–1959* (Cambridge: Cambridge University Press, 1967), 87.

26. [Charles Leslie], *A new and exact account of Jamaica* [Edinburgh, ca. 1740], 353.

27. Burnard, "'Prodigious Riches,'" 517.

28. CO 137/19, 137/27/24, 137/70/88; Long, *History of Jamaica*, 1:494–96; "Evidence of John Ellis," in *The Substance of the Evidence of the Petition Presented by the West-India Planters and Merchants to the House of Commons* (London, 1775), 66–67. For cattle pens, see Verene Shepherd, "Pens and Pen-keepers in a Plantation Society: Aspects of Jamaican Social and Economic History, 1740–1845" (Ph.D. diss., Cambridge University, 1988).

29. Burnard, "'Prodigious Riches,'" 517–20.

30. Trevor Burnard and Kenneth Morgan, "The Dynamics of the Slave Market and Slave Purchasing Patterns in Jamaica, 1655–1788," *WMQ*, 3d ser., 58 (2001): 205–7.

31. For slavery in Jamaica, see Higman, *Slave Population and Economy in Jamaica*; Michael Craton, *Searching for the Invisible Man: Slaves and Plantation Life in Jamaica* (Cambridge, Mass.: Harvard University Press, 1978); Kenneth F. Kiple, *The Caribbean Slave: A Biological History* (New York: Cambridge University Press, 1984); Roderick A. McDonald, *The Economy and Material Culture of Slaves: Goods and Chattels on the Sugar Plantations of Jamaica and Louisiana* (Baton Rouge: Louisiana State University Press, 1993); B. W. Higman, *Montpelier, Jamaica: A Plantation Community in Slavery and Freedom, 1739–1912* (Kingston: Press University of the West Indies, 1998); Barbara Bush, *Slave Women in Caribbean Society, 1650–1838* (London: James Currey, 1990); Michael Mullin, *Africa in America: Slave Acculturation and Resistance in the American South and the British Caribbean, 1736–1831* (Urbana: University of Illinois Press, 1992); Ward, *British West Indian Slavery*; Richard D. E. Burton, *Afro-Creole: Power, Opposition, and Play in the Caribbean* (Ithaca, N.Y.: Cornell University Press, 1997); Franklin W. Knight, ed., *General History of the Caribbean*, vol. 3, *The Slave Societies of the Caribbean* (London: UNESCO, 1997); and Richard B. Sheridan, *Doctors and Slaves: A Medical and Demographic History of Slavery in the British West Indies, 1680–1834* (Cambridge: Cambridge University Press, 1985). For an argument about the heterogeneous origins of Jamaican slaves, see Trevor Burnard, "E Pluribus Plures: African Ethnicities in Seventeenth and Eighteenth Century Jamaica," *Jamaican Historical Review* 21 (2001): 8–22, 56–59. See also David Eltis, *The Rise of African Slavery in the Americas* (Cambridge: Cambridge University Press, 2000), 224–57.

32. Trevor Burnard, "European Migration to Jamaica, 1655–1780," *WMQ*, 3d ser., 53 (1996): 769–96; Trevor Burnard, "'The Countrie Continues Sicklie': White Mortality in Jamaica, 1655–1780," *Social History of Medicine* 12 (1999): 45–72.

33. Trevor Burnard, "A Failed Settler Society: Marriage and Demographic Failure in Early Jamaica," *Journal of Social History* 28 (1994): 63–82.

34. Burton, *Afro-Creole*, 20–21. See also Ira Berlin, *Many Thousands Gone: The First Two Centuries of Slavery in North America* (Cambridge, Mass.: Harvard University Press, 1998), 107–12, 170–74, 190–91.

35. Long, *History of Jamaica*, 2:279, 328; Burnard, "'Countrie Continues Sicklie,'" 63–64.

36. "Statistics of Jamaica, 1739–1775," Long Papers, Add. MSS 12435, f. 41, BL.

37. Edmund S. Morgan, *American Slavery, American Freedom: The Ordeal of Colonial Virginia* (New York: W. W. Norton, 1975); James Horn, *Adapting to a New World: English Society in the Seventeenth-Century Chesapeake* (Chapel Hill: University of North Carolina Press, 1994).

38. James Ramsay, "Motives for the Improvement of the Sugar Colonies," Add. MSS 27621, f. 44, BL; Leslie, *New and exact account*, 38; Long, *History of Jamaica*, 1:6, 397, 438, 570, 2:135, 266, 287; James Knight, "The Natural, Moral and Political History of Jamaica and the Territories thereon depending," Long Papers, Add. MSS 12418–19, BL; Long, *History of Jamaica*, 1:88, 239, 2:78; [Edmund Burke], *An Account of the European Settlements in America*, 2 vols. (London, 1757), 2:128, 130.

39. *An Essay concerning Slavery and the Danger Jamaica is expos'd to from too great Number of Slaves . . .* (London, 1746), vi, 18, 38; Leslie, *New and exact account*, 41; *The Works of James Houston, M.D.* (London, 1753), 254.

40. John Fothergill, *Considerations Relative to the North American Colonies* (London, 1765), 41–42; Patrick Browne, *The Civil and Natural History of Jamaica* (London, 1756), 23.

41. 21 July 1751; Long, *History of Jamaica*, 1:39, 77, 178, 393, 2:234, 262–65, 281–84; Leslie, *New and exact account*, 319. For the Jamaican love of freedom, see Jack P. Greene, "The Jamaica Privilege Controversy, 1764–1766: An Episode in the Process of Constitutional Definition in the Early Modern British Empire," *Journal of Imperial and Constitutional History* 22 (1994): 16–53, and Jack P. Greene, "Liberty, Slavery, and the Transformation of British Identity in the Eighteenth-Century West Indies," *S&A* 21 (2000): 1–31.

42. Edwards, *History, Civil and Commercial*, 2:6–7.

43. Knight, "Natural, Moral and Political History," Add. MSS 12419, f. 71; Leslie, *New and exact account*, 28; Long, *History of Jamaica*, 2:262–63, 280–83; Browne, *Civil and Natural History*, 22–23.

44. CO 137/19; R. C. Dallas, *The History of the Maroons*, 2 vols. (London, 1803); Craton, *Testing the Chains*, 67–98, 211–23; 1 June 1750, 8 January 1751.

45. CO 137/19, 137/28/160, 137/87; "Statistics of Jamaica," Inventories, 1732–86, IB/11/3/16, 24, 25, 33, 56, 63, JA.

46. These manuscripts were purchased by William John Monson, 6th Lord Monson (1796–1862), from J. S. Padley, who had acquired them from the Reverend J. F. Wray of Horncastle, the husband of Thistlewood's great-great-niece, in 1853 (Monson 31/91).

47. In transcribing and quoting from Thistlewood's diaries, I have adopted the interpretative practices explained in Douglas Hall, *In Miserable Slavery: Thomas Thistlewood in Jamaica, 1750–1786* (London: Macmillan, 1989), xviii–xix.

48. V. A. C. Gatrell, *The Hanging Tree: Execution and the English People, 1770–*

1868 (Oxford: Oxford University Press, 1994), 284–92; William K. Wimsatt Jr. and Frederick A. Pottle, eds., *Boswell for the Defence, 1769–1774* (London: William Heinemann, 1960), 300.

49. Lawrence Stone, *The Family, Sex, and Marriage in England, 1500–1800* (New York: Harper and Row, 1977), 546–47.

50. 10 November 1759.

51. Diary of John Thistlewood, 3 February 1765, Monson 31/38.

52. 17 July 1757.

53. Robert A. Fothergill, *Private Chronicles: A Study of English Diaries* (London: Oxford University Press, 1974), 22.

54. Alan Macfarlane, *The Family Life of Ralph Josselin, a Seventeenth-Century Clergyman* (Cambridge: Cambridge University Press, 1970), 8.

55. 5 February 1768.

56. Leslie, *New and exact account*, 38; Long, *History of Jamaica*, 2:266.

57. 5 May 1778, 18 January 1780.

58. Leslie, *New and exact account*, 41.

59. Stanley Milgram, *Obedience to Authority: An Experimental View* (London: Tavistock, 1974); Arthur G. Miller, *The Obedience Experiments: A Case Study of Controversy in the Social Sciences* (New York: Praeger, 1986), 179–90.

60. The classic work is Christopher Browning, *Ordinary Men: Reserve Police Battalion 101 and the Final Solution in Poland* (New York: Harper Collins, 1992).

61. Fothergill, *Considerations*, 41–42; *Works of James Houston*, 285; J. B. Moreton, *Manners and Customs in the West India Islands* (London, 1790), 78, 81.

62. Abbe Guillaume Raynal, *A Philosophical and Political History of the Settlements and Trade of the Europeans in the East and West Indies*, 5 vols., translated by J. Justamond (Dublin, 1779), 5:48; [Burke], *Account of the European Settlements in America*, 2:154; *Essay concerning Slavery*, 19.

63. Knight, "Natural, Moral and Political History," Add. MSS 12419, f. 85.

64. Long, *History of Jamaica*, 2:354.

65. Primo Levi, *The Drowned and the Saved*, translated by Raymond Rosenthal (London: Abacus, 1988), 27–32.

66. Jack P. Greene, *Pursuits of Happiness: The Social Development of Early Modern British Colonies and the Formation of American Culture* (Chapel Hill: University of North Carolina Press, 1988), 193–206.

Chapter Two

1. 27–28 March 1749.

2. Trevor Burnard, "European Migration to Jamaica, 1655–1780," *WMQ*, 3d ser., 53 (1996): 781–83.

3. 26 February, 8 March 1751.

4. Jack P. Greene, *Imperatives, Behaviors, and Identities: Essays in Early American*

Cultural History (Charlottesville: University Press of Virginia, 1992), 101, 188; [John Norris], *Profitable Advice for Rich and Poor* (London, 1712), 55, 61–62; Thomas Nairne, *A Letter from South Carolina* (London, 1710), 3, 56.

5. In 1773, Thistlewood, as executor of the estate, sold 30 slaves and 117 acres belonging to his partner, Samuel Say, for £2,988.48 in currency—£287.06 more than Thistlewood's executors received for his 34 slaves and 160 acres in the late 1780s (28 September 1773).

6. This may be a substantial underestimate, as Thistlewood may have benefited considerably from the will of his friend Samuel Hayward, who died on 4 June 1781. On 14 June 1781, he remitted to Britain £801.77, along with a copy of Hayward's will. On 7 February 1786, he sent to London bills of exchange for the Hayward estate of £1,524.25 sterling (£2,133.95)—the first installment of Herring's payment for Hayward's slaves. It is unclear whether this money should be counted as part of Thistlewood's estate. On his own account, Thistlewood also remitted to Britain a total of £774.74 on 20 August and 1 September 1781, 24 August 1784, and 12 April 1785. On 12 May 1786, Thistlewood agreed to pay six equal annual payments totaling £1,800 for the great house of Theodore Stone and 25 acres, suggesting that some of Hayward's money had devolved to Thistlewood. If this is correct, Thistlewood's landed estate needs to be increased by the amount he had paid for Stone's property. Thistlewood may have had as much as £5,000 at his death.

7. Inventories, 1787, IB/11/3/71/200, JA; Deeds, 1789, 374/75, IRO.

8. Trevor Burnard, "'Prodigious Riches': The Wealth of Jamaica before the American Revolution," *Economic History Review* 54 (2001): 506–24.

9. Richard B. Sheridan, *Sugar and Slavery: An Economic History of the British West Indies, 1623–1775* (Bridgetown, Barbados: Caribbean Universities Press, 1974), 230.

10. Philip D. Morgan, *Slave Counterpoint: Black Culture in the Eighteenth-Century Chesapeake and Lowcountry* (Chapel Hill: University of North Carolina Press, 1998), 41; Allan Kulikoff, *Tobacco and Slaves: The Development of Southern Cultures in the Chesapeake, 1680–1800* (Chapel Hill: University of North Carolina Press, 1986), 331, 338.

11. See Trevor Burnard, "Not a Place for Whites?: Demographic Failure and Settlement in Comparative Context, Jamaica, 1655–1780," in Kathleen Monteith and Glen Richards, eds., *Jamaica in Slavery and Freedom: History, Heritage, and Custom* (Kingston: Press University of the West Indies, 2002), 73–86.

12. Trevor Burnard, "'The Countrie Continues Sicklie': White Mortality in Jamaica, 1655–1780," *Social History of Medicine* 12 (1999): 45–72.

13. M. F. Lloyd Prichard, ed., *The Collected Works of Edward Gibbon Wakefield* (Auckland: Auckland University Press, 1969).

14. Burnard, "European Migration," 787–89.

15. 5 May 1750.

16. 29 April, 15 May 1750, 27 June 1757.

17. Quarter deficiency taxes, Westmoreland Vestry Minutes, 1780–81, IB/2/7/1, JA.

18. Richard B. Sheridan, *Doctors and Slaves: A Medical and Demographic History of Slavery in the British West Indies, 1680–1834* (Cambridge: Cambridge University Press, 1985), 148–84.

19. "Mr. Richard Beckford's Instructions to Messrs. John Cope, Richard Lewing, [and] Robert Mason," 10 April 1754, Monson 31/86.

20. 7, 10, 26 May, 9, 29 June 1750.

21. 13 May 1750, 8 March 1751, 1 September 1757.

22. 20 March, 6 June 1756.

23. 18 June 1757.

24. 12 August 1770, 19 June 1779. On 11 April 1777, Woolery bought Midgeham from George Poyntz Ricketts for the astonishing sum of £80,000.

25. Diary of John Thistlewood, 29 June 1763, Monson 31/38.

26. 20, 29 October, 8 November, 2–5 December 1760.

27. For the functioning of debt in the Chesapeake, see T. H. Breen, *Tobacco Culture: The Mentality of the Great Tidewater Planters on the Eve of the Revolution* (Princeton: Princeton University Press, 1985).

28. Sheridan, *Sugar and Slavery*, 262–305; Richard Pares, *Merchants and Planters*, supplement no. 4, *Economic History Review*, (Cambridge: Cambridge University Press, 1960).

29. Inventories, 1753, IB/11/3/19, 23, JA.

30. 12 June 1756.

31. 23 June 1764.

32. 25 May 1762, 31 December 1769.

33. 24 May, 11 July 1751.

34. 6 October, 17 December 1751, 11 May 1753. See also 19 September 1771.

35. His inventory may have been understated since no slaves were included in the tally. His son, who died two years later, left a personal estate worth £5,803.71, including twenty-seven slaves, valued at nearly £2,000. See Inventories, 1792, IB/11/3/78/162; 1794, IB/11/3/81/228, JA. For Cope's fear of being seized by the marshal for nonpayment of debts, see 25 November 1765, 15 April 1767.

36. Harry Weech gave one explanation for Cope's behavior toward Crookshanks: "Crookshanks Accomodated Mr. Cope with his Sister in England, which is the Reason off his being a Favourite" (30 July 1758).

37. 13 September 1759.

38. Cope's affairs were becoming desperate: on 15 August 1765, Thistlewood was served a summons as a result of a dishonored bill of exchange given by Cope to Kingston merchants Thomas Hibbert and Samuel Jackson in 1764.

39. 23 May 1763.

40. 12–13 November, 17 December 1761.

41. 7–8 January, 8 February 1761.

42. 3–5 November, 17 December 1761.

43. 17 April 1759, 31 December 1765, 13 August 1766.

44. 13 November 1760. The mean wealth of twenty-six tavern keepers who left inventories between 1732 and 1787 was £516.21 sterling (£722.69 Jamaica currency). See Inventories, 1732–87, IB/11/3/16, 20, 26, 56, 63, JA.

45. 2 June 1750, 18 September 1751, 13 May 1756.

46. "List of Slaves on York Estate, Jamaica, 1 Jan. 1778," Gale-Morant Papers, 3/c, University of Exeter Library, Devon, England.

47. 21 December 1772.

48. Inventories, 1735, 1774, IB/11/3/20, 56, JA. For the increasing number of transatlantic slave arrivals in Jamaica in the third quarter of the eighteenth century, see David Eltis, "The Volume and Structure of the Transatlantic Slave Trade: A Reassessment," and Trevor Burnard and Kenneth Morgan, "The Dynamics of the Slave Market and Slave Purchasing Patterns in Jamaica, 1655–1788," *WMQ*, 3d ser., 58 (2001): 45, 205–8. For the rise in sugar production in Jamaica after mid-century, especially in the far western and far eastern parishes, and the increasing profitability of sugar, see J. R. Ward, "The Profitability of Sugar Planting in the British West Indies, 1650–1834," *Economic History Review* 21 (1978): 207, and Burnard and Morgan, "Dynamics of the Slave Market," 211.

49. Sheridan, *Doctors and Slaves*, 132–33.

50. Not surprisingly, Richardson thought that most slave owners "succeed from a lucky combination of circumstances" (6 July 1784).

51. 17 August 1773.

52. 17 March 1761.

53. Higman estimates that slave productivity averaged £11.58 per annum between 1800 and 1834. The highest returns—£25.90 per annum—were from slaves working in sugar, and slaves working in livestock pens brought in £10.90 per annum. See B. W. Higman, *Slave Population and Economy in Jamaica, 1807–1834* (Cambridge: Cambridge University Press, 1976), 213, 217. Sheridan based his figures on Jamaican data from inventories and a methodology based on modern capital theory. See Sheridan, *Sugar and Slavery*, 260. Thistlewood earned approximately 1 shilling per day for hiring out adult hands to sugar plantations, implying a maximum annual return of £22 per adult male. Of course, this figure is based on the assumption that the slaves were healthy adults who worked in the most profitable sector of the Jamaican economy.

54. Sheridan, *Doctors and Slaves*, 136.

55. Douglas Hall, "Botanical and Horticultural Enterprise in Eighteenth-Century Jamaica," in Roderick A. McDonald, ed., *West Indies Accounts: Essays on the History of the British Caribbean and the Atlantic Economy in Honour of Richard Sheridan* (Kingston: Press University of the West Indies, 1996), 101–25.

56. 6 August 1775, 13 November 1784, 12 May 1786.

57. Alan Karras, *Sojourners in the Sun: Scottish Migrants in Jamaica and the Chesapeake, 1740–1800* (Ithaca, N.Y.: Cornell University Press, 1992).

58. It is unclear whether the money gained by Hayward's slaves went to Thistlewood or not. If it did, Thistlewood would have derived £411 from hiring out slaves that year.

59. 10 June 1780.

60. By way of comparison, Joseph Massie calculated in 1759 that a family needed an annual income of at least £50 to aspire to membership in the middling ranks of English society. Only the top 3 percent of English families were reputed to earn over £200 per annum—mainly the families of gentlemen, merchants, and superior tradesmen and master manufacturers. See Peter Mathias, *The Transformation of England: Essays in the Economic and Social History of England in the Eighteenth Century* (London: Methuen, 1979), 186–87.

61. 16 January 1763.

62. Census of St. James Parish (ca. 1774), Long Papers, Add. MSS 12435, BL.

63. 7 December 1772, 12 February, 2, 28 September 1773.

64. 25 March 1767. For attorneys, see Edward Brathwaite, *The Development of Creole Society in Jamaica, 1770–1820* (Oxford: Clarendon Press, 1971), 139–42.

65. 14, 21 February, 11 June, 29 July 1778.

66. 9, 19 April, 13 August 1771, 29, 31 March, 5, 11 April 1772; Wills, 1787, 52/77, IRO; Hall, "Botanical and Horticultural Enterprise," 120.

67. Sheridan, *Sugar and Slavery*, 230; Edward Long, *History of Jamaica . . .* , 3 vols. (1774; reprint, London: Frank Cass, 1970), 1:456–63. William Belgrave valued Barbadian sugar estates at a higher level: £31,525 (£22,518 sterling) for a 500-acre plantation with 300 slaves. He calculated annual expenses to be approximately £3,000 and the total capital costs for fitting out a plantation (excluding slaves and land) to be £7,300. See William Belgrave, *A Treatise upon Husbandry or Planting* (London, 1755), 42. Thistlewood copied Belgrave's calculations in his diary on 26 July 1759.

68. 1 September 1757.

69. Inventories, 1778, IB/11/3/60/168, JA.

70. 23 October 1765.

71. Inventories, 1805, IB/11/3/104/33, JA.

72. Samuel Martin, *An Essay On Plantership etc.* (London, 1773), i–xii.

73. Ward, "Profitability of Sugar Planting," 207.

74. 10 September 1770.

75. 29 September 1780, 24 October, 20 December 1782, 13 November 1784, 12 May 1786.

76. 3, 4 October, 8 November, 31 December 1780, 21 February 1781.

77. Barbara Solow, "Slavery and Colonization," in Barbara Solow, ed., *Slavery and the Rise of the Atlantic System* (Cambridge: Cambridge University Press, 1991), 21–42.

78. *An Essay concerning Slavery and the Danger Jamaica is expos'd to from too great Number of Slaves . . .* (London, 1746), 18.

Chapter Three

1. On 18 June 1766, he "reprimanded [Henry] McCormick for encouraging mean white people to come to the still house to him."

2. 16, 23 July, 20 August 1777, 29 March 1780, 30 August 1785.

3. 24 May, 17 December 1751, 11 May 1753.

4. 18, 21 April, 7 October 1766.

5. 26 November 1765, 19 May 1784.

6. Edward Long, *History of Jamaica . . .* , 3 vols. (1774; reprint, London: Frank Cass, 1970), 1:351, 2:294–95.

7. Philip D. Morgan, *Slave Counterpoint: Black Culture in the Eighteenth-Century Chesapeake and Lowcountry* (Chapel Hill: University of North Carolina Press, 1998), 258.

8. Walter Bagehot, *The English Constitution* (London, 1867), 236, 238; J. G. A. Pocock, "The Classical Theory of Deference," *American Historical Review* 81 (1976): 516; J. R. Pole, "Historians and the Problem of Early American Democracy," *American Historical Review* 67 (1962): 626–46.

9. 29 December 1770, 23 January 1785.

10. Thistlewood was aware that he was not a gentleman. On arrival at Antigua, for example, en route to Jamaica, he noted that "the gentlemen went ashore (I also went in the barge). One of these gentlemen is a clergyman, one a captain of a ship, and the other is a very old gentleman [Christopher Codrington], who is chief owner of the island of Barbuda" (13 April 1750).

11. See, in particular, Edmund S. Morgan, *American Slavery, American Freedom: The Ordeal of Colonial Virginia* (New York: W. W. Norton, 1975); Jack P. Greene, "'Slavery or Independence': Some Reflections on the Relationship between Liberty, Black Bondage, and Equality in Revolutionary South Carolina," *South Carolina Historical Magazine* 80 (1979): 193–214; and James Oakes, *Slavery and Freedom: An Interpretation of the Old South* (New York: Alfred A. Knopf, 1990).

12. Jack P. Greene, "The Jamaica Privilege Controversy, 1764–1766: An Episode in the Process of Constitutional Definition in the Early Modern British Empire," *Journal of Imperial and Constitutional History* 22 (1994): 22.

13. Richard Renny, *A History of Jamaica* (London, 1807), 209.

14. David Ramsay, *History of the Revolution of South-Carolina*, 2 vols. (Trenton, N.J., 1785), 1:11.

15. Bryan Edwards, *The History, Civil and Commercial, of the British Colonies in the West Indies*, 2d ed., 3 vols. (London, 1793), 3:7.

16. Ibid.

17. Patrick Browne, *The Civil and Natural History of Jamaica* (London, 1756), 22.

18. William Beckford, *A Descriptive Account of the Island of Jamaica*, 2 vols. (London, 1790), 2:348.

19. Jack P. Greene, "Liberty, Slavery, and the Transformation of British Identity in the Eighteenth-Century West Indies," *S&A* 21 (2000): 13–14, 27–28.

20. Trevor Burnard, *Creole Gentlemen: The Maryland Elite, 1691–1776* (New York: Routledge, 2002), 167–204; Stephanie McCurry, *Masters of Small Worlds: Yeoman Households, Gender Relations, and the Political Culture of the Antebellum South Carolina Low Country* (New York: Oxford University Press, 1995), 92–129.

21. Gordon J. Schochet, *Patriarchalism in Political Thought: The Authoritarian Family and Political Speculation and Attitudes Especially in Seventeenth-Century England* (Oxford: Blackwell, 1975), 165.

22. Rhys Isaac, "Communication and Control: Authority Metaphors and Power Contests on Colonel Landon Carter's Virginia Plantation, 1752–1778," in Sean Wilentz, ed., *Rites of Power: Symbolism, Ritual, and Politics since the Middle Ages* (Philadelphia: University of Pennsylvania Press, 1985), 275–302; Philip D. Morgan, "Three Planters and Their Slaves: Perspectives on Slavery in Virginia, South Carolina, and Jamaica, 1750–1790," in Winthrop D. Jordan and Sheila L. Skemp, eds., *Race and Family in the Colonial South* (Jackson: University Press of Mississippi, 1987), 54–68; Kathleen M. Brown, *Good Wives, Nasty Wenches, and Anxious Patriarchs: Gender, Race, and Power in Colonial Virginia* (Chapel Hill: University of North Carolina Press, 1996), 319–66; Robert Olwell, *Masters, Slaves, and Subjects: The Culture of Power in the South Carolina Low Country, 1740–1790* (Ithaca, N.Y.: Cornell University Press, 1998), 181–219; Kenneth A. Lockridge, *On the Sources of Patriarchal Rage: The Commonplace Books of William Byrd and Thomas Jefferson and the Gendering of Power in the Eighteenth Century* (New York: New York University Press, 1992).

23. These figures are based on 1,389 inventories made between 1732 and 1782, of which 1,105 included slaves. See Inventories, 1732–82, IB/11/3/16, 24, 25, 33, 56, 63, JA.

24. Sir William Gooch, *A Dialogue Between Thomas Sweet-Scented, William Orinoco, Planters . . . and Justice Love-Country* (Williamsburg, Va., 1732), cited in Jack P. Greene, *Negotiated Authorities: Essays in Colonial Political and Constitutional History* (Charlottesville: University Press of Virginia, 1994), 268.

25. 18 December 1751, 4 April 1755, 26 May 1757, 25 September 1758.

26. 7 January 1752, 14 August 1760, 9, 15, 21, 23 March 1775.

27. 19 December 1745, 23 February 1767, 31 December 1769, 17 December 1775, 9 January 1776; Westmoreland Parish Copy Register, Baptisms, Marriages, and Deaths, vol. 1, 1 December 1786, f. 98, JA.

28. 27 September 1763.

29. 15 August, 15 October 1768.

30. Thistlewood listed the results for elections held on 5 December 1754, 18 April 1766, 15 October 1768, 23 February 1770, 19 March 1770, 26 November 1771, 3 November 1777, 28 February 1781, and 9 April 1781.

31. Robert J. Dinkin, *Voting in Provincial America: A Study of Elections in the Thirteen Colonies, 1689–1776* (Westport, Conn.: Greenwood Press, 1977), 144–80; John Gilman Kolp, *Gentlemen and Freeholders: Electoral Politics in Colonial Virginia* (Baltimore: Johns Hopkins University Press, 1998), 48. Andrew O'Shaughnessy cautions that in Barbados only about 20 to 25 percent of adult white males were qualified to vote. In Jamaica, the franchise was limited to twenty-one-year-old white Christian males who were British subjects and owned either a minimum of ten acres of land or a house with an annual taxable value of £10 in local currency. The 8 percent of the population who were Jewish and the larger percentage who were not landowners were excluded. See Andrew O'Shaughnessy, *An Empire Divided: The American Revolution and the British Caribbean* (Philadelphia: University of Pennsylvania Press, 2000), 132, and Edward Brathwaite, *The Development of Creole Society in Jamaica, 1770–1820* (Oxford: Clarendon Press, 1971), 44. In 1788, the white population of Westmoreland was 1,495, of whom around 58 percent were adult males (extrapolating from age and sex breakdowns in Clarendon Parish in the same year). If we allow for some growth of white population between 1781 and 1788 and assume that the number of people able to vote increased from 170 in 1781 to approximately 200 in 1788, this suggests that around 23 percent of white adult men were able to vote. See "Return of number of Inhabitants . . . in Jamaica, November 1788," CO 137/87, and "Statistics of Jamaica, 1739–1775," Long Papers, Add. MSS 12435, f. 41, BL.

32. 26 April 1766, 15 October 1768. For treating in North America, see Alan Tully, *Forming American Politics: Ideals, Interests, and Institutions in Colonial New York and Pennsylvania* (Baltimore: Johns Hopkins University Press, 1994), 201, 328, 343.

33. James Knight, "The Natural, Moral and Political History of Jamaica and the Territories thereon depending," Long Papers, Add. MSS 12419, 1:71, BL.

34. Beckford, *Descriptive Account*, 1:267.

35. 27 April, 1, 4–5 May 1750.

36. 24 January, 19, 25 February, 13 March, 27 April 1752, 19 April 1754.

37. John Stewart, *A View of the Past and Present State of the Island of Jamaica* (Edinburgh, 1823), 189–94.

38. 18 February, 17 June 1780. For other dinners with Blake, see 25 December 1781 and 9 October 1782.

39. "Statistics of Jamaica."

40. 28 October, 25 December 1768, 24 February 1770.

41. 12 March 1755, 27 November 1756, 25 September 1758, 18 August 1761, 14 July 1778. For other times when Thistlewood drank too much, see 10 January 1755, 20–21 September 1762, 22 October 1768, and 7 February 1774.

42. Peter W. Bardaglio, *Reconstructing the Household: Families, Sex, and the Law in the Nineteenth-Century South* (Chapel Hill: University of North Carolina Press, 1995), 34.

43. Morgan, "Three Planters and Their Slaves," 39.

44. Gerda Lerner, *The Creation of Patriarchy* (New York: Oxford University Press, 1986), 238–39.

45. William J. Cooper, *Liberty and Slavery: Southern Politics to 1860* (New York: Alfred A. Knopf, 1983); George Fredrickson, *The Black Image in the White Mind: The Debate on Afro-American Character and Destiny, 1817–1914* (New York: Harper and Row, 1971), 61–70; McCurry, *Masters of Small Worlds*, 240.

46. James Ramsay, "Motives for the Improvement of the Sugar Colonies" (ca. 1778), Add. MSS 27621, f. 74, BL.

47. Lowell J. Ragatz, *The Fall of the Planter Class in the British Caribbean, 1763– 1833* (New York: Century, 1928); Brathwaite, *Development of Creole Society in Jamaica*, 9–62; Thomas Holt, *The Problem of Freedom: Race, Labor, and Politics in Jamaica and Britain, 1832–1938* (Baltimore: Johns Hopkins University Press, 1992), 215–312.

48. "Mr. Richard Beckford's Instructions to Messrs. John Cope, Richard Lewing, [and] Robert Mason," 10 April 1754, Monson 31/86.

49. 17–20 April 1757.

50. 12 December 1760.

51. 16 December 1767. For other visits of governors, see 2 April 1754, 20 March 1772, 2 March 1775, and 15 February 1786.

52. 19 March 1767.

53. 19 September 1771.

54. 1 June 1768, 11 April, 9, 11 July, 29 August 1769.

55. 9 April 1768, 19 March 1770, 15 October 1778.

56. 26, 30 November 1771.

57. Alan L. Karras, *Sojourners in the Sun: Scottish Migrants in Jamaica and the Chesapeake, 1740–1800* (Ithaca, N.Y.: Cornell University Press, 1992).

58. 13 August 1762, 20 August 1774, 27 July 1776, 5 September 1781. For Scots, see Richard B. Sheridan, "The Role of the Scots in the Economy and Society of the West Indies," in Vera Rubin and Arthur Tuden, eds., *Comparative Perspectives on Slavery in New World Plantation Societies* (New York: New York Academy of Sciences, 1977), 94–106.

59. Long, *History of Jamaica*, 2:28.

60. 14–15 June 1756, 25 July 1766, 8 March, 3 November 1775, 12 July 1776, 2 October 1780.

61. Edward Ward, *A Trip to Jamaica: With a True Character of the People and Island* (London, 1700), 13; [James White to Bishop Robinson, ca. 1720], Fulham Papers, American Colonial Section (microfilm), 18:220–27, Lambeth Palace Library, London; *The groans of Jamaica . . .* (London, 1714), v.

62. Trevor Burnard, "European Migration to Jamaica, 1655–1780," *WMQ*, 3d ser., 53 (1996): 780–89.

63. Edwards, *History, Civil and Commercial*, 3:7; Browne, *Civil and Natural History*, 22; Renny, *History of Jamaica*, 127.

64. Samuel Johnson, *A Dictionary of the English Language*, 8th ed., 2 vols. (London, 1799).

65. Michael Wayne, "An Old South Morality Play: Reconsidering the Social Underpinnings of the Proslavery Ideology," *Journal of American History* 77 (1990): 843, 860–63.

66. O'Shaughnessy, *Empire Divided*, 34–57.

67. Jack P. Greene, *Imperatives, Behaviors, and Identities: Essays in Early American Cultural History* (Charlottesville: University Press of Virginia, 1992), 199, 268–89.

68. Soame Jenyns, *A Free Enquiry Into the Nature and Origin of Evil*, cited in Olwell, *Masters, Slaves, and Subjects*, 192.

69. 21 July, 13 December 1751, 11 July 1752, 11 May 1753, 23 February 1754, 12 January 1768.

70. O'Shaughnessy, *Empire Divided*, 170, 233.

71. 28 October 1776, 14 February 1778, 11 July 1780.

72. 22 August 1754, 1, 22 June, 21 December 1766. For the privilege controversies, see George Metcalf, *Royal Government and Political Conflict in Jamaica, 1729–1783* (London: Longmans, 1965), 160–72.

73. 19 July 1785; Monson 31/76, pp. 36–41.

74. 31 January, 18 February 1763, 19 March 1770, 21, 26 December 1771, 15 October 1778, 23 October 1779, 31 October, 23 September 1782; Monson 31/76, pp. 4–6.

75. 31 December 1768.

76. Rhys Isaac, *The Transformation of Virginia, 1740–1790* (Chapel Hill: University of North Carolina Press, 1982). See also A. G. Roeber, *Faithful Magistrates and Republican Lawyers: Creators of Virginia Legal Culture, 1680–1810* (Chapel Hill: University of North Carolina Press, 1981).

77. Isaac, *Transformation of Virginia*, 324–25.

78. Elsa V. Goveia, "The West Indian Slave Laws of the Eighteenth Century," *Revista de ciencas sociales* 4 (1960): 75–105; John H. Howard, ed., *The Laws of the British Colonies in the West Indies . . .* , 2 vols. (London, 1827); Thomas D. Morris, *Southern Slavery and the Law, 1619–1860* (Chapel Hill: University of North Carolina Press, 1996), 210–20.

79. 18 May 1751.

80. 27 December 1752, 11 January 1762, 9 March, 14 June 1765, May 1775, 20 April 1776, 30 April 1785, 26 July 1786.

81. See Olwell, *Masters, Slaves, and Subjects*, 57–102.

82. 26 July 1786.

83. 22 November 1765, 3 September 1770, 16 April 1777.

84. Ira Berlin, *Many Thousands Gone: The First Two Centuries of Slavery in North America* (Cambridge, Mass.: Harvard University Press, 1998), 99.

85. "Blue-coat boys" were apprentices sent to Jamaica after being educated at Christ's Hospital in Horsham, Surrey.

86. 5 June, 30 July 1754, 13, 23 February, 15 October 1755, 24 February 1756.

87. 4 June, 17 August 1761.

88. 6–8 January, 12 November 1761, 23 May 1763.

89. J. B. Moreton, *Manners and Customs in the West India Islands* (London, 1790), 81. Most whips were made out of cowhide, hence the reference to cowskin. See Edwards, *History, Civil and Commercial*, 3:7.

Chapter Four

1. "Dr. Anthony Robinson formed a collection of several hundred figures and descriptions of Jamaican plants and animals, correcting the errors of Sloane and Brown, and supplying their deficiencies, but he died before it could be digested into a regular series for publication. He invented a vegetable soap, for which he obtained a premium of a thousand pounds sterling from the House of Assembly and prepared the sago and tapioca from that species of palm which is commonly used only as thatch" (Rev. George Wilson Bridges, *Annals of Jamaica*, 2 vols. [London, 1826], 1:25).

2. 12, 13, 20 May 1768.

3. [Charles Leslie], *A new and exact account of Jamaica* [Edinburgh, ca. 1740], 41.

4. 1 November 1766. For Scottish conjectural history, see Adam Ferguson, *An Essay on the History of Civil Society* (Edinburgh, 1767), and Christopher J. Berry, *Social Theory of the Scottish Enlightenment* (Edinburgh: Edinburgh University Press, 1997).

5. 19 June, 17–18, 29 July, 3 August, 2 September, 31 December 1760, 3 August 1761; Bryan Edwards, *The History, Civil and Commercial, of the British Colonies in the West Indies*, 2d ed., 3 vols. (London, 1793), 2:66–67.

6. 24 May 1768.

7. 26 May, 23, 24, 30, 31 July, 1, 4, 27 August, 5 October 1756.

8. 1 August 1750, 22 November 1764.

9. Norbert Elias, *The Civilizing Process*, translated by Edmund Jephcott (Oxford: Blackwell, 2000). Elias argued that this self-regulating and empathetic personality arose as a result of the growth of the modern state. I prefer Thomas Haskell's interpretation that it was the result of the ethical outworkings of market capitalism. See Thomas Haskell, "Capitalism and the Origins of the Humanitarian Sensibility," *American Historical Review* 90 (1985): 339–61, 547–66. See also V. A. C. Gatrell, *The Hanging Tree: Execution and the English People, 1770–1868* (Oxford: Oxford University Press, 1994), 17.

10. Michel Foucault, *Discipline and Punish: The Birth of the Prison*, translated by Alan Sheridan (London: Allen Lane, 1977).

11. G. J. Barker-Benfield, *The Culture of Sensibility: Sex and Society in Eighteenth-Century Britain* (Chicago: University of Chicago Press, 1992); John Mullan, *Sentiment and Sociability: The Language of Feeling in the Eighteenth Century* (Oxford: Clarendon Press, 1988); Lawrence E. Klein, *Shaftsbury and the Culture of Politeness: Moral Discourse and Cultural Politics in Early Eighteenth Century England* (New York: Cambridge University Press, 1994).

12. Joyce E. Chaplin, "Slavery and the Principle of Humanity: A Modern Idea in the Early Lower South," *Journal of Social History* 24 (1990): 299–315.

13. Lady Knutsford, ed., *Life and Letters of Zachary Macaulay* (London, 1908).

14. Fred Anderson, *Crucible of War: The Seven Years' War and the Fate of Empire in British North America, 1754–1766* (New York: Alfred A. Knopf, 2000), 287, 781–82.

15. Gatrell, *Hanging Tree*, 7; G. M. Trevelyan, *English Social History* (London: Longmans, 1942), 281.

16. David B. Davis, *The Problem of Slavery in the Age of Revolution, 1770–1823* (Ithaca, N.Y.: Cornell University Press, 1975); Roger Anstey, *The Atlantic Slave Trade and British Abolition, 1760–1810* (London: Macmillan, 1975).

17. Catherine Hall, *Civilising Subjects: Metropole and Colony in the English Imagination, 1830–1867* (Cambridge: Polity Press, 2002).

18. Robert Darnton, "History of Reading," in Peter Burke, ed., *New Perspectives on Historical Writing* (Cambridge: Polity, 1991), 157–86.

19. The evidence about books and reading in the West Indies is ambiguous. An analysis of inventories suggests that very few whites owned books. Fewer than 1 in 15 inventories listed books, and around 1 in 50 indicated that the person being inventoried owned a library. See Inventories, 1753, IB/11/3/33, JA. Nevertheless, shipping records suggest that the West Indies received more books from London than its population warranted. Between 1701 and 1780, the West Indies received 51,769 hundredweight of books, which was 24.5 percent of all books by weight sent to the colonies. It is possible that the percentage of books sent to the West Indies is overstated since customs clerks recorded only the first destination of any boat and thus ships stopping in the West Indies and then unloading books in the mainland colonies would have all their books recorded as having landed in the islands. Nevertheless, by any measure, the volume of books sent to the West Indies far surpassed the volume sent to other regions. See James Raven, "The Importation of Books in the Eighteenth Century," in Hugh Amory and David D. Hall, eds., *A History of the Book in America*, vol. 1, *The Colonial Book in the Atlantic World* (Cambridge: Cambridge University Press, 2000), 183, 186.

20. Monson 31/82.

21. Monson 31/85.

22. 9 October, 6 November 1780.

23. "Inventory of Thomas Thistlewood," Inventories, 1787, IB/11/3/71/200, JA.

24. For Bourke, see Jack P. Greene, *Negotiated Authorities: Essays in Colonial Po-*

litical and Constitutional History (Charlottesville: University Press of Virginia, 1994), 370–71. By way of comparison, William Byrd II of Virginia had a library of 3,500 books at his death in 1744. See Amory and Hall, *Colonial Book in the Atlantic World*, 426.

25. "Every gentleman [going to the West Indies] almost [always] takes out his own library with him and what books may be wanted are generally sold in the store of merchants who import them from England with their other goods" (Leman Thomas Rede, 1789 survey of the American book trade, in Stuart C. Sherman, ed., "Leman Thomas Rede's 'Bibliotheca Americana,'" *WMQ*, 3d ser., 4 [1947]: 349).

26. 11 July 1756. See also 16 April 1785, when Thistlewood "bought a parcel of old books at vendue—mostly religious books."

27. 31 December 1758, 29 June 1765, 3 February 1766, 11, 28 April 1771, 1 May 1772, 1 May 1774, 7 June 1779, 7 August 1780.

28. 2, 8, 12, 29 April, 29 May 1756.

29. 3 March 1777.

30. 6 July 1757. Thistlewood clearly read Leslie since he quoted from him less than a month later, on 31 July 1757.

31. 15 August 1781. Matthew Lewis was the father of the much better known Matthew "Monk" Lewis, the Gothic novelist.

32. John Brewer, *The Pleasures of the Imagination: English Culture in the Eighteenth Century* (London: Harper Collins, 1997), 167–200. See also James Raven et al., eds., *The Practice and Representation of Reading in England* (Cambridge: Cambridge University Press, 1996).

33. 1 September 1767.

34. 27 December 1752.

35. Brewer, *Pleasures of the Imagination*, 181.

36. Monson 31/73/88–96.

37. Brewer, *Pleasures of the Imagination*, 193.

38. 11 June 1778.

39. Mark Goldie, "Priestcraft and the Birth of Whiggism," in Nicholas Phillipson and Quentin Skinner, eds., *Political Discourse in Early Modern Britain* (Cambridge: Cambridge University Press, 1993), 210.

40. Roy Porter, *Enlightenment: Britain and the Creation of the Modern World* (London: Allen Lane, 2000), xxxii, 11.

41. Bernard Bailyn, *The Peopling of British North America: An Introduction* (New York: Vintage, 1986), 113.

42. Joseph Addison and Richard Steele, *The Spectator*, 5 vols., edited by Donald Bond (Oxford: Clarendon Press, 1965), 1:293.

43. Edward Long, *History of Jamaica . . .* , 3 vols. (1774; reprint, London: Frank Cass, 1970), 2:287; *The Works of James Houston, M.D.* (London, 1753), 276–79.

44. Long, *History of Jamaica*, 2:262–63.

45. Ibid., 1:374–75, 413, 2:32.

46. Ibid., 2:64–65.

47. Leslie, *New and exact account*, 37–38.

48. Andrew O'Shaughnessy, *An Empire Divided: The American Revolution and the British Caribbean* (Philadelphia: University of Pennsylvania Press, 2000), 5–6; James E. McClellan, *Colonialism and Science: Saint-Domingue in the Old Regime* (Baltimore: Johns Hopkins University Press, 1992); Richard Drayton, "Knowledge and Empire," in P. J. Marshall, ed., *The Oxford History of the British Empire: The Eighteenth Century* (Oxford: Oxford University Press, 1998), 245.

49. Leslie, *New and exact account*, 31; Lord Adam Gordon, "Journal of an Officer who Travelled in America and the West Indies in 1764 and 1765," in Newton D. Mereness, ed., *Travels in the American Colonies* (New York: Macmillan, 1916), 381.

50. Long, *History of Jamaica*, 2:76–78.

51. Richard Drayton, *Nature's Government: Science, Imperial Britain, and the "Improvement" of the World* (New Haven: Yale University Press, 2000), 64–65, 79–80; Edwards, *History, Civil and Commercial*, 1:xxxiv; Arthur Broughton, *Hortus Eastensis, or a Catalogue of Exotic Plants in the Garden of Hinton East, Esq.* (Kingston, 1792).

52. Edward Gibbon, *The Decline and Fall of the Roman Empire*, edited by D. M. Low (London: Chatto and Windus, 1960), 530.

53. 5 October 1769.

54. 4 October 1777.

55. Inventories, 1787, IB/11/3/71/200, JA.

56. 23 October 1773.

57. 9 June 1762, 6 July 1763, 4 February, 19 April 1768, 25 January 1770, 25 January, 3 May 1778, 19 June 1779.

58. 15 May 1759, 14 May 1770, 9 January 1777.

59. Porter, *Enlightenment*, 144.

60. Drayton, *Nature's Government*, 138.

61. Douglas Hall, "Botanical and Horticultural Enterprise in Eighteenth-Century Jamaica," in Roderick A. McDonald, ed., *West Indies Accounts: Essays on the History of the British Caribbean and the Atlantic Economy in Honour of Richard Sheridan* (Kingston: Press University of the West Indies, 1996), 101–25.

62. "Thomas Thistlewood's Meteorological Observations," Long Papers, Add. MSS 18275A, BL.

63. Hall, "Botanical and Horticultural Enterprise," 122.

64. 20 January 1762, 12 May 1770.

65. 19 April, 13–14 August 1771. Asparagus was his most successful transplantation, accounting for over one-quarter of the money he made from the sale of garden produce. See Hall, "Botanical and Horticultural Enterprise," 121.

66. 29 March, 11 April 1772.

67. Long Papers, Add. MSS 18275A, f. 10, BL.

68. 10 September 1770, 30 June, 1 July 1775; Douglas Hall, *In Miserable Slavery: Thomas Thistlewood in Jamaica, 1750–1786* (London: Macmillan, 1989), 238.

69. 15 October, 7 November 1773.

70. 23 May, 22 July 1775.

71. Drayton, *Nature's Government*, 26.

72. 12 May 1768.

73. Long Papers, Add. MSS 18275A, ff. 112–15, BL.

74. A. Gerard, *An Essay on Taste* (1759), 86, cited in Gatrell, *Hanging Tree*, 228.

75. Gatrell, *Hanging Tree*, 229; Porter, *Enlightenment*, 281–83.

76. Gatrell, *Hanging Tree*, 234–35; David Hume, *Treatise of Human Nature*, 2d ed., edited by L. A. Selby-Bigge (1739–40; reprint, Oxford: Clarendon Press, 1978); Adam Smith, *The Theory of Moral Sentiments*, edited by D. D. Raphael and A. L. Macfie (1759; reprint, Oxford: Clarendon Press, 1976).

77. 24 December 1766, 7 August 1767, 22 July 1770, 20–21 October 1775.

78. 29 June 1750, 30 March 1765, 12 May 1768, 7 September 1780, 4 June 1781. For Jamaican fatalism toward death, see Trevor Burnard, "'The Countrie Continues Sicklie': White Mortality in Jamaica, 1655–1780," *Social History of Medicine* 12 (1999): 68–70.

79. 17 July 1757.

80. "Mr. Richard Beckford's Instructions to Messrs. John Cope, Richard Lewing, [and] Robert Mason," 10 April 1754, Monson 31/86.

81. Gordon K. Lewis, *Main Currents in Caribbean Thought: The Historical Evolution of Caribbean Society in Its Ideological Aspects, 1492–1900* (Baltimore: Johns Hopkins University Press, 1983), 109–15; Davis, *Problem of Slavery*, 184–98; David Eltis, *The Rise of African Slavery in the Americas* (Cambridge: Cambridge University Press, 2000), 59–62, 77–84.

82. John Lean, "The Racialisation of Society in Eighteenth-Century Jamaica" (essay, University of Canterbury, 1998).

83. James H. Sweet, "The Iberian Roots of American Racist Thought," *WMQ*, 3d ser., 54 (1997): 144–45; Alden T. Vaughan and Virginia Mason Vaughan, "Before Othello: Elizabethan Representations of Sub-Saharan Africans," *WMQ*, 3d ser., 54 (1997): 32, 42.

84. Richard Ligon, *A True and Exact History of the Island of Barbadoes . . .* (London, 1657), 50–51; Hans Sloane, *A Voyage to the Islands Madera, Barbados, Nieves, S. Christophers and Jamaica . . .* , 2 vols. (London, 1707), 2:lii.

85. Long, *History of Jamaica*, 2:353–54.

86. Ligon, *True and Exact History*, 12.

87. James Knight, "The Natural, Moral and Political History of Jamaica and the Territories thereon depending," Long Papers, Add. MSS 12418–19, ff. 79–87, BL; Leslie, *New and exact account*, 322–27, 336–38.

88. 17 July 1750.

89. 6 January, 10 May, 3, 17 July 1751. See also Philip D. Morgan, "Slaves and Livestock in Eighteenth-Century Jamaica: Vineyard Pen, 1750–1751," *WMQ*, 3d ser., 52 (1995): 69–72.

90. See Michael Mullin, *Africa in America: Slave Acculturation and Resistance in the American South and the British Caribbean, 1736–1831* (Urbana: University of Illinois Press, 1992), 79–88.

91. 15 August 1750, 8 March 1751.

92. 12 June 1757.

93. 11 June 1752.

94. Morgan, "Slaves and Livestock," 77.

95. 1 July 1751.

96. 20 May 1751.

97. Morgan, "Slaves and Livestock," 74; Karl Jacoby, "Slaves by Nature?: Domestic Animals and Human Slaves," *S&A* 15 (1994): 89–99; Trevor Burnard, "Slave Naming Patterns: Onomastics and the Taxonomy of Race in Eighteenth-Century Jamaica," *Journal of Interdisciplinary History* 31 (2001): 325–46.

98. Lean, "Racialisation of Society."

99. Smith, *Theory of Moral Sentiments*, 61.

100. Haskell, "Capitalism and the Origins of the Humanitarian Sensibility."

101. Hume, *Treatise of Human Nature*.

Chapter Five

1. Rev. Robert Robertson of Nevis, *A Letter to the Right Reverend the Lord Bishop of London* (London, 1730), 12–13.

2. 30 March–5 April 1765.

3. James C. Scott, *Domination and the Arts of Resistance: Hidden Transcripts* (New Haven: Yale University Press, 1990).

4. Richard B. Sheridan, *Sugar and Slavery: An Economic History of the British West Indies, 1623–1775* (Bridgetown, Barbados: Caribbean Universities Press, 1974).

5. Bryan Edwards, *The History, Civil and Commercial, of the British Colonies in the West Indies*, 2d ed., 3 vols. (London, 1793), 1:13.

6. For slave resistance in the Caribbean, see Michael Craton, *Testing the Chains: Resistance to Slavery in the British West Indies* (Ithaca, N.Y.: Cornell University Press, 1982); David Barry Gaspar, *Bondmen and Rebels: A Study of Master-Slave Relations in Antigua* (Baltimore: Johns Hopkins University Press, 1985); Eugene D. Genovese, *From Rebellion to Revolution: Afro-American Slave Revolts in the Making of the Modern World* (Baton Rouge: Louisiana State University Press, 1979); Mary Turner, *Slaves and Missionaries: The Disintegration of Jamaican Slave Society, 1787–1834* (Urbana: University of Illinois Press, 1982); Michael Mullin, *Africa in*

America: Slave Acculturation and Resistance in the American South and the British Caribbean, 1736–1831 (Urbana: University of Illinois Press, 1992); Hilary Beckles, Black Rebellion in Barbados: The Struggle against Slavery, 1627–1838 (Bridgetown, Barbados: Antilles Publications, 1984); Gad Heuman, ed., Out of the House of Bondage: Runaways, Resistance, and Marronage in Africa and the New World (London: Frank Cass, 1986); and Emilia Viotti da Costa, Crowns of Glory, Tears of Blood: The Demerara Slave Rebellion of 1823 (New York: Oxford University Press, 1994).

7. Peter Kolchin, Unfree Labor: American Slavery and Russian Serfdom (Cambridge, Mass.: Harvard University Press, 1987), 253.

8. Eugene Genovese, Roll, Jordan, Roll: The World the Slaves Made (New York: Pantheon, 1974), 594.

9. An Essay concerning Slavery and the Danger Jamaica is expos'd to from too great Number of Slaves . . . (London, 1746), 18.

10. Trevor Burnard, "A Failed Settler Society: Marriage and Demographic Failure in Early Jamaica," Journal of Social History 28 (1994): 64–65.

11. Mullin, Africa in America, 268.

12. 31 August 1751.

13. 15 July 1769, 7 October 1780.

14. 30 September 1760, 19 November 1764.

15. 15 November, 4, 27 December 1752, 8 April 1754.

16. See, for example, 31 May 1755, 18 April 1756, and 16 March 1761.

17. 28 January 1752.

18. 31 October 1758. Lincoln turned into such a fine marksman that Thistlewood recommended him as a "Baggage Negroe in the expected Expedition under pocock" (11 May 1762).

19. 16 March 1761. See also 31 October 1764.

20. 27 December 1752.

21. [Charles Leslie], A new and exact account of Jamaica [Edinburgh, ca. 1740], 327. Leslie repeats, almost word for word, statements on slave divisions made by Richard Ligon nearly a century earlier. See Richard Ligon, A True and Exact History of the Island of Barbados . . . (London, 1657), 46.

22. Craton, Testing the Chains, 99–160; Mullin, Africa in America, 40–49.

23. 6 July 1757.

24. Melville J. Herskovits, The Myth of the Negro Past (1941; reprint, Boston: Beacon Press, 1958), 81.

25. John Thornton, Africa and Africans in the Making of the Atlantic World, 1400–1680 (New York: Cambridge University Press, 1992), 192–205; Mervyn Alleyne, Roots of Jamaican Culture (London: Pluto Press, 1988), 122–30.

26. Olaudah Equiano, The Interesting Narrative of the Life of Olaudah Equiano, or Gustavus Vassa, the African, Written By Himself (1789), edited by Vincent Carretta (London: Penguin, 1996). Carretta has raised important questions about the iden-

tity of Equiano and whether he misrepresented himself. See Vincent Carretta, "Olaudah Equiano or Gustavus Vassa?: New Light on an Eighteenth-Century Question of Identity," *S&A* 20 (1999): 96–105.

27. "Slaves must have known a good deal more about the intimate daily affairs of the masters than the masters could have known about the slaves" (Sidney W. Mintz and Richard Price, *An Anthropological Approach to the Afro-American Past: A Caribbean Perspective* [Philadelphia: Institute for the Study of Human Issues, 1976], 9).

28. Beckles, *Black Rebellion in Barbados*, 29–30.

29. 27 December 1752.

30. See, for example, Thistlewood's exclamation after the terror of Tackey's revolt: "But one Negroe Come to me for a Ticket the rest go without no person questioning them! 500 Negroes on the Road to Leeward every Sunday with plantanes, etc few have Tickets" (9 November 1760). For British West Indian slave laws, see Elsa Goveia, *The West Indian Slave Laws of the Eighteenth Century* (Kingston: Caribbean Universities Press, 1970).

31. 25 October 1751.

32. Every white man between the ages of fifteen and sixty was supposed to serve in the militia unless exempted.

33. Governor Robert Hunter to the Council of Trade and Plantations, 4 July 1730, in *Calendar of State Papers, Colonial Series: America and the West Indies*, vol. 39, no. 311.

34. Leslie, *New and exact account*, 327.

35. 12 April 1763. Cudjoe was the leader of the Maroons. See Craton, *Testing the Chains*, 77–78, 81–82, 85–93.

36. 4 April 1757.

37. 30 July 1776.

38. Craton, *Testing the Chains*, 211–23.

39. 2 September 1756, 18 November 1760, 17 January, 8 October 1762.

40. See Genovese, *Roll, Jordan, Roll*, 25–97; Robert Olwell, *Masters, Slaves, and Subjects: The Culture of Power in the South Carolina Low Country, 1740–1790* (Ithaca, N.Y.: Cornell University Press, 1998), 189–217; Lorena S. Walsh, *From Calabar to Carter's Grove: A History of a Virginia Slave Community* (Charlottesville: University Press of Virginia, 1997); and Elsa Goveia, *Slave Society in the British Leewards at the End of the Eighteenth Century* (New Haven: Yale University Press, 1965).

41. Philip D. Morgan, *Slave Counterpoint: Black Culture in the Eighteenth-Century Chesapeake and Lowcountry* (Chapel Hill: University of North Carolina Press, 1998), 284–96.

42. Drew Gilpin Faust, *James Henry Hammond and the Old South: A Design for Mastery* (Baton Rouge: Louisiana State University Press, 1982), 72–73.

43. Ibid., 69–104.

44. Gordon K. Lewis, *Main Currents in Caribbean Thought: The Historical Evo-

lution of Caribbean Society in Its Ideological Aspects, 1492–1900 (Baltimore: Johns Hopkins University Press, 1983), 94–170; Larry E. Tise, *Pro-Slavery: A History of the Defence of Slavery in America, 1701–1840* (Athens: University of Georgia Press, 1987), 90–96; Edward Long, *The History of Jamaica . . .* , 3 vols. (1774; reprint, London: Frank Cass, 1970), 2:351–485.

45. Faust, *James Henry Hammond*, 72.

46. "Mr. Richard Beckford's Instructions to Messrs. John Cope, Richard Lewing, [and] Robert Mason," 10 April 1754, Monson 31/86.

47. 5 September 1759.

48. 26 May 1760, 6–8 January 1761.

49. Dr. George Pinckard, *Letters from Guiana* (Georgetown, Guyana: Daily Chronicle, 1942), 18–19.

50. 9 October 1751, 9 February 1752, 15 August 1753, 9 March 1765.

51. 2 November 1771.

52. In addition, between 300 and 400 slaves lost their lives in the revolt. See Craton, *Testing the Chains*, 139. For the later history of "rebels from Tackey's revolt sent to Honduras and eagerly purchased," see "A Narrative of the Publick Transactions in the Bay of Honduras from 1784 to 1790 by Edward Marcus Despard, Esq.," CO 123/10/105–6.

53. 31 May–30 September 1760.

54. "The Care Off White Servants," Monson 31/86.

55. 25 September 1759.

56. Sidney W. Mintz and Douglas Hall, *The Origins of the Jamaican Internal Market System* (New Haven: Yale University Press, 1960), 1–26. See also Roderick A. McDonald, *The Economy and Material Culture of Slaves: Goods and Chattels on the Sugar Plantations of Jamaica and Louisiana* (Baton Rouge: Louisiana State University Press, 1993); Ira Berlin and Philip D. Morgan, eds., *The Slaves' Internal Economy: Independent Production by Slaves in the Americas* (London: Frank Cass, 1991); Mullin, *Africa in America*, 126–58; and G. Melvin Herndon, *William Tatham and the Production of Tobacco* (Coral Gables, Fla.: University of Miami Press, 1969), 104–5.

57. Mullin, *Africa in America*, 127.

58. For food-provisioning systems in British America and their effects on patterns of work organization, see Philip D. Morgan, "Task and Gang Systems: The Organization of Labor on New World Plantations," in Stephen Innes, ed., *Work and Labor in Early America* (Chapel Hill: University of North Carolina Press, 1988), 189–220. For the British Caribbean, see B. W. Higman, *Slave Populations of the British Caribbean, 1807–1834* (Baltimore: Johns Hopkins University Press, 1984), 188–217. West Indian planters' awareness that the provision-ground system gave slaves unwanted independence is clear from comments made by Barbadian planters in the aftermath of Bussa's rebellion in 1816 that masters' indulgence of slave commerce had "induced the Negroes to assume airs of consequence, and put a value on

themselves unknown amongst the slaves of former periods" (Craton, *Testing the Chains*, 258). It is important, however, not to overstate the amount of independence that the provision-ground system gave slaves. Planters used the practice to reduce the food demands that slaves made on them. The introduction of the provision-ground system in Jamaica principally meant that slaves had to work much harder there than they did in Barbados, where a rationing system prevailed. Higman estimates that Jamaican slaves worked 800 hours more a year than Barbadian slaves and argues that "the provision ground system was simply an added imposition for the Jamaican slave, in no way compensated by extra 'free' days" (*Slave Populations of the British Caribbean*, 188). Moreover, Barbadian slaves developed as vibrant an internal marketing system as did Jamaican slaves without having a well-developed provision-ground system.

59. "Care Off White Servants." Of course, it was standard in all slaveholding societies for slaves to be allowed to own property. Orlando Patterson explains: "In all slaveholding societies the slave was allowed a *peculium*," which "may be defined as the investment by the master of a partial, and temporary, capacity in his slave to possess and enjoy a given range of goods" (*Slavery and Social Death: A Comparative Study* [Cambridge, Mass.: Harvard University Press, 1982], 182).

60. Barry W. Higman, "African and Creole Slave Family Patterns in Trinidad," *Journal of Family History* 3 (1978): 163–80.

61. Mullin, *Africa in America*, 164–65.

62. 17 March 1754.

63. 29 August 1784.

64. Olwell, *Masters, Slaves, and Subjects*, 177–78.

65. "Sex Uncovered," London *Observer*, 27 October 2002.

66. This figure excludes Phibbah, whom he never paid for sex.

67. 9 April 1768.

68. 8 January 1751.

69. 20 March 1753.

70. 2–5 May 1756.

71. Barbara Bush, *Slave Women in Caribbean Society, 1650–1838* (London: James Currey, 1990), 33–45.

72. 4–6 February 1764.

73. 11 December 1774.

74. Richard Price finds that among the eighteenth-century Saramakas Maroons in Surinam, the proportion of adult men who at any given time had two or more wives was close to 20 percent. See Richard Price, *Alabi's World* (Baltimore: Johns Hopkins University Press, 1991), 382–83. Price's estimates indicate what percentage of polygamy would have been likely if slave men had been free to choose their types of marital practices.

75. 8, 22 October 1757; Mullin, *Africa in America*, 171; Madeleine Manoukian, *Akan and Ga-Adangme Peoples* (London: Oxford University Press, 1950), 26–31;

M. D. McLeod, *The Asante* (London: British Museum Publications, 1981), 30–31. For the demoralization of male slaves, see Bertram Wyatt-Brown, "The Mask of Obedience: Male Slave Psychology in the Old South," *American Historical Review* 93 (1988): 1228–52.

76. 16 March 1752, 30 June 1755, 2 April 1757.

77. 7 February, 17 November, 11 December 1763.

78. 14 June 1765.

79. Alex Lichtenstein, "'That Disposition to Theft, with Which They Have Been Branded': Moral Economy, Slave Management, and the Law," *Journal of Social History* 21 (1988): 425.

80. Mullin, *Africa in America*, 268.

81. Genovese, *Roll, Jordan, Roll*, 599–609.

82. 5 November 1758.

83. 2 December 1759.

84. 4 October 1756, 25 October 1764.

85. 28 September 1765.

86. 4, 11 May 1753.

87. Craton, *Testing the Chains*, 138. The American Revolution was a greater shock, but it was not so much a revolt from below as a challenge made by one established authority to another.

88. Long, *History of Jamaica*, 2:447.

89. Ibid., 447–65; Craton, *Testing the Chains*, 127–38.

90. 16 August, 24 October 1760.

91. 29 July, 18 October 1760.

92. Long, *History of Jamaica*, 1:462; Turner, *Slaves and Missionaries*, 148, 173.

93. Theodore Faulks, *Eighteen Months in Jamaica; with Recollections of the Late Rebellion* (London, 1833), 76.

94. 31 May 1760.

95. The hesitation that Thistlewood's slaves demonstrated during the rebellion of 1760 was also adopted by the greatest of revolutionary slave leaders, Toussaint L'Ouverture, in the 1791 St. Domingue revolution. Toussaint, a small property owner, did not join the initial frenzy of slave destructiveness. Instead, he kept his master's slaves in order and prevented them from burning down the plantation. Only when the rebellion was well advanced did he join the rebel cause. See C. L. R. James, *The Black Jacobins* (New York: Vintage, 1963), 90–93.

Chapter Six

1. J. H. Lawrence Archer, *Monumental Inscriptions etc* (London, 1875).

2. Thistlewood told an extraordinary tale relating to Cope's dual experiences of slavery in Africa and Jamaica in the aftermath of Tackey's rebellion in 1760. It involved Apongo or Wager, leader of the rebels in Westmoreland: "Wager, alias Apongo,

was a Prince in Guinea, tributary to the King of Dome [Dahomey]. The King of Dome had Conquer'd all the County for miles round him. Apongo Come to visit the late John Cope, my employer's father, when governor of Cape Coast Castle, attended by a guard of 100 men, Well-armed. He was supriz'd and took prisoner when hunting, and Sold for a Slave, brought to Jamaica and sold to Capt. Forest. In Jamaica Mr. Cope knew him again and Wager used when a Slave Sometimes to go to Strathbogie to see Mr. Cope, who had a Table Set out, a Cloth land etc for him, and would have purchased him and sent him home had Capt. Forest come to the island. Wager came to this country 6 or 7 years ago" (4 December 1760).

3. Masters in colonial Virginia and South Carolina were also lax in allowing slaves to carry firearms. But their complacency was somewhat justified by the fact that in an emergency masters could depend on a large adult white male community to come to their rescue. See Philip D. Morgan, *Slave Counterpoint: Black Culture in the Eighteenth-Century Chesapeake and Lowcountry* (Chapel Hill: University of North Carolina Press, 1998), 389–91.

4. Ira Berlin, *Many Thousands Gone: The First Two Centuries of Slavery in North America* (Cambridge, Mass.: Harvard University Press, 1998), 2–3.

5. Richard S. Dunn, "A Tale of Two Plantations: Slave Life at Mesopotamia in Jamaica and Mount Airy in Virginia, 1799–1828," *WMQ*, 3d ser., 34 (1977): 64.

6. 8 December 1756.

7. 8 August 1754.

8. 1–2 November 1771.

9. These debates have a long history. The initial positions were set down in the early 1940s in Melville J. Herskovits, *The Myth of the Negro Past* (1941; reprint, Boston: Beacon Press, 1958), and E. Franklin Frazier, *The Negro Family in the United States* (Chicago: University of Chicago Press, 1948), 1–69. For representative views that stress slave agency in developing slave culture, see Sidney W. Mintz and Richard Price, *An Anthropological Approach to the Afro-American Past: A Caribbean Perspective* (Philadelphia: Institute for the Study of Human Issues, 1976); Mervyn Alleyne, *Roots of Jamaican Culture* (London: Pluto Press, 1988); and Michael Mullin, *Africa in America: Slave Acculturation and Resistance in the American South and the British Caribbean, 1736–1831* (Urbana: University of Illinois Press, 1992). For representative views of the second position, see Orlando Patterson, *The Sociology of Slavery: An Analysis of the Origins, Development, and Structure of Negro Slave Society in Jamaica* (London: Macgibbon and Kee, 1967).

10. See Jerome S. Handler, "Life Histories of Enslaved Africans in Barbados," *S&A* 19 (1999): 129–40, and Vincent Carretta, ed., *Unchained Voices: An Anthology of Black Authors in the English Speaking World of the Eighteenth Century* (Lexington: University Press of Kentucky, 1996).

11. For an important attempt at reconstructing individual slave life, see Lorena S. Walsh, "A 'Place in Time' Regained: A Fuller History of Colonial Slavery through Group Biography," in Larry E. Hudson Jr., ed., *Working toward Freedom: Slave So-

ciety and the Domestic Economy in the American South (Rochester, N.Y.: University of Rochester Press, 1994), 1–32. For a sophisticated analysis of the personal experience of slavery, see Rhys Isaac, "Stories of Enslavement: A Person-Centered Ethnography from an Eighteenth-Century Virginia Plantation," in Bruce Clayton and John Salmond, eds., *Varieties of Southern History: New Essays on a Region and Its People* (Westport, Conn.: Greenwood Press, 1996), 3–20.

12. For Thistlewood's slave-management practices at Vineyard Pen, see Douglas Hall, "Thomas Thistlewood in the Vineyard, 1750–51," and "The Vineyard Slaves," *Jamaica Journal* 21, no. 3 (1988): 16–29, and 21, no. 4 (1988–89): 2–16, and Philip D. Morgan, "Slaves and Livestock in Eighteenth-Century Jamaica: Vineyard Pen, 1750–51," *WMQ*, 3d ser., 52 (1995): 47–76.

13. Egypt was a marginal sugar estate. At the end of the 1766 harvest, Thistlewood tabulated its annual production since 1754. Production varied greatly, from no crop at all in 1756 to 194,837 pounds of sugar, 700 gallons of rum, and 7,000 gallons of molasses in 1758. In that year, Egypt yielded tropical produce worth £3,531.78 sterling. Thistlewood supplied John and Molly Cope with 55 hogsheads of sugar and 33 puncheons of rum or molasses worth £1,595.28 sterling in an average year. Top-quality estates produced well over 100 hogsheads of sugar. See 27 March 1757 and 1 September 1766. Values have been calculated using data supplied in David Beck Ryden, "Producing a Peculiar Commodity: Jamaican Sugar Production, Slave Life, and Planter Profits on the Eve of Abolition, 1750–1807" (Ph.D. diss., University of Minnesota, 1999), 279–84, 299–301.

14. For commodity production in Jamaica at the time of Thistlewood's arrival, see David B. Ryden, "An Analysis of the Slave Economy in Jamaica's St. Andrew Parish," *S&A* 21 (2000): 48; "Statistics of Jamaica, 1739–1775," Long Papers, Add. MSS 12435, ff. 31–32, BL; and Douglas Hall, *In Miserable Slavery: Thomas Thistlewood in Jamaica, 1750–1786* (London: Macmillan, 1989), 138–39.

15. Richard B. Sheridan, *Sugar and Slavery: An Economic History of the British West Indies, 1623–1775* (Bridgetown, Barbados: Caribbean Universities Press, 1974), 230; Michael Craton, *Searching for the Invisible Man: Slaves and Plantation Life in Jamaica* (Cambridge, Mass.: Harvard University Press, 1978), 37.

16. B. W. Higman, *Slave Population and Economy in Jamaica, 1807–1834* (Cambridge: Cambridge University Press, 1976), 123. For amelioration, see J. R. Ward, *British West Indian Slavery, 1750–1834: The Process of Amelioration* (New York: Oxford University Press, 1988).

17. Richard S. Dunn, "'Dreadful Idlers' in the Cane Fields: The Slave Labor Pattern on a Jamaican Sugar Estate, 1762–1831," *Journal of Interdisciplinary History* 17 (1987): 797.

18. Betty Wood and T. R. Clayton, "Slave Birth, Death, and Disease on Golden Grove Plantation, Jamaica, 1765–1810," *S&A* 6 (1985): 100; Inventories, 1776, IB/11/3/56/72, JA; "List of Slaves on York Estate, Jamaica, 1 Jan. 1778," Gale-Morant Papers, 3/c, University of Exeter Library, Devon, England.

19. Ryden, "Producing a Peculiar Commodity," 73–80; Dunn, "Tale of Two Plantations," 54; Lucille Mathurin Mair, "Women Field Workers in Jamaica during Slavery," Elsa Goveia Memorial Lecture, Department of History, University of the West Indies, Mona, Jamaica, 1986.

20. A good contemporary description of sugar making can be found in Bryan Edwards, *The History, Civil and Commercial, of the British Colonies in the West Indies*, 2d ed., 3 vols. (London, 1793), 2:259–75.

21. Richard B. Sheridan, "Slave Medicine in Jamaica: Thomas Thistlewood's 'Receipts for a Physick,' 1750–1786," *Jamaican Historical Review* 17 (1991): 6.

22. Jerome S. Handler and Frederick W. Lange, *Plantation Slavery in Barbados: An Archaeological and Historical Investigation* (Cambridge, Mass.: Harvard University Press, 1978). For how slaves celebrated Christmas, see Cynric Williams, *A Tour through the Island of Jamaica* (London, 1826), 21–26.

23. "Mr. Richard Beckford's Instructions to Messrs. John Cope, Richard Lewing, [and] Robert Mason," 10 April 1754, Monson 31/86. See also Richard B. Sheridan, *Doctors and Slaves: A Medical and Demographic History of Slavery in the British West Indies, 1680–1834* (Cambridge: Cambridge University Press, 1985), 148–84, and B. W. Higman, *Slave Populations of the British Caribbean, 1807–1834* (Baltimore: Johns Hopkins University Press, 1984), 158–203. For Thistlewood's care of sick slaves, see Sheridan, "Slave Medicine in Jamaica." An example of slave management on the Egypt estate can be found in Mullin, *Africa in America*, 85–88.

24. See Verene Shepherd, "Alternative Husbandry: Slaves and Free Labourers on Livestock Farms in Jamaica in the 18th c. and 19th c.," *S&A* 14 (1993): 41–66; Higman, *Slave Population and Economy*, 122–25; and Higman, *Slave Populations of the British Caribbean*, 324–29.

25. Morgan, *Slave Counterpoint*, 174–75, 193–94, 240–56.

26. John Stewart, *A View of the Past and Present State of the Island of Jamaica* (Edinburgh, 1823), 234.

27. Thistlewood's slave force was more productive than most. The percentage of slaves between the ages of fifteen and forty-four on three large sugar estates in the 1770s ranged from 54.1 percent to 67.8 percent. See "Bayly v. Edwards," CO 107/68; "List of Slaves on York Estate, 1 January 1778"; and Inventories, 1776, IB/11/3/56/72, JA.

28. Thirty of these receipts are listed in Sheridan, "Slave Medicine in Jamaica," 10–13. For white medical treatment of slaves, see Sheridan, *Doctors and Slaves*.

29. I have found only one other inventory—Alexander Reed's of 1732—in which slaves are grouped according to household (IB/11/3/16/132, JA).

30. The four listings are 29 September 1767, 19 October 1770, 13 July 1776, and Inventories, 1787, IB/11/3/71/200, JA.

31. I have not included shipmates as fictive kin here because the relatively small size of Thistlewood's holdings and the comparatively large percentage of slaves that he bought at one time (notably 10 slaves in 1765) make it likely that shipmates

would have lived together at some point. For the importance of shipmates, see Mintz and Price, *Anthropological Approach*, 22–23.

32. Sometimes slaves decided who would live together, but at other times Thistlewood made the decision. Slaves had to ask for Thistlewood's permission if they wanted to be "kept" by slaves at other plantations. Thus, after Abba "slyly" made a match with John Rickett's Cudjoe, her "new sweetheart" asked Thistlewood for "leave to have her" and he consented (30 December 1770). Generally, however, slaves were free to make their own matches within the plantation and set up household together. Solon and Maria did this in the 1760s, but Thistlewood never records that Solon asked for permission. Occasionally, Thistlewood made a match between two slaves. On 4 July 1768, for example, he wrote that he "Made a match between Chub and Sally." It was not a success.

33. The leading authority on West Indian slave family structure is Barry Higman. See his "Household Structure and Fertility on Jamaican Slave Populations: A Nineteenth-Century Example," *Population Studies* 27 (1973): 527–50; "The Slave Family and Household in the British West Indies," *Journal of Interdisciplinary History* 6 (1975): 261–87; "African and Creole Slave Family Patterns in Trinidad," *Journal of Family History* 3 (1978): 163–80; *Slave Populations of the British Caribbean*, 365–74; and *Montpelier, Jamaica: A Plantation Community in Slavery and Freedom, 1739–1912* (Kingston: Press University of the West Indies, 1998), 116–24. See also Orlando Patterson, "Persistence, Continuity, and Change in the Working-Class Family," *Journal of Family History* 7 (1982): 135–61; Karen Fog Olwig, "Finding a Place for the Slave Family: Historical Anthropological Perspectives," *Folk* 23 (1981): 345–58; and Michael Craton, "Changing Patterns of Slave Families in the British West Indies," *Journal of Interdisciplinary History* 10 (1979): 1–35.

34. Sheridan, *Doctors and Slaves*, 83–89.

35. 14 July 1758, 30 January 1762, 22 October 1769.

36. 19 July 1765, 24 August 1766, 23 January 1767, 9 September 1768, 10 July 1769, 9 August 1771, 15 October 1772, 19–21 October 1775.

37. 29 June 1768.

38. Fernando Ortiz, *Cuban Counterpoint: Tobacco and Sugar*, translated by Harriet de Onis (New York: Alfred A. Knopf, 1947), 65.

39. Morgan, *Slave Counterpoint*, 334.

40. 21 September 1767, 21 November 1764.

41. Morgan, *Slave Counterpoint*, 244.

42. 9 December 1767.

43. 15 February, 5 March, 26 May, 8, 27 June, 6 July 1770, 20 October 1775.

44. 7 July 1768.

45. 29 December 1781.

46. Inventories, 1787, IB/11/3/71/200, JA.

47. *Jamaica Royal Gazette*, 9 May 1795, cited in Mullin, *Africa in America*, 89.

48. 14 November 1786.

49. Eugene Genovese, *Roll, Jordan, Roll: The World the Slaves Made* (New York: Pantheon, 1974), 3.

50. Orlando Patterson, *Slavery and Social Death: A Comparative Study* (Cambridge, Mass.: Harvard University Press, 1982), 12.

51. Patterson, *Sociology of Slavery*.

52. Isaac, "Stories of Enslavement," 10–16; Jack P. Greene, ed., *The Diary of Colonel Landon Carter of Sabine Hall, 1752–1778* (Charlottesville: University Press of Virginia, 1965), 953.

53. Hall, *In Miserable Slavery*, 181.

54. 22 July 1770.

55. 5 December 1768, 16 July 1770, 6 October 1786.

56. See, for example, 25 December 1768.

57. On 4 September 1767, for example, Thistlewood gave Lincoln his old coat.

58. 26 August 1757.

59. 5, 20, 22, 26 January 1756.

60. For problems of slave subsistence during and after the American Revolution, see Richard B. Sheridan, "The Crisis of Slave Subsistence in the British West Indies during and after the American Revolution," *WMQ*, 3d ser., 33 (1976): 615–41. See also Mullin, *Africa in America*, 88.

61. 5 December 1768. See also 16 July 1770 and 6 March 1781.

62. 26–30 May 1760.

63. 23 February 1756, 14 August 1786.

64. 4 September, 9 December 1767, 10, 30 January 1776, 13 February, 2, 6 March 1781, 3 April 1778.

65. 25, 29 January 1776.

66. 7 May 1776.

67. For South Carolina, see Morgan, *Slave Counterpoint*, 240–43, and Peter H. Wood, *Black Majority: Negroes in Colonial South Carolina from 1670 through the Stono Rebellion* (New York: Alfred A. Knopf, 1974), 123. For the Caribbean, see Richard Price, "Caribbean Fishing and Fishermen: A Historical Sketch," *American Anthropologist* 67 (1966): 1363–83.

68. R. Smith, "The Canoe in West African History," *Journal of African History* 11 (1970): 515–33.

69. 5 June 1760, 17 April 1781.

70. 2 July 1768.

71. 2 May 1777, 5 July 1779. See also 19 October 1778 and 13, 15 February 1781.

72. 7 May 1776, 3 April 1778.

73. Robert Olwell, *Masters, Slaves, and Subjects: The Culture of Power in the South Carolina Low Country, 1740–1790* (Ithaca, N.Y.: Cornell University Press, 1998), 145–58; Alex Lichtenstein, "'That Disposition to Theft, with Which They Have Been Branded': Moral Economy, Slave Management, and the Law," *Journal of So-*

cial History 21 (1988): 413–40. For different understandings of privileges and rights by whites and blacks in the antebellum South, see Drew Gilpin Faust, "Culture, Conflict, and Community: The Meaning of Power on an Antebellum Plantation," *Journal of Social History* 14 (1980): 83–97. For an ethnographic analysis of master-slave contestation, see Rhys Isaac, "Communication and Control: Authority Metaphors and Power Contests on Colonel Landon Carter's Virginia Plantation, 1752–1776," in Sean Wilentz, ed., *Rites of Power: Symbolism, Ritual, and Politics since the Middle Ages* (Philadelphia: University of Pennsylvania Press, 1985), 275–302. For the Caribbean, see Emilia Viotti da Costa, *Crowns of Glory, Tears of Blood: The Demerara Slave Rebellion of 1823* (New York: Oxford University Press, 1994), 61–85.

74. Sidney Mintz, "Slavery and the Rise of Peasantry," *Historical Reflections* 1 (1979): 240–41.

75. Trevor Burnard, "Theater of Terror: Domestic Violence in Thomas Thistlewood's Jamaica, 1750–1786," in Christine Daniels and Michael V. Kennedy, eds., *Over the Threshold: Intimate Violence in Early America* (New York: Routledge, 1999), 248.

76. 22 July 1770.

77. 19 November 1778.

78. 22 February 1756, 12 October, 3 December 1757, 20 July 1758.

79. 11 May 1773.

80. 10 September 1771.

81. 7–10 August 1770.

82. 14 April 1757, 12 June 1759, 7, 23 January, 2 June, 29 December 1760.

83. 4 July 1785.

84. 5 February 1767.

85. For the strength of West African patriarchalism, see Sandra E. Greene, *Gender, Ethnicity, and Social Change on the Upper Slave Coast* (Portsmouth, N.H.: Heinemann, 1996), 20–47, and Remi Clignet, *Many Wives, Many Powers: Authority and Power in Polygynous Marriages* (Evanston, Ill.: Northwestern University Press, 1970), 46–61.

86. 3 November 1782.

87. 10 September 1780.

88. The transfer of African kinship patterns to slave communities in the New World is a matter of intense debate in the modern historiography of slavery, in part because of its seeming significance to present-day politics and social policy. For some initial findings on Africa, see Shula Marks and Richard Rathbone, "The History of the Family in Africa: Introduction," *Journal of African History* 24 (1983): 145–61, and Patrick Manning, *Slavery and African Life: Occidental, Oriental, and African Slave Trades* (Cambridge: Cambridge University Press, 1990), 116–17. For the Caribbean slave family, see the works cited in note 33. For the antebellum American South, see Ann Patton Malone, *Sweet Chariot: Slave Family and Household*

Structure in Nineteenth-Century Louisiana (Chapel Hill: University of North Carolina Press, 1992). For colonial North America, see Michael A. Gomez, *Exchanging Our Country Marks: The Transformation of African Identities in the Colonial and Antebellum South* (Chapel Hill: University of North Carolina Press, 1998).

89. Mullen, *Africa in America*, 171.

90. Burnard, "Theater of Terror," 246; Trevor Burnard, "The Sexual Life of an Eighteenth-Century Jamaican Slave Overseer," in Merril D. Smith, ed., *Sex and Sexuality in Early America* (New York: New York University Press, 1999), 182.

91. For "Quashie" behavior by slaves, see Michael Craton, *Testing the Chains: Resistance to Slavery in the British West Indies* (Ithaca, N.Y.: Cornell University Press, 1982), 52–57, and Patterson, *Sociology of Slavery*, 174–81.

92. 6–8 May 1771.

93. Willie Lee Rose, *Slavery and Freedom*, edited by William W. Freehling (New York: Oxford University Press, 1982), 23. The shift from patriarchalism to paternalism in slave owners' treatment of slaves over time is skillfully discussed in Morgan, *Slave Counterpoint*, 273–300, and Philip D. Morgan, "Three Planters and Their Slaves: Perspectives on Slavery in Virginia, South Carolina, and Jamaica, 1750–1790," in Winthrop D. Jordan and Sheila L. Skemp, eds., *Race and Family in the Colonial South* (Jackson: University Press of Mississippi, 1987), 37–79. See also Berlin, *Many Thousands Gone*, esp. 95–99, 142–76.

94. 3 December 1771, 20 November 1773. For music in Jamaica, see Mullin, *Africa in America*, 66; Richard Cullen Roth, "African Music in Seventeenth-Century Jamaica: Cultural Transit and Transaction," *WMQ*, 3d ser., 50 (1993): 700–726; and Richard D. E. Burton, *Afro-Creole: Power, Opposition, and Play in the Caribbean* (Ithaca, N.Y.: Cornell University Press, 1997), 18–19, 22, 26, 29–30. For another example of Thistlewood destroying a banjo, see 3 February 1764. For the African origins of the banjo, see Michael Theodore Coolen, "Senegambian Archetypes for the American Folk Banjo," *Western Folklore* 43 (1989): 117–32, and Dena J. Polacheck Epstein, *Sinful Times and Spirituals: Black Folk Music in the Civil War* (Urbana: University of Illinois Press, 1977), 34–38.

95. Genovese, *Roll, Jordan, Roll*, 646–47.

96. G. W. F. Hegel, *The Phenomenology of Mind*, trans. J. B. Baillie (New York: Harper and Row, 1967).

Chapter Seven

1. Trevor Burnard, "Theater of Terror: Domestic Violence in Thomas Thistlewood's Jamaica, 1750–1786," in Christine Daniels and Michael V. Kennedy, eds., *Over the Threshold: Intimate Violence in Early America* (New York: Routledge, 1999), 237–53.

2. Dr. Collins, *Practical Rules for the Management and Medical Treatment of Negro Slaves in the Sugar Colonies* (London, 1803), 35.

3. David Barry Gaspar, "Working the System: Antigua Slaves and Their Struggle to Live," *S&A* 13 (1992): 134–35. See also Alex Lichtenstein, "'That Disposition to Theft, with Which They Have Been Branded': Moral Economy, Slave Management, and the Law," *Journal of Social History* 21 (1988): 413–40; Michael A. Gomez, *Exchanging Our Country Marks: The Transformation of African Identities in the Colonial and Antebellum South* (Chapel Hill: University of North Carolina Press, 1998), 120–21; and Barbara Bush, "Hard Labor: Women, Childbirth, and Resistance in British Caribbean Slave Societies," in David Barry Gaspar and Darlene Clark Hine, eds., *More Than Chattel: Black Women and Slavery in the Americas* (Bloomington: Indiana University Press, 1996), 208.

4. Michel-Ralph Trouillot, "In the Shadow of the West: Power, Resistance, and Creolization in the Making of the Caribbean Region," in Wim Hoogbergen, ed., *Born out of Resistance: On Caribbean Cultural Creativity* (Utrecht, Netherlands: ISOR-Publications, 1995), 9.

5. Michel de Certeau, "On the Oppositional Practices of Everyday Life," *Social Text* 3 (1980): 3–43; Michel de Certeau, *The Practice of Everyday Life* (Berkeley: University of California Press, 1984).

6. Michel Foucault, "The Ethic of Care for the Self as a Practice of Freedom," in James Bernauer and David Rasmussen, eds., *The Final Foucault* (Cambridge, Mass.: Harvard University Press, 1994), 12.

7. "A tactic is a calculated action determined by the absence of a proper locus. No delimitation of an exteriority, then, provides it with the condition necessary for autonomy. The space of the tactic is the space of the other" (de Certeau, *Practice of Everyday Life*, 38).

8. Arlene Gautier, "Les Esclaves femmes aux Antilles françaises, 1635–1848," *Reflexions Historiques* 10 (1983): 409–35.

9. Barbara Bush, *Slave Women in Caribbean Society, 1650–1838* (Bloomington: Indiana University Press, 1990); Bush, "Hard Labor," 193–217.

10. Robert Dirks, *The Black Saturnalia: Conflict and Its Ritual Expression on British West Indian Slave Plantations* (Gainesville: University Presses of Florida, 1987), 160–61.

11. Hilary McD. Beckles, *Centering Women: Gender Discourses in Caribbean Slave Society* (Kingston: Ian Randle, 1999), 162.

12. William Beckford, *Remarks upon the Situation of the Negroes in Jamaica* (London, 1788), 13.

13. Richard S. Dunn, "Sugar Production and Slave Women in Jamaica," in Ira Berlin and Philip D. Morgan, eds., *Cultivation and Culture: Labor and the Shaping of Slave Life in the Americas* (Charlottesville: University Press of Virginia, 1993), 49–72.

14. Richard B. Sheridan, *Doctors and Slaves: A Medical and Demographic History of Slavery in the British West Indies, 1680–1834* (Cambridge: Cambridge University Press, 1985), 178–90; B. W. Higman, *Slave Populations of the British Caribbean,*

1807–1834 (Baltimore: Johns Hopkins University Press, 1984), 158–99; Richard S. Dunn, "'Dreadful Idlers' in the Cane Fields: The Slave Labor Pattern on a Jamaican Sugar Estate, 1762–1831," *Journal of Interdisciplinary History* 17 (1987): 795–822.

15. Elsa Goveia, *Slave Society in the British Leeward Islands at the End of the Eighteenth Century* (New Haven: Yale University Press, 1965), 244–45. See also Ira Berlin, *Many Thousands Gone: The First Two Centuries of Slavery in North America* (Cambridge, Mass.: Harvard University Press, 1998), 143.

16. Philip D. Curtin, *Economic Change in Pre-Colonial Africa: Senegambia in the Era of the Slave Trade* (Madison: University of Wisconsin Press, 1975); Clare Robertson and Martin Klein, eds., *Women and Slavery in Africa* (Madison: University of Wisconsin Press, 1983).

17. Inventories, 1732–82, IB/11/3/16, 24, 25, 33, 56, 63, JA.

18. *An Essay concerning Slavery and the Danger Jamaica is expos'd to from too great Number of Slaves . . .* (London, 1746), vi, 18.

19. Kenneth F. Kiple, *The Caribbean Slave: A Biological History* (New York: Cambridge University Press, 1984), 120–34.

20. Ibid.; Bush, "Hard Labor," 198; Lucille Mathurin Mair, "A Historical Study of Women in Jamaica from 1655 to 1844" (Ph.D. diss., University of the West Indies, 1974). Higman traces the higher levels of morbidity among females to occupation and to females' tendency to outlive males in *Slave Populations of the British Caribbean*, 299–300.

21. Bush, "Hard Labor," 197–98.

22. For example, he had sex with Maria when she was eight months pregnant on 26 June 1770 and again on 9 and 15 July 1770. Maria gave birth on 6 August 1770.

23. Bush, "Hard Labor," 210; Richard S. Dunn, "A Tale of Two Plantations: Slave Life at Mesopotamia in Jamaica and Mount Airy in Virginia, 1799–1828," *WMQ*, 3d ser., 34 (1977): 61.

24. John Lean and Trevor Burnard, "Hearing Slave Voices: The Fiscals' Reports of Berbice and Demerara-Essequebo," *Archives* 27, no. 106 (2002): 48–50.

25. Bush, "Hard Labor," 205.

26. 11 June 1758, 9 April 1764, 14 February 1775.

27. Trevor Burnard, "The Sexual Life of an Eighteenth-Century Jamaican Overseer," in Merril D. Smith, ed., *Sex and Sexuality in Early America* (New York: New York University Press, 1999), 163–89.

28. 14 September 1763.

29. 21 March 1772.

30. 9 August 1766.

31. 27 March, 18 April, 25 May 1767.

32. 3 October 1770, 3 November 1771, 22 June 1775.

33. 30 September, 7 October, 14 November 1782.

34. 11 May 1781. Sally would have been twenty-eight or twenty-nine.

35. These figures underestimate the number of miscarriages and stillbirths and do not include abortions. He refers to only one abortion, by Mountain Lucy, who took an herbal mixture to induce an abortion on 17 July 1767.

36. Marietta Morrissey, *Slave Women in the New World: Gender Stratification in the Caribbean* (Lawrence: University of Kansas Press, 1989), 96–98; Bush, *Slave Women in Caribbean Society*, 137–42, 150.

37. Matthew Lewis, *Journal of a West India Proprietor . . .* (1816; reprint, Oxford: Oxford University Press, 1999), 54.

38. 30 August, 13 September, 11, 17, 31 October, 14, 21 November, 2 December 1778, 28 April, 27 May, 2, 9 June 1781.

39. 2 August 1784.

40. 2 July 1770.

41. Dunn, "Tale of Two Plantations," 43; Dunn, "'Dreadful Idlers,'" 165.

42. For the demographic performance of slaves in the Caribbean in the early nineteenth century, see B. W. Higman, *Slave Population and Economy in Jamaica, 1807–1834* (Cambridge: Cambridge University Press, 1976); Sheridan, *Doctors and Slaves*, 222–48; Kiple, *Caribbean Slave*, 89–124; and Stanley Engerman and B. W. Higman, "The Demographic Structure of the Caribbean Slave Societies in the Eighteenth and Nineteenth Centuries," in Franklin W. Knight, ed., *General History of the Caribbean*, vol. 3, *The Slave Societies of the Caribbean* (London: UNESCO, 1997), 45–104.

43. Inventories, 1739, IB/11/3/20/1–8, JA.

44. Fanny, who died shortly after childbirth on 6 December 1782, had two children who survived her. At his death, Thistlewood owned sixteen slaves who were the offspring of his slave women, all younger than fifteen except for Mary, who was twenty-five. Of these, five were either Abba's children or her grandchildren.

45. 30 December 1770.

46. 3 May 1771.

47. Edward Long, *History of Jamaica . . .* , 3 vols. (1774; reprint, London: Frank Cass, 1970), 2:435–37, 441; Bryan Edwards, *The History, Civil and Commercial, of the British Colonies in the West Indies*, 2d ed., 3 vols. (London, 1793), 2:148.

48. 10 April 1756, 11 August 1758, 12 July 1759, 17, 24 October 1771, 9 April 1774, 10 March 1776.

49. See, for example, 27 May 1762, 11 May 1767, and 9 February 1769.

50. 7 July 1771.

51. 11 July, 13 September 1770, 31 December 1785.

52. Gilbert Mathison, *Notices Respecting Jamaica in 1808, 1809, 1810* (London, 1811), 30–31.

53. *Essay concerning Slavery*, 38.

54. 23 September 1770.

55. Orlando Patterson, *The Sociology of Slavery: An Analysis of the Origins, Development, and Structure of Negro Slave Society in Jamaica* (London: Macgibbon

and Kee, 1967), 228–29; Richard B. Sheridan, "The Crisis of Slave Subsistence in the British West Indies during and after the American Revolution," *WMQ*, 3d ser., 33 (1976): 615–41; Sheridan, *Doctors and Slaves*, 154–73.

56. 4 February 1775, 22 August 1779, 7 February 1780.

57. 3 July, 4 August, 30 November 1784, 23 July 1785, 25 October 1786.

58. 6 September, 25 December 1777.

59. 29 September 1781, 20 June, 23 July, 5 November 1785, 29 June, 20 July, 30 October 1786.

60. Higman, *Slave Populations of the British Caribbean*, 364; Bush, *Slave Women in Caribbean Society*, 102.

61. Wills, 1787, 52/77, IRO; Manumissions, 1792, 7/119, JA.

62. Inventories, 1787, IB/11/3/71/200, JA.

63. 5 August 1755, 29 April 1760.

64. 10 May, 29 June, 8 October 1752, 27 January, 26 March 1753.

65. Eugene Genovese, *Roll, Jordan, Roll: The World the Slaves Made* (New York: Pantheon, 1974), 359–61; William Dusinberre, *Them Dark Days: Slavery in the American Rice Swamps* (New York: Oxford University Press, 1996), 190–99.

66. 20 November 1768, 7 September 1780.

67. Higman, *Slave Populations of the British Caribbean*, 332–36, 667–70.

68. Hilary McD. Beckles, *Natural Rebels: A Social History of Enslaved Black Women in Barbados* (New Brunswick: Rutgers University Press, 1989), 65–68.

69. When house slaves did form liaisons with slave men, they usually did so with light-skinned tradesmen or mulatto house servants. Phibbah confined her attentions solely to white men, having relations not only with Thistlewood but also with Thistlewood's employer, John Cope, and Thistlewood's predecessor at Egypt, John Filton. See 4 May 1752, 3 October, 15 November, 22 December 1754, and 5 August 1755.

70. John Gabriel Stedman, *Stedman's Surinam: Life in an Eighteenth-Century Slave Society*, edited by Richard and Sally Price (Baltimore: Johns Hopkins University Press, 1992), 20–21.

71. 5 May 1764, 22 March, 16 April 1769, 29 December 1780; Beckford, *Remarks upon the Situation of Negroes in Jamaica*, 13; Long, *History of Jamaica*, 2:278–79; Mullin, *Africa in America*, 159–73, 271–73.

72. 21–22 August 1755.

73. See also 10 July 1755 and 16 June 1781.

74. For punishments, see 7 August 1770 and 2 November 1771. For forgiveness, see 16 June 1781.

75. 1 November 1755, 4 January 1758.

76. 16 February 1779; John Stewart, *A View of the Past and Present State of the Island of Jamaica* (Edinburgh, 1823), 173.

77. Deborah Gray White, *Ar'n't I a Woman?: Female Slaves in the Plantation South* (New York: W. W. Norton, 1985), 119.

78. 29 April, 1 May 1760, 3 September 1769, 8 April 1776.

79. 24 August 1761.

80. 9 May 1767, 31 January 1768.

81. 12 July, 23 August 1777, 3–21 September 1780, 3 January 1782; Douglas Hall, *In Miserable Slavery: Thomas Thistlewood in Jamaica, 1750–1786* (London: Macmillan, 1989), 215. For creolization, see Edward Brathwaite, *The Development of Creole Society in Jamaica, 1770–1820* (Oxford: Clarendon Press, 1971), 296–305.

82. See 31 January, 28 June, 2 July, 28 October 1777, 6 January, 6, 8 May, 3, 8, 31 July, 29 December 1778, and 26 May 1779.

83. Gad Heuman, *Between Black and White: Race, Politics, and the Free Coloreds in Jamaica, 1792–1865* (Westport, Conn.: Greenwood Press, 1981).

84. Bush, *Slave Women in Caribbean Society*, 116.

85. 14 February 1764, 27 September 1767, 1 March 1771, 29 August 1774, 9 March 1776, 26 September 1779, 1–16 September 1780.

86. 21 August 1772. Thistlewood was often exasperated at his son's behavior. Nevertheless, he was devastated when John died, exclaiming, "I am exceeding dejected and low spirited etc a parched mouth and great inward heat" (13 September 1780).

87. 24 March, 6 June 1752, 31 December 1753, 5 December 1757, 23 March 1774, 9 March 1776, 5 May 1777, 22 April 1778, 5 September 1779.

88. 24 July 1765; Hall, *In Miserable Slavery*, 116; Wills, 1786, 52/77, IRO.

89. Sidney W. Mintz, "The Jamaica Internal Marketing Pattern: Some Notes and Hypotheses," *Social and Economic Studies* 4 (1955): 95–103; Sidney W. Mintz, "Was the Plantation Slave a Proletarian?," *Review* 2 (1978): 81–98; Sidney W. Mintz and Douglas Hall, *The Origins of the Jamaican Internal Market System* (New Haven: Yale University Press, 1960), 1–26; Jean Besson, "A Paradox in Caribbean Attitudes to Land," in Jean Besson and Janet Momser, eds., *Land and Development in the Caribbean* (London: Macmillan, 1987), 18.

90. Brutality was not confined to men. Thistlewood related on 13 August 1780 that "Mrs. Allwood, dr. Allwoods wife, has flogged another wench to death and buried her in the buttery, this is said to be the 3rd she has killed."

91. 31 December 1765, 20–21 November 1775, 31 July 1778, 8 October 1781, 25 August 1782.

92. 4 May 1752, 3 October, 15 November, 22 December 1754, 5 August 1755.

93. 17 April, 4 October, 19 November 1754, 7 February, 6 July, 26 August 1755, 17, 31 August 1759.

94. 1 April 1765, 18–24 November 1768. See also 27 May–3 June 1775.

95. 19, 22 June 1757.

96. 17 July 1757.

97. 17, 23, 25 July, 13, 27 August, 23 September, 8 October, 4, 19 November, 3 December 1757.

98. 3 July 1757, 10 January, 5 February, 23 April 1758.

99. 10 July 1755, 4 January 1758, 2 November 1771, 19 December 1776.

Chapter Eight

1. Wills, 1787, 52/77, IRO; Inventories, 1787, IB/11/3/71/200, JA.

2. For the distinction between societies with slaves and slave societies, see Keith Hopkins, *Conquerors and Slaves: Sociological Studies in Roman History* (Cambridge: Cambridge University Press, 1978), 99, and Moses Finley, *Ancient Slavery and Modern Ideology* (New York: Viking, 1980), 79–80.

3. Frank Tannenbaum, *Slave and Citizen: The Negro in the Americas* (New York: Vintage, 1946), 117.

4. Cited in Sheila Duncker, "The Free Coloureds and the Fight for Civil Rights in Jamaica, 1800–1830" (master's thesis, University of London, 1960), 231–32.

5. For the contribution of eighteenth-century whites to long-standing Jamaican cultural patterns, see Edward Brathwaite, *The Development of Creole Society in Jamaica, 1770–1820* (Oxford: Clarendon Press, 1971), 296–305.

6. Trevor Burnard, *Creole Gentlemen: The Maryland Elite, 1691–1776* (New York: Routledge, 2002), 237–64.

7. Edward Long, *History of Jamaica . . .* , 3 vols. (1774; reprint, London: Frank Cass, 1970); Bryan Edwards, *The History, Civil and Commercial, of the British Colonies in the West Indies*, 2d ed., 3 vols. (London, 1793).

8. Edwards, *History, Civil and Commercial*, 3:7.

9. Trevor Burnard, "Not a Place for Whites?: Demographic Failure and Settlement in Comparative Context, Jamaica, 1655–1780," in Kathleen Monteith and Glen Richards, eds., *Jamaica in Slavery and Freedom: History, Heritage, and Custom* (Kingston: Press University of the West Indies, 2002), 73–86.

10. Barbara Solow, "Slavery and Colonization," in Barbara Solow, ed., *Slavery and the Rise of the Atlantic System* (Cambridge: Cambridge University Press, 1991), 21–42.

11. Governor George Nugent to William Sullivan, 30 April 1803, CO 137/110.

12. William Dorrill's will suggests that Molly Cope was his natural daughter by Elizabeth Anderson, thus implying that Molly was either a quadroon or lighter skinned but still free colored rather than white (Wills, 1754, 52/77, IRO).

13. For assertions that whites in the Caribbean did not create anything of lasting value, see Richard S. Dunn, *Sugar and Slaves: The Rise of the Planter Class in the English West Indies, 1624–1713* (Chapel Hill: University of North Carolina Press, 1972), xv, 340.

14. Richard S. Dunn, "A Tale of Two Plantations: Slave Life at Mesopotamia in Jamaica and Mount Airy in Virginia, 1799–1828," *WMQ*, 3d ser., 34 (1977): 64.

15. Ira Berlin, *Many Thousands Gone: The First Two Centuries of Slavery in North*

America (Cambridge, Mass.: Harvard University Press, 1998), 2–4; Eugene Genovese, *Roll, Jordan, Roll: The World the Slaves Made* (New York: Pantheon, 1974).

16. 16 July, 1 August 1750.

17. Charles Oscar Hardy, *The Negro Question in the French Revolution* (Menasha, Wis.: Collegiate Press, George Banta Publishing Company, 1919), 51–52, 57–58.

18. Gordon K. Lewis, *Main Currents in Caribbean Thought: The Historical Evolution of Caribbean Society in Its Ideological Aspects, 1492–1900* (Baltimore: Johns Hopkins University Press, 1983), 109.

19. Jack P. Greene, "'Slavery or Independence': Some Reflections on the Relationship among Liberty, Black Bondage, and Equality in Revolutionary South Carolina," *South Carolina Historical Magazine* 80 (1979): 193–214.

20. Winthrop D. Jordan, *White Over Black: American Attitudes toward the Negro, 1550–1812* (Chapel Hill: University of North Carolina Press, 1968), 3–268.

21. Trevor Burnard, "A Failed Settler Society: Marriage and Demographic Failure in Early Jamaica," *Journal of Social History* 28 (1994): 77.

22. Douglas Hall, *In Miserable Slavery: Thomas Thistlewood in Jamaica, 1750–1786* (London: Macmillan, 1989), 180–213.

23. 11 August 1782.

24. Judith Lewis Herman, *Trauma and Recovery: The Aftermath of Violence—From Domestic Abuse to Political Terror* (New York: Basic Books, 1992). For a contrary view, see Ian Hacking, *Rewriting the Soul: Multiple Personality and the Sciences of Memory* (Princeton: Princeton University Press, 1995).

25. *The Works of James Houston, M.D.* (London, 1753), 354; [Charles Leslie], *A new and exact account of Jamaica* [Edinburgh, ca. 1740], 41; Thomas Jefferson, *Notes on the State of Virginia* (1787; reprint, New York: W. W. Norton, 1972), 162; *Jamaica, a poem, in three parts written in that Island in the Year 1776* (London, 1777), 43, cited by Thistlewood in Monson 31/86.

26. Thistlewood marked all of his slaves. The youngest recorded was Bristol, the son of Phibbah's slave Bess, who was apprenticed to be a carpenter and marked with Thistlewood's distinctive triangular symbol on his left shoulder when he was seven and a half and "just 4 ft 1 inch high" (13 February 1780).

27. 25 January 1778, 28 June, 1 July 1780, 19 June 1781, 23 January, 25 February, 8 August, 30 November 1784.

28. Alex Bontemps, *The Punished Self: Surviving Slavery in the Colonial South* (Ithaca, N.Y.: Cornell University Press, 2002), ix. On slavery as "soul murder," see Nell Irvin Painter, *Southern History across the Color Line* (Chapel Hill: University of North Carolina Press, 2002), 15–39.

29. Bontemps, *Punished Self*, 117; Primo Levi, *The Drowned and the Saved*, translated by Raymond Rosenthal (London: Abacus, 1988), 27–32.

30. Orlando Patterson, *Slavery and Social Death: A Comparative Study* (Cambridge, Mass.: Harvard University Press, 1982), 1–101.

31. Philip D. Morgan, *Slave Counterpoint: Black Culture in the Eighteenth-Century Chesapeake and Lowcountry* (Chapel Hill: University of North Carolina Press, 1998), 284–96.

32. Long, *History of Jamaica*, 2:353–56, 407–9.

33. Douglas Hay, "Property, Authority, and the Criminal Law," in Douglas Hay et al., eds., *Albion's Fatal Tree: Crime and Society in Eighteenth-Century England* (London: Allen Lane, 1975); E. P. Thompson, *Whigs and Hunters: The Origin of the Black Act* (London: Allen Lane, 1975). See also V. A. C. Gatrell, *The Hanging Tree: Execution and the English People, 1770–1868* (Oxford: Oxford University Press, 1994), and J. M. Beattie, *Policing and Punishment in London, 1660–1720: Urban Crime and the Limits of Terror* (Oxford: Oxford University Press, 2001).

34. William Paley, *Principles of Moral and Political Philosophy* (London, 1785), cited in Hay, "Property, Authority, and the Criminal Law," 25–26.

35. J. Langbein, "*Albion's* Fatal Flaws," *Past and Present* 98 (1983): 96–120; Frank O'Gorman, *The Long Eighteenth Century: British Political and Social History, 1688–1832* (London, 1997), 288–94.

36. Catherine the Great's aphorism—"I work on human skin"—is noted in Louis Philippe, Comte de Segur, *Memoires, ou souvenirs et anecdotes*, 5th ed., 2 vols. (Paris, 1844), 2:127, cited in Robert Olwell, *Masters, Slaves, and Subjects: The Culture of Power in the South Carolina Low Country, 1740–1790* (Ithaca, N.Y.: Cornell University Press, 1998), 99. For the Barbados slave code of 1688, see Dunn, *Sugar and Slaves*, 242. For Lejeune, see Jacques Thibau, *Le Temps de Saint-Domingue: L'Esclavage et la revolution française* (Paris: Editions Jean-Claude Lattès, 1989), 17–93. See also Edwards, *History, Civil and Commercial*, 2:169–70.

37. Olwell, *Masters, Slaves, and Subjects*, 69.

Index

Toyne, Elizabeth, 8–9
Toyne, Thomas, 8
Trelawney, Governor William, 124–25
Trouillot, Michel-Ralph, 212
Turner, Nat, 139
Tyranny, 75–78, 271

Underwood, John, 87

Vassall, Florentius, 3, 44–45, 50, 62,
   81, 87, 94, 255 .
Vassall, Mrs., 87, 124
Vassall, Richard, 62, 82, 87, 124, 126
Venereal disease, 95, 218–19
Vineyard Pen, 3, 45, 50
Voting, 70, 72, 78–79, 92
Vyner, Robert, 7–8

Wade, James, 81
Wakefield, Edward Gibbon, 41
Wallace, William, 44, 110
Wallen, Matthew, 118–19
Ward, Edward, 90
Warlow, Mr., 83
Watt, Mr., 216
Weech, Harry, 47, 53–54, 63, 161,
   237–38
Westmoreland: description and history,
   22–24
White, Christopher, 53
White, Hugh, 78

White, James, 90
Whitehead, Mr., 199
Whites: demand for white labor, 47–
   49, 52–54; interactions of, 49–50,
   85–90, 92; labor problems of, 50–
   54; labor turnover of, 43–44; mortality of, 17, 44–45, 129; and politics, 76–78, 93–95; poor whites,
   75–76, 78, 85–88; and punishment,
   105; and religion, 20; and social origins, 90; and status, 61; and stewardship, 76; value of whiteness, 21, 75;
   wealth of, 6, 12, 14–15, 19, 23–24,
   40–41, 45–49, 51, 54, 58–59, 60–
   65, 115, 247–48; white supremacy,
   75, 91, 146–52, 249–50, 270–71;
   white women, 18
Williams, George, 47, 168
Williams, John, 64
Williams, Martin, 47, 59
Williams, Thomas, 6, 87, 89
Wilson, Hugh, 93, 107, 113, 194, 237,
   243
Witter, Norwood, 77
Witter, William, 70–72
Woolery, Edward, 78
Woolery, Robert, 47
Woolery, William, 119
Wright, John, 32

York estate, 5